Snowboarding Bodies in Theory and Practice

Global Culture and Sport Series

Series Editors: **Stephen Wagg** and **David Andrews**

Titles include:

John Harris
RUGBY UNION AND GLOBALIZATION
An Odd-Shaped World

Roger Levermore and Aaron Beacom (*editors*)
SPORT AND INTERNATIONAL DEVELOPMENT

Jonathan Long and Karl Spracklen (*editors*)
SPORT AND CHALLENGES TO RACISM

Pirkko Markula (*editor*)
OLYMPIC WOMEN AND THE MEDIA
International Perspectives

Global Culture and Sport
Series Standing Order ISBN 978–0–230–57818–0 hardback 978–0–230–57819–7 paperback
(*outside North America only*)

You can receive future titles in this series as they are published by placing a standing order. Please contact your bookseller or, in case of difficulty, write to us at the address below with your name and address, the title of the series and the ISBN quoted above.

Customer Services Department, Macmillan Distribution Ltd, Houndmills, Basingstoke, Hampshire RG21 6XS, England

Snowboarding Bodies in Theory and Practice

Holly Thorpe
University of Waikato, New Zealand

palgrave
macmillan

First published 2011 by
PALGRAVE MACMILLAN

Palgrave Macmillan in the UK is an imprint of Macmillan Publishers Limited, registered in England, company number 785998, of Houndmills, Basingstoke, Hampshire RG21 6XS.

Palgrave Macmillan in the US is a division of St Martin's Press LLC, 175 Fifth Avenue, New York, NY 10010.

Palgrave Macmillan is the global academic imprint of the above companies and has companies and representatives throughout the world.

Palgrave® and Macmillan® are registered trademarks in the United States, the United Kingdom, Europe and other countries.

ISBN: 978–0–230–57944–6 hardback

This book is printed on paper suitable for recycling and made from fully managed and sustained forest sources. Logging, pulping and manufacturing processes are expected to conform to the environmental regulations of the country of origin.

A catalogue record for this book is available from the British Library.

Library of Congress Cataloging-in-Publication Data
Thorpe, Holly.
   Snowboarding bodies in theory and practice / Holly Thorpe.
     p. cm.
   Includes index.
   ISBN 978–0–230–57944–6 (hardback)
    1. Snowboarding. 2. Snowboarding – Social aspects. I. Title.
GV857.S57T46 2011
796.939—dc22
2011001488

10 9 8 7 6 5 4 3 2 1
20 19 18 17 16 15 14 13 12 11

Transferred to Digital Printing in 2012

For Catherine Kells (1978–2007)

An inspirational woman, board-sport enthusiast, and dearly missed friend

Contents

Illustrations

Acknowledgments

The process of writing this book has been greatly facilitated by the generous intellectual, professional, and personal support offered by many wonderful people. Firstly, I would like to acknowledge my deepest gratitude to Douglas Booth for his enduring mentorship throughout this academic journey. Toni Bruce, Richard Pringle, and Belinda Wheaton have also supported and informed my intellectual growth throughout the project. For academic friendship, support, and/or inspiration, I also thank Karen Barbour, Becky Beal, Susan Birrell, Megan Chawansky, Hamish Crocket, Jim Denison, Bevan Grant, Mark Falcous, John Horne, Pirkko Markula, Kirsten Petrie, Gertrud Pfister, Cassie Phoenix, Clive Pope, Rebecca Olive, Bob Rinehart, and Emma Wensing. For professional support, I am grateful to my colleagues in the Department of Sport and Leisure Studies at the University of Waikato, and the Chelsea School at the University of Brighton. I am also thankful for the financial support provided by the Faculty of Education at the University of Waikato, the Leverhulme Trust, and the New Zealand Postgraduate Study Abroad Award, which helped make various stages of my research possible. Many thanks also to Olivia Middleton and Philippa Grand at Palgrave Macmillan, and to Professor David Andrews, for their expert editorial assistance and advice at various stages of the project. Thanks also to the team at Newgen Publishing, and particularly Vidhya Jayaprakash.

Secondly, to my family – Kris, Geoff, Anna, Brook, Jack, George and Taylor-Blue. Without you, none of this could have been possible. I am forever grateful for your endless love and encouragement. I would also like to thank José Borrero for his intelligence, humor, patience, and companionship during this project. A great deal of appreciation is also owed to the Thorpe, Robertson, McNeice, Walker, Borrero, and Clissold families, with a particularly special mention to my loving grandparents – Joyce and Jack Thorpe, and Margaret and Clive Robertson. Many thanks also to my fabulous friends in Raglan and around the world, particularly Marie McCoy and Hariet Waffenschmidt.

Lastly, I express my sincere gratitude to the participants in this project who willingly dedicated their time, energy, and knowledge, as well as the photographers who generously offered the images that appear in these pages. Special thanks also to my past and present snowboarding friends, who have supported and inspired this project in more ways than they know.

1

Introducing a Sociology of Snowboarding Bodies

February 17, 2010. Standing atop of the super-pipe wearing baggy denim pants, a plaid-style jacket, long disheveled auburn hair, and a stars-and-stripes-patterned bandana around his neck, 23-year-old snowboarder Shaun White prepares for his second and final Olympic run. The announcer has declared it a victory lap. I stand in the bleachers at the base of the half-pipe, absorbing the energy of the crowd, anxiously awaiting action. A camera boom sweeps across our heads. Flags wave wildly. The babble of the commentators is interspersed with blasts of music. The dancing, stomping, cheering bodies around me blur. On the big screen, I catch Shaun read-justing his goggles and readying his legs. I quickly double-check the zoom on my camera, my right index finger itching in anticipation. Effortlessly, Shaun jumps his snowboard into position and begins to slide toward the pipe, quickly gaining speed and momentum. I inhale the cold night air with a sense of urgency, and hear others gasp around me; as if collectively holding our breath, there is a moment of silence. Pumping down into the half-pipe, Shaun slices across the transition and up the icy wall, and then launches into flight. As he soars more than 20 feet through the Vancouver skyscape and performs a dizzying array of highly technical maneuvers, including the infamous 'double McTwist' – a 1260 degree rotation with two flips – the crowd explodes. Furiously snapping photos and scribbling notes, I recognize this as a significant moment in snowboarding's short, but vibrant, history.

Snowboarding – the act of standing sideways on a board and sliding down a snow-covered slope – has gone from a marginal activity for a few diehard participants to an Olympic sport with mass appeal in the past four decades. Developing in a historically unique conjuncture of transnational mass communications and corporate sponsors, entertainment indus-tries, and an increasingly affluent young population, snowboarding has spread around the world at a phenomenal rate and far faster than many established sports and physical cultures. Since its emergence in North America in the late 1960s and 1970s, snowboarding has become a highly visible feature of popular culture. Images, narratives, and representations associated with snowboarding as a cultural form are often rich, evocative and wide-reaching. Snowboarders appear on the covers of *Rolling Stone*, *Sports Illustrated*, and *FHM*, and feature in advertisements for a plethora of corporate sponsors such as Nike, Mountain Dew, Red Bull, Hewlett-Packard, and American Express; they feature in blockbuster movies, and have their own video games and reality television shows. The broader cultural significance of snowboarding was particularly evident during the 2010 Winter Olympic Games in Vancouver (Canada) with a snowboarder officially launching the opening ceremony by performing a spectacular jump through the Olympic rings. Media sources identified Shaun White as the most popular athlete at the games (Ebner, 2009), and NBC coverage of the men's snowboard half-pipe final drew over 30 million viewers in the United States alone (Dillman, 2010).

The mainstream exposure of snowboarding has had a significant influence on cultural demographics. Snowboarding attracts participants from around the world, and from different social classes and age groups, as well as females and minority groups. Between 1988 and 2003 snowboarding experienced a 385 percent increase in participation, and during the early 2000s, snowboarding was one of America's fastest growing sports ('Fastest growing', 2005; 'Select snow', 2004). Although snowboarding demographics are changing, privileged white youth continue to constitute a dominant force at the core of the culture. In America, for example, more than 75 percent of snowboarders are 24 or younger (NGSA, 2005a) and only approximately 11 percent are members of racial or ethnic minority groups (NGSA, 2001). Reliable international statistics are rare, yet some recent estimates suggest that there are nearly 70 million snowboarders worldwide (Wark, 2009). Contemporary participants range from novices and weekend warriors, to lifestyle sport migrants, to professional athletes. Snowboarders demonstrate various levels of physical prowess and cultural commitment, and engage in an array of styles (e.g., alpine, freestyle, big mountain, jibbing, and snow-skating) in various snow-covered spaces (e.g., on and off piste at ski resorts, half-pipes, terrain parks, backcountry, indoor ski slopes, and urban environments). Styles of participation and competition are constantly evolving, with boarders creating new and ever more technical maneuvers, and snowboarding companies and ski resorts going to greater lengths to cater to the diverse demands of this highly fragmented, yet lucrative, physical culture.

I have three primary objectives in this book. First, I provide an in-depth analysis of the global phenomenon of snowboarding culture. Drawing upon an extensive collection of artifacts and sources, each chapter offers fresh insights into the snowboarding culture, including the sport, lifestyle, industry, media, and gender relations, in both historical and contemporary contexts. Second, I offer a multidimensional analysis of the physical cultural body via the case of snowboarding. To facilitate understandings of boarding bodies as historical, material, mediated, cultural, symbolic, inter-acting, gendered, moving, traveling, sensual, affective, and political, I draw upon, and extend, various critical sociological approaches and theoretical perspectives – cultural memory studies, Marxist political economy, post-Fordism, Foucauldian theorizing, Pierre Bourdieu's theory of embodiment, feminism, sociology of mobilities, and nonrepresentational theory. In so doing, I hope to contribute to contemporary debates surrounding the body and embodiment in sociology. It is also through this empirically grounded, theoretical examination of snowboarding culture that I address the third aim of this book, to bring social theory 'to life' for wider audiences. By making social theories and concepts more accessible via the case of snow-boarding, I hope this book empowers readers to use social theory more con-fidently and reflexively to understand, analyze, and perhaps change, the social world around them.

Sociology, physical cultural studies, and the snowboarding body

Since the mid-1980s, the body has become a major domain for sociological inquiry and it remains 'one of the most contested concepts in the social sci-ences' (Shilling, 2005, p. 6). As Turner (2008), one of the preeminent body theorists, explains:

> Sociological theory can be said to be organized around a number of perennial contrasts – agency and structure, the individual and society, nature and culture, mind and body. ... The importance of the sociology of the body is that it lies at the axis of these theoretical tensions and it is thus a necessary component of any genuine sociology. The difficulty of providing a coherent account of what we mean by 'the body' is an effect of these theoretical problems. (p. 209)

The analysis of the body and embodiment has produced 'an intellec-tual battlefield' over which 'the respective claims of post-structuralism and postmodernism, phenomenology, feminism, sociobiology, sociology and cultural studies have fought' (Shilling, 2005, p. 6; see also Csordas, 1994; Davis, 1997; Featherstone et al., 1991; Shilling, 2007; Turner, 2008; Williams & Bendelow, 1998). Increasingly, scholars have drawn upon an array of theoretical and methodological perspectives to shed new light on various aspects of the body. Yet, as Williams and Bendelow (1998) suggest, this has led to some conceptual ambiguity and disciplinary fragmentation:

> Recent years have witnessed a veritable explosion of interest in the body within social theory ... [But] the more the body is studied and written

about the more elusive it becomes: a fleshy organic entity and a natural symbol of society; the primordial basis of our being-in-the-world and the discursive product of disciplinary technologies of power/knowledge; an ongoing structure of lived experience and the foundational basis of rational consciousness; the well-spring of human emotionality and the site of numerous 'cyborg' couplings; a physical vehicle for personhood and identity and the basis from which social institutions, organizations and structures are forged. The body, in short, is all these things and much more. At best this has served to capture the multifaceted nature of the body in society. At worst it has led to a fragmentation of perspectives and a dispersal of approaches which, for the most part, talk *past* rather than *to* each other. (pp. 1–2)

Despite numerous theoretically sophisticated and empirically nuanced analyses of particular dimensions of the body and embodiment, contemporary sociological studies have yet to provide a theoretical approach that satisfactorily explains the various dimensions of the body. Rather, in each of these studies particular aspects of embodiment are foregrounded while others 'fade into the background' (Shilling, 2005, p. 6). Arguably, many of the criticisms leveled at mainstream sociological research on the body also apply to studies of sporting bodies.

The sociology of sport – a field of critical inquiry dedicated to the empirical and theoretical analysis of sport and human movement cultures – 'came of age' during the mid-1960s and 1970s (Coakley & Dunning, 2000). It was not until the late 1980s and early 1990s, however, that the physically active body (re)gained the attention of sociology of sport researchers (Gruneau, 1991; Hargreaves, 1987; Harvey & Sparkes, 1991; Loy, 1991; Loy et al., 1993; Theberge, 1991). The body and embodiment increasingly became the 'empirical core' of the field (Andrews, 2008, p. 52), such that today, sociology of sport boasts an array of theoretically and empirically insightful research on various aspects of the moving body in local, national, global, and virtual contexts. Since the late 1990s, however, a number of scholars have expressed concern that the overspecialization and fragmentation of the parent field of kinesiology is limiting understandings of the 'body in motion' (Duncan, 2007, p. 56; see also Andrews, 2008; Booth, 2009; Hargreaves & Vertinsky, 2007; Ingham, 1997; Woodward, 2009). Arguably, Physical Cultural Studies (PCS) – 'an emergent intellectual project with an interdisciplinary and multidimensional commitment toward critical and theoretically informed engagement with various expressions of the physical' (Silk & Andrews, 2010) – has the potential to reinvigorate and reconceptualize understandings of the physically active body.

The term 'Physical Cultural Studies' (PCS) was initially coined in the late 1990s (Ingham, 1997), but has recently (re)gained momentum among scholars seeking more multidimensional understandings of the politics and practices of active embodiment in all its myriad forms (such as sport, dance, exercise, fitness, health, and leisure). While the PCS agenda continues to evolve, Andrews (2008) offers a preliminary definition:

> Physical cultural studies is...a synthesis of empirical, theoretical and methodological influences (drawn from, among other sources, the sociology and history of sport and physical activity, the sociology of the body, and cultural studies) that are focused on the critical analysis of active bodies and specifically the manner in which they become organized, represented, and experienced in relation to the operations of social power. (p. 45)

The emerging field of PCS advocates 'a multi-method approach toward engaging the empirical (including ethnography and autoethnography, participant observation, discourse and media analysis, and contextual analysis)', and advances 'an equally fluid theoretical vocabulary, utilizing concepts and theories from a variety of disciplines (including cultural studies, economics, history, media studies, philosophy, sociology, and urban studies) in engaging and interpreting the particular aspect of physical culture under scrutiny' (Andrews, 2008, p. 55). In the remainder of this chapter I explain the PCS-inspired interdisciplinary methodological and theoretical approaches I employ to help capture the multifaceted nature of the snowboarding body. I then offer a brief overview of the book.

Understanding physical cultural bodies: some methodological and theoretical considerations

Contemporary physical cultures are complicated and multidimensional phenomena interwoven with numerous political, cultural, social, and economic events and processes. Understanding and explaining such complexities can make for challenging social research. Sociological investigations seeking to construct nuanced social explanations of the body in contemporary physical cultures must embrace theoretical and conceptual reflexivity, and methodological and analytical dynamicism and openness. Here I outline the multi-methodological and multi-theoretical approach I employ in this study of snowboarding bodies. Of course, there is a plethora of ways in which socially meaningful and insightful analyses of contemporary physical cultures may transpire. The following is by no means a prescriptive account of how to research physical cultures. However, I hope that the insights gleaned from my embodied research experiences prove useful for others embarking on their own projects on sport and physical cultures in global and/or local contexts.

Researching physical cultural bodies: a multimethodological approach

My understanding of the complexities of snowboarding bodies derives from multiple modes of data generation, a type of methodology used extensively by Bourdieu and which he describes as 'discursive montage' of '*all sources*' (Bourdieu & Wacquant, 1992, p. 66, emphasis added). Bourdieu (1992) adds that this is 'the only possible attitude toward theoretical tradition' (p. 252). Similarly, Grossberg (2001) recommends using 'any and every kind of empirical method, whatever seems useful to the particular project' in order to 'gather more and better information, descriptions, resources', and improve one's interpretations (cited in Wright, 2001, p. 145). Throughout this project I seized all types of data, evidence, sources, and artifacts to shed light on my inquiry into snowboarding bodies. According to Mills (1959), sociologists do not study projects, rather they become tuned, or sensitive, to themes that 'they see and hear everywhere in [their] experience' (p. 211). As I became increasingly sensitive to the themes of the snowboarding body, I gathered evidence from personal observations and experiences, magazines, websites, newspapers, interviews and personal communications, videos, Internet chat rooms, promotional material, television programs, press releases, public documents, reports from snowboarding's administrative bodies, and promotional material from sporting organizations and from associated industries.[1] I will now briefly discuss some of the practical, ethical, and reflexive considerations for employing such methods in contemporary physical cultures.

Snowboarding bodies in global and local contexts: doing transnational ethnography

In light of fundamental transformations of space, place, and time, anthropologists and sociologists are increasingly calling into question traditionally defined ethnography – as an 'intensively-focused-upon single site of ethnographic observation and participation' (Marcus, 1995, p. 96). They urge scholars to embrace more broadly based research strategies, what some variously refer to as 'globalizing methods' (Stoller, 1997), 'mobile ethnography' (Fincham et al., 2010; Marcus, 1995), multisite 'transnational fieldwork' (Knowles, 1999), and 'global ethnography' (Burawoy et al., 2000). Arguably, transnational ethnography provides us with new tools to study the flows of physical cultural commodities, images, discourses, power and populations across local, regional, national, and international fields (Canniford, 2005; Nayak & Kehily, 2008). Thus, with the goal of further examining the values, practices, and interactions of snowboarding bodies in local snowboarding cultures, as well as regional, national, and global flows of people, objects, value systems, information, and images within and across these places, I conducted 15 'ethnographic visits' – ranging from one week to one month – in an array of snowboarding communities and ski resorts in Canada (Whistler), France (Chamonix, Tignes), Italy (the Dolomites), New Zealand (Methven, Ohakune, Queenstown, Wanaka), Switzerland (Saas Fee, Zermatt), and the United States (Mt Hood, Oregon; Salt Lake City, Utah; Telluride, Colorado) between 2004 and 2010. The prolonged nature of this project allowed me to observe cultural change, as well as providing time for reflection on the data gathered and my conceptual interpretations.

Attempting to understand how snowboarders experience their bodies in (and across) local snowboarding fields, I made observations on and off the snow (including lift lines, chairlifts, resort lodges, snowboard competitions, prize-giving events, video premiers, bars, cafes, local hangouts, snowboard shops, bus shelters, train stations, and airports). During this fieldwork, I observed, listened, engaged in analysis, and made mental notes, switching from snowboarder to researcher depending on the requirements of the situation. Of course, the covert nature of some aspects of these participant-observation phases raises many ethical issues. As Sands (2008) explains, 'when or if the ethnographer reveals his/her role as a fieldworker and informs those being observed of the intent of the ethnographer is a matter of ethical concern' (p. 369). While all participants have the right to know when their behavior is being observed for research purposes, in some situations it was not feasible (or, indeed, safe) to declare my researcher identity or ask for informed consent from *all* participants (e.g., observations from the chairlift of unidentifiable snowboarders and skiers interacting in the terrain park below, or at a Big Air snowboarding event with thousands of young, intoxicated spectators). Rather, I negotiated my way through the various social situations differently depending on the dynamics of the interaction and my role in the relationships. In so doing, I regularly engaged in 'situated ethics', that is, I made ethical decisions regarding the overt and covert nature of my research based on the dynamics and complexities of the particular social, cultural and/or physical environment (Simons & Usher, 2000; Wheaton, 2002).

In light of the recent sensual turn in the social sciences and humanities, scholars have begun to question the bias toward the visual in ethnography. They are increasingly calling for greater attention to the 'multi-sensoriality of the ethnographic process' (Pink, 2010, p. 1). Terms used to describe this shift in ethnographic research and representation include an 'anthropology of the senses' (Howes, 2003), 'sensuous scholarship' (Stoller, 1997), 'sensuous geography' (Rodaway, 1994), and 'sensory ethnography' (Pink, 2010). For Pink, the process of sensory ethnography can help us account for 'multisensoriality' in both the 'lives of people who participate in our research' and 'our craft' (Ibid., p. 1). During my transnational fieldwork I observed and jotted notes in various social and snow-covered environments, and I was also a participant. Thus my fieldwork was a form of 'sensual research' that offered new opportunities for experiencing, observing, and sharing the bodily and social pleasures, as well as the pains and frustrations inherent in snowboarding (Evers, 2006, p. 239). During phases of participant-observation I further adopted a 'sensory ethnographic' sensitivity by paying particular attention to the unique sights, as well as the sounds, smells, tastes, and touch, of various spaces and places. To facilitate more vivid recall of the multisensual aspects of the research experience upon returning 'home' from the field, I also employed an array of creative strategies using my notebook, camera and Dictaphone (Azzarito, 2010). For example, while conducting fieldwork at some snowboarding events and competitions (such as an urban rail-jam in downtown Queenstown, a Big Air event in Whistler, and a slopestyle event at the European X-Games in Tignes) I used my dictaphone to capture some of the multilayered sounds (e.g., commentators, music, snowmobiles, helicopters, crowd), thus freeing me to focus on other social and sensual dimensions of the occasion. Indeed, listening to these recordings, while viewing my photos and annotating my field notes, evoked more multidimensional memories of these socially, physically and sensually loaded phases of fieldwork.

Each of the locations I visited for this project posed different opportunities *and* challenges, such as language, localism, cultural access, accommodation, preexisting contacts in the field, and funding. According to Stoller (1997), the key to doing research in complex transnational spaces is 'suppleness of imagination' (p. 91). Thus I attempted to respond and adapt flexibly to the unique conditions of each field, and to remain open to a wide variety of relationships and interactions as they arose in various locations (e.g., on chairlifts, in snowboard shops, on buses). Particular ethnographic methods became more important when conducting research in some spaces and places than in others. For example, language barriers in France, Italy, and Switzerland made the communicative and auditory aspects of fieldwork more difficult. While conducting fieldwork in social spaces such as lift lines and resort cafes in these locations, my observations became much more important – I paid more attention to the signs and symbols, posturing and interactions of snowboarding bodies, as well as the tones and inflections of voices. In this way, it was typically the 'circumstance that defined the method rather than the method defining the circumstance' (Amit, 2000, p. 11).

I developed my transnational and sensual ethnographic methods in dialogue with 60 participants (32 female and 28 male) from an array of countries, including Australia, Canada, England, France, New Zealand, South Africa, Switzerland, and the United States.[2] Participants ranged from 18 to 56 years of age, and included novice snowboarders, weekend warriors, committed/core boarders, professional snowboarders, an Olympic snowboarder, an Olympic judge, snowboarding journalists, photographers, film-makers, magazine editors, snowboard company owners, snowboard shop employees and owners, snowboard instructors and coaches, and event organizers and judges. The snowball method of sampling proved effective with many participants helping me gain access to other key informants by offering names, contact details (e.g., email addresses, phone numbers), and even vouching for my authenticity as 'a researcher who actually snowboards' (Field notes, November 2005). During the interviews, I asked participants to reflect on their beliefs about various aspects of the snowboarding culture and encouraged them to express their attitudes, ideas, and perceptions about, and memories of different aspects of the snowboarding body (such as gender, media, performance, competition, travel, pleasure, risk, injury, consumption, and lifestyle). Interviews ranged from 30 minutes to 4 hours in length, depending on the willingness of participants. To accommodate the nomadic existence of many snowboarders, I also distributed follow-up interviews by email to 35 participants living or traveling abroad. The majority of respondents wrote freely and in colloquial tones, their degree of comfort with this medium perhaps reflecting the time spent on the Internet emailing and chatting in their everyday lives.

In conjunction with my multisited transnational fieldwork and interviews, I also gathered evidence from cultural sources, such as magazines, films, newspapers, television, and websites,[3] to help deepen my understanding of cultural complexities of the global–local nexus in snowboarding. Instead of focusing solely on the detailed structuring of individual texts, I examined the evolving patterns of discourse traceable across the various forms of snowboarding media. Integrating this analysis with participant-observations and interviews further enabled me to examine the ways particular discursive constructions of the snowboarding body were created, reinforced, amplified, and negotiated within the culture. In other words, I analyzed both the content of the texts and 'the everyday life of media representations, their contexts of production and circulation, and the practices and discourses of reception that envelop them' (Spitulnik, 1993, cited in Frohlick, 2005, p. 177). As I did so, the study of documentary and visual sources enabled me to refine and develop the analytical themes that simultaneously emerged during the phases of transnational fieldwork and interviews, as well as to produce new areas of inquiry. Furthermore, combining the empirical evidence with secondary sources (especially scholarly research relating to the kindred activities of surfing, skateboarding, and windsurfing) also helped me to construct the social and cultural contexts of the snowboarding body. Secondary sources included theoretical and empirical literature covering the body and embodiment, social and cultural change, sport and leisure, and youth cultures.

The reflexive researching body

Research is a process that occurs through the medium of a person: 'the researcher is always and inevitably present in the research' (Stanley & Wise, 1993, cited in Wheaton, 2002, p. 246; see also Bourdieu & Wacquant, 1992).

This was certainly true in this project. Prior to commencing this study of snowboarding bodies, I had already spent approximately 600 days snowboarding on more than 30 mountains in New Zealand, Canada, and the United States. Between 1999 and 2004, I held many roles in the snowboarding culture (novice, weekend warrior, and lifestyle sport migrant) and industry (semiprofessional athlete, snowboard instructor, terrain park employee, and journalist). Thus, upon embarking on this project, I could have been considered a cultural insider. My physical abilities and knowledge about snowboarding gave me access to the culture and a head start in recognizing the significant issues and sensitizing themes and concepts, and in discerning relevant sources. However, this 'insider knowledge' also carried potential pitfalls. Perhaps one of the hardest tasks during the early phases of this research was negotiating the path that allowed me to understand and acknowledge the participants' worldviews and their subjectivities, while also gaining the 'critical distance' necessary to contextualize those views and actions (Wheaton, 2002, p. 262). This involved not only 'demystifying the familiar' but also 'analyzing respondents' views' (Ibid.) and engaging with them from a number of different theoretical perspectives. Moreover, as my research progressed I spent less time on the mountains and more time reflecting in my study, which helped me acquire greater analytical distance. The length of this project and the dynamic nature of the snowboarding culture also meant that, as my research progressed, I became further removed in terms of age and generation (as exemplified by clothing style and language) from the majority of core participants, who are mostly in their late teens and early twenties. In a way that I had not anticipated, my personal experiences of a progressive physical, social, and psychological 'distancing' from the core of the snowboarding culture, prompted me to further reflect on issues relating to cultural access and participant rapport while conducting research in the field, as well as individual participants' embodied experiences of movement into, within, and out of, the snowboarding culture.

Acknowledging that the 'theorist is also embodied', and reflexively exploring some of the bodily tensions that can occur within the field, can 'open up' new areas of inquiry, as well as 'possibilities for exploring new ways of doing theory – ways which use embodiment as a theoretical resource' (Davis, 1997, p. 14; see also Thomas & Ahmed, 2004). During the early phases of my research, my insider knowledge and cultural identity undoubtedly influenced my ability to develop rapport with participants during interviews and participant-observation. For example, while in the United States completing fieldwork, I bought a cap from a snowboard store in Portland, Oregon. Admittedly, I liked its style and color, and was naive about the fact that this was one of the most 'authentic' core brands within the local snowboarding scene at the time. Core snowboarders are masters of reading bodies and their symbols, and wearing this cap seemed to give me instant cultural credibility among some local core snowboarders and facilitate my rapport with interviewees. During my participant-observation phase in Whistler, Canada, I experienced the flipside of this scenario. Due to unforeseen circumstances, I was forced to rent an outdated snowboard. Interestingly, the tone of chair-lift conversations changed when core snowboarders observed this board, as it was a clear sign of outsider status and hindered my rapport with some snowboarders (interestingly, noncore participants rarely noticed). While this was somewhat frustrating, it provided me with a fresh perspective on the cultural intricacies and social hierarchies, and the effect these can have on those outside the snowboarding culture. These examples illustrate the capricious nature of some of my interactions with participants. While I made attempts to manage my impressions (e.g., by wearing snowboard-specific clothing, employing snowboarding argot, and sharing snowboarding experiences), I could not control the interpretations that others drew from my performances. In this sense, as Shilling (2003) notes, I was 'caught in a web of communication irrespective of individual intentions' (p. 85). The key point here is that throughout my fieldwork, I self-consciously reflected on my constantly shifting positions as an (increasingly less) active snowboarder and a young, white, heterosexual, middle-class, female researcher and academic from New Zealand, and on how these roles influenced my relationships in the field, as well as the theoretical and empirical development of the study. While the focus of this book is the corporeal experiences of 'other' snowboarders, it is important to acknowledge that my own embodied snowboarding experiences – as a participant and researcher – influenced every phase of this study, from conducting participant-observations and interviews, to theorizing, to representing my research.

As Knowles (1999) explains, 'fieldwork offers the transnational researcher the prospect of reconnection with a former life or the prospect of escape; it sustains the possibility of an alternate sense of belonging and self, deftly busied in conceptions of work and intellectual enterprise' (p. 60). While I certainly enjoyed moments of escapism, nostalgia, adrenalin, and joy during my fieldwork, the practice of global ethnography should not be romanticized. Transnational ethnography has the potential to be 'humiliating, belittling, at times dull, boring and downright exhausting' (Silk, 2005, p. 75), as well as dangerous. When conducting global (and local) fieldwork the researcher – particularly the female researcher – should be prepared for an array of potentially high-risk or threatening situations in which instantaneous decisions may need to be made (e.g., witnessing violent, sexist and/ or criminal behaviors, or hiking out of bounds from a ski resort despite avalanche warnings). In such situations, researchers need to protect both the right of their participants to anonymity and their own safety. When confronted with situations requiring an almost immediate ethical response, the researcher should draw upon all of his/her senses to interpret the dynamics and complexities of the particular social, cultural and physical environment.

In sum, my study drew upon all types of data, evidence, sources, and artifacts to illuminate the theoretical inquiry into snowboarding bodies that follows. 'Even the humblest material artifact is', as Eliot (1947) explains, 'an emissary of the culture out of which it comes' (cited in Vamplew, 1998, p. 268). Using cultural sources, such as magazines, films, and websites, in conjunction with transnational multisited fieldwork and interviews, certainly helped deepen my understanding of snowboarding's cultural complexities and the multidimensional snowboarding body. But even the richest caches of primary source materials 'will speak only when they are properly questioned' (Bloch, 1952, cited in Hardy, 1999, p. 91). Similarly, Bourdieu et al. (1991) remind us, no matter how sophisticated one's 'techniques of observation and proof', unless they are accompanied by a 'redoubling of theoretical vigilance', they will only 'lead us to see better and better fewer and fewer things' (p. 88). In this case of the snowboarding body, the range and diversity of theories structured my evidence, and in so doing helped me to see better and better more and more things.

Explaining physical cultural bodies: using social theory

Theory is the heart and soul of sociology and central to the discipline's contribution to 'the development of self-knowledge and the guidance of human society' (Waters, 2000, p. 1). Similarly, Wilson (1983) says that 'good sociological research without theory is unthinkable' (p. xi), while Hall (1996) believes that theory can better 'help us understand our culture' (p. 30). Thus social theory is a 'tool' (Mouzelis, 1995, p. 3), a 'heuristic device' (Blaikie, 2000, p. 141) and a 'framework for interpretation' (Tosh, 2000, p. 134) which sets out questions, directs practitioners to particular sources, organizes evidence and shapes explanation, and thereby gives 'impetus to an inquiry and influences its outcomes' (Munslow, 1997, p. 46). Theory helps scholars understand and critique society, and point to new directions and perhaps reform. In this book, broadly following in the sociological tradition, I employ social theory to understand the multidimensional snowboarding body.

A wide range of opinions exists as to the prime concerns of social theory. Some argue for a microanalysis of behaviors and interaction in specific contexts; some advocate macro approaches that examine structures and processes. Others strive to reconcile micro and macro analyses. Some see the multiplicity of approaches as problematic (Turner, 1991), or the source of endless disputes and conflicts (Cuff et al., 1990). Others find virtue in diversity. Among the latter, Merton (1981) said that diverse theoretical orientations help the field deal with 'diverse kinds of, and aspects of, sociological and social problems' (p. 1), and Wallace and Wolf (1991) believe that 'different perspectives offer different and often complementary insights' (cited in Waters, 2000, p. 345). According to Shilling (2005), while no theoretical approach has proved adequate to explain all dimensions of the body and embodiment, diverse theoretical and methodological approaches can 'heighten our sensitivity to various aspects of the body's multiple dimensional relationship with society' (p. 71). With Shilling, I believe there is merit in strategically juxtaposing a selection of conceptual perspectives from commensurate paradigms in order to construct a better and more multi-dimensional representation of the social, cultural, political, gendered, practiced, lived, and interacting body.

In this book I employ an array of theories from compatible paradigms to help explain various dimensions of the snowboarding body, including cultural memory studies, Marxist political economy, post-Fordism, Foucauldian theorizing, Pierre Bourdieu's theory of embodiment, feminism, sociology of mobilities, and nonrepresentational theory. Of course, the social sciences and humanities are host to a wide variety of theories and theoretical perspectives, and I had to make judgments about which theories to include. My selection of these theories was informed by both my existing cultural knowledge of snowboarding, and my theoretical knowledge. I selected the theories that I believed would shed light on various aspects of the snowboarding body and help me capture some of the complexities of the global phenomenon of snowboarding. The chosen concepts were those that remain flexible enough for appropriation and application to this contemporary phenomenon. This approach is in the spirit of the PCS agenda, where the aim is not 'finding the "right theory"' or 'demonstrating one's theoretical acumen', but finding 'whatever theoretical positions' will best facilitate the task of 'understanding what is going on' (Wright, 2001, cited in Andrews, 2008, p. 57). I do not pretend to provide an exhaustive account of each theory. It would be impossible to analyze all the strengths and shortcomings of each theory in detail in the space available. Moreover, such an analysis would not contribute to my goal of providing a more nuanced explanation of the practices and politics of the physical cultural snowboarding body. Instead I have cast my net widely, and I focus on selected critical concepts from a range of sociocultural theoretical perspectives. The chapters which follow extend existing knowledge of the body in physical culture by painting a fuller, more complete picture of snowboarding bodies than could have been achieved by focusing on one theory, but this does not mean that I have sealed all the gaps.

The various theoretical approaches adopted in this book offer different perspectives on, and often complementary insights into, the body in contemporary popular physical culture. Yet no single theory could adequately explain all aspects of the multidimensional body. Furthermore, because all 'theories are created by individuals in their search for meaning' in response to concrete material conditions (Alexander, 1995, pp. 79–80), some theories prove more suitable for explaining some aspects of the physical cultural body at the current historical moment than others. But, as Slack (1996) explains, 'successful theorizing is not measured by the exact theoretical fit but by the ability to work with our always inadequate theories to help us move understanding "a little further down the road" ' (p. 112). Thus, in this book I 'work with' theory to enhance understanding of physically active bodies in global snowboarding culture.

Theoretical conversations with snowboarding bodies

Balancing theory and empirical research is a prime goal of sociology, yet its practice is 'all too rare' (Waters, 2000, p. 4). Not only do critical social theories often appear as a 'clash or confrontation of ideas', they rarely involve 'a productive interchange [of] empirical evidence' (Layder, 2004, p. 118). Concerned that many intellectual projects have lost their analytical dynamism and openness, and remain bent on 'illustrating the applicability of *their* framework' (Baert, 2004, p. 362, emphasis added), philosopher Richard Rorty (1980) pleads for a critical approach that challenges 'accepted taxonomies and lenses rather than merely reiterating them' (cited in Ford & Brown, 2006, p. 146). Baert, like Rorty, is concerned by the contemporary trend that measures theory-inspired research by the 'extent to which a theory...neatly...fits the data...and to which the various components of the theory...weave easily into the myriad of empirical experiences' (Baert, 2004, p. 367). Instead, he proposes that the success of such research should be measured by its ability to 'see things differently' (Ibid.). This is one of the goals of this project. Rather than employing one theoretical perspective to frame the phenomenon of the snowboarding body, I attempt to make multiple theoretical ideas 'live' through 'empirical discussions' (Alexander, 2003, pp. 7–8) with the culture.

Throughout this project, I 'move[d] back and forth between theorizing and researching, between interpretations and explanations, between cultural logics and pragmatics' (Alexander, 2003, p. 6). In other words, at the centre of this project I placed dialogue between theoretical knowledge and cultural knowledge, which was gained from previous and current cultural participation and combined with multiple modes of data generation. In sum, the empirical evidence gathered through a transnational multimethodological approach was refined and developed in conversation with the theoretical concepts. While each of the theoretical chapters which follow is informed by my 'discursive montage' of *all* the sources (Bourdieu & Wacquant, 1992, p. 66), each of the theories I have adopted in this project asks different questions of the evidence. Thus, each chapter approaches and analyzes the same (and different) sources in different ways, according to the sociological questions being asked. Nonetheless, throughout my research, I continually sought 'negative instances or contradictory cases' from *all* the sources in order to avoid including only those elements of the snowboarding culture that would substantiate my analyses (Mason, 2002, p. 124).

In some cases, I also extend and synthesize theoretical perspectives to help make sense of nuanced (or contradictory) evidence, and to make a further contribution to theoretical conversations surrounding the body and embodiment. Theoretical synthesis arguably provides a fruitful strategy for analyzing multidimensional social and physical cultural phenomena.[4] As Giulianotti (2005) writes, 'the research object of sociologists – human societies – can be better explained through working relationships with other disciplines rather than insisting upon the hypocritical, asocial conceit of splendid isolation' (p. 211). In recent years there has been a significant abatement of hostility and a fundamental shift towards synthesis in the humanities, even while fundamental disagreements remain: 'The borrowing and intertwining of once rival traditions is readily apparent in recent empirical work. It is also the new agenda for a wide range of robust and ambitious efforts in sociological theory' (Alexander, 1991, p. 152). As will become apparent in some chapters of this book, I found theoretical syntheses between feminism and the work of Pierre Bourdieu particularly insightful for understanding issues relating to gender, the body and embodiment, power, culture, agency, and reflexivity in snowboarding culture.

The politics of embodied theorizing

Davis (1997) believes that much theorizing about the body has been cerebral, esoteric, and ultimately, disembodied, and as such ironically 'distances us from individuals' everyday embodied experiences' (p. 14). Similarly, Williams and Bendelow (1998) argue that it is only through a shift from theorizing *about* bodies 'in a largely disembodied, typically male way (e.g., a sociology of the body, which objectifies and subjectifies the body from outside, so to speak), to a new mode of social theorizing *from* lived bodies' (p. 3), that a 'truly embodied sociology [will] have any real hope of putting minds back into bodies, bodies back into society and society back into the body' (p. 3). Thus, by grounding theoretical discussions of the body in the global phenomenon of snowboarding, I offer an account of 'the body in everyday life as well as in social theory' (Davis, 1997, p. 13).

Adopting an embodied theoretical approach that engages theoretical concepts in dialogue with numerous examples and evidence from an array of sources from the snowboarding culture, I also hope to make social theory more accessible. While the various social theories adopted in this study have much to offer in terms of providing frameworks for a range of descriptions and explanations of the body in the contemporary social world, they are often largely inaccessible, in their current form, to the majority of those outside academe. Social theories are too often presented as highly abstract and disembodied, such that many students and new researchers experience social theory as intimidating, overwhelming, and tedious. A central aim of this book is to show that much pleasure can be gained from using social theory to reflexively interpret the social conditions of our existence and inform our involvement in related practical and political issues.

This text seeks to make social theory more accessible, yet it does not claim to offer an introduction to, or an overview of, modern sociological theory; a number of excellent resources already achieve this (Elliott, 2008; Layder, 2006; Turner, 1996; Waters, 2000). While the theoretical discussions offered in the chapters which follow briefly introduce theoretical schemas and key concepts, the focus is on illustrating their applicability through the example of snowboarding culture. Moreover, some chapters build upon, extend, and synthesize theoretical perspectives to further reveal some of the corporeal complexities in contemporary physical culture. In other words, I am less concerned with outlining the 'rules' for using social theory or achieving theoretical closure, and more interested in exploring the possibilities of engaging in more reflexive, dynamic, and creative embodied theorizing.

I hope that my resulting theoretical and practical 'adventures' in the field of physical cultural studies highlight the rich potential of social theory for producing new knowledge and understanding of physically active bodies in global and local contexts, and inspire others to embark on their own theoretical journeys with confidence and a sense of excitement. Like Foucault (1974), I hope readers find in this book 'a kind of toolbox' which they can 'rummage through to find a tool which they can use however they wish in their own area' (p. 523). Importantly, a political impetus also underpins this project. It is hoped that some readers – particularly those less familiar with social theory – will be inspired to use these 'tools' to identify and analyze – and perhaps seek to intervene in – the 'operation and experience of power and power relations' in the social world around them (Andrews, 2008, p. 58), and particularly in those sporting and physical cultures that have captured their 'sociological imagination' (Mills, 1959), as snowboarding did mine.

Snowboarding bodies in theory and practice: an overview

The remainder of this book consists of nine chapters. Each chapter draws upon one (or two) principal theoretical approaches to examine a different dimension of the snowboarding body, offering fresh insights into the snowboarding culture, and identifying some of the strengths and limitations of the selected theoretical perspective(s) for explaining physical cultural bodies. While each chapter is based on a solid understanding of the extensive theoretical and empirical literature from various disciplines that examines the particular aspect of the body under investigation (e.g., mediated physical cultural bodies, or masculinity), it is beyond the scope of this book to review all of this work. Just as I made decisions about which methodological and theoretical approaches to use based on an understanding of the strengths and limitations of various possibilities, in each chapter I employ only those studies that most facilitate my analysis of the particular dimension of the snowboarding body under discussion.

Chapter 2 offers a brief history of the development of snowboarding culture. This is followed by a critical discussion of the cultural politics involved in the construction and reproduction of this historical narrative. In the process, it examines how some snowboarding bodies are remembered while others are forgotten, and reveals that the production of the snowboarding cultural memory is an implicitly political process complicated by various sociocultural-economic factors. Building upon this interdisciplinary analysis of cultural memory construction, Chapter 3 draws upon traditional Marxist and post-Fordist perspectives to illustrate how the snowboarding body has become a malleable marker of commercial value subject to the fragmentation of the snowboarding market and the vagaries of fashion. Various case studies illustrate the processes of production and consumption of snowboarding bodies by the owners and employees of companies such as Burton Snowboards, professional athletes, and various groups of cultural consumers (i.e., the female niche market).

Further exploring the complex relationship between the snowboarding culture and economy, Chapter 4 explains how the highly fragmented snowboarding media produce multiple representations of snowboarding bodies and, in so doing, support new niche markets necessary for ongoing economic growth. The chapter begins with a description of snowboarders' engagement with various forms of mass, niche, and micro media. Drawing upon Michel Foucault's concepts of power, power/knowledge and discourse, I then examine some of the multiple discursive constructions of snowboarding bodies in various forms of mass and niche media, focusing on representations of female snowboarding bodies. In the latter part of this chapter I engage with Foucault's concept of 'technologies of self' to examine how women (and men) make sense of the multiple and contradictory mediated discourses of femininity and sexuality in the snowboarding media.

Chapter 5 draws on the work of French social theorist Pierre Bourdieu to explain how distinctions among snowboarders, expressed as differences in embodied tastes and styles, and uses of cultural products and commodities, are practiced, performed, and regulated, on the mountain and in various other social spaces. More specifically, this chapter explains embodied dress and language practices, as well as displays of cultural commitment, physical prowess and risk-taking, as contributing to the social construction and classification of group identities (e.g., skiers, snowboarders, poseurs, professionals, freestyle riders) within the alpine snow field.

In Chapters 6 and 7, I draw upon recent feminist engagements with some of Bourdieu's key concepts to offer fresh insights into the gendered snowboarding body. Chapter 6 begins with an introduction to recent feminist critiques of, and conversations with, Bourdieu's conceptual schema, and then proceeds to examine female snowboarders' embodied experiences of physical and social agency, reflexivity and constraint within the male-dominated snowboarding field. In Chapter 7, I extend this discussion to argue that a gendered (re)reading of Bourdieu's conceptual schema also has the potential to shed new light on men and masculine identities in sport and physical culture. Here I offer a description of some of the practices and performances of different masculinities identifiable across the global snowboarding field, and the power relations between and within these groups. In both chapters, I consider the potential of the gender-habitus-field complex for explaining how some female and male snowboarders come to critically reflect upon problematic aspects of the hypermasculine snowboarding culture.

Chapter 8 explores the discourse of transnationalism within the snowboarding culture with a discussion of the corporeal mobilities and migration of snowboarders. Engaging with some of Urry's (2000) suggestions for a 'sociology of mobilities', I begin by offering a description of the various travel patterns of snowboarders (e.g., snow-sport tourists, professional athletes, and core participants). In the latter part of this chapter I draw upon recent work by human geographers, and Pierre Bourdieu's key concepts of field, capital and habitus, to enhance our understanding of privileged youth's lifestyle sport migration experiences. I conclude with a brief discussion of the local mobilities and interactions of snowboarding bodies within three transnational mountain resort destinations.

Located at the intersection between the recent sensual, affective and spatial turns in the social sciences and humanities, Chapter 9 examines the lived experiences of participants within various physical spaces and social places, focusing particularly on three distinct geographies – snowboard terrain parks, the backcountry, and the après-snow culture. Each section begins with a description of the interactions and experiences within these places, and concludes with a brief autoethnographic tale of the sensual and affective experiences in these unique geographies. Here I point to some of the possibilities of alternative ways of reflexively engaging with theory and representing the sensual and affective dimensions of the lived physical cultural body.

The final chapter consists of two main parts. In the first, I draw on two theoretical approaches – nonrepresentational theory and third-wave feminism – to reveal some of the creative and embodied approaches employed by contemporary youth to produce new forms of passionate and affective politics in local and global contexts. Lastly, I offer some concluding comments about the opportunities and challenges of theorizing the body and researching physical cultures into the twenty-first century, as well as possibilities for disseminating potentially empowering forms of knowledge to wider audiences.

In sum, this project is an intellectual and personal statement on both contemporary snowboarding culture *and* social theory. It is the result of my ongoing critical reflections on snowboarding culture *and* the usefulness of modern social theory for explaining the myriad ways the active body is 'culturally regulated, practiced, and materialized' (Andrews, 2008, p. 53).

Drawing inspiration from the burgeoning field of Physical Cultural Studies, I adopt an interdisciplinary, multimethodological, and 'fluid' theoretical approach to help make sense of the complex and highly nuanced snowboarding culture and the multidimensional snowboarding body. Engaging multiple theoretical concepts in conversation with my empirical evidence, gathered over seven years from local, national, transnational, and virtual snowboarding sites, I seek to 'identify and analyze how dominant power structures become expressed in, and through, [the] socially and historically contingent embodied experiences, meanings, and subjectivities' of snowboarders (Ibid.). It is hoped that, through recognizing and understanding the various forms of power operating within contemporary physical cultures, such as snowboarding, we can begin to imagine more effective strategies for intervening, disrupting, and challenging power inequalities in local, national, and global contexts.

2
Remembering the Snowboarding Body

There is a growing interest in the history of snowboarding because our sport is finally at a point where we can look back and speculate. Now I feel there is actually a history. Ten years ago it seemed silly to think of snowboarding in any historical sense, as it was still so young. Now there is some depth, people have stories...There is a lot of interest for me personally in the history of snowboarding because these were the years that shaped my life. (Steve, personal communication, June 2009)

The history of snowboarding definitely seems to be getting more important to me as I get older. Possibly it could be more about me trying to maintain a connection to the sport...or a longing for the good old days...When I read stories or watch footage from earlier periods it provides that nostalgic feeling. I remember making my first pair of pants...sawing off parts of my bindings...cutting the toes out of my boot liners....The young kids today have no idea, and I don't think many of them really care, but I do. This is *our* history, and I feel like I was part of something special. (Nathan, personal communication, June 2009)

Dating the birth of snowboarding is impossible. People have been standing on sleds and trying to slide on snow for hundreds of years; recent 'discoveries' include a board dating back to the 1920s and a 1939 film of a man riding a snowboard-type sled sideways down a small hill in Chicago. Snowboarding as we understand the activity today, however, emerged in the late 1960s and 1970s in North America with a new piece of equipment that appealed to the hedonistic desires of a new generation of youth. In this chapter I offer a brief history of the development of snowboarding culture. This is followed by a critical discussion of the cultural politics involved in the construction and reproduction of this historical narrative, which examines how some snowboarding bodies are remembered while others are forgotten, and reveals the production of the snowboarding cultural memory as an implicitly political process complicated with various socio-cultural-economic factors. First, however, I offer some brief comments on the importance of history and context for understanding contemporary physical cultures.

How history informs sociology

For decades sociologists have debated the role of history in the discipline (see Abbott, 1991; Abrams, 1982; Eliot, 1922; Goldthorpe, 1991; Griffin, 1995). C. Wright Mills (1959) described history as the 'shank of social study' and critical to grasping the 'problems of our time' (p. 143), while Griffin (1995) subscribes to the view that it is important to 'get the history right' not only for its own sake but also for that of sociology (p. 1274). Despite proclaiming history as important to sociological analysis and explanation, many practitioners continue to theorize social processes, patterns, and trends with scant regard for history (Rojek & Turner, 2000). An important segment of the discipline does, however, place real importance on the power of history, and more specifically context, to elucidate sociological research. Foucault's genealogical work, or writing a 'history of the present', is a good example (Goldstein, 1994). Writers such as Abrams (1982) and Skocpol (1984) have also been powerful advocates of 'historical sociology'. This type of thinking was also central to research carried out by Eric Dunning and his colleagues at the Centre for Research into Sport and Society, University of Leicester (see Dunning, 1994; Maguire, 1995). More recently, some Physical Cultural Studies scholars have been attempting to take history and context seriously by adopting the 'dialectic method and approach' of articulation (Andrews, 2008, p. 56). Each of these, and other, approaches to incorporating history into socio-cultural analyses has its strengths and limitations. It is not my intention to examine these approaches in any detail (for examples see Goldthorpe, 1991; Griffin, 1995; Thorpe, 2006). Rather, in this chapter I adopt an interdisciplinary approach to history and memory to reveal contemporary snowboarding culture as 'produced from specific social and historic contexts', and snowboarding bodies as 'actively engaged in the ongoing constitution of the conditions out of which they emerge' (Andrews, 2008, p. 57). Building upon this discussion, the subsequent chapters, particularly Chapters 3 and 4, further position snowboarding bodies within the hyper-commercial and highly mediated contemporary context.

The history of snowboarding: a realist tale

The popularization of the Malibu surf-board and the escapism and hedonism of surfing, with its antiestablishment countercultural values and do-it-yourself philosophies, inspired many of the early snowboarders. In 1964, Sherman Poppen invented the Snurfer when he bolted two skis together and added a rope for stability. Jake Burton Carpenter experimented with foam, fiberglass, steam-bent solid wood and vertically laminated wood with the goal of making a board that was more maneuverable and faster than the Snurfer (Howe, 1998). In 1978, he established Burton Boards. The early Burton boards had a rubber water-ski binding for the front foot which allowed greater control and maneuverability; turns became easier and more stable (Reed, 2005). Thus Burton modified both the board and the action.

Burton was not the only one to experiment with board designs; other pioneers included Dimitrije Milovick (Utah), Tom Sims and Chuck Barefoot (California), Chris and Bev Sanders (California), and Mike Olsen (Washington) who established Winterstick, Sims Snowboards, Avalanche Snowboards, and GNU Snowboards, respectively. While all these early board-makers wanted 'an alternative' to the elitist culture associated with skiing, their plans for the sport and styles of participation varied (Chris Sanders cited in Howe, 1998, p. 31). Well into the 1980s boards varied extensively in shape and design which in turn influenced the style of snowboarding. It was a period of trial and error, and groups of boarders adopted their own version of snowboarding shaped by local climate and terrain, equipment, and background (skiing, skateboarding, surfing, BMX biking, or mountaineering). Yet most of these pioneers embodied the idealism of the bygone counterculture and, in direct contrast to skiing (which was an expensive and bourgeois sport framed by a strict set of rules of conduct), embraced snowboarding as a free, fun, cooperative and individualistic activity (Humphreys, 1996, 1997).

Difficult beginnings

Ski resorts initially banned snowboarders. Owners, managers, and their skiing clientele defined the snowboarding cohort as '13–18 year olds with raging hormones' who liked skateboarding and surfing (Hughes, 1988, para. 11). Negative images of surfing and skateboarding from the 1970s contributed to the public dislike and distrust of snowboarding. According to David Schmidt, the national sales manager for Burton Snowboards, 'most people visualize snowboarders as a bunch of skate rats who are going to terrorize the mountain' (cited in Nelson, 1989). While bans made participation difficult, they did not stop determined and passionate devotees.

In 1983, Stratton Mountain, Vermont, became the first major ski-field to open its piste to snowboarders. Others quickly followed. This new-found access was the result of two major factors. First, a number of snowboarders actively campaigned for access (Howe, 1998). Second, skiing had reached a growth plateau and snowboarding offered ski-fields a new youth market and ongoing economic prosperity. Hughes (1988) described snowboarding as the 'biggest boost to the ski industry since chairlifts' (para. 8). But even after gaining access to the ski-fields, snowboarders continued to see themselves as 'different' to skiers. According to early U.S. snowboarder Todd Richards (2003), the interactions between skiers and snowboarders during this period were playful and relatively harmless: 'It was fun to toy with unsuspecting wanker-two-plankers; I'm certain they considered us equally pathetic. Snowboarders were a novelty to skiers, and skiers were old news to snowboarders. There was an utter lack of understanding, which made the early days so much fun' (p. 73). But, as the number of snowboarders increased during the 1980s, so too did tensions between the two groups.

Snowboarding continued to develop in opposition to the dominant ski culture. Skiing was an expensive sport with participants being mostly white and middle- or upper-class. Snowboarders were typically younger, less educated, single, male, earning lower incomes, or students (Williams et al., 1994). Summarizing the cultural differences during this period, Humphreys (1996) wrote that whereas 'skiing embodied technical discipline and control', snowboarding 'embodied freedom, hedonism and irresponsibility' (p. 9). Drawing inspiration from other alternative youth cultures, such as punk or skateboarding, many early snowboarders subscribed to antiestablishment, do-it-yourself and countercultural philosophies. Ben, an early snowboarder, recalls the antiestablishment mentality among snowboarders as 'ruining all the fixtures at resorts...running into skiers and telling them to screw off...' (cited in Anderson, 1999, p. 62). Jake Blattner recollects the do-it-yourself mentality prevalent in early snowboarding culture: 'there were no boards being made for what we wanted to do...so we took matters into our own hands and cut the noses off our boards' (cited in Howe, 1998, p. 86). Terje Haakonsen, a snowboarder of legendary status, best captured the countercultural ideology among early boarders when he described snowboarding as about making 'fresh tracks and carving powder and being yourself' rather than 'nationalism and politics and big money' (cited in Lidz, 1997, p. 114). Snowboarding was, in the words of cultural commentator Jamie Brisick (2004), 'an expansion of surfing and skateboarding, a way to explore different terrain with the same mind-set' (p. 69).

The long history and acceptance of skiing as a legitimate pastime and sport bestowed social authority on the mountain to skiers (Humphreys, 1996). One running joke among skiers went: 'What's the difference between a boarder and a catfish? One is a bottom-dwelling, disgusting, rejected muck sucker and the other is a fish' (cited in Coleman, 2004, p. 206). Physical confrontations and fights between skiers and snowboarders were not unusual as the two groups vied for territory and eminence (Anderson, 1999). Although snowboarders seriously challenged skiers' power, snowboarding remained a minor activity (Humphreys, 1996). In 1985, only seven percent of American resorts allowed snowboarders and in 1988 snowboarders still only comprised six percent of the ski resort population (Crane, 1996). However, participants formed a unified front and, as professional boarder Peter Line recalls, 'every other boarder was your buddy' (cited in Coyle, 2004, p. 115).

While there were undoubtedly geographical variations in approach, commentators in the early years frequently referred to a pervasive community spirit based on 'a fun, nonjudgmental scene that valued personal style' (Howe, 1998, p. 23). Although still in the minority, women found space within this scene. As Ste'en, an early New Zealand snowboarder, recalls: 'There were really no attitudes towards women snowboarding when I started; any attitude was leveled at boarders in general' (personal communication, May 2003). Similarly, early American snowboarder Jennifer Sherowski (2005a) recollects, 'it didn't seem like gender divisions really mattered. There were so few of us snowboarders, we were all just in it together' (p. 54). Another early American snowboarder Tina Basich (2003) remembers meeting other male and female snowboarders on the mountain and 'instantly becoming friends' (p. 36). She also adds that there was 'always … support from the guys' (p. 39).

Early competitions

Modern competitive snowboarding began in 1981 with the first American national titles held at Suicide Six, Vermont. The next year the resort hosted the first international snowboard race. Snowboard competitions during the mid- to late-1980s embodied an inclusive ideology. Basich (2003) recollects one of the first regional competitions in 1986 in which 'everybody', from both genders and all ability levels, competed together. Snowboarding historian Susanna Howe (1998) describes these events as 'cultural hotbeds' that effectively ironed out any notions of social stratification (p. 51). Everyone, she adds, was 'drunk and disorderly' (Howe, 1998, p. 43). Early snowboard competitions were typically poorly organized and, in keeping with countercultural traditions, privileged fun over serious competition and individualism.

Snowboarding also gained popularity among groups of youths wherever there was snow. The Japanese held their first national snowboarding contest in 1982, and in 1986 the Europeans organized regional events such as the Swiss Championships in St. Moritz. More than 100 male and female competitors from 17 nations competed in the World Championships at Livigno (Italy) and St. Moritz (Switzerland) in January 1987. At the end of the 1980s, however, the organization of snowboarding competitions was chaotic. For example, two World Championships were held simultaneously in 1987, one shared between Livigno and St. Moritz, the other in Breckenridge, Colorado. However, recognizing the commercial opportunities in developing the sporting side of snowboarding, groups of sporting-inclined snowboarders and manufacturers formed the North American Snowboard Association (NASBA) and Snowboard European Association (SEA) later that year. Their goal was to work together to create a unified World Cup tour, similar to that of skiing. In 1988 devotees formed the United States of America Snowboarding Association (USASA) to standardize rules and organize events in the United States. Similar organizations emerged in snowboarding countries worldwide.

Growing pains

Significant change occurred in the late 1980s and early 1990s. The convergence of several factors contributed to the escalating number of boardsport participants. More ski resorts opened their pistes to snowboarders, the mainstream media started reporting favorably on snowboarding culture, and snowboarding magazines (e.g., *Absolutely Radical* (1985), renamed *International Snowboarder Magazine* six months later; *Transworld Snowboarding* (1987), *Snowboarder* (1988), *Blunt* (1993), and movies such as *The Western Front* (1988), *Totally Board* (1989), *Snowboarders in Exile* (1990), and *Critical Condition* (1991)) communicated images, attitudes and styles to snowboarding cultures around the world. Technological advances and an increasingly competitive market also provided participants with a cheaper and wider variety of equipment. Economic growth and further institutionalization accompanied higher levels of participation. Television and corporate sponsors also started to identify the huge potential in extreme sports as a way to tap into the young male market. Mainstream companies quickly began appropriating the alternative, hedonistic, and youthful image of the snowboarder to sell products ranging from chewing gum to vehicles.

Yet institutionalization and commercialization angered many snowboarders: some overtly resisted the process. Jeff Galbriath, senior editor of *Snowboarder Magazine*, recalls one Professional Snowboard Tour of America (PSTA) event sponsored by clothing company Body Glove where top U.S. snowboarder Shaun Palmer 'hit the main sponsor guy in the face...with a hot dog'. Body Glove subsequently 'pulled out': 'culturally, none of the riders were prepared to deal with contest structure' (cited in Howe, 1998, p. 56). For some, competitive boarding stood in symbolic juxtaposition to 'soul boarding'. For example, in 1990 U.S. snowboarder and world champion Craig Kelly retired at the peak of his career from the competitive circuit that he likened to 'prostitution' (Ibid., p. 82). As he put it: 'Snowboarding is something that I think should be done on your own terms. Society is full of rules, and I use the time I spend in the mountains as an opportunity to free myself of all constraints...I decided that competing on the World Tour restricted the freedom that I found with snowboarding in the first place' (cited in Reed, 2005, p. 54). Debates over the institutionalization process in snowboarding came to the fore in the lead-up to the 1998 Winter Olympics.

The inclusion of snowboarding in the 1998 Winter Olympics signified a defining moment in snowboarding's short history and boarders were divided as to their opinion on this topic. Many were infuriated by the International Olympic Committee's (IOC) decision to include snowboarding under the International Ski Federation (FIS) rather than the International Snowboard Federation (ISF) – an organization established in 1990 by 120 snowboarders from more than five nations, and dedicated to hosting elite-level competitions around the world. The loudest voice of opposition came from Terje

Haakonsen – undoubtedly the world's best half-pipe rider at the time – who criticized the IOC's lack of understanding of snowboarding culture and consideration of snowboarders' needs: 'Snowboarding is not a discipline of skiing' (cited in *Transworld Snowboarding*, March 2010, p. 78). Haakonsen refused to enter the games because he believed, quite correctly in the eyes of many (see, e.g., Bale & Krogh-Christensen, 2004), that the IOC comprised a group of Mafia-like officials and that participation in the event was tantamount to joining the army. Haakonsen protested against snowboarders being turned into 'uniform-wearing, flag-bearing, walking logo[s]' (Mellegren, 1998, para. 8). Other snowboarders expressed similar sentiments: 'The Olympics will change the sport altogether. I didn't get into snowboarding to go to the Olympics. I don't think it sounds so great. Snowboarding is great because it's so different from other sports. Now it will get too serious, training, competing, working out in gyms. There's nothing wrong with that but snowboarding isn't like that, and it'll be sad when it becomes like that' (Cara Beth Burnside, cited in Howe, 1998, p. 151); 'I think the Olympics are way too big and are going to change snowboarding. They are going to make us fit their mold. They aren't fitting into our mold...it will create a reality for snowboarding that millions will swallow and accept' (Morgan Lafonte, cited in Howe, 1998, p. 151).

While many snowboarders resisted snowboarding's inclusion in the Olympics, it is important to note that some embraced these changes: 'I want to go to the Olympics...be the first snowboarder to win a gold medal and be written into the history books' (Jimi Scott, cited in Howe, 1998, p. 151). Todd Richards (2003) also admitted, 'I'd be a liar if I said the thought of being on the first U.S Olympic Snowboard team didn't fire me up. Wheaties boxes, international prestige, the best half-pipe in the world – and let's not forget the cold hard cash that goes with it all' (p. 185). Continuing, Richards (2003) conceded that 'finally snowboarding is becoming lucrative' (p. 107). As Doug Palladini, publisher of *Snowboarder* magazine, observes:

> The Olympics are a fascinating little microcosm of the whole mainstreaming fear. We've always shied away from the political structure, the rigidity, and all the things in competition that don't really apply to the concept of our sport. But having the opportunity to go to the Olympics has made all the riders assess what they want to do. When an opportunity like this comes along, you're not so prone to be a cool guy...you just want to go. (cited in Howe, 1998, p. 155)

Debates among snowboarders over the institutionalization process, and the 1998 Winter Olympics more specifically, are illustrative of the growing divisions and cultural fragmentation within snowboarding culture during this period (see Humphreys, 2003; Thorpe & Wheaton, In Press).

Snowboarding becomes mainstream

Inevitably, incorporation continued regardless of snowboarders' opposition. By the late 1990s television and corporate sponsors were appropriating the alternative, hedonistic, and youthful image of the snowboarder to sell products to both youth and mainstream markets. During this period snowboarding increasingly became controlled and defined by transnational media corporations like ESPN and NBC via events such as the X-Games, Gravity Games, and the Winter Olympics. According to Todd Richards:

> The X-Games marked the end of one era but simultaneously gave birth to a whole new world of possibilities. It was sort of sad to say good-bye to being a bunch of misunderstood outcasts. A lot of joy was derived from the punk-rock-spirit, and once the masses join your ranks ... it's over. The image had already begun to change but the X-Games put the icing on the mainstream cake. (2003, p. 182)

In 1998, ESPN's sport channels beamed the X-Games to 198 countries in 21 languages (Rinehart, 2000). According to a Leisure Trends survey, 32 percent (nearly 92 million people) of the U.S. population watched the 2002 Olympic snowboarding half-pipe competition in which Americans won gold (Ross Powers), silver (Danny Kass), and bronze (J. J. Thomas) in the men's event (this was the first U.S. Winter Olympic medal sweep since 1956) and gold (Kelly Clark) in the women's event. Of those viewers 18.6 million Americans said they wanted to try snowboarding (Snowboarding and the Olympics, 2004). The incorporation of snowboarding into mega-events such as the X-Games and Olympics, video games including Playstation's *Cool Boarders* and *Shaun Palmer Pro-Snowboarder*, and blockbuster movies such as *First Descent* (2005), helped further expose the sport to the mainstream.

As snowboarding became popularized and incorporated into the mainstream, it assumed many of the trappings of other modern sports including corporate sponsorship, large prize monies, 'rationalized systems of rules', hierarchical and individualistic 'star systems', win-at-all-costs values, and the creation of heroes, heroines and 'rebel' athletes who look like 'walking corporate billboards' (Messner, 2002, p. 82). Unlike earlier generations, many current boarders embrace commercial approaches or, in the more colorful words of Todd Richards (2003), are 'milk[ing] it while it's lactating' (p. 178). Professional snowboarders including Gretchen Bleiler, Torah Bright, Kelly Clark, Tara Dakides, Lindsey Jacobellis, Danny Kass, Hannah Teter, and Shaun White have benefited from the recently commercialized form of snowboarding. They have achieved superstar status within the culture, attracting major corporate sponsors including Target, Visa, Nike, Mountain Dew, Campbell's Soup, and Boost Mobile. Indeed, a report by *Forbes* identified White as the most highly paid athlete entering the 2010 Winter Olympics with an annual salary of more than US$9 million; Bleiler and Teter were seventh equal on the list, each netting more than US$1 million a year (Settimi, 2010).

But with major corporate sponsors offering large prize monies, the focus of many boarding competitions is no longer fun; extreme forms of individualism and egocentricity prevail. Olympic silver medalist Gretchen Bleiler believes the 'industry pressure' and 'ultra-high' level of snowboarding ability are creating an 'extremely competitive' atmosphere in snowboarding, and decries a younger generation who, in their hunger to win, are 'changing the overall feel at the top of the half-pipe' (cited in Sherowski, 2003a, p. 146). Indeed, many contemporary young 'up-and-comers' participate in different ways to boarders from the past; they train under the guidance of coaches in highly organized structures in which snowboarding is not only an Olympic sport but also a highly profitable career.

Despite the increasing professionalism at the elite level, many athletes continue to celebrate snowboarding's countercultural past. Arguably the most professional competitive snowboarder, Shaun White downplayed the professionalism of snowboarding in an interview with *Rolling Stone*: 'We are still the dirty ones in the bunch, the sketchy snowboard kids. I don't think I'd have it any other way' (Edwards, 2006, p. 45). Of course, neither would the corporate sponsors who have profited enormously from the commodification of snowboarding's perceived irresponsible and uncontrolled image (see Thorpe & Wheaton, In Press).

Cultural fragmentation

The influx of new participants during the late 1990s and early 2000s fueled struggles within the snowboarding culture between insiders, newcomers, and various subgroups. Andy Blumberg (2002), editor of *Transworld Snowboarding*, explains that 'once united we seem today divided' (p. 16). Core participants include males and females whose commitment to the activity is such that it organizes their whole lives. Snowboard instructor, lift operator, park crew, journalist, photographer, competition judge, and coach, are among the jobs held by passionate snowboarders committed to the lifestyle rather than the economic rewards (see also Wheaton & Tomlinson, 1998). In contrast to core boarders, snowboarders who are less committed – including male and female novices, poseurs, or weekend warriors – have lower cultural status. Rather than demonstrating commitment via participation, poseurs consciously display brand-name clothing and equipment. A dominant mode of thinking among many committed male and female boarders is that the only 'authentic' cultural identity is that of the 'core' snowboarder who demonstrates commitment to the activity itself, not just the snowboarding style. Members of the snowboarding industry, however, understand increasing participation rates and cultural fragmentation as vital for economic growth. 'Obviously, for self-interested business reasons I think the more people who snowboard the better', proclaims Jake Burton (cited in Hagerman, 2002, p. 21).

Various identities and preferred styles of participation (e.g., free riding, free-styling, jibbing, and alpine) exist within the core group. Freeriders prefer to hike, ride a snowmobile, or pay for a helicopter ride, to access remote backcountry terrain, where they might drop off rocks or cliffs, ride down chutes, and snowboard in powder and among trees. Others, including free-style boarders, prefer to ride the more accessible, yet typically crowded, ski resort slopes. Freestyle riding, which includes snowboarding on man-made features such as half-pipes and terrain parks, is currently the most popular form of participation. This style is based on creative and technical maneuvers such as spins, grabs, or inverts, many of which have their roots in skateboarding. In response to this trend, the typical ski resort invests in equipment and personnel to create and maintain features such as terrain parks and half-pipes to attract snowboarding patrons. Some core snowboarders also enjoy jibbing, a substyle of freestyle snowboarding that involves performing various skateboarding-inspired maneuvers on obstacles including trees, stumps, and rails. Jibbing in urban environments has also become a popular activity among core boarders; jibbers locate a handrail (e.g., down a flight of stairs outside a school, hospital, or mall), shovel snow at the top and bottom of the rail (to create a run-in and landing), and then perform technical maneuvers while jumping onto, sliding down, and jumping off the rail. Alpine, another style of participation, privileges speed and carving over jumping or jibbing, but it is the least popular style among core snowboarders who tend to dismiss participants as skiers on boards.

In sum, the story of snowboarding began a little over four decades ago with a new piece of equipment that appealed to the hedonistic desires of a new generation. Developing in a historically unique conjuncture of mass communications, corporate sponsors, entertainment industries, and an increasingly, young affluent population, snowboarding has spread around the world at a phenomenal rate. While many early participants regret snowboarding having been subjected to the forces and constraints of the commercialization process, contemporary participants typically accept major corporate sponsorship, mass-mediated events (e.g., Olympics and X-Games), and hierarchical and individualistic 'star systems' as endemic to the sport in the twenty-first century. Many current boarders accept that 'the snowboarding industry sold itself out to the corporate world' (Question, 2006, para. 2). However, this does not necessarily diminish the enjoyment they derive from participation; many acknowledge the benefits offered to athletes and participants in this hypercommercial context (e.g., opportunities for athletes to travel, well organized and widely publicized events, more affordable equipment). The sport, culture, and industry of snowboarding have experienced rapid change over the past four decades. With participants constantly developing new styles and seeking out new spaces and technologies, it seems inevitable that the activity will continue to evolve for many years to come.

A story of snowboarding: virtue or vice?

Historical narratives such as the story of snowboarding told above have explanatory virtues. As Appleby et al. (1994) note, 'the human intellect demands accuracy while the soul craves meaning. History ministers to both with stories' (p. 263). Yet paradoxically, the story format is precisely the Achilles' heel of the historical narrative. The explanation that appears to emerge 'naturally' from the raw data is in fact the result of my mediation of the past, of my arranging ideas and sorting evidence. The range and volume of evidence bearing on the history of snowboarding is so large that I could not avoid selecting evidence to compose this narrative. As Phillips (2004) explains, 'objectivity is illusory because history is a discursive form of interpretation from the moment a topic is conceived through to narrative creation in which the actions, behavior and thoughts of the historian cannot be expunged from the process of representing the past' (p. 63). Moreover, the numerous political, cultural, social, and economic events and processes inherent in the story of snowboarding unfold simultaneously and interactively and complicate the narrative account of the development of snowboarding. Thus, this short history of snowboarding is merely one interpretation of the past and it invariably excludes other, equally valid personal, local, regional, and national stories and forms of knowledge. The primary intention of this chapter, however, is not to establish the 'veracity of the historical facts' but rather to explore the ways in which 'the past is understood and appropriated within contemporary consciousness' (Nora, 1996, cited in Schultz, 2007, p. 716). Thus in the second part of this chapter I examine how and why this particular historical narrative has become an integral part of the snowboarding collective memory, suggesting that the way the snowboarding body is remembered is an implicitly political process located as much in the present as the past.

The politics of remembering the snowboarding body: an interdisciplinary approach to physical cultural memory

Recording personal and collective memory is an ancient practice. In recent years, however, there has been a 'passion for memory' in the social sciences (Nora, 1996). Employing an array of methodological and theoretical approaches, sociologists, anthropologists, cultural studies scholars, psychologists, and historians have all offered explanations of how social memory is generated, maintained, reproduced, and embodied through texts, images, sites and experiences. Some critical sport historians have also helped reveal the important nexus between cultural practice and memory-making via investigations of sporting museums, monuments, stadiums, films and photos (Osmond & Phillips, 2004; Osmond et al., 2006; Schultz, 2007). In the remainder of this chapter I build on their work to consider how we might further understand the complex processes of producing and consuming snowboarding cultural memories[1] (See Thorpe, 2010a).

I begin with some definitions. History and memory are two different ways of knowing the past. Misztal (2003) defines history as 'an intellectual, critical [*sic*] activity, which emerges as the primary mode of knowledge about the past when tradition weakens and social memory is fading' (p. 101). Memory, on the other hand, is the 'unavoidable gap between experiencing an event and remembering it, filled up by our creative interpretation of the past' (Ibid.). The relationship between history and memory is complex. While some insist on the opposing natures of history and memory, the cultural turn in the social sciences and humanities has led to the 'blurring of the boundaries between history and memory' and alerted us to the complex relationships between memory and time, memory and power, and memory and imagination (Misztal, 2003).

While memory has both individual and collective dimensions, in this chapter I focus on collective or cultural memory. Collective memory is 'the representation of the past, both that shared by a group and that which is collectively commemorated, that enacts and gives substance to the group's identity, its present conditions and its vision of the future' (Misztal, 2003, p. 7). Collective memory is passed on to us in various cultural practices, routines, institutions, and artifacts, and is always contested. For Misztal (2003), 'seeing collective memory as the creative imagining of the past in the service of the present and an imagined future, studying the fluidity of images, the commodification of memory and the acceptance of the debate-ability of the past', introduces 'a new dynamic to the interactions between memory and historiography in the representation of the past' (p. 103). Recently, a plethora of studies of collective memory have shed light on the way representations of the past help construct shared cultural knowledge in present conditions.

Despite the richness of collective memory studies, the field faces some heavy critiques. According to Confino (1997), collective memory studies lack a clear focus and have become somewhat predictable. In his words, 'the often-made contention that the past is constructed not as fact but as myth to serve the interest of a particular community may still sound radical to some, but it cannot (and should not) stupefy most historians' (Ibid., p. 1387). Continuing, he notes that the field has become highly fragmented, defined largely in terms of topics of interest (e.g., monuments, films, museums). Kansteiner (2002) is also concerned that cultural memory studies lack critical reflection on method and theory, as well as a systematic evaluation of the field's problems, approaches, and objects of study. The work of Barbara Misztal, however, is a notable exception, and thus deserves further comment.

In *Theories of Social Remembering* (2003), Misztal offers an insightful analysis of four theoretical strands underpinning past and present studies of social or collective memory. First, she describes Maurice Halbwachs' original theory of social memory which draws on the Durkheimian perspective to systematically explore the ways in which present concerns determine what we remember of the past. A second approach, known as the 'invention of tradition perspective' or 'theory of the politics of memory', explains the past as molded to suit present interests. While the 'Halbwach tradition' argues that we remember collectively and selectively, the 'invention of tradition' approach engages with those who control or impose the content of social memories; 'invented' memories serve the purposes of those in power. The third approach, known as 'popular memory', is less deterministic than 'invention of tradition' and allows space for other solutions to the conflict over memory than just its manipulation and control from above. Taking inspiration from Foucault's concepts of popular memory and countermemory, and from the work of British cultural studies theorists, the 'popular memory' approach is critical of top-down understandings of memory, and recognizes that groups (in some circumstances) assert their own version of the past. Arguably, the fourth approach, 'dynamics of memory', has the most potential for future studies of cultural remembering. The 'dynamics of memory' approach conceptualizes memory as 'never solely manipulated or durable; instead, the role of agency and the temporal dimensions of memory as well as the historicity of social identities are stressed and analyzed' (Misztal, 2003, p. 69; see also Shapiro, 1997). Collective memory is understood as the outcome of multiple and competing discourses within a particular historical conjuncture in which people are 'neither solely rational actors who use history to their own ends, nor are they merely cultural dopes' (Misztal, 2003, p. 72). According to Misztal, the dynamics of memory approach is more 'aware of the flexibility and ambiguities of memory' and thus runs a lower risk of political reductionism and functionalism (Ibid., p. 73).

Each of these theoretical approaches offers a different explanation of the dynamics of remembering, and different answers to the question of *who* is a remembering subject and *what* is the nature of the past. Underpinning each of the four theories are different assumptions about power and the relationship between structure and agency in the remembering process. In this way, explanations of social remembering appear to mirror some of the major trends in sociology and in social theory more broadly (Urry, 1996). Arguably, of the four different theoretical strands of cultural remembering, the 'dynamics of memory' approach directs the most attention to time, power, structure, agency, social change, and the historicity of cultural memory construction.

None of the four theories of social remembering, however, give sufficient attention to the *interpreting self* (Misztal, 2003). Some scholars are concerned by the trend in memory studies to focus on the representation of specific events within particular chronological, geographical, and media settings, without reflecting on how an audience interprets a particular representation. Kansteiner (2002) argues that too much attention is paid to the mediation of memory via discursive and visual objects, and to the production of objects of memory, and too little to the 'consumers' of memory; we cannot assume that 'facts of representation coincide with facts of reception', nor should we forget that audiences 'use, ignore or transform' memory artifacts according to their own interests (p. 180). Kansteiner proposes addressing some of these problems by adopting and further developing the methods of media and communication studies, especially with respect to audience reception. Drawing upon a more interdisciplinary approach, we can begin to examine the *interaction* among memory makers, memory users, and visual and discursive objects and traditions of representations (or what he refers to as 'media of memory'). According to Kansteiner (2002) this 'hermeneutical triangle' implies an 'open dialogue between the object, the maker, and the consumer in constructing meaning' (p. 197). Adopting such an approach, cultural memory might be recast as a 'complex process of cultural production and consumption that acknowledges the persistence of cultural traditions as well as the ingenuity of memory makers and the subversive interests of memory consumers' (p. 179). While there is nothing particularly new in pointing out the importance of audience reception for our understandings of cultural artifacts, these arguments have yet to be made in relation to collective memory in sport and physical culture. Thus, in the remainder of this chapter I apply Kansteiner's (2002) model to an examination of the production *and consumption* of cultural memory in snowboarding.

'Media of memory' in snowboarding culture

In recent years a palpable sense of nostalgia has emerged among ageing snowboarders. A plethora of cultural memory products, including museums, books, films, documentaries, magazines, and websites, work to frame representations of the snowboarding past and evoke cultural memories. These are examples of what Kansteiner (2002) calls 'media of memory'.

According to Radley (1990), 'remembering is something which occurs in a world of things...artifacts play a central role in the memories of cultures and individuals... In the very variability of objects, in the ordinariness of their consumption and in the sensory richness of relationships people enjoy through them, they are fitted to be later reframed as material images for reflection and recall' (p. 57). This is certainly the case in snowboarding museums which feature an array of early equipment, such as snowboards and boots, and other cultural artifacts, such as photos, magazines, trophies, and clothing. Like many sporting museums, snowboarding museums are typically organized by passionate snowboarders with little curatorial expertise (see Vamplew, 1998). According to the founder of the Living Room Snowboard Museum in Mühlbach am Hochkönig, Austria, 'the goal of the museum is to document the spirit of snowboard history'. Continuing, he explains his initial motives and current collecting practices: 'I love snowboarding and that is what this museum is all about. ... I am not buying all old boards I find on the internet, I am searching for people who share my passion for snowboarding and want to make their board a part of history' (retrieved from www.snowboardmuseum.net). In contrast, with the aim to 'document and preserve the early history of snowboarding', Dennis Nazari actively uses the internet (particularly EBay) to source, bid for, and purchase early snowboards which he then exhibits at his snowboard museum/retail shop in Salt Lake City, Utah.[2] With more than 1000 vintage snowboards hanging from the roof and attached to the walls, and the latest snowboard products displayed on racks and hangers throughout the store, the Salty Peaks Snowboard Museum and Snowboard and Skateboard Shop offers a fascinating multidimensional and temporal cultural experience.[3] As the product of a passionate snowboard collector *and* creative businessman, it also offers support for Vamplew's (1998) claim that 'commercialism and modern museums are bedfellows' (p. 273).

Another interesting example of the complex relationship between media of memory and commercialism in the snowboarding culture is the 'Aries2010 Project'. The brainchild of snowboarding photographer and designer, Trevor Graves, and produced in collaboration with Nike, the Aries2010 project involved the creation of a time capsule storing cultural artifacts ranging 'from photographs and historical discourse to trick schematics and some of the sport's most pivotal gear' (Graves, 2010, p. 4). The capsule was launched during the 2010 Winter Olympics in Vancouver and is scheduled to be reopened in 2020. The opening and closing 'parties' hosted by Nike, and attended by many past and present snowboarding athletes and industry members, including journalists, photographers, and company owners, featured presentations from various snowboarding pioneers, as well as extensive displays of cultural artifacts, including early equipment, such as boots, boards, and bindings, and other cultural artifacts (e.g., videos and DVDs, magazines, event posters, race bibs, photos, early video footage, and clothing) (see Figure 2.1). The Aries2010 project also includes an interactive website which is intended to 'act as a beacon to draw out the stories, images and art that form our history' (Graves, 2010, p. 3; see www.ARIES2010.com). According to Graves, it is hoped that this 'social media platform' will be 'easy and fun for all snowboarders to upload their historical stories' and engage in 'conversation and arguments about the facts that should be presented' (personal communication, March 2010). Arguably, the Aries2010 project offers an excellent example of both the highly creative and the variegated forms of media of memory being created by passionate snowboarders and amateur curators.

Interestingly, early snowboards tend to dominate many spaces of nostalgia (i.e., museums, the Aries2010 display). According to Sam, a committed snowboarder and journalist, the technological changes are important because they form a 'timeline' for the sport. He explained that 'by piecing together...technological developments, we can map out the early years of

Figure 2.1 Displays of cultural artifacts (a) snowboard boots and photos, and (b) snowboards at the Aries2010 Project 'time capsule' closing 'party' held in a snowboard shop in Vancouver during the 2010 Winter Olympics (photograph taken and used with permission of Author)

snowboarding, pretty much to the month, if not the day' (personal communication, June 2009). Similarly, Trevor Graves identified the 'Kidwell R 1985 Red Roundtail' snowboard as one of the most culturally significant artifacts featured in the Aries2010 project: 'it resonated the strongest because all generations can relate to the pioneering of the sport of snowboarding [represented by] that board, that rider, and that place in time' (personal communication, March 2010). But the process of remembering is 'not only a faculty of the brain, since the body remembers too' (Chronis, 2006, p. 293; see also Urry, 1996). Following Chronis (2006) and Urry (1996), I suggest that early snowboards are allocated the most space within snowboarding museums because they 'evoke the senses', either real or imaginary, of the remembering snowboarding body. The website for 'The Living Room Snowboard Museum' in Austria, for example, invites snowboard enthusiasts to visit the museum where they can '*see* the boards for real, *touch* them, *feel* how heavy the boards were' and '*feel* how the boards have changed over the years' (retrieved from www.livingroom-hochkoenig.at, emphasis added). Put simply, some material artifacts in museums, such as snowboards, 'provide the medium through which sensory experiences of the past are transmitted to the present generation' (Chronis, 2006, p. 270).

An array of books and films also describe and illustrate the history of snowboarding. Some of these are extensively researched cultural histories – for example, *Sick: A Cultural History of Snowboarding* (Howe, 1998) – while others are more autobiographical accounts of snowboarding pioneers and athletes, including Tina Basich (*Pretty Good for a Girl*, 2003), Tara Dakides (*Against the Grain*, DVD, 2008), Craig Kelly (*Let it Ride*, DVD, 2007) and Todd Richards (*P3: Pipes, Parks, and Powder*, 2003). Snowboarding magazines increasingly include images and stories from the (not so distant) past. Websites and other electronic media also offer an array of personal and collective histories of snowboarding. In his widely cited book, *Theatres of Memory*, Samuel (1994) explains that the function of memory keeping and presentation is 'increasingly assigned to the electronic media' (p. 25). This is particularly true in snowboarding where hundreds of websites offer an array of textual, visual and interactional personal and collective histories of snowboarding. It is beyond the scope of this chapter to offer a detailed examination of websites as spaces of snowboarding cultural memory production. Nonetheless, I concur with Urry (1996) who argues that the 'electronification' of memory provides another twist in understanding how societies and cultures remember their past within an extraordinarily changing present.

The key point here is that collective memory in the contemporary snowboarding culture is cultivated via an array of mass, niche and micro 'media of memory', each with different production processes and audiences. Comments from Misztal (2003) and Herview-Leger (2000) seem pertinent in relation to cultural memory construction in the highly mediated and rapidly evolving snowboarding culture. According to Misztal (2003), 'the immediacy of communication, information overload, and the speed of changing images, the growing hybridity of media, all further expand and problematize the status of memory. We have unlimited access to facts, sources and information which we can store, freeze and replay' (p. 25). For Herview-Leger, (2000) 'digital technology, interactive media and information systems have greatly changed the facets of memory practices in our time, and as a result today's memory is "composed of bits and pieces"' (p. 129). Indeed, as the following comment from Nick, an ex-core New Zealand snowboarder, illustrates, collective memories are 'multimedia collages':

> My understanding of snowboarding history comes from personal experience, magazines, videos/DVDs, and the odd book. It's a cumulative mash of various sources and wouldn't be totally accurate but it reflects my involvement and opinions. It's biased by my experiences and the few forms of media available to me through my time in the sport. (personal communication, June 2009)

The production processes of these amateur and commercial cultural histories might perturb some professional historians. But, as Huyssen (2003) reminds us: 'There is no pure space outside of commodity culture, however much we may desire such a space... [and] the problem is not solved by simply opposing serious memory to trivial memory' (p. 19). A two-minute video clip on the 'history of snowboarding' on YouTube, for example, has been viewed more than 160,000 times! Thus, with the increasing 'fluidity of images [and] commodification of memory', scholars seeking to understand the production of historical narratives in sport and physical culture must give due consideration to both traditional and new 'media of memory' (Misztal, 2003, p. 103).

Interestingly, a dominant snowboarding narrative is being constructed as 'cultural truth' through repetition across these various 'media of memory'. Contemporary snowboarders the world over appear to be (temporarily) settling on a global cultural narrative that ignores local differences and reinforces the sport's rebellious, countercultural, do-it-yourself, antiauthoritarian roots. While this narrative appears to emerge 'naturally' from the raw data, it is of course the result of various historical agents' mediations of the past, of arranged ideas and sorted evidence. This narrative is the outcome of multiple and competing historical discourses; it is the result of complex and political processes of cultural remembering and forgetting. Perhaps this story is finding its way into popular cultural imagination simply because it fits the needs of contemporary participants who are seeking an 'alternative' identity via snowboarding. This narrative also appears to work well for marketing and media agents, who know that the alternative, hedonistic, and youthful image of snowboarding is an important selling point in the highly competitive sport and youth cultural industries. Since I am adopting a dynamic and interdisciplinary approach to understanding cultural memory, however, I am less interested in the historical 'facts' or the commemorative practices stabilizing particular cultural memories, and more concerned with the ongoing negotiations between those producing *and* consuming various narratives of the history of snowboarding.

'Key agents' in the production of cultural memory

Journalists, editors, photographers, cinematographers, directors and producers, and museum curators, all employ – either consciously or unconsciously – 'framing strategies and devices' in their construction of snowboarding memories (Irwin-Zarecka, 1994). Arguably, we can garner fresh insights into the cultural politics involved in the production of snowboarding narratives by examining the 'framing strategies' employed by key agents in the industry.

For example, Burton Snowboards, which currently accounts for approximately 40 percent of the global snowboarding industry, is at the forefront of much of the nostalgia in the snowboarding culture (see Chapter 3). Snowboarding pioneer and company founder Jake Burton ensures his central position in these histories with a wide range of subtle and not so subtle strategies, such as eagerly providing interviews and photos to those creating historical narratives and representations. In fact, every historical source in my collection acknowledges the assistance given by Burton Snowboards and/or Jake Burton himself (e.g., Curtes et al., 2001; Howe, 1998; Reed, 2005). When I visited Salty Peaks Snowboard Museum in Salt Lake City it was clear that Burton Snowboards had donated a significant proportion of the early equipment on display. Jake was acknowledged in this museum for his 'generous' contributions. Furthermore, the Burton Snowboards' website contains a 19-page document, readily accessed by journalists, students and snowboarders, detailing the integral roles of Jake and Burton Snowboards in the development of snowboarding. Burton Snowboards also entered into a partnership with media conglomerate Mandalay Entertainment to produce a range of media (theatrical features, television programming, reality, and event coverage) that, according to the press release, will 'detail the evolution of the sport and culture' and 'showcase Burton's vast history and position as the *leader and true innovator in snowboarding*' (Press release, October 2004).

Burton has been so successful at writing himself into the history of snowboarding, that he is popularly known as the 'father of snowboarding'. He played a key role in the technical development of snowboarding, but so too did many others who are now being written out of the sport's history. Snowboarding pioneer Tom Sims laments: 'It's ironic...that so many of the early pioneers of the sport have gone by the wayside. The history of snowboarding is', he says, 'being written by the winners' (Reed, 2005, p. 41). The 'framing' of the history of snowboarding has important political and economic effects. Jake's centrality in the history of snowboarding works to connect his company to its cultural roots. Reinforcing the company's 'authenticity' is critical to deflecting charges of industry domination and is, therefore, integral to the company's economic success. But, as Misztal reminds us, distortion of memory can occur for various reasons, and we should be cautious of assuming manipulative motives in advance; cultural memories are 'never solely manipulated or durable' (2003, p. 69). Moreover, these narratives are not being imposed on a public without consent; in some instances, individuals and groups are attempting to assert their own versions of the past.

Consuming 'media of memory'

In their efforts to reveal some of the complexities of producing 'memory projects', historians often overlook the various ways in which audiences consume and make meaning of cultural products. This is problematic, however, because neither the characteristics of a 'memory artifact', nor the objectives of the makers of these products, are good indicators of subsequent reception processes. Indeed, media and communication scholars have clearly shown that media representations are often ignored or read against the grain of their intended or intrinsic messages. There is also a tendency for cultural memory scholars to assume that group members adopt similar readings of these 'texts'. But many groups, including contemporary snowboarding culture, are highly fragmented and in a constant state of flux; thus we should not assume identical or stable readings of these 'technologies of memory'.

Adopting Kansteiner's (2002) dynamic model of cultural memory production and consumption, we are invited to examine the ways snowboarders make meaning of multiple (and sometimes competing) historical narratives and representations. Snowboarders' responses to 'media of memory' range from passive consumption to reflexive consumption, and cultural production (see also Chapter 4). Their readings are influenced by an array of factors including past snowboarding experiences, position within the snowboarding culture (e.g., core snowboarder, weekend warrior, novice boarder) or industry (e.g., journalist, company employee), age, nationality, education, and so on. In contrast to many marginal participants, such as weekend warriors or novices, who tend to be unfamiliar with (or less interested in) the history of snowboarding, some core and ex-core participants are critical of the dominant historical narrative that is being repeated across various 'media of memory' products and that ignores local differences. For example, Nathan draws upon his lived experiences to question the exaggerated accounts of physical confrontations between early skiers and snowboarders:

> I think it's funny how many snowboarders reflect on those times ... they always seem to *bend perception*. If you read the histories of snowboarding, or listen to people tell their stories about the 'old days', it always seems

like there were piles of burly skiers trying to beat the stuffing out of snowboarders and bully them off the slopes. Maybe that was the case at a few resorts in America, but it certainly was not the case in New Zealand. From my memory, skiers were only trying to protect themselves from out of control snowboarders... If you slammed near a lift, a chorus would go up from the skiers above, but it was mostly in good humor. (personal communication, June 2009, emphasis added)

Continuing, Nathan also reveals his critical awareness of the 'Americanization' of snowboarding media and cultural memory products:

The American presence in snowboarding was there right from the beginning and they quickly took control of the communication of it. At the time I started, the only magazines were American; the few videos available were American; most of the popular riders were American. So they [Americans] were positioned very early as the pioneers and leaders in snowboarding. All of the histories I've read have focused on American pioneers, but I think a *fairer representation* is starting to come about as some websites and magazine articles are starting to tell the stories of some of the early Euro riders. (personal communication, June 2009, emphasis added)

Similarly Ste'en comments on the dominance of American memories in representations of the snowboarding history:

Most of the stories we read are actually American snowboarding histories. But this has a lot to do with the fact that [in New Zealand] our language, culture, and interest in board sports has tended to look to America more than anywhere else – and you must admit, they (USA) are pretty good at pumping it out! There is, however, plenty of European snowboarding history once you start looking for it. Many of the early developments were happening simultaneously, if not earlier, in Europe, and gradually some of these stories are coming to the surface. (personal communication, June 2009)

The following comments further reveal the critical historical reflexivity of some core and ex-core participants who are aware of the broader cultural politics within which these historical narratives are produced:

I think it comes down to how motivated people are to tell their stories. Burton obviously is motivated and it directly relates to his companies image, and therefore sales. Good on him, but his story will always appear to have an agenda. It doesn't greatly bother me as I accept I'm watching a single account of what happened and that other stories are likely to conflict with it. (James, personal communication, June 2009)

The stories most visible are the ones told by the 'biggest' industry people in our sport, and it comes as no surprise that they are using their own history to springboard the credibility of themselves and their product. In today's world of media use (often verging on propaganda!), I think it becomes a responsibility of the reader to be slightly wary of this element in anything they see or hear. (Simon, personal communication, June 2009)

As these comments suggest, some (though certainly not all) snowboarders are critically aware of the highly political and context-based framings of snowboarding histories. Perhaps, as Baer (2001) suggests: 'The massive presence of media products, the variety of genres, styles and interpretations of the past, might be creating a richer understanding of history and collective memory and a more reflexive and self-conscious historical subject' (p. 499).

My key argument here is that cultural memory in snowboarding is the result of an ongoing process of negotiation between at least three historical factors: cultural memory products, producers, and consumers. To illustrate the *dynamic nature* of the production and consumption of cultural memories in the contemporary snowboarding culture, I want to offer two brief examples. The first is a recent dialogue that appeared in *New Zealand Snowboarder* magazine. During an interview with an ex-core New Zealand snowboarder, Nathan noted: '[The editor] has written some good stuff about the fledgling New Zealand snowboard community, which interestingly was argued as inaccurate from a reader who sent in photos and his own account. That was good. It became like an open forum' (personal communication, February 2009). A follow-up conversation with the editor of the magazine and author of this article, Ste'en Webster, revealed further details:

In 2006 I had a ten page story published in American magazine *Snowboard Journal* documenting the early history of snowboarding in New Zealand. My story, 'Kiwi Dawn', covered the late 80s and early 90s, which was the period when things really started to take shape. I was aware there were some earlier rumblings, and made reference as such, but I had no specific information or material so let the details slide. I was pretty proud with the finished article, thinking I'd managed to sum things up nicely. Then, a few months later, out of the blue, an email from old Queenstown buddy Simon Clayton turned up

He argued that I had missed out a whole chapter of the history of New Zealand snowboarding. What he didn't know was that I had a 3000 word limit set by the magazine, and so had to make some pretty tough choices about what to include and exclude. Obviously, I couldn't re-write my history, but we published his account in *NZ Snowboarder*. In this way he was able to add detail that predated the information I presented in my story...

detail that may not have come to the surface had he not read my story. (personal communication, June 2009)

According to Kansteiner (2002), 'all media of memory, especially electronic media, neither simply reflect nor determine collective memory but are inextricably involved in its *construction and evolution*' (p. 195). This seems particularly true in snowboarding where niche cultural media such as magazines and websites – which are produced and consumed by active snowboarders – provide space for participants to share lived memories, and actively discuss and debate the accuracy of particular historical narratives. And, as this particular example illustrates, these new media also provide space for countermemories to emerge.

The second example is the recent publication of a children's comic book describing Jake Burton as the 'inventor of snowboarding' which caused considerable controversy within the snowboarding culture and industry (see Figure 2.2). Shortly after the book's release, an anonymous email was sent to hundreds of members of the North American snowboard industry accusing Burton of 'team[ing] up with a kids' book publisher to create a skewed version of snowboard history for very young kids to "learn" from in early elementary school. Probably so that they'll be inclined to buy Burton product as they get older....Burton is trying to brainwash little kids these days that Jake invented snowboarding'. The email concludes by asking recipients to 'forward this message to anyone who you think cares about Burton twisting snowboarding's history for their own gain, and post it on any blogs you participate on' (cited in Crane, 2008, para. 2). In an effort to 'see if there really was some kind of conspiracy in play', *Transworld Business* journalist Mike Lewis became the self-proclaimed 'fact checker' in this cultural debate. Comments from his interviews with some of the key agents in the (passive) production and (reflexive) consumption of this controversial 'media' of cultural memory are revealing. For example, Capstone senior product planning editor John Rahm, explained:

> Although Burton may not be the official inventor of the snowboard, we feel his story fits into this series because of his important contribution to the sport...That said no one from Burton Snowboards was involved with this project. (cited in Lewis, March 2008, para. 6)

Somewhat surprisingly, the author of the comic book, Michael O'Hearn, openly admits to relying exclusively on easily accessible secondary sources to produce this historical narrative:

> I didn't talk to Burton or anyone else for my research. I used what books I could find and a lot of articles...That was primarily it. I felt there was

Figure 2.2 Cover design of 'Jake Burton Carpenter' cartoon book that described Burton Carpenter as the 'inventor' of snowboarding, and evoked much controversy within the snowboard culture and industry (image used with permission of Capstone Press)

enough publicly available information, and didn't think an interview was really within the scope of the book. (cited in Lewis, 2008, para. 4)

Less surprisingly, Burton's Senior Vice President of global marketing, Bryan Johnston, adamantly denies any company involvement in the production of the comic:

> Just like everyone else, we think this book is misleading. We wish it wasn't out there, but it is. We're limited in what we can do because Jake is a public figure and anyone can choose to write about him. There's nothing we can do about the copies that are already out there. But we are going to recommend the publisher work with us... to make corrections if the book is re-printed. (cited in Lewis, 2008, para. 8)

Interestingly, on his personal blog Lee Crane (2008), past editor of *Transworld Snowboarding* magazine and cited as consultant for the comic book, contextualizes the debate within broader cultural politics:

> So far this 'email' has shown up on Burton's Forums, TransworldSnow-boarding.com, the GroupY marketing club blog, and Transworldbusiness. com. In other words, people are talking about it. The reaction to this email really says more about the current state of the snowboard industry than it does anything else. Burton has been doing a great job of combining and conquering action sports lately and this has many business people frightened; even big people. While I'm all for being critical when it comes to companies like Burton, it would be better if those critiques were based on something other than fear and ignorance. (Crane, 2008, para. 7)

He concludes by stating that 'anyone who has read the comic' would likely 'laugh out loud' at the suggestion that it is 'some kind of insidious conspiracy by the evil marketers at Burton to subjugate the minds of America's youth into only buying Burton products' (Crane, 2008, para. 7).

As this example illustrates, constructing cultural narratives is never an innocent activity. All 'media of memory', even children's comic books, have the potential to be highly political. The processes involved in the production and consumption of such cultural products can never be understood outside the cultural context, nor can we assume individual agents' involvement or motives a priori. This example also highlights the significance of new 'electronic' media, such as email, blogs, and websites, as spaces for engaging in debates about the production of cultural memory.

In sum, cultural memories in snowboarding culture are constructed through 'a process of co-narration, a social process of telling and enacting in which teller and listener are not stable and permanent positions but moments of an interplay whose outcome remains open' (Brockmeier, 2002, p. 35). Importantly, the focus of contests over representations of snowboarding history in various 'media of memory' (e.g., magazines, comic books, websites) is not necessarily conflict about what actually happened in the past so much as questions of 'who or what is entitled to speak for the past in the present' (Hodgkin & Radstone, 2003, p. 1). Struggles over representations of the snowboarding past thus reveal some of the complex power relations in the contemporary snowboarding culture, sport and industry.

Physical cultural memory: boarding bodies in the past, present and future

In this chapter I have argued for greater attention to be paid to the processes by which we come to understand what stories of the past matter to whom, and how these cultural narratives are produced *and* consumed. I propose that understanding the social *and* individual dimensions of collective memory, and the media through which memory is experienced, produced, conveyed, and negotiated, requires an interdisciplinary approach to physical cultural memory studies (Hodgkin & Radstone, 2003). To this end, Wulf Kansteiner offers a useful heuristic device to examine the dynamic relations between media of memory, memory makers, and memory users in contemporary sport and physical cultures. Arguably, this model provides sport historians and sociologists with new opportunities to acknowledge historical representations as 'negotiated, selective, present-oriented, and relative, while insisting that the experiences they reflect cannot be manipulated at will' (Kansteiner, 2002, p. 192). As this discussion has revealed, the cultural politics involved in the production and consumption of snowboarding historical narratives cannot be separated from the broader sociocultural-economic context. In the next chapter I draw upon Marxist and post-Fordist theoretical perspectives to further examine the commercial forces operating on and through snowboarding bodies in historical and contemporary contexts.

3
Producing and Consuming the Snowboarding Body

I remember when I was 13 years old...the infatuation with the new product – a new board, a new jacket, a new pair of goggles – the brand-names, the colors, the smell, it all sticks with me. For kids getting into snowboarding, getting all the new gear is addicting and the companies depend on that. (Ste'en, personal communication, October 2005)

It's just marketing, marketing, marketing...stuffing these kids' minds with 'coolness.' It's really big business. [As a professional snowboarder] if you do it right, you can really go far. It all depends on who your sponsors are and how good you are at talking, because even a mediocre athlete can go far if they know how the industry works, on the flipside the best snowboarder ever can get absolutely nothing if he or she doesn't market themselves right. (Zane, personal communication, November 2005)

When I was younger I used to think: 'Why is everybody so obsessed with growth?' I used to have this debate in my head, and then I just sort of ultimately said: 'Just go for it. Just grow, that's what everybody wants. It's what makes the world go round.' So I sort of just sold out on that regard. ... [But] that's just how [business] works. You want to hire ambitious people. And those people will want to make more money and if everybody in the company wants to make more money there's just one way that's going to happen. You will have to grow. (Jake Burton, founder and chairman of Burton Snowboards, cited in Benedek, 2009, para. 10)

Within four short decades the snowboarding market has flourished, rapidly developing from a medley of backyard businesses to a global industry worth US$2.4 billion per annum (Morris, 2008). In this chapter I examine the snowboarding body as a malleable marker of commercial value subject to the fragmentation of this snowboarding market and the vagaries of fashion.

Here I am particularly interested in the production and consumption of snowboarding bodies by company owners and employees, professional athletes, and various groups of cultural consumers. The following discussion consists of two main parts. The first examines snowboarding as a capitalist phenomenon through the works of political revolutionary and social theorist Karl Marx (1818–1883). Here I employ three of Marx's basic principles of capitalism to explain how snowboarding propagates capitalist accumulation, competition, and exploitation in its modes of economic and political organization. I bring these theoretical concepts 'to life' using the case of Burton Snowboards. While this analysis reveals the inextricable links between snowboarding culture and the capitalist system, serious questions remain over the ability of Marx's work to explain culture and cultural politics. Thus in the second part I draw upon a more recent post-Fordist perspective to further explain the relationship between the snowboarding economy and culture, illustrating this with the case of the female niche market.

Karl Marx and the political economy of snowboarding

Karl Marx has been a major influence on the development of sociology and as often a subject of criticism as of inspiration. Although Marx's writings cover an enormous spectrum, he remains the preeminent theorist of capitalist society. Importantly for this project, he is also the 'best known critic of the effects of capitalism on our bodily "species-being"' (Shilling, 2007, p. 5). *Capital: A Critique of Political Economy* (1970[1885]), his most detailed work, spells out the economic mechanisms of capitalist society, developing the labor theory of value, the theory of capital accumulation, and the theory of capitalism's possible internal collapse. Simply put, for Marx the economy is the main determinant of social phenomena. Inevitably, since Marx's death in 1883, the structure of social life has undergone significant changes. Against this background, the relevance of his theories for explaining contemporary social and economic phenomena is hotly debated. As Bottomore (1956) states, 'after a century of turbulent economic and political changes, and in the face of entirely new problems, we have to ask what is still living and what is dead in Marx's theory' (p. 4). Whereas some argue that Marx's theories belong in the dustbin of history, others believe his fundamental critique of political economy 'still holds a vibrant, untapped potential for critical sociological study' (Beamish, 2002, p. 38). Harvey (1989) claims that 'the invariant elements and relations that Marx defined as fundamental to any capitalist mode of production still shine through, and in many instances with an even greater illuminosity than before' (p. 187). Giulianotti (2005), for example, believes that Marxist perspectives retain 'explanatory currency' in explaining the 'hyper-commodification' of sport (p. 41). Arguably, Marx's conditions for the capitalist mode of production remain relevant to understanding contemporary society (Mandel, 1976).

In *Capital*, Marx demonstrated that three conditions – and three only – determine the existence of capitalist mode of production. First, there must be continuous economic growth. A basic driver of the capitalist mode of production is 'the drive to accumulate capital' (Mandel, 1976, p. 60). Second, accumulation of capital fuels competition between capitalists, and leads them to seek new technology and new ways of organizing and controlling labor. 'Capitalism' wrote Harvey (1989) 'is necessarily technologically and organizationally dynamic. This is so in part because the coercive laws of competition push individual capitalists into leap-frogging innovations in their search for profit' (p. 180). Third, the quest for accumulation by the owners of the means of production (capitalists) leads them to extort maximum surplus value from those who own only their labor power (workers). What Marx's *Capital* explained was, above all, the 'ruthless and irresistible impulse to growth which characterizes production for private profit and the predominant use of profit for capital accumulation' (Mandel, 1976, p. 11). Marx also showed that these three conditions necessary for capitalism were inconsistent and contradictory, thus rendering this mode of production necessarily crisis-prone.

Marx's three conditions have the potential to inform our understanding of the effects of capitalism on snowboarding bodies in contemporary material culture. Thus, in the following discussion I apply Marx's three premises to snowboarding to explain the ongoing processes of capital accumulation, competition, and exploitation in snowboarding. My analysis is divided into three parts. First, Marx's first condition that growth is inevitable guides a discussion of Burton Snowboards and its quest for continual capital accumulation in periods of growth and crisis. Marx's second condition, that accumulation of capital fuels competition between capitalists and leads them to seek new technologies and new ways of organizing and controlling labor, guides my subsequent investigation into new trends and innovations in the highly competitive snowboarding marketplace. Lastly, Marx's third condition, that growth in real value rests on the exploitation of productive labor, informs my examination of the effects of capitalism on the bodies of professional snowboarding athletes.

Capital accumulation: the case of Burton Snowboards

Twenty-three-year-old Jake Burton Carpenter established Burton Snowboards in 1977 in Londonderry, Vermont.[1] Having recently graduated from New York University with a degree in economics, and with work experience at a New York business broker company, Burton wanted to start his own business. An avid Snurfer in his teenage years, Burton saw the activity as an untapped opportunity for capital accumulation (Helmich, 2000). Indeed, he confessed that his primary drive was to 'create a successful business' (Burton, 2003, p. 403) and 'make a good living...like 100 grand a year or something' (Burton Carpenter & Dumaine, 2002, para. 12). He calculated that by producing 50 boards a day, he could make at least a comfortable living (Burton Carpenter & Dumaine, 2002). Only now does he admit to being 'blindly optimistic': 'I didn't do any market research; I didn't talk to any competitors. I just bought a little saber saw and started making boards in my apartment. I didn't know what I was doing... It was trial and error' (Burton Carpenter & Dumaine, 2002, p. 64). Burton worked mostly alone, relying on some part-time high-school worker help. After making the boards, he became a 'travelling salesman', loading his station wagon and driving to ski and sports stores across the eastern States trying to market and sell his product (Bailey, 1998, para. 28). Within the first year the fledgling company had sold 300 boards for US$88 each, although 'everyone said it was too much' (Burton, cited in Howe, 1998, p. 11). Burton responded with a cheaper version, the 'Backyard', which sold (without bindings) for US$45. The following year, 1979, he sold 700 boards but continued to struggle financially. In his own words: 'I started the business as a get-rich-quick scheme, but very soon I had even less money than when I started' (Burton, cited in Morris, 2008, para. 5).

By 1981 Burton had spent his $120,000 inheritance and was $130,000 in debt but orders for his boards climbed into the thousands over the next few years. In the early and mid-1980s Burton shifted his focus from selling boards to promoting snowboarding as a physical activity. To create a market, Burton also lobbied the local ski resorts to open their slopes to snowboarding. Paul Alden, who worked for Burton Snowboards from 1984 to 1990, recalls that Burton 'spent hundreds of thousands of dollars to put this sport on the map' (cited in Bailey, 1998, para. 32). In 1983, Stratton Mountain, Vermont, became the first major ski-field to open its piste to snowboarders. Others quickly followed. Sensing the growing momentum, Burton turned his attention back to his product. With financial backing from his wife's family, he added better bindings, a high-tech base and steel edges to his boards, making them more maneuverable. Burton continued to develop snowboarding technologies, and to improve his marketing and distribution practices. In 1984 sales of Burton Snowboards reached US$1 million.

Burton Snowboards was not alone in the early snowboarding industry. Dimitrije Milovick (Utah), Tom Sims and Chuck Barfoot (California), Chris and Beverly Sanders (California), and Mike Olsen (Washington), also recognized opportunities in snowboarding. They established Winterstick (1975), Sims Snowboards (1978), Avalanche Snowboards (1982), and GNU Snowboards (1984) respectively. While the early board-makers shared an 'alternative' motivation, their plans for the activity and styles of participation varied. As Howe (1998) explains:

> Burton's reserved but determined East Coast personality and ski racing background informed his vision of snowboarding... while the Californian lifestyle was at the core of [Tom] Sim's plan. Having been immersed for over

a decade in the volatile skateboard industry and its media-based structure, Sims, with all the right media contacts, was poised to build a personality-driven hero-worship machine of promotion for snowboarding. (p. 23)

Burton and Sims hosted two major annual contests, the Nationals and the Worlds respectively, in the early 1980s. Not only did such contests contribute to fostering a larger, national, and international community, they also had a significant impact on the commercial success of their companies (Howe, 1998). The rivalry between Burton Snowboards and Sims Snowboards continued to grow and as the competitive arena opened up in the 1980s, Burton and Sims regularly butted heads. The following comment from Tom Hsieh, editor of the first snowboarding magazine, *International Snowboarder Magazine* (established in 1985 and now defunct), is illuminating:

> There was a lot of struggle between Burton and Sims. Jake's whole thing at the time was that the sport needed credibility and professionalism. He hated the whole thrash, 'skate and destroy' attitude. [Tom] Sims was all, 'Hey, this is my roots,' skating, half-pipes, vertical. That early conflict was great for me as a publisher. I was in the middle of these two guys, the devil on one shoulder and the angel on the other. I would get calls at three in the morning from those guys. Jake would call up and say that I had too many guys in the air, not enough guys on the ground. That basically meant that I had too many Sims (freestyle) riders and not enough Burton (alpine) riders. (cited in Howe, 1998, p. 46)

Howe (1998) argues that, ultimately, 'the Sims–Burton, West–East Coast rivalry would prove healthy for snowboarding's advancement' (p. 23). Howe's comment echoes Marx's premise that without competition 'the "driving fire" of growth would become extinguished ... totally monopolized capital would essentially be stagnating capital' (Mandel, 1976, p. 60); the snowboarding market was definitely not stagnating.

Snowboarding continued to grow in popularity during the 1980s and into the mid-1990s. By the mid-1990s snowboarding had developed a cohesive industry complete with its own media, international events and competitions, trade shows, fashions, and professional and amateur athletes. Burton Snowboards grew 'on average about 100% per year' during this period (Burton Carpenter & Dumaine, 2002, p. 64). By 1995 it employed 250 workers and was worth well over US$100 million. The potential for growth in overseas markets was considerable during this period and Burton Snowboards established offices in Innsbruck in 1986 and Tokyo in 1995. Brad Steward, an employee at Sims Snowboards, recalls that everyone thought Burton was 'nuts for going to Europe' (cited in Bailey, 1998, para. 34) but he admitted that Jake 'always had vision' and knew how to 'look at the much bigger picture' (para. 34). Burton's wife, Donna Burton Carpenter, was the company's first European sales and operations manager, later becoming company chief financial officer. Through geographical expansion, Burton Snowboards was able to fulfill Marx's premise of the basic drive of the capitalist mode of production – growth – as it is only through growth that profits can be assured and capital accumulation sustained.

The growth of the sport and industry during this period attracted an influx of new companies, many of which had their roots elsewhere, in surfing (such as Billabong and Ripcurl), skateboarding (DC, Etnies, and Airwalk) and skiing (Rossignol, Soloman, and Voikal). By 1995 the North American snowboard retail industry was worth US$750 million (Randall, 1995). That same year more than 300 companies peddled snowboard equipment, apparel and accessories at the industry trade show, compared with just 90 companies two years earlier. Industry sources predicted that retail snowboard market sales would double to US$1.5 billion by the end of the 1990s (Ibid.). When Ride Snowboards became the first snowboard company to go public on the NASDAQ stock exchange in 1994, it sold all 500,000 shares in the first two weeks; it then released another 75,000. Within a month the shares had reached US$28 each, six times the release price. Despite massive growth during this 15-year period, some warned that consolidation was inevitable. Rodger Madison Jr, chairman of Ride Snowboards, predicted: 'this is a textbook example of an early-stage, fast-growth market. You're going to see a major shakeout. Instead of 100 companies, in five years you might have 12' (cited in Randall, 1995, p. 46). Madison's prophecy proved correct. Sagging sales in Asia (particularly Japan) during their economic downturn, and overproduction, triggered a 'shakeout' in the late 1990s. Larger companies acquired many smaller snowboarder-owned companies around this time. In 1998 Quicksilver (a surf company) purchased Lib Technologies and Gnu Snowboards (both snowboard manufacturers), Arcane (snowboard boot manufacturers), and Bent Metal (snowboard binding manufacturers). Similarly, K2 (a ski company) acquired Ride Snowboards and Morrow Snowboards. Others downsized. Joyride Snowboards reduced the number of its employees from 120 to 6. Still others exited the market (e.g., Millennium Three [snowboard manufacturer], Belligerent [bindings manufacturer], and Random Snowboards) (Deemer, 2000). This crisis seems to support Marx's premise that accumulation is a contradictory process in which the rate of profit can also fall and thus retard capital accumulation.

Not only is the ability to read the market a prerequisite for financial success, but at times of economic difficulty and intensifying competition the 'well organized corporation has marked competitive advantages' through its ability 'to make swift decisions' (Harvey, 1989, p. 230). During this financial downturn Burton remained the industry leader because, as Burton boasted:

> We don't have much moneyed competition. The pure snowboarding companies don't have a lot of money, don't have real [research and

development], don't have great operations. And the ski companies, who are very well financed, don't really understand the sport, and they don't have the focus. We've got the focus that the little guys have, we've been around the sport, we understand the image. We have roundtables with pro riders who help us design our boards and keep us ahead of the market. And we've got all the [technology], [research and development], financing, and operational know-how of the big guys. That's why we've been successful. (Burton Carpenter & Dumaine, 2002, p. 64)

Burton Snowboards is currently the leading snowboard company in North America, Europe and Japan ('Jake Burton Carpenter Interview', 2008). The company remains privately owned by Jake and Donna Burton Carpenter, and thus does not release financial information. However, in a recent financial review it was revealed that Burton Snowboards currently controls approximately 40 to 70 percent of the multibillion-dollar global market, depending on the specific category of goods (Brooks, 2010); foreign sales account for 60 percent of volume, with a very profitable Japanese segment (Burton history, 2005).

   Burton Snowboards is a good example of a successful 'transnational company' (Pries, 2001). From its offices in Australia, Austria, California, and Japan, and headquarters in Burlington, Vermont, Burton Snowboards distributes via independent Burton representatives to authorized specialty retailers in 36 countries including the United States, Canada, 28 countries in Europe, two countries in South America, Japan, Korea, Australia, and New Zealand ('Fact sheet', 2003). In 2010, Burton Snowboards and its subsidiary companies – RED (helmets and body protection equipment), Gravis Footwear (shoes and bags), Anon Optics (goggles), Analog Clothing (casual apparel line), Forum Snowboards (snowboard equipment, clothing and accessories), Special Blend (snowboard clothing and accessories), Four Square (snowboard clothing), and Jeenyus (snowboard equipment and clothing) – employed 962 people globally (Burton Reports, 2009). Burton Snowboards also recently expanded into the broader board-sports industry by founding Channel Islands Surfboards and acquiring DNA Distribution, an umbrella company for various skateboarding brands including Alien Workshop, Habitat Skateboards, and Reflex.

   While the broader board-sports and youth fashion industries offer new opportunities for economic growth, the North American snowboarding market is currently at 'saturation point' and the Japanese market is steadily shrinking (Robinson, 2006, para. 5). The company has recently identified China as 'the next step', and is employing an array of innovative marketing strategies to raise both the sport's and its own profile among the rapidly growing Chinese middle-class youth (William Avendon of Burton Snowboards, cited in Robinson, 2006, para. 5). For example, in 2005, Burton Snowboards signed a three-year deal to sponsor China's national snowboard team, which consists of six boys and six girls selected solely on their athletic (rather than snowboarding) abilities. According to Bryan Johnston, vice president of global marketing for Burton Snowboards, 'snowboarding's expansion into China presents a huge opportunity in the sport's overall growth...and we're extremely pleased to have the chance to work with the National Snowboard Team of China' (cited in 'Burton sponsors', 2005, para. 4). In 2008, Burton Snowboards also became the title sponsor of the Burton Quiabo Mellow Park, a new indoor year-round terrain facility in Beijing. Clearly Burton Snowboards understands the laws and rules of capital accumulation.

Continual innovation in a competitive marketplace

In an increasingly competitive and volatile market, Burton Snowboards has embraced innovative marketing strategies, technologies, and ways of organizing labor to maintain its leadership position. Marx's second principle of capitalism – that under the coercive laws of competition, technological and organizational progress is both inevitable and good – informs the following discussion of these strategies.

Since the late 1990s the snowboarding market has been infiltrated by large, mainstream companies; Burton Snowboards faces intense competition from Nike, K2, Quiksilver, and Adidas-Salomon. These companies are very well financed and invest significant amounts of money in their marketing programs. They sponsor groups of elite boarders and invest heavily in advertising, product design, and packaging. However with the influx of new companies from outside the culture, perceptions of 'cultural authenticity' have become a central concern among core boarders (see Wheaton & Beal, 2003). As the president of one mainstream company stated, 'it's a difficult category. It's highly technical, and core snowboarders are loyal to core snowboard brands. They are not really open to mainstream brands' (Dick Baker, Ocean Pacific president, cited in Deemer, 2000, para. 17). To core boarders – the most savvy of consumers – the 'authenticity' of a snowboarding company is central to their consumption choices. Moreover they shy away from companies that appear too commercially successful. According to one cultural commentator, core snowboarders base their consumption decisions on 'values such as loyalty and commitment':

> Riders will typically consider the nature of the company: Is the company committed to snowboarding? Does the company truly understand snowboarding? Companies that are seen to have ulterior motives or as not part of the snowboarding culture will generally be boycotted. Such companies cannot be trusted. ('The principles of snowboarding', 2002, para. 2)

Burton Snowboards holds a significant share of the market and perceptions of its being too commercially successful exist in some quarters. For example, anti-Burton sentiments regularly appear on snowboarding websites: 'I would rather ride on a Glad garbage bag than ride a Burton' (posted by ULLiGaN151, March 11, 2005); 'I personally do not like [Burton] because they're trying to take over the sport and they're only in it for the money that's not what snowboarding is all about' (posted by grrlboarder, October 30, 2004); 'It's rad that Jake Burton still owns em and they've been around for so long but it just seems lame how they dominate sh*t so much, even though that is business, they just seem too geared towards the dollar' (posted by SsKnAoTwE July 18, 2004), (all on www.snowboard.com). Not surprisingly, competitors help fuel this sentiment.

In a highly competitive industry, it is not simply products but the corporate image itself that becomes essential. Image building is a central characteristic in contemporary capitalist systems (Harvey, 1989). Snowboarding companies such as Burton employ various strategies to create and re-create a culturally authentic corporate image. They use niche media, especially magazines and films, extensively to advertise their products and, more importantly, for corporate image work (see Chapters 2 and 4). Like advertising in broader society, much of the snowboarding advertising does not 'inform or promot[e] in the ordinary sense' but is 'geared to manipulating desires and tastes that may or may not have anything to do with the product sold' (Ibid., p. 287). This is evident in advertisements for Burton Snowboards, which regularly appear as an expensive double-page spread inside the front cover of an array of national and international magazines. As Booth (2005) writes, 'as well as a tool for producers and retailers to manipulate desire, advertising helps ensure company and brand recognition in competitive markets' (p. 324). Advertisements for Burton Snowboards typically emphasize the high status and skill levels of their sponsored riders, combined with a focus on either the snowboarding lifestyle or the innovative design and technology of their product. The first two strategies help connect the company to its cultural roots; reinforcing the company's 'authenticity' is critical to deflecting charges of industry domination.

More recently, the demand for growth and continual capital accumulation has shifted attention from the production of goods to the production of events that have an 'almost instantaneous consumption time' (Harvey, 1989, p. 157). In 2006 Burton Snowboards established the Burton Global Open Series, which built upon the success of longstanding events, such as the Burton U.S. Open and European Open Snowboarding Championships, and includes the Nissan X-Trail Nippon Open, New Zealand Burton Open, and the Burton Australian Snowboarding Open Championships. The company also invests heavily in the highly esteemed Arctic Challenge (Norway) and regularly establishes novel events such as the Burton Abominable Snow Jam (Mt. Hood, Oregon). Further raising the visibility of the company, Burton Snowboards has recently partnered with various ski resorts – Killington Ski

Resort (Vermont, United States), Northstar (Tahoe, United States), Avoriaz (France), The Remarkables (New Zealand), and Flachauwinkel (Austria) – to develop the Burton Stash series of 'organic snowboard terrain parks' featuring natural obstacles such as rocks, stumps and logs (see www.thestash. com). Burton Snowboards also partners with various media agencies to produce snowboarding films, such as *The B Movie*, television programming (Burton TV), and interactive web-based media, for example, Burton Studios with iTunes, to further 'showcase Burton's vast history and knowledge to new and expanded audiences' (Press release, 2004). Burton Snowboards' expansion into the production of events, spaces, and media is an innovative attempt at, to paraphrase Harvey (1989), mastering or actively intervening in the volatile snowboarding market by 'saturating the market with images' (p. 287).

As with all snowboarding companies, Burton Snowboards also invests in other forms of image building, including sponsorship and direct marketing, which further enable it to 'manipulate taste and opinion' (Harvey, 1989, p. 287). Burton Snowboards and its subsidiary companies sponsor over 100 snowboarders worldwide, approximately 30 of whom are women.[2] Burton Snowboards also conducts an annual 'World Tour' marketing campaign, traveling to major cities throughout North America, Europe and Japan with a selection of its top athletes. Burton Snowboards' sponsorship of events and athletes illustrates the company's commitment to snowboarding, and thus does important corporate image work. Burton Snowboards clearly understands that, in a competitive capitalist system, the need to invest in image building never ceases, and they continue to produce new and innovative advertising and marketing campaigns.

Faced with strong market volatility, heightened competition, and narrowing profit margins, employers in the contemporary capitalist system have 'taken advantage of weakened union power and the pools of surplus (unemployed or underemployed) labourers to push for more flexible work regimes and labour contracts' (Harvey, 1989, p. 150). In this context, Burton Snowboards obliges its employees to work much longer hours during periods of peak demand (winter), and compensates with shorter hours at periods of slack demand (summer). Benefits for employees at the headquarters in Burlington, Vermont include a free season pass to Stowe Mountain Resort and flexibility in their work regimes. For example, if it snows two feet overnight employees can take a few hours off in the morning to go snowboarding but are expected to work late in the evening. The work environment is accommodating toward young employees; the dress code is casual, dogs are allowed, and a skateboard ramp is available for use during breaks. Despite the relaxed workplace appearance, however, a former employee asserts that Burton Snowboards is famous for 'burning out the bright-eyed young workers who flock to the company' and adds that 'there is nothing light about it, the work is serious as hell' (cited in Goodman, 2003, para. 19).

From a Marxist perspective, it might be argued that the quest for accumulation by Burton Snowboards leads them to extort maximum surplus value from their workers. The current trend in labor markets is to 'reduce the number of "core" workers and rely increasingly upon a labor force that can quickly be taken on board and equally and costlessly be laid off when times get bad' (Harvey, 1989, p. 152). The labor structure of Burton Snowboards is similar to that described by Harvey; it is 'made up of core and periphery groups' (Ibid., p. 150) and relies heavily upon part-time, temporary, or sub-contracted work arrangements. This labor structure allows Burton to remain flexible in a highly volatile industry. For example, in 2002, following the September 11 terrorist attacks and a poor snow year in North America, Europe, and Japan, Burton Snowboards underwent a restructuring and 102 employees were laid off ('Snowboard shocker!', 2002). Burton conceded that 'the people side of these moves suck' but that it is nonetheless necessary to remain competitive in a capitalist system (Ibid., para. 5). More recently, Burton Snowboards responded to the 'challenging global economic situation' in 2009 by cutting staff salaries, cancelling raises and bonuses, and laying off approximately five percent of their North American staff, including a number of high-profile professional athletes; Jake and Donna further demonstrated their commitment to the company by temporarily foregoing their own salaries (*Business Week*, 2009, para. 1).

Summarizing Burton Snowboards' business philosophy, the company website touts: 'We never stop innovating. We never stop creating. And we never stop listening to snowboarders' (www.burton.com, 2005). Indeed, Burton Snowboards' strategic marketing, production, and labor processes are a good example of 'capitalists ... leap-frogging innovations in their search for profit' (Harvey, 1989, p. 180), thus supporting Marx's second premise of capitalism. I will now expand on the third aspect of Marx's premise of capitalism with a discussion of the labor processes in the snowboarding industry.

Professional snowboarding and labor power: alienation and the millionaire athlete

The snowboarding industry comprises many jobs, including snowboard instructor, park crew, journalist, photographer, competition judge, coach, and event organizer. However, few are highly paid. I will explore the attraction of such occupations shortly. Here, however, I will focus on the top tier of the snowboard industry job market, the potentially financially lucrative labor of the professional snowboarder. Snowboard companies maintain close contact with consumers by sponsoring a team of professional and amateur snowboarders. According to Zane, a core U.S. snowboarder and cinematographer, the companies 'spend so much money on their team because the team influences the kids, and the kids see a team riding a certain type of product, and that sells products' (personal communication, November 2005). Professional boarder Todd Richards (2003) also elaborates on the functions of the sponsored athletes and their role in a snowboarding company's commercial success:

> Snow was a business, and I was essentially selling snowboarding. Magazine editors, for the most part, looked at contest results to help them figure out who deserves to be on their covers. Kids looked at magazines and bought snowboards based on who was riding them. The marketability, and thus the success of all companies, was directly related to the exposure their team riders were able to secure. (p. 136)

Manufacturers and retailers hire riders on the basis of physical skills, personality, and attitude that reflect positively on the company. The perceived marketability of a snowboarder is also very important, a point alluded to by David Carrier-Porcheron, a professional snowboarder sponsored by Burton: 'I've been asking Burton, "Why don't you pick up Gaetan? He's so sick!" They're like, "No, we couldn't...the name Gaetan Chanut is just not selling"' (cited in Dresser, 2005, p. 148).

The notion that professional snowboarding is the 'dream job' pervades the snowboarding culture. While professionalism certainly bestows status, prestige, the opportunity to travel, and an enviable lifestyle, one can also discern elements of exploitation in the relationship between manufacturers and athletes. The relationship between snowboarding manufacturers (capitalists) and professional snowboarders (workers) appears to support Marx's third premise of capitalism, namely that the quest for accumulation by the owners of the means of production (capitalists) leads them to extort maximum surplus value from those who only own their labor power (workers). As Marx explains, growth in real value rests on the exploitation of productive labor. This is not to say that professional snowboarders confront gross exploitation. On the contrary, some earn six- and seven-figure salaries. But those amounts have to be contextualized by the relationships between what boarders receive and what they create (Harvey, 1989). A recent promotional document sheds some light on the harsh realities of professional snowboarding, which include 'repetitive risk, lack of health insurance, shortness of careers, and lack of any type of pension' (Buyers Guide, 2004/2005, p. 16). In his autobiography, Todd Richards referred to negotiating his 'employment' contract with Morrow (snowboarding company):

> For a few months, 'Mr. Jerk' had been dropping hints to me about the company's budget and how I needed to be a 'team player', obviously trying to soften me up for the negotiating table. I was thinking, *Screw you. You just sold 30,000 boards with my name on them. I've been with this company for nine years. The Olympics are a once-in-a-lifetime opportunity, and if you want me to flash the Morrow logo around the world, you need to pay me!* And that's what I intended to tell him as the big sit-down approached.

It amazed me how a meeting about one basic issue can drag on for hours. The point was ... I wanted a three-year one-million-dollar contract. Period. I was getting pretty pissed off that Morrow wasn't stepping up to the plate. I was about to say, 'Pay me, or I'm riding for Airwalk,' when Mr. Jerk finally spoke up. 'You know what Todd ... we want you to ride Morrow at the Olympics. And we want to thank you for all these years. We're going to give you what you want.' I went nuts inside. I was shitting my pants. Basically, Mr. Jerk had the ability to pay the amount the whole time but he wanted me to crumble and take less. When I didn't give in he had no choice but to agree to the million-dollar contract. (Richards, 2003, p. 192, emphasis in original)

Professional snowboarder Kris Jamieson observes 'some people making so much money and some so little' in the snowboarding industry (cited in Howe, 1998, p. 101) and draws a perceptive conclusion: 'It just goes to show you that snowboarding is just like any other capitalist venture. People don't get what they deserve. They get what they negotiate' (cited in Ibid.).

When contextualizing the relationship between what boarders receive and what they create, some professional snowboarders appear exploited by their employers. For example, when asked if she receives adequate financial compensation, professional snowboarder Morgan Lafonte replied, 'God, no! Hell, no! K2 thinks my niche is backcountry, [but] anybody that goes into the backcountry is putting [themselves] at risk right away. ... For what you do to your body and yourself, no, you're definitely not paid what you need to be' (cited in Baccigaluppi et al., 2001, p. 96). As workers who rely solely upon their labor power, professional snowboarders are also vulnerable to the processes associated with capitalist accumulation. Notwithstanding the essential role of the professionals, pro-snowboarder Tom Burt remarks that they are 'the first ... to hit the floor when companies fall ... [they're] just a marketing tool' (cited in Ibid., p. 97). Even youth cultural marketing phenomenon Shaun White lost sponsorship deals with American Express and Hewlett-Packard as the companies responded to the global recession of 2009 and 2010 (Settimi, 2010). The capitalist economy is, in Mandel's (1976) words, 'a gigantic enterprise of dehumanization, of transformation of human beings from goals in themselves into instruments and means for money-making and capital accumulation' (p. 65).

According to Marx's concept of alienation, the capitalist mode of production alienates workers from the act of production (see Marx, 1964, 1982). Working becomes an alien activity without intrinsic satisfaction; external constraints compel workers to produce and production ceases to be an end in itself (see Petrovic, 1991). Work in fact becomes a commodity that is sold and its only value to the worker is its saleability. Indeed, in a capitalist society, professional sport is also reduced to the status of work (Rigauer, 1981[1969]). Professional sport assumes the same relations as the workplace: 'The athlete is the producer, the spectators the consumers' (Ibid., pp. 68–69). As with the worker, sport dehumanizes the professional sportsperson. Rigauer (1981[1969]) claims that the athlete is alienated at the point at which sporting performances are transformed into a commodity. As professionals, 'athletes forfeit control over their labour power, and are forced to maximize productivity' (Giulianotti, 2005, p. 32). Beamish (2002) agrees, arguing that this insight is central to the study of sport and physical activity because

> if sporting activity is so rich with creative potential – so robust with opportunities for individuals to explore their own limits and the limitations of human physical performances – the loss of control of the product can have devastating consequences for the creative potential of physical activity (p. 37).

Simply put, market-structured sport restricts the expressive and creative potential of the athletes themselves. In 1994, *Flakezine* magazine predicted that

> in the hands of the 'mainstream,' snowboarding will become exactly like skiing, golf, inline skating, NASCAR, and tennis...boring, dull, and staid. Sure, snowboarders, snowboard companies, and the snowboard media will make a lot more money (yippee) but it will be in exchange for their souls, creativity, and individuality. (cited in Baccigaluppi et al., 2001, p. 145)

Many of the changes forecast by *Flakezine* in 1994 can be observed in contemporary professional snowboarding, as journalist Cody Dresser notes:

> The existence of a professional snowboarder has degraded into a serious, high pressure situation over the years....*Stress levels rose as the fun factor slowly crumbled.* Snowboarding has been sterilized and neutered by the mainstream, the Olympics, the X-Games...*homogenized* by way of professionalism practiced in team sports like football or track and field – *tainted by training and endless competition.* (Dresser, 2004b, p. 125, emphasis added)

In a discussion about the pressures he faces to meet sponsors' demands to produce video footage, professional snowboarder Marc Frank Montoya comments:

> It's a *lot* harder [today] 'cause there's more competition out there. A lot of new blood coming in...just like any other sport, it's like a big ol' production. It's definitely not as much fun as it used to be when you could go to a resort and ride all day. Now you have to work, hike [and] build some big

ol' jump...I didn't start to snowboarding to be pro [or] to watch myself on film but *I have to now because that's what I get paid to do.* I busted my ass this winter...filming, filming, filming...I got burned out on it. (cited in Yant, 2001a, para. 22, emphasis added)

Whereas Montoya pursued snowboarding primarily as a means of self-expression and self-exploration, as a professional snowboarder (worker) he has become alienated from his labor; the market now shapes and restricts his snowboarding experiences.

Jean Brohm (1978) maintains that the physical demands placed on the sportsperson in training and in sporting contexts amounts to bodily oppression. The inhumanity of this situation is itself, he says, a form of alienation. From this perspective it might be argued that professional snowboarders experience a form of alienation when they confront serious injury and even death in order to 'get the shot,' and thus 'earn' a wage. Snowboarding journalist Jennifer Sherowski (2003b) observes that professional snowboarding is increasingly 'dangerous', with 'riders...put[ting] their lives on the line to get the gnarliest footage and photos' (p. 48). Early professional snowboarder Mike Basich reveals the risks associated with his job:

A lot of people say I'm lucky for what I do for a living. Sure, maybe that's true. I get to travel the world and not have a nine-to-five job. But when I get to work, my worries are not about giving a report to my boss or something. I worry about making it through the day without breaking a bone or getting stuck in an avalanche (knock, knock). Your body takes a beating. You're never home. Lots of lag time at the airports. You're in the cold all the time. (cited in Baccigaluppi et al., 2001, p. 95)

Professional snowboarder Travis Parker sums up the situation when he says that 'we have to risk our lives to make a paycheck' (cited in Sherowski, 2003b, p. 48).

Despite the potential for alienation in professional snowboarding, with significant sponsorships on offer many boarders happily embrace commercial approaches. The rewards from selling one's labor power are alluring, as Richards (2003) makes clear: 'I'd be a liar if I said the thought of being on the first U.S. Olympic Snowboard team didn't fire me up. Wheaties boxes, international prestige, the best half-pipe in the world – and let's not forget the cold hard cash that goes with it all' (p. 185). He adds: 'I wanted to make more money, stay ahead of the other guys, drive the nicest car, and have the nicest house' (Ibid., p. 270). Similarly, professional snowboarder Tara Dakides describes her good fortune as simply 'amazing': 'I never thought in a million years that I would be able to buy things that I'm able to buy [a new home, a condominium, a new sports-utility vehicle]' (cited in Roberts, 2002, p. A1).

Arguably, snowboarding reflects the three key aspects of capitalism: growth, competition and exploitation. In this capitalist system some snowboarders struggle with the capitalist/worker relationship, others have reaped the financial benefits of their cultural authenticity, and a few have established their own companies and become capitalists themselves. While an examination of Marx's three conditions of capitalism illuminates how snowboarding reflects the key premises of capitalism, it would be remiss to ignore some of the serious criticisms leveled at his work. The most common criticisms of Marx centre on 'unfulfilled predictions (global communism never occurred), over-simplification of social stratification (class relations are more complex than dichotomous), and his "economism", which viewed the economic base as determining all other "superstructures" (cultural activities, for example, are not always commodified)' (Giulianotti, 2005, pp. 30–31). While many critics 'over-simplify Marx's thinking' (Ibid., p. 31), the latter two arguments – the limitations of traditional Marxism for explaining class and culture – hold some weight in relation to contemporary snowboarding.

Critiquing Marx: class

The concept of class is central to Marxism. According to Bottomore (1956), Marx showed, by empirical investigation, 'how the development of modern capitalism necessarily leads to a social transformation in which the working-class movement will abolish all classes' (p. 21). But Marx's analysis of class and class struggle has proved less than satisfying. Contemporary society is not split, as Marx predicted, into two hostile classes. Rather a much more complex class structure has evolved (Gurley, 1984). Moreover, it has been argued that class struggle has little to do with change from one society to another (Abercrombie et al., 2000). Arguably, Marx's analysis of class and class struggle is of little relevance for explaining contemporary society, or snowboarding culture per se.

The majority of snowboarders are white (89 percent)[3] and from the middle and upper classes.[4] Despite a general lack of awareness of, or concern about, class-related issues among snowboarders, some boarders do recognize the privileged nature of the sport. Zane surprised me in an interview when he declared: 'I think snowboarding is still a rich kid sport; it's really hard for poor kids to come up in snowboarding and get a chance to ride enough to be good' (personal communication, November 2005). Continuing, he revealed:

My parents weren't well off, so when I started snowboarding, I had a job just so I could afford to go riding. We [my brother and I] definitely found ways around the money though, we would drive 3.5 hours to go riding with fifty bucks in our pockets, find a cheap hotel or sleep in the car, scam lift tickets…we'd do anything to do what we loved.

Marc Frank Montoya, the first Mexican American professional snowboarder, is critical of the whiteness and exclusivity of snowboarding:

> There are so few Latinos involved in the sport because they are in the cities, and no one is up in the mountains. Also, the ones that are close to the slopes don't have the money to go snowboarding. It's an outrageous sport – mad expensive – and few people have access to the equipment and lift tickets. It's almost a rich man's sport, pretty much like skiing. (cited in Rossi, 2002, para. 1)

In another article he complains about expensive lift tickets that exclude the lower classes from the resorts: 'They charge like 50 or 60 bucks. That's how they [resorts] keep the city kids from going up and snowboarding' (cited in Yant, 2001a, para. 13). As a lower-class youth, Montoya went to great lengths to snowboard, admitting, 'I jacked [stole] a snowboard and I'd clip tickets. And I'd jack gas. I stole my food everyday on the way up there. Went to 7-Eleven, jacked a bunch of Lunchables – threw 'em down my pants' (cited in Ibid.).[5] Despite a six-figure salary, Montoya still 'clips tickets' in order to not 'let them get away with that bullshit' (cited in Ibid.). Nonetheless, such acts of symbolic resistance tend to be isolated in the snowboarding culture; certainly there are no signs of a revolution among lower-class snowboarders.

The application of Marx's analysis of social class to snowboarding in contemporary capitalist society is also problematic because of the difficulties of fitting professional snowboarders into a two-class scheme. The financial success of some professional snowboarders illustrates a key feature of the political economy of snowboarding, in that 'wealth derives not from ownership of the means of production and control over wage labour but from ownership of aesthetic ingenuity and the ability to create and mobilize cultural authenticity' (Booth, 2005, p. 328). As Ste'en explained, 'now the successful riders are marketing themselves through any other means than competition ... videos, books, video games; there are so many new ways of turning your name into profit' (personal communication, October 2005). Professional U.S. snowboarder and skateboarder, Shaun White, offers a good example of an athlete owning much more than his labor power. White earns a multimillion-dollar salary from prize money and his relationships with an array of mainstream (Red Bull, Target, HP, Mountain Dew, Ubisoft) and board-sport (Burton, Oakley) companies (Borden, 2009). Importantly, White exercises his agency within these relationships; he works closely with key staff to produce marketing campaigns that are consistent with his personal style and cultural values; he also partners with companies to design and develop his own signature products, including goggles with Oakley, snowboarding equipment (snowboards, bindings, and boots), clothing (jackets and pants) and accessories (helmets and gloves) with Burton, a line of urban-style clothing sold in Target stores throughout North America, and two editions of his signature video games, *Shaun White Snowboarding: Road Trip* and *World Tour*, with Ubisoft. Critically aware of the importance of 'cultural authenticity' within the highly discerning board-sports market, White carefully protects his image by refusing to be associated with companies or projects that could damage his appeal to young consumers: 'A lot of people will just put their name on anything, and you can tell. I just can't do that' (White, cited in Ebner, 2009, para. 18). According to White's former agent, Mark Ervin, 'every week we get presented with a big opportunity from someone. Shaun turns down a lot of money' (cited in Ibid., para. 17). Clearly, production relations in the snowboarding economy cannot be simply divided into those who own and control the means of production and are able to take the profit (capitalists), and those who depend on their own labor alone (workers). The key issue here is that a Marxist position does not take social actors' critical faculties and interpretive capacities into account. As Giulianotti (2005) explains of sport more broadly, 'many professional athletes are not passive cogs in sport's commercial wheel but have won improved industrial conditions and often superlative financial rewards for their erstwhile commodification' (p. 42).

Another limitation of a Marxist perspective is the tendency to focus on the negative, and ignore the positive, aspects of capitalism. The Marxist approach adopted in this chapter, for example, overlooks the enjoyment and opportunities that professionalism offers some snowboarders. According to U.S. professional snowboarder Bjorn Leines:

> The best thing about being a professional snowboarder is probably all the opportunities that come along with it. Like being able to travel, meet new people, and see different things. And you're pretty much your own boss, so you can do anything you want. It's really cool being able to do what you love. (cited in Bridges, 2005, para. 40)

The worker–capitalist relationship in professional snowboarding consists of opportunities and constraints and therefore cannot be explained solely by the concepts of alienation and exploitation that focus exclusively on the negative elements of this relationship. This pessimistic approach is also apparent in the Marxist analysis of Burton Snowboards.

Certainly, Jake Burton is a capitalist who has embraced and benefited from capitalist accumulation and exploitation of his staff. Yet Burton also takes risks, works hard and provides a product enjoyed by millions of consumers around the world. Many snowboarders appreciate Burton's contribution to the development of the sport and culture, and the opportunities his company offers its sponsored athletes are second to none. 'Without Burton, snowboarding would not be as progressive as it is today ... lots of people don't want to believe that because Burton has lots of money. But Burton pays its riders so well. Every single one of the Burton riders is on the snow 200 plus days a year', claims one core female snowboarder (Melissa, personal communication, November 2005). Burton Snowboards also has a philanthropic bent. For example, the company raised and donated US$152,000 to disaster relief efforts to help those affected by the hurricanes in North America and earthquakes in Pakistan during 2005, and has also established 'Chill', an international nonprofit intervention program for at-risk inner-city youth aged 10–18.[6] Arguably, Marx's analysis of class and class struggle is limited because it splits society into two hostile classes, workers and capitalists. But as the previous examples illustrate, Jake Burton and Burton Snowboards are not simply the capitalist villains that a Marxist perspective might suggest. Moreover, professional snowboarders do not necessarily confront gross exploitation, and they have access to a degree of creative capital unknown to the factory worker.

Critiquing Marx: culture

For all the evidence supporting snowboarding as a model of capitalist enterprise, many aspects of the culture run contrary to the capitalist model. Snowboarding still retains some connections to the leisure movement of the 1960s that espoused cooperation, fun and freedom as its principal tenets. Snowboarders tend to embrace the somewhat idealistic philosophy that snowboarding is about 'fun, self-expression, and getting back to nature, not making money' (Humphreys, 2003, p. 416). Although a select few professional snowboarders embrace commercialized forms of snowboarding and have benefited from them, the majority of participants view money as merely a means to an end – the snowboarding lifestyle. The majority of jobs in the snowboarding industry – snowboard instructor, ski lift operator park crew, journalist, photographer, competition judge, coach, and event organizer – are not highly paid. These jobs tend to be held by passionate snowboarders committed to the lifestyle rather than the economic rewards. In the words of top snowboarding photographer Trevor Graves: 'If you're shooting to maintain the lifestyle, it's worth it. That's all you can do with the time constraints anyway. It's not a huge cash-maker, like fashion or rock photography. It's really about living snowboarding' (cited in Howe, 1998, p. 107). After professional snowboarder Leanne Pelosi finished university she relocated to 'Whistler to be a poor snowboarder while all [her] university friends were making cashola' (cited in Sherowski, 2005b, p. 168). Instead of 'sitting behind a desk working some white-collar job', she is 'living [her] dream, meeting amazing people, and snowboarding year-round'. 'My choice was definitely better...I love it', she adds (cited in Ibid.). Such examples of snowboarders refusing to embrace opportunities for capital accumulation illustrate that snowboarders still privilege culture and lifestyle over financial wealth. But how does traditional Marxism deal with culture, particularly cultural ideologies and politics? The answer lies in the base–superstructure model.

Marx and Engels employed the building-like metaphor of base and superstructure to further propound the idea that the economic structure of society conditions the existence and forms of the state and social consciousness (Bottomore, 1991). Economic relations represent the base while the superstructure consists of the various political and cultural institutions of society. From an orthodox Marxist perspective, the superstructure is not autonomous; it does not emerge out of itself, rather it is founded in the social relations of production; the economy determines the superstructure. Marxist theorists stress economic processes and, in particular, assume that change in the mode of production initiates societal developments. One key function of the superstructure, however, is to act as a framework for ideologies that justify and stabilize the modes of production and consumption under capitalism.

The base and superstructure metaphor, as well as being a fruitful analytical device, has also excited a great deal of debate both inside and outside Marxism. One bone of contention is that the model entails economic determinism.[7] According to Bottomore (1991), the base–superstructure model treats the superstructure of ideas as 'secondary phenomenon...a mere reflection whose reality is ultimately to be found in the production relations. Consciousness is thus emptied of its specific content and significance and is reduced to economic relations' (p. 47). It is as though the superstructures (politics, ideology and culture) do not in themselves need to be analyzed. Put simply, the base–superstructure metaphor does not succeed in conveying an adequate understanding of culture. This is especially problematic in a contemporary social system in which 'no artificial separation can be maintained between the "light" sphere of culture and symbols and the "heavy" world of economics and material objects' (Rowe, 2004, p. 68). According to Rowe, under conditions where the economies and social structures of advanced capitalist societies grow increasingly dependent on cultural processes, we must see culture, social relations, and economics as 'inextricably linked in a manner that defies a simple equation involving arrows pointing in a single, determining direction' (2004, p. 68). Clearly the base–superstructure model can only explain to a limited extent contemporary social phenomena such as snowboarding which, although demonstrating many of the basic tenets of capitalism, have a significant cultural component.

As this discussion has suggested, the snowboarding cultural industry is both similar to, and different from, other industries. On the one hand, it is a clearly organized industry and is part of the general productive economic system. On the other hand, the snowboarding industry does not simply make commodities; as Murdock (1997) argues about the cultural industries in general, it also 'makes available the repertoire of meanings through which the social world, including the world of commodities, is understood and acted on' (p. 68). Hence, as Murdock (1997) claims, it is 'not enough simply to acknowledge this duality [between the economy and culture], we need

to conceptualise the relations between the material and discursive organization of culture without reducing one to the other' (p. 68). Thus, building on this discussion of the political economy of snowboarding within a
capitalist system, in the second part of this chapter I draw on a post-Fordist
perspective to offer a fuller explanation of the causal connections between
the snowboarding economy and culture. In the process, we move from an
understanding of the snowboarding body as commodity or alienated worker
within a capitalist system to an analysis in which snowboarding bodies are
important consumer groups whose cultural desires and aspirations must be
acknowledged and catered for. In contrast to the Marxist approach, which
gives little scope for the recognition of the agency of snowboarders, a post-
Fordist theoretical approach helps us recognize that some snowboarding
bodies have – to varying degrees – the ability to dictate what they consume
and produce.

Post-Fordism and the snowboarding culture

Post-Fordist theory purports to describe a restructuring of capitalism in
the final quarter of the last century. According to post-Fordists, the worldwide economic crisis of 1973, sparked in large part by the Arab oil embargo,
prompted a reconfiguration of Fordism and the emergence of a highly flexible post-Fordist system (Amin, 1994; Kumar, 1995). The earlier Taylor-Fordist
system that had emphasized high volume and standardized mass production changed to one based on rapid and often highly specialized responses.
In other words, 'economies of scope' superseded 'economies of scale' and
capitalist production began to rapidly respond to, and take full advantage
of, fast-changing fashions (Harvey, 1989, p. 155). Though economic changes
lie at its core, in the hands of several of its proponents post-Fordism includes
wide-ranging political and cultural changes.[8] According to Hall and Jacques
(1989), 'diversity, differentiation and fragmentation' – the hallmarks of post-
Fordism – are replacing 'homogeneity, standardization and the economies
and organization of scale' in more than simply the economic sphere (p. 12).
Similarly, Harvey (1989) explains that the relatively stable aesthetic of Fordist
modernism has 'given way to all the ferment, instability, and fleeting qualities of a postmodern aesthetic that celebrates difference, ephemerality, spec-
tacle, fashion, and the commodification of cultural forms' (p. 156). The shift
from Fordism to post-Fordism has also had an impact on the *Zeitgeist*, the
social mood or tempo of the times. Whereas Fordism encouraged conformity in the *Zeitgeist*, post-Fordism fostered the rise and promotion of individu-
alist modes of thought and behavior (Kumar, 1995).

   If post-Fordism carries any merit, then snowboarding, which emerged in
the 1970s and 1980s, has always been a part of the post-Fordist economy, culture and *Zeitgeist*. Hence I do not attempt to theorize the motors of change
in post-Fordism.[9] Rather, I draw upon Krishan Kumar's (1995) post-Fordist

theoretical approach to facilitate an analysis of the production and consumption of snowboarding bodies within the contemporary economic and cultural system. Kumar (1995) draws selectively from the wide-ranging post-Fordist literature to articulate a blend of post-Fordism that gives equal weight to changes in the economy, politics and industrial relations, and culture and ideology. He stresses that we must combine these changes because it is unlikely that they are occurring independently. Moreover, it is just as likely that 'changes in culture and politics are pushing on changes in the economy as the other way around – or, at least, that the causal connections are two way' (Ibid., p. 65). Thus, taken as a conglomerate of contemporary economic, political, and cultural circumstances, a Kumarian post-Fordist theoretical approach becomes a particularly insightful framework for analyzing cultural phenomena such as snowboarding because it expands the locus of power away from economic classes to social classes and their cultural attributes. In short, post-Fordism has the potential to facilitate a fuller explanation of the relationship between the snowboarding economy – outlined in the first part of this chapter – and snowboarding culture. This is particularly important for understanding snowboarders' (often contradictory) positions as consuming (and producing) subjects within a post-Fordist system.

Post-Fordism and physical culture:
flexible production and specialized consumption

In contrast to the rigid Fordist system, post-Fordism rests on flexibility in the key areas of labor markets, products, and patterns of consumption (Murray, 1989). More specifically, the post-Fordist regime of accumulation required shifts from mass production to flexible production and from mass consumption to specialized consumption (Lash, 1990). Flexible production is a key feature of post-Fordism. Under the conditions of recession and heightened competition, the drive to explore new, small-scale markets became fundamental to capitalism's survival. Within a post-Fordist capitalist system, the snowboarding market has become highly fragmented, consisting of an array of small-scale consumer groups, such as children, youth, women, freeriders, backcountry, jibbers, and alpine. This market fragmentation is evident in the diversification of the snowboarding industry. Many small companies specialize in producing boards (e.g., GNU, Option, Morrow), boots (e.g., 32, Osiris), clothing (e.g., NFA, Bonfire, Dub, 686, Sessions, Holden), or accessories (e.g., Grenade Gloves, Dragon) targeted at specific market segments. Some of these niche companies are the creations of professional snowboarders attempting to capitalize on their cultural status (e.g., Air-Blaster and Grenade), whereas other companies, such as Burton, DC and Quiksilver, target every segment of the snowboarding market by offering various lines of equipment, clothing and accessories often under the guise of a confederation of small specialist firms. In the post-Fordist system, small-batch production and subcontracting bypass the rigidities of the Fordist system and satisfy a far greater range of market needs. Of course, accelerating turnover time in production would be useless without an accompanying reduction in the turnover time of consumption. Thus, post-Fordism has also witnessed rapidly changing fashions and the mobilization of all the 'artifices of need inducement', such as the continual repackaging and branding and advertising of products, and cultural transformation that this implies (Harvey, 1989, p. 156). The shift from mass consumption to specialized consumption is also characteristic of the post-Fordist system. Post-Fordist marketers invest commodities with meaning according to what segment of the population they aim to reach. They pay close attention to the styles favored by their niche markets and appropriate those styles as commodities.

In the post-Fordist system, culture and cultural activity, especially leisure and recreation, increasingly became cultural industries, that is, commodities sold in the market to individual consumers who, in turn, increasingly identify cultural gratification with consumption (Amin, 1994). As the comments from Ste'en at the head of this chapter suggest, contemporary youth are particularly susceptible to commodity fetishism: recalling his own 'infatuation' with 'new product', he recognizes that for many young boarders 'getting all the new gear' is an alluring and highly affective experience (personal communication, October 2005). According to ex-professional snowboarder and snowboard graphic designer Seth Neary, snowboard graphics are 'such an important part of the snowboard because when you walk into a shop, they're going to *talk* to you…. [Snowboard graphics] give you an emotional response….When I look down at my board, I want to be *stoked*' (cited in Picard, 2008, para. 7, emphasis in original).

In the post-Fordist system, lifestyles based on consumption also tend to have a significant effect on one's sense of self-worth and broader social status (see Chapter 5). Post-Fordist producers and marketers not only cope with rapidly and continually changing lifestyles and fashions, they capitalize on them no matter how short-term or limited their influence. In a post-Fordist system, the continuous creation of new needs and wants, and new niche markets, can 'alert us to new cultural possibilities' (Harvey, 1989, p. 109). Thus when companies identified women's snowboarding as a new and untapped niche market in the mid-1990s, they turned to the female boarding body as a 'new cultural possibility'. In the remainder of this chapter I consider some of the implications for female snowboarders as consumers and producers within this post-Fordist culture and economy.

'Shrink it and pink it': post-Fordism and the female niche market

Prior to the early 1990s, female snowboarders used equipment, and wore clothing, designed by men for men. Tina Basich (2003) recalls the lack of clothing available to female boarders during the early years, complaining that all the boys' clothes were 'super-huge': 'I'd have to roll up the sleeves and the pants and wear a belt to hold them up ... my pants would get stuck in my bindings and I'd go to do a trick in the pipe only to have my coat ride up and blind my view for landing' (p. 102). In the logic of post-Fordism, however, female snowboarders are a valuable niche market and an important consumer group whose cultural desires and aspirations must be acknowledged and catered for. In the mid- to late 1990s, the snowboarding industry recognized the untapped potential in this niche market and started accommodating the needs of female snowboarders by designing and producing equipment and clothing specifically for women.

A good example of the snowboarding industry attempting to cater to female boarders is the production of female-specific snowboards and boots. Physical and technical considerations are critical to board and boot design. Women typically have smaller feet thus influencing board width, and are often lighter and shorter with a narrower stance, effecting board length; their feet also tend to be narrower and have a higher arch, influencing boot design ('Women's tech', 2006). In the early 1990s Nitro created the Petra Mussig race board and Checker Pig marketed the Lisa Viciguerra freestyle board (Gasperini, 1996). These boards sold for a season in Europe but never reached the American market. In 1993, Burton made the first women's snowboard boots, which sold out in the first two months. In 1994, Sims tested the U.S. market and launched a full-scale marketing campaign, touting its 'first women's pro model snowboard' with Shannon Dunn as the rider. It was a success and Sims surpassed its estimated financial goals five times over (Sosienski, 1995). Kemper Snowboards also released a Tina Basich pro model. Recalling these exciting developments, Basich (2003) states:

> We were able to help design the boards to our specifications and design our own art for the graphics.... I remember finding a list of goals that I had made a few years earlier that lists 'My own pro model snowboard' with a 'ha ha!' next to it. At the time I thought it was a long shot because only the guys had pro model snowboards. I was proving myself wrong and that became a big deal in so many ways. Professional and Olympic women skiers were shocked. It turned the heads of corporate sports manufacturers like Nike and Trek. Other than basketball shoes and tennis rackets, not many other manufacturers had professional female-endorsed sporting equipment. (pp. 101–102)

By 1995, numerous snowboarding companies catered for the female consumer with specific boots and boards with graphics and colors chosen and designed by women.

Post-Fordist marketers invest commodities with meaning according to what segment of the population they want to reach. In the broader society, marketers often target the young female market by using 'girl power' sentiments or, rather, 'commodified feminism' in a way that positions young women as creators of their own identities and life chances, and as liberated by their participation in the consumer culture that surrounds them (see Cole and Hribar, 1995). The girl power market not only relies on young women as its key consumer group but also 'sells an image of savvy girlness to them in the process' (Harris, 2004a, p. 166). Similar marketing strategies are employed by snowboarding companies in their attempts to reach the female consumer. Companies often use language that connotes girl power sentiments of autonomy, rights, independence, and power. For example, Rossignol promoted its top-of-the-range female freestyle board, Amber, as 'provocatively feminist! This demanding board is for girls with tough per-sonalities, militating for committed riding', and described the graphics as ' "Bad Girl" pink and black cosmetics' that will 'stand out in the snow-parks' (Rossignol Winter 2004–2005 brochure, p. 23). Another current theme in marketing to female snowboarders has been the use of traditionally femi-nine graphics and colors. Missy Samiee, co-owner of Goddess Snowboards, described their product as 'designed by women with women in mind', claiming they 'don't have guns or ugly graphics like a lot of guys' boards. Ours are pastel colors with classic looks' (cited in Sosienski, 1995, para. 14). Women's boards traditionally featured feminine designs and names (e.g., Empress, Feather, Nymph, Zen Purity, Zen Peace, Wild Flower, Bella, Liberty, and Diva). Graphics on female boards often include flowers, birds and but-terflies, and the most prevalent color schemes are white, pink and pastels. By comparison male boards generally feature scary, morbid, or creepy images of skulls, skeletons, flames, devils, dragons, monsters, and naked women, with black and red the dominant colors and labels like Destroyer, Nomad, Tribal Fear, Machine, Zen Energy, Fury, Bonehead, Evil Cluster, and Punisher ('Buyers guide', 2003).

The female niche market continued to grow throughout the late 1990s and, by 2001 the women's market comprised the 'fastest growing aspect of snowboarding' ('Women's market', 2001, para. 4). Most of the companies that entered the boarding industry to cater for male boarders broadened their product lines to tap into the female market (e.g., Rossignol, Nitro, and Ride Snowboards). Some large companies, seeking to further capitalize on the growing female market, established separate female divisions. Examples in 2007 included Quiksilver (Roxy Snow) and Volcom (Volcom Girls). Interestingly, Volcom Girls contributed 32 percent to Volcom's US$110.6 mil-lion revenues in 2004, a 200 percent increase since 2002 (Stassen, 2005b). Other smaller companies, including Cold as Ice (outerwear and accessories), Betty Rides (outerwear), Nikita (street clothing) and Chorus (snowboards), focus solely on the female niche market; women own and operate many of these companies. The contemporary female market contains numerous subcategories that cater for different levels of ability and styles. According to Donna Burton Carpenter, the notion of a homogenous women's market was a figment of the male imagination and was responsible for the 'shrink it and pink it' mentality among many male-dominated companies during the late 1990s ('Volvo sports', 2005, para. 7). In the contemporary snowboard market, however, the smartest companies seeking capital accumulation invest heavily in expanding their product ranges and embracing innovative marketing strategies to target new subgroups of female boarders, such as girls, novices, core freestyle riders, athletes, and backcountry riders.

With the influx of companies trying to capture the female consumer, the women's snowboarding market has become increasingly competitive. Moreover, as Kathleen Gasperini, youth market trend forecaster and president of Label Networks, stated: 'Girls today are so much more demanding and so much [savvier] than just ten years ago. Girls can sense brands that are cool and core. They seek them out and are very brand conscious' ('Volvo sports', 2005, para. 6). In order to appeal to this increasingly savvy female consumer, snowboard companies must prove their 'cultural authenticity' and demonstrate their commitment to women's snowboarding. Hence, snowboarding manufacturers are investing heavily in sponsoring female athletes, women-specific events (e.g., Roxy Chicken Jam, Nikita Chickita Snowdown, Queen of the Mountain), and media. For example, *Dropstitch* (2004), an all-female snowboarding video, was sponsored by Roxy, Nikita, Billabong, Saloman, Burton, Oakley, Vans, *White Lines* magazine, Powderroom.com, *Method Magazine*, and Peugeot. Others demonstrate their commitment to women by donating a percentage of their global sales to female-specific charities, such as breast cancer research.

New opportunities

The success of the female niche market has opened up new opportunities for women within the snowboarding industry. In 1987, Bev Sanders, Lisa Hudson, and Donna Burton Carpenter were among the only women in the industry, manufacturing Avalanche snowboards, Airwalk boots, and Burton Snowboards respectively. Hudson recalls going to board meetings with 40 men in suits and being 'the only female in upper management' (cited in Howe, 1998, p. 118). But the recent boom in female-specific products has helped women find new spaces within the snowboarding economy. Women increasingly hold positions of responsibility in the industry as manufacturers, CEOs, film-makers, publishers, journalists and event organizers. In 2005, women held 50 percent of the top positions at *Transworld Snowboarding*, including associate editor, associate art director, photography department manager and senior contributing editor. In 2001 Jake Burton observed that his company had 'become male-dominated without us really realizing it' (cited in Stassen, 2005a, para. 22). Since then, Burton Snowboards has adopted a women-led philosophy, established and directed by Donna Burton Carpenter, which seeks to 'recruit, promote and retain women in leadership positions...in the marketplace, and in the field [athletes]' ('Volvo sports', 2005, para. 12). Much of this progress can be attributed to the growth of the female niche market that has provided opportunities previously unavailable to women in the snowboarding industry and sport.

As well as offering women opportunities for consumption and employment, the female niche market also offers new space for female entrepreneurialism. Indeed, some female snowboarders are founding their own snowboard clothing, equipment and accessory companies, producing their own media (e.g., magazines, films, and websites), and organizing snowboarding events and clinics. Some of these projects are established by women seeking to improve the conditions for women within the sport and culture; economics provides the basic motives for others. Leanne Pelosi, professional snowboarder and cofounder of MGT Snowboard Camps – female-specific snowboard coaching programs held in Whistler, Canada – admits, 'I just wanted to snowboard as much as possible but I didn't have a job and I wasn't getting paid ... so I used my savings and Joanna and I came up with MGT ... it helps pay my rent' (cited in Floros, 2004, para. 10). Pelosi has clearly adopted the individualistic and entrepreneurial attitude so characteristic of the post-Fordist *Zeitgeist*. The key issue here, however, is that, within a post-Fordist system, female agents have space to both earn an income and reconstruct and recreate new cultural meanings for female snowboarding. For example, having bought her ex-husband out of her business, Janet Freeman, owner and operator of Betty Rides, proudly affirms 'snowboarding pays for this house, for my kids' school, for the food on the table' (cited in Lewis, 2005, para. 24). It is important to reiterate, however, that these women (like most female snowboarders) tend to be among a very small middle-class core, and such opportunities are not available to all women.

Post-Fordism, empowerment and critical consumption

The post-Fordist industrial, economic and cultural transformations ushered in since the 1970s across the Western world have been the backdrop against which privileged women have embraced new roles in education, work, sport, and leisure. Or, as Kumar (1995) puts it, in a post-Fordist system women are able to achieve 'more in business and professional life and ... to make their way in society independently of men' (p. 170). Despite structural limitations of the new economy that differentially affect young women's educational and employment opportunities, choice and self-invention have become central to the ways in which many young women think about their identities and futures within the new post-Fordist system (Aapola et al., 2005). Many young women 'sit[ting] at the intersection of feminist discourse and economic reality' are taking seriously messages of self-invention, choice and flexibility (Ibid., p. 76). Ideas of girl power, freedom, choice and individualism translate easily into the post-Fordist economic context (see Cole & Hribar, 1995). In the words of one journalist: 'Girl power is flexing its economic muscles' through the spending power of 'single, professional, independent and confident young women' (Lambert, 2003, cited in Harris,

2004a, p. 166). But are the new consumption and participation opportunities available to young women empowering them?

On the one hand, it might be argued that every choice situation involves acts of selection and rejection that give the consumer a sense of power. On the other hand, it might be said that through consumption, women are experiencing, paradoxically, 'an increased sense of control with minimal impact of the oppressive social context within which they are located' (Cavanagh, 2005, p. 1424). 'Empowerment and consumption,' says Harris (2004b), are 'closely linked through the associations made between products for young women and being confident, strong, assertive, a leader, a role model, and in charge' (p. 90). In these ways, consumption is seen as a 'shortcut to power' (Ibid.). Young women's power is defined 'only as a power to buy, rather than a power to create, think and to act' (Taft, 2001, cited in Harris, 2004b, p. 90). As such, it 'promotes another barrier to girls' expression of social critique and their political and civic participation' (Ibid.). Adopting a Marxist perspective, it might be argued that female boarders are not empowered by these new opportunities for consumption, rather they are duped and 'alienate[d] embodied subjects' (Shilling, 2007, p. 5). In contrast, a Kumarian post-Fordist perspective gives more room for their agency and tends to sway towards optimism.

In a post-Fordist system, female snowboarders are not passive consumers, or cultural dupes, rather they appropriate space to dictate what is produced and consumed. Professional snowboarder Barrett Christy believes 'snowboarding as an industry has been pretty supportive of its girls, we've had signature boards, boots, clothes, shoes, etc and *we've created a market* for women's specific products' (cited in Hakes, 2000, para. 70, emphasis added). Similarly, Jake Burton alludes to the power of the female consumer in the snowboarding economy: 'It wasn't me that made girls' riding happen. It was the girls themselves. And once they made that choice, we didn't shy away from the investments needed to make women's products happen and develop in the right way' ('Volvo sports', 2005, para. 13). But how does a signature snowboard equate to empowerment? How much power lies in choosing one particular board, pair of boots or jacket over another?

The cultural responses by female snowboarders to economic developments ultimately depend on their position within both snowboarding culture and the broader society. The positions of women within the snowboarding culture range from the novice and marginal boarder (who participates once or twice a year) to the professional rider (who may board more than 200 days a year). These various cultural positions give rise to a range of cultural responses, including passive consumption, reflexive consumption, and cultural production. Certainly many young women, particularly novice boarders, appreciate the opportunity to purchase clothing and equipment designed specifically for their technical, physical and/or cultural snowboarding needs. Yet some female snowboarders, particularly core participants, remain cautious of some of the opportunities (for consumption) available in the post-Fordist context. Indeed, Pamela complains: 'Too many of these companies still rely on male perspectives of what women want. I don't want butterflies, flowers and birds on my snowboard...and everything doesn't have to be pink' (personal communication, February 2005). Similarly, snowboarding journalist and snowboarder Tracey Fong (2000) called the 'stereotypical girlie' pastel pinks, baby blues, 'glam' fabrics and fake fur being promoted by some snowboard clothing companies a 'disturbing trend' (para. 1). Fong, like many other female riders, does not regard snowboarding as 'cute' (para. 4). Comments posted on a snowboarding website (www.snowboard.com) further reflected this sensibility:

> I wouldn't want a girly board because I have a hard enough time proving to guys that I'm on the mountain for the same reason they are...to board (not to pick up boys), and having girly sh*t just puts me into a category of 'girly girl'. (posted by michele9993, May 26, 2004)

> As a girl who doesn't fit the girl build, I am not an A cup for Nikita clothing or 110 pounds for the nice 143–148 [length in cm] boards, and I ride more than 100 days a year, longer than most girl boards last...I have always purchased guy boards. Since I'm not the stick figure Barbie snowboarder and actually ride more than most I need a harder board. For some girls it's great, but not for me. (posted by shayboarder, August 10, 2005)

As these comments show, production and marketing techniques that tout girl power messages, employ lower quality construction and traditionally feminine designs, and put cultural and physical limits on women's snowboarding, do not satisfy all female consumers. Put simply, we must be wary of interpreting changes within the post-Fordist system too optimistically. Not all female snowboarders are in a position to benefit, or be empowered, by these economic and cultural changes. While post-Fordism struggles to explain the different levels of access female snowboarders have to reflexive consumption and cultural production, it does alert us to the complex 'dialectic of exploitation and empowerment' rooted in contemporary youth's practices of physical cultural consumption and participation (Latham, 2002, p. 4).

Producing and consuming the snowboarding body: some final thoughts

In this chapter I employed two different theoretical approaches to shed light on various practices and processes involved in the production and consumption of the material snowboarding body. First, using a Marxist perspective, I examined the snowboarding body as a source of economic relations and considered the destructive effects of capitalism (i.e., alienation) on the bodies of professional snowboarders who own their labor power as well as a degree of creative capital unknown to the factory worker. Second, I drew on a more recent post-Fordist perspective to reveal the snowboarding body as a surface phenomenon, a malleable marker of commercial value subject to the fragmentation of the snowboarding market and the vagaries of fashion. Exploring these ideas through the case of the female niche market, this part highlighted aspects of the two-way relationship between the snowboarding economy and culture. Although the economy helps define the cultural opportunities and meanings for female snowboarders, the cultural responses by female snowboarders may exert a dialectical influence on economic developments, facilitating and perhaps even contradicting them. This supports Kumar's (1995) claim that it is 'just as possible that changes in culture and politics are pushing on changes in the economy as the other way around' (p. 65). This approach also showed that, within a post-Fordist system that celebrates new niche markets, female snowboarders have (to varying degrees) the ability to dictate what they consume and produce.[10]

In the post-Fordist snowboarding industry, the media are integral to corporate image building, as is the case with Burton Snowboards, and supporting new niche markets, such as female snowboarders. In the next chapter, I draw upon Michel Foucault's concepts of power and discourse to examine the highly fragmented snowboarding media as an important cultural institution where multiple representations of snowboarding bodies are communicated, consumed, and contested, within and across global and local contexts.

4
Representing the Boarding Body: Discourse, Power, and the Snowboarding Media

> After a few runs, I was hiking back up the pipe when a guy who looked almost as dorky as me approached. He was skinny and pimple-faced, and he had a camera around his neck. 'Hi, I'm Trevor Graves with *International Snowboard Magazine*. You're ripping', he said, holding up his camera to convey the point. At that moment, I thought I was part of something huge. After all, here was this guy from *'International' Snowboard Magazine* taking photos of me. ... That little bit of Kodak motivation got me riding harder than I ever had. (Todd Richards recalls an early half-pipe competition in February 1988 in New Hampshire; Richards, 2003, pp. 57–58)

> Snowboard videos were always playing in [my] house [in Whistler]. The early videos were like primers: how to board, how to look, how to be. The design was gritty and the soundtrack raucous; this rawness, of course, was in keeping with the snowboard ethic. The fact that these videos were so difficult to come by made them even cooler; watching them felt like being a member of an exclusive little club. [We would] watch the same videos over, and over, and over. ... We even made our own videos, and those were in rotation at the chalet as well. (Ross Rebagliati reflects on the use of early snowboard videos during the late 1980s; Rebagliati, 2009, p. 46)

The media has always played a decisive role in the lives of snowboarders, by confirming, spreading and consolidating cultural perceptions. While the heavily circulated image of the teenage male snowboarder with spiky hair, multiple piercings, tattoos and wearing over-sized clothing continues to loom large in the public imagination, representations of snowboarding bodies are in fact diverse and dynamic. In the first part of this chapter I offer a brief discussion of the processes through which snowboarding bodies are represented and consumed differently across the mass, niche, and micro media. Here I argue that new approaches are required to make meaning of the dynamic power relations between various agents involved in the production and consumption of snowboarding media. In this chapter I consider the potential of Michel Foucault's unique conceptualization of power to reveal some of the multiple, variegated, and dialectical relations between snowboarders and the media.[1] The second part of the chapter consists of two main sections. The first draws on Foucault's concepts of power and discourse to examine some of the discursive constructions of snowboarding bodies in the media. The second explores these ideas further with an examination of the discourses of femininity and (hetero)sexuality in the snowboarding media. Drawing on Foucault's notion of 'technologies of self', I also examine how women (and men) make sense of the multiple and contradictory mediated discourses of femininity in snowboarding culture. The resulting discussion critically evaluates the sexualized images of women in the snowboarding media and the discursive effects these have on women's snowboarding experiences. Taking inspiration from Foucault's unique approach to knowledge and power, the later part of this chapter voices a long ignored question: are sexualized images of women *really* at the heart of gender problems in contemporary society?

Snowboarding bodies in the mass, niche, and micro media

The *mass media* (television, newspapers, and mainstream magazines), *niche media* (sport-specific magazines, films, and websites), and *micro media* (flyers, posters, homemade videos, and online zines) cater for different audiences, and have different consequences and 'markedly different cultural connotations' for youth and physical cultural participants (Thornton, 1996, p. 122; see also Wheaton & Beal, 2003). Here I offer a brief introduction to some of the cultural complexities involved in the production and consumption of the mass, niche, and micro media, respectively, in snowboarding. The Foucauldian theoretical analysis which follows will discuss some of these issues in more depth.

Snowboarding and the mass media

The mass media tend to be produced by nonsnowboarding journalists and producers for a mass audience with, often, little knowledge of snowboarding. The mass media typically gloss over cultural complexities and reinforce stereotypes of snowboarders as young, white, hedonistic, rebellious males (Heino, 2000; Stone & Horne, 2008). This was particularly obvious in the late 1980s and early 1990s when the mass media began reporting on snowboarding. The exaggerated mass-mediated image of snowboarding during this period was such that in 1988, *Time* magazine declared snowboarding 'the worst new sport'. While negative mass media contributed to the general public's dislike of snowboarding and its participants, it had the opposite effect on 'alternative' young people who were attracted to the activity. In the words of Todd Richards (2003), 'we were outcasts, viewed negatively – or at least warily – by public opinion. [But] this only fuelled the fire of the snowboarding youth movement' (p. 67).

In the mid- and late 1990s, however, snowboarding became increasingly controlled and defined by transnational media corporations like ESPN and NBC via events such as the X-Games and Gravity Games. But as the comments from one early participant suggest, snowboarders were not passive in this process:

> [Our] sponsors quickly learned all they had to do was dress us up in Day-Glo and catch somebody on camera saying, 'Gnarly air, dude', and they were guaranteed 15 seconds on the evening news. We all knew the sponsors and the media had no idea what the sport was about, but if dressing up like clowns and posing for MTV meant a few days of free-riding, most of us were in. (David Alden, cited in Howe, 1998, p. 56)

The incorporation of snowboarding into the Winter Olympics, video games including Xbox' *Amped Freestyle* and Ubisoft *Shaun White Snowboarding*, and blockbuster movies such as *Out Cold* (2001) and *First Descent* (2005), helped further expose the sport to the mainstream, as well as contributing to the creation of the 'star system'. Indeed, the mass media coverage of some snowboarding stars is such that Shaun White was identified as the 'most popular' and 'recognizable athlete' attending the 2010 Winter Olympic Games (Ebner, 2009).

In this hyper-commercial context of the X-Games, Gravity Games, Olympic Games and prime-time television exposure, new competition formats and boarding disciplines that lend themselves to television coverage emerged, including boarder-cross, slope-style, and big air competitions. These events are 'spectacular to watch and you're more or less guaranteed to see someone crash' (Reed, 2005, p. 95). Many contemporary professional snowboarders embrace these new opportunities for increased media exposure and celebrity. But there are inherent dangers for the athlete within this highly mediatized context. For example, when professional snowboarder Tara Dakides appeared on *The Late Show with David Letterman* in February 2004, various contingencies and convergences resulted in a significant and unforeseen event. Having recently won a silver medal in the X-Games slope-style event and featured on the cover of *FHM*, Dakides was invited to become the first female to complete a live stunt on the show. The producers built a massive wooden ramp outside the studio in the middle of 53rd Street and then covered it in snow. Various factors including lack of building materials, warm weather melting the snow and the pressure of a big-time production, however, diminished Dakides' chances of successfully completing the 360-degree spin over the 20-foot gap she had planned. Falling on asphalt from an estimated height of 25 feet, Dakides was knocked unconscious and split her head in front of a stunned crowd and live national audience. The mass media response to this event was phenomenal. 'It just spread like wildfire' says Dakides (cited in Reed, 2005, p. 161). The event was covered by every major American newspaper and became the lead story on local news programs across the country. Dakides later returned to the *Letterman Show, sans* snowboard, and appeared on *Last Call, The Early Show, Deborah Norville Tonight,* and *The Howard Stern Show.* Much to the dismay of many inquisitive snowboarders, Letterman banned any further re-runs of the incident, obviously wanting to 'erase this little mishap from everyone's minds' (Roenigk, 2004, para. 1). According to Dakides, footage of the accident was censored because it challenged mainstream America's assumptions about appropriate risk-taking for young women: 'Nobody wants to see a girl hit the concrete, hard on *David Letterman.* Is that supposed to be funny?' (cited in Roenigk, 2004, para. 7). An unforeseen benefit from this incident, according to Dakides, was that 'a lot more people know my name now' (cited in Roenigk, 2004, para. 12). But Dakides also observed the risks for the athlete within this highly mediated context: 'they build these big obstacles to watch us do gnarlier and gnarlier tricks, and I'm risking my entire season and all my other goals...lying in bed for a month is not fun' (cited in Ibid., para. 4).

Snowboarding and the niche media

In contrast to mass media representations of snowboarding bodies, which are often ignored, parodied, or resisted by core participants, niche snowboarding media are instrumental to committed snowboarders' cultural identity construction. The term 'niche media' refers to magazines (e.g., *Transworld Snowboarding, Snowboarder*), films (e.g., *Resistance, Commitment*) and websites (e.g., www.snowboard.com) typically created by journalists, editors, photographers, and film-makers who are, or were, active snowboarders. According to Howe (1998), niche photographers and film-makers are 'the real image makers' because their work 'creates the dream that is snowboarding' and 'sells lifestyle' (p. 107). Doug Palladini, publisher of *Snowboarder* magazine, believes snowboarding magazines are 'not just something you pick up at the airport'; to core participants they are 'the bible' (cited in Ibid., p. 104). Similarly, Reed (2005) describes snowboarding films as 'windows into the culture of snowboarding...Through these films viewers can connect with the best [snowboarding] personalities, styles, destinations, and tricks, taking virtual journeys around the world of snowboarding, living it, if only for an hour or so' (p. 114). Niche snowboarding websites also offer important spaces for the sharing of information and communication across local and national fields. For example, www.snowboard.com is the world's largest snowboarding website, hosting 550,000 registered members – 313,000 from the United States, 98,000 from Canada, and 144,000 from other countries around the world (Media man, no date).

As the following comments from Richards (2003) illustrate, coverage in the niche media, particularly magazines and films, plays an important role in both the financial and social reward systems within the snowboarding industry and culture:

> You could never have enough coverage. Tricks and logo shots you got published in magazines or included in films were used to negotiate your sponsorship the following year…. I wanted to be in the videos [because it paid well], but it was more about gaining respect from my friends. If a rider pulled a 900 [degree spin] and nobody saw it, he didn't want to run up and say, 'Did you see that? The videos did the talking for him. The name of the game was acting like you didn't give a shit, but I think everyone wants to get noticed when they pull off something big. Videos let us maintain that cool facade with minimal outward conceit. (p. 156)

Niche snowboarding films and magazines not only communicate snowboarding discourses and knowledge across local, national, and global fields; they also contribute to the construction and maintenance of the cultural hierarchy through the allocation of social, symbolic and economic capital (see Chapter 5).

Though the niche media reside closest to the culture, commercial processes also complicate their production. In 2004 *Transworld Snowboarding* had a circulation of 207,000, featured a total of 1333 pages of advertisements, and generated US$21.9 million in revenue, up from US$14.9 million in 2000 (Stableford, 2005). Responding to concerns about the amount and type of advertising featured in the magazine, Cody Dresser (2004a), associate editor of *Transworld Snowboarding*, acknowledged that 'editorial and advertising are two separate departments – we're often bitching about the corporate ads diluting our magazine' (p. 26). Ste'en Webster, editor of *New Zealand Snowboarder*, admits to similar tensions, but as a smaller, snowboarder-owned and -operated company with a circulation of 10,000, he retains more control over the final product: 'Our goal is to represent what's happening within New Zealand snowboarding. I think that is an important goal, a lot of magazines get distracted and rather than portray what's going on [in the culture] they tend to dictate [based on] what they think the advertiser wants them to say' (personal communication, October 2005). Snowboard journalists Matt Barr, Chris Moran, and Ewan Wallace describe local niche magazines such as Spain's *Snow Planet*, Sweden's *Transition*, and the U.K.-based *White Lines*, as 'labours of love … sustained only by the passion of the staff and the avidity with which their generally low readership devours each issue' (Barr et al., 2006,

Angry Snowboarder' also cites 'tweets' from professional snowboarder, ex-Olympian, and television presenter Todd Richards' recent 'Twitter' postings:

> All the media attention for Kevin Pierce is amazing, but it seems like they are trying to label snowboarders as reckless and wacky again....It really pisses me off that these fools at ABC call someone with no ties to what is actually happening in the sport to report facts. Call me, I'll tell you what's up ABC. Shit, Disney owns ESPN and I work for ESPN....I am so pissed about this ABC fiasco [because] I think of myself as one of the credible mouth pieces for snowboarding on TV. I really take pride in having snowboarding being shown with integrity to the masses. (cited in 'The mainstream', 2010, para. 4, edited for clarity)

As these brief examples suggest, 'representation wars' are occurring with increasing frequency in part because 'new communication technologies are enabling more people to receive and compare differing local, regional, national, and "global" representations' of snowboarding bodies (Frow & Morris, 2003, p. 502). But how do we explain the complex social, cultural, and economic processes involved in representing snowboarding bodies in the mass, niche, and micro media? How do we make meaning of the dynamic power relations between various agents involved in the production and consumption of the snowboarding media?

In recent years, cultural studies scholars, anthropologists, and sociologists have employed an array of innovative methodological and theoretical approaches (e.g., content analysis, critical discourse analysis, feminist media studies, media ethnography, visual anthropology, and visual cultural studies) in their attempts to understand and explain text-based media, photography, video, and hypermedia as representations of cultural knowledge and/ or sites of production, social interaction, and individual experience (see, for example, Lister & Wells, 2005; Pink, 2006, 2007). While I see value in many of these approaches, I am concerned by the tendency for many contemporary media analysts, particularly those following in the cultural studies tradition (e.g., du Gay et al., 1997), to view the production, circulation, and consumption of media as a cyclical process. As the previous examples suggest, contemporary youth and sports cultural participants use various forms of mass, niche, and micro media in dynamic and multifarious ways. In the early twenty-first century, media producers and consumers do not constitute two separate groups. Media producers and consumers can also be passive, critical or resistant in different sociocultural-temporal moments. Arguably, Michel Foucault's unique conceptualization of power has the potential to help us move beyond cyclical explanations of the media and examine some of the multiple, variegated, and dialectical relations between snowboarders and the media.

Foucault, power, and the snowboarding media

Many scholars regard Michel Foucault as one of the 'most influential think-ers of contemporary times' (Markula & Pringle, 2006, p. 5). His writings, according to Dreyfus and Rabinow (1982), represent 'the most important contemporary effort both to develop a method for the study of human beings and to diagnose the current situation of our society' (p. xiii). While Foucault's work is often insightful, 'it is sometimes difficult to know how best to use it' (Mills, 2003, p. 110). Perhaps this is because he does not develop one fully thought-out theory but instead tries to 'think through ways of thinking without the constraints of a systematized structure' (Ibid.). Foucault (1975) encourages readers to make what they can of his work rather than slavishly following his ideas: 'All my books are little toolboxes. If peo-ple want to open them, to use this sentence or that idea as a screwdriver or spanner to short-circuit, discredit systems of power...so much the better' (cited in Mills, 2003, p. 7). Following this recommendation, many theorists and critics have used Foucault's ideas as a way of approaching a subject rather than as a set of principles or rules. Here I employ a selection of con-cepts from Foucault's toolbox to facilitate an analysis of the media and the production of cultural knowledge in snowboarding culture.

Foucault rarely wrote specifically about the media. Nonetheless, his understanding of power, power/knowledge, and discourse offers 'a variety of insights into the media's current strategies for communicating with their publics' (Macdonald, 2003, p. 2). Here I concur with Myra Macdonald, one of the few to explore media discourse from a Foucauldian perspective, who argues that Foucault contributes to our understanding of media operations through his attention to 'the historical evolution of discourses; shifting discursive constellations, and relation between these and socio-cultural change; [and] the relation between media discourses and wider public dis-courses' (Ibid., p. 25). Thus in this section I critically evaluate the efficacy of Foucault's concepts of power and discourse, as vehicles for understanding the discursive constructions of snowboarding bodies.

Power

Foucault has had a major influence on contemporary understandings of power, as often as a subject of criticism as of inspiration. Foucault's model of power caught the attention of many scholars and activists because it radi-cally reconceptualized earlier notions. Traditionally, many scholars thought of power in solely repressive terms whereby the powerful repress the power-less (e.g., Althusser, 1977; Poulantzas, 1978; Weber, 1978). Foucault, however, moved beyond this one-sided view of power by examining the operation of power within everyday relations between people and institutions. Power, he suggested, is not a possession that can be 'acquired, seized, or shared' (Foucault, 1978, p. 94); power is not a 'group of institutions...that ensure the subservience of the citizens of a given state' (p. 92), nor is it a manner of subjugation that operates through laws or a 'system of domination exerted by one group over another' (p. 92). While governments, social institutions, laws, and dominant groups are commonly assumed to hold power, Foucault (1978) emphasized that they represent 'only the terminal forms' of power (cited in Markula & Pringle, 2006, p. 34). Foucault (1978) rejected the idea that power was easily locatable and that a binary division existed between the ruled and rulers; there is 'no such duality extending from the top down and reacting on more and more limited groups to the very depths of the social body' (p. 94). Rather, Foucault recognized power as 'a relational effect of a network of localized social practices which shape the conduct of everybody but belong to nobody' (Crossley, 2005, p. 220).

Foucault's concept of power as relational presupposed multiple forms of power. Of particular interest to Foucault (1991[1977]) was 'disciplinary power', a form of power that focuses on the control and discipline of bodies and that is exercised fundamentally 'by means of surveillance' (p. 104). Foucault (1991) saw 'the existence of a whole set of techniques and institutions for measuring, supervising and correcting the abnormal' (p. 199). These techniques and institutions are architecturally embodied in the 'panopticon' (p. 200).[2] For Foucault, panopticism refers to a 'political anatomy' where the mechanisms of surveillance and discipline are no longer locked within specific buildings or institutions but 'function in a diffused, multiple, polyvalent way throughout the whole social body' (pp. 208–209). A number of sports scholars have drawn on Foucault's concept of panopticism to examine how the media functions as part of the 'apparatus of technologies of domination' (see, for example, Chapman, 1997; Duncan, 1994; Markula & Pringle, 2006). While these studies have contributed much to our understanding of the mass media as a technology of domination, some scholars express concern that research focusing on 'technologies of dominance' results in 'pessimistic representations of sport and exercise practices' (Markula & Pringle, 2006, p. 48). Gruneau (1993), for example, claims that such a focus 'can too easily deflect attention from analyzing the creative possibilities, freedoms, ambiguities, and contradictions also found in sport' (cited in Markula & Pringle, 2006, p. 48). Moreover, such an approach does not adequately explain the media in physical cultures such as snowboarding; it overlooks the various forms of media (mass, niche, and micro) and their production and reproduction of multiple, and often conflicting, discourses of physical cultural bodies. Furthermore, this top-down understanding of power ignores the dialectical relationship between the media and the snowboarding culture. Hence, rather than focusing on the media as a 'technology of discipline' (which is only one form of power discussed by Foucault), I seek to draw more broadly upon Foucault's unique conceptualization of power and, in so doing, facilitate a discussion of the media in snowboarding culture as not always repressive but also potentially positive and productive. I now outline five key assumptions underlying Foucault's distinctive theories of power in relation to the snowboarding media.

Firstly, Foucault conceptualized power as *omnipresent*, as it was 'produced from one moment to the next, at every point, or rather in every relation from one point to another' (1978, p. 93). 'Power is everywhere', declared Foucault, 'not because it embraces everything but because it comes from everywhere' (p. 93). He focused on the microforms of power exercised at the level of daily life and stressed the importance of local, specific struggles. As Harvey and Sparks (1991) note, according to Foucault, 'power...arises in a capillary-like fashion from below, expressed in people's concrete knowledges, dispositions, interactions and relations' (cited in Andrews, 1993, p. 157). When applied to the snowboarding media, such an understanding of power helps us recognize that no binary division exists between those with power, such as media producers, and those without power, such as media consumers. Rather, media power relations in the snowboarding culture are better understood as part of an entanglement of localized social practices, interactions, and performances, which 'shape the conduct of everybody but belong to nobody' (Crossley, 2005, p. 220). Secondly, power, from a Foucauldian perspective, refers to *relations between people*. Foucault defined a relationship of power as one person acting upon the actions of another, rather than directly on the other person. However, an individual's actions within a relationship of power do not determine or physically force the actions of others. This is related to the third important aspect of Foucault's understanding of power relations, that is, *the way power is exercised*. For Foucault (1983), 'power is exercised only over free subjects, and only insofar as they are free' (p. 221).

Fourthly, rather than simply viewing power in a negative way, as constraining and repressing, Foucault argued that even at their most constraining, oppressive measures may be productive, 'giving rise to new forms of behaviors rather than simply closing down or censoring' others (Mills, 2003, p. 34). Power produces *particular types of behaviors*, by regulating people's everyday activities. Foucault (1975) describes this as the 'microphysics of power' (cited in O'Farrell, 2005, p. 101). Furthermore, Foucault claimed that what allows power to exert such a grip is that it is not merely a repressive force but it is also creative: 'What makes power hold good, what makes it accepted, is simply the fact that it doesn't weigh on us as a force that says no but that it traverses and produces things, it induces pleasure, forms knowledge, produces discourse' (Rabinow, 1984, cited in O'Grady, 2005, p. 15). The niche media are particularly powerful in the snowboarding culture not only because they produce forms of cultural knowledge, but also because they offer a 'fertile ground for the imitative transmission of affect' (Thrift, 2008, p. 245). For Russian snowboard photographer Dasha Stecenko (2009), 'getting the shot' can offer a highly affective experience: 'I enjoy the process... the self-expression... the chance to show something in a way that you can't describe with any words... capturing feelings, emotions and rare moments... as well as the reaction you get from people looking at the photos' (cited in Almendros, 2009, para. 11). Snowboarding films can also become prime conductors of affect. For example, a snowboarding journalist present at the premiere of *As If*, a female-only snowboarding video, acclaimed the occasion: 'The place was packed.... The movie got the crowd hyped, left us wanting more and f–king stoked' (Fast, 2005, para. 2). Mel, a committed New Zealand snowboarder, also described the film as 'sick' [awesome]: 'it got me so amped to go riding' (personal communication, October 2006). Not dissimilar from the highly affective surfing magazines described by Booth (2008), snowboard niche media producers employ a variety of photographic, editorial and design techniques to produce a final product (e.g., magazine cover, snowboard film, website homepage) that evokes the highest affective response from the viewer ('stoke' or 'amp', a sense of freedom, fear, danger, thrill, and/or sexual titillation).

Fifthly, the existence of power relations depends on a *multiplicity of points of resistance*. 'Where there is power, there is resistance,' Foucault (1978, p. 95) declared. It is important to note here that, while most social theorists think of resistance as a reaction to power, Foucault understood resistance as a power form in its own right. Continuing, he explained that within relations of power 'there is necessarily the possibility of resistance, for if there were no possibility of resistance – of violent resistance, of escape, of ruse, of strategies that reverse the situation – there would be no relations of power' (1987, p. 12). Snowboarders, for example, demonstrate resistance at the local level when they voice their concerns in the editorial pages of specialist snowboarding niche magazines, on snowboarding websites, and in everyday conversations. Charles' analysis of the relationship between niche snowboarding magazines and the boarding culture, in a letter to the editor published in *Snowboarder Magazine*, is particularly insightful:

> For a snowboarding magazine to be profitable, it has to sell magazines and ads. In other words, snowboarding magazines must market a 'lifestyle' and 'attitude'... That is why a certain snowboarding magazine is filled with personality-centric interviews with pro-riders, plus articles of music, fashion, and snowboarding culture. In turn, corporations appreciate the magazine's efforts to sell (as in SELLOUT) the snowboard lifestyle to the mainstream and these companies respond by filling the magazine with ads for street shoes, cologne, rock bands, and fashion accessories, as well as traditional snowboarding equipment. People in the mainstream who aren't a natural part of snowboarding culture will then, of course, buy a snowboard magazine to try to learn how to be part of this lifestyle. (February 2003, p. 42)

Others challenge the cultural meanings promoted by snowboarding magazines. For example, writing to *Transworld Snowboarding*, a correspondent named PJ asked: 'Why do half the snowboarders in advertisements throw ghetto poses and directional hand signs' when there are no 'ghetto kids on the mountain?' (Mail, 2005, p. 48). The editor's response highlights the significance of the broader social context (and the mass media) on snowboarding culture: 'Because it sells... turned on MTV lately? Hip-Hop has the world by the balls' (Ibid.). Snowboarders have also expressed concern over the recent recruitment efforts by the U.S. Army: 'You guys are letting the military pay to put pictures of soldiers standing in the snow wearing snowboard goggles and beanies complete with machine guns in your magazine... and you're advertising this to teens all over the country... this is wack [uncool]!' (Mike, cited in Mail, 2005, p. 48).

Simply put, micropolitics between the media and members of the snowboarding culture are 'everywhere' (Foucault, 2000). According to Mills (2003), Foucault's 'bottom-up model of power,' that is, his focus on the way power relations permeate all relations within a society, 'enables an account of the mundane and daily ways in which power is enacted and contested, and allows an analysis which is focused on individuals as active subject, as agents rather than passive dupes' (p. 34). Indeed, Foucault's unique conceptualization of power has the potential to facilitate fresh insights into the representation of physical cultural bodies in the media, primarily because it directs attention to dialectical, dynamic, and nuanced relationships between multiple forms of media and physical cultural participants.

Discourse

Foucault linked his schema of power and its exercise to the workings of discourse: 'it is in discourse that power and knowledge are joined together' (Foucault, 1978, p. 100). Discourse, he continued, 'transmits and produces power; it reinforces it but also undermines and exposes it, renders it fragile and makes it possible to thwart it' (p. 101). While discourse is one of the most frequently used terms from Foucault's work, it is also one of the most ambiguous (Mills, 2003). Here I draw on the interpretation he employed in *The Archaeology of Knowledge* (1972) and in *The Order of Discourse* (1981) to examine the role of the media in producing 'conceptual understandings' of snowboarders, 'individualized groups of statements' or discourses in the snowboarding culture, and 'unwritten rules and structures' which produce and regulate particular utterances and statements of snowboarding bodies.

Of particular interest to Foucault in his analysis of discourse were the processes by which some statements gain currency and others evaporate. Thus, rather than seeing discourse as simply a set of relatively coherent statements, we should look at it as something that exists due to 'a complex set of practices which... keep them in circulation and other practices which... fend them off from others and keep those statements out of circulation' (Mills,

2003, p. 54). The notion of exclusion is important in Foucault's (1981) thinking about discourse, and he described a range of external and internal procedures that constrain some discourses while highlighting and producing others. These procedures, he argued, are all concerned with 'classifying, distributing and ordering discourse, and their function is ultimately to distinguish between those who are authorized to speak' and 'those who are not' (Mills, 2003, p. 58).

Various processes work to constrain some discourses, and produce others, within the snowboarding media. *Blunt* magazine, for example, was established in 1993 by U.S. snowboarders Ken Block and Damon Way, and gained more cultural authenticity among core snowboarders than any other magazine because it was seen as providing a 'truthful' representation of snowboarding culture. Targeting the young, core, male snowboarder, *Blunt* magazine promoted juvenile pranks, soft-core pornography, and disregard for authority (see Attwood, 2005). Professional snowboarder Todd Richards described the *Blunt* formula as 'alcohol, party, party, party, oh, and snowboarding', and added, 'it was really popular among snowboarders and really unpopular among ski resorts, parents, and snowboarding companies because of its blatant disregard for authority. It also covered the most progressive snowboarders and turned down advertising from big companies like Burton and Morrow' (2003, p. 162). However, in 1998 *Blunt* folded under political and economic duress. According to one industry insider, 'distributors and advertisers wanted mainstream readers, while mainstream readers' parents wanted a more subdued, politically correct publication' (Blehm, 2003, p. 33). Despite *Blunt*'s appeal to core snowboarders, the magazine challenged authorities within the snowboarding industry, particularly those snowboarding companies, such as Burton Snowboards, and organizations, such as United States of America Snowboarding Association (USASA) and the International Ski Federation (FIS), that were actively promoting snowboarding as a legitimate sport, and touting participants as 'responsible athletes' in the lead-up to the 1998 Winter Olympics (see Humphreys, 1996). Thus *Blunt* was subjected to what Foucault (1981) termed the processes of 'exclusion' that effectively removed it from circulation.

The niche media also contribute to the 'classifying, distributing and ordering' of discourses of whiteness in snowboarding culture. While the snowboarding bodies appearing in niche magazines and films are almost exclusively white, there are some notable exceptions. The North American snowboarding media and associated commercial interests have seized images of some nonwhite professional snowboarders – for example, Marc Frank Montoya (Latino) and Gabby Maiden (African American) – and placed them at the centre of cultural discourse. The athletes exposed to such 'selective incorporation' tend to be those who have been identified by snowboard companies and media firms as having the potential to help them access new and expanding niche markets, such as the Latino market in Southern

California. As will be explained further in Chapter 5, the novelty of being a racial 'other' in the predominantly white snowboarding culture can offer some nonwhite professionals additional opportunities to convert symbolic capital into economic capital in a highly competitive market (also see Brayton, 2005; Kusz, 2007a). For example, as the first professional African American female snowboarder, Gabby Maiden features in a plethora of fashion and action images and advertisements in snowboarding magazines to such an extent that she was recently identified as one of the most 'recognizable' snowboarders in the United States ('MLK Day', 2009; see Figure 6.1 of this book). As the first professional Mexican American snowboarder, Montoya is aware of the commodity value of his nonwhite snowboarding body, and he consciously embodies practices, styles and tastes from hip-hop, urban gangster, and Latino cultures to create a highly marketable snowboarding identity that appeals to the desires of young, white, privileged male snow-boarders, as well as snowboarders from 'other' groups, such as Latino snow-boarders (Athlete Bio, no date). According to *Snowboard* magazine editor Pat Bridges, 'Marc Frank is always a good interview because his voice is so *distinct*' (cited in Whyte, 2009, para. 17, emphasis added).

The visibility of professional athletes such as Maiden and Montoya inspires many nonwhite snowboarders. A snowboarder from Puerto Rico, for exam-ple, recently wrote to Montoya thanking him for 'opening up this sport for Latinos everywhere' ('Ask Dr Marco', 2003). Yet discourses of whiteness con-tinue to dominate the snowboarding niche media, such that participants from other racial or ethnic groups are often expected to justify their inclu-sion to predominantly white audiences. For example, some snowboarders question the 'authenticity' of Montoya's cultural identity and accuse him of 'performing' a faux racial persona for financial gain: 'Marc Frank, I'm tired of all your wannabe-black shit. You aren't black – get over it.... you're damn good at snowboarding, but I think you would be hella cooler if you didn't try to be so gangster' (Shale, cited in 'Ask Dr Marco', 2006, p. 200). Montoya is scathing in his response: 'That's real messed up you're such a racist. You should be ashamed of yourself' (cited in Ibid.). The magazine editor also adds: 'For the record: Marc Frank Montoya is neither black nor white – he's a *Latino*, ya heard!' (Ibid.). The key point here, of course, is that white profes-sional snowboarders are rarely questioned about the authenticity of their cultural identities, or the privileges offered by their white snowboarding bodies.

The concept of discourse is central to Foucault's understanding of the 'material connections' between 'power, knowledge of self, and regimes of truth' (Cole et al., 2004, cited in Pringle, 2005, p. 260). More specifically, it aids our examination of the particular way 'power/knowledge complexes operate at a microlevel in order to produce regimes of truth' (McNay, 1992, p. 27). Foucault's concepts of discursive formations, power, and exclusion can help reveal some of the many ways in which the snowboarding media determines which snowboarding bodies are authorized to speak and be seen, and which are not. A Foucauldian approach thus has the potential to expand our understanding of the role of the media, as a social institution, in producing and reproducing cultural knowledge of physical cultural bodies. In the second part of this chapter I further examine how snowboarding bodies are subject to the workings of various mediated discourses via a case study of the media portrayals of female snowboarders.

Discourses of femininity in the snowboarding media

A plethora of media forms currently cover women's snowboarding, yet the mass, niche, and micro media offer multiple (and often competing) representations of women's snowboarding bodies. Foucault's approach to discourse, however, suggests that attempting to investigate the 'truthfulness' of any of these media representations of female snowboarders can produce 'only a wild goose chase' (Macdonald, 2003, p. 17). Thus the following discussion is not a search for a single 'truthful' representation of the female boarder but rather an examination of multiple and competing discourses of femininity being produced in the snowboarding media. This discussion is guided by Foucault's (1978) 'cautionary prescriptions' for understanding the workings of discourse. Foucault was opposed to binary conceptualizations of power, and thus precluded the possibility of 'dominant' discourses ranged against other sets of relatively powerful 'alternative' or 'oppositional' ones. He warned that it was not a simple task to identify a specific discourse, and explained that discourses are difficult to decipher, partly because 'multipl[e] discursive elements...can come into play in various strategies' (Foucault, 1978, cited in Markula & Pringle, 2005, p. 215). Indeed, identifying with any certainty the 'prevailing' or 'dominant' discourses of female snowboarding is a difficult task. Compounding this difficulty is the rapid expansion of media outlets and distribution channels. Cultural understandings surrounding the identities of female snowboarders cannot be divided into accepted and excluded discourses. Rather, audiences confront numerous and even contradictory discourses. Put simply, while the mass and niche media undoubtedly influence the negotiation of femininities in the snowboarding culture, these negotiations 'do not produce a simple dominating discourse' (Pringle & Markula, 2005, p. 472) of femininity. In the remainder of this chapter I illustrate how the mass media and niche media create and recreate multiple discourses of female snowboarders, before examining how female (and male) snowboarders read (and sometimes resist) different portrayals of female boarding bodies.

Female boarding bodies in the mass media

When the mass media first started reporting on snowboarding in the late 1980s, participants tended to be described as young, white, hedonistic, rebellious males. Women rarely appeared and, when they did, journalists typically cast them as token 'tomboys' or 'wild women,' and in so doing, reinforced the discourse of snowboarding as an activity best suited to young males. Today, with increased participation rates and the rapidly closing performance gap between the top female and male boarders, the mass media pay female snowboarders greater attention. However, despite well-meaning strategies to promote snowboarding for girls and women, the widespread practice of foregrounding heterosexually attractive women tends to symbolically erase women who appear lesbian, bisexual, 'queer', or 'unfeminine.' As a result, the mass media's representation of women's snowboarding tends to be a routine manifestation of wider public and sporting discourses of femininity.

The sports media and associated commercial interests occasionally seize images of female athletes and place them at the 'centre of cultural discourse, at least temporarily' (Messner, 2002, p. 109). The media 'seem most likely to do so when there is high profit potential (and this usually means that the women can be neatly packaged as heterosexually attractive)' explains Messner. Torah Bright and Gretchen Bleiler exemplify such 'selective incorporation'. Their roles as snowboarding superstars derive from a combination of athletic skill and marketability. Prior to winning an Olympic gold medal in the 2010 Vancouver Games, Torah Bright was already widely acknowledged as 'one of Australia's most recognized snowboarders' and the 'most exciting young snowboarder in the world' (Irish, 2003, para. 12). Bright regularly features in mainstream newspapers and magazines and on billboards, and is a character in multiple video games. While her new-found success is 'a testament to the fact that she is much more than a pretty face,' her 'fresh-faced good looks' have propeled her to become 'one of the hottest properties in the extreme sports world' (Press release, 2002, para. 3). American snowboarder Gretchen Bleiler is also a hot commodity in contemporary popular culture and after winning a silver medal in the 2006 Winter Olympic half-pipe event she featured in *FHM* and *Maxim* magazines. In these photographs she interestingly combines cultural icons (beanie, goggles, snowboard, and snowboard boots) with symbols of traditional femininity (bikini, passive and sexually suggestive poses). It should be noted, however, that in these images Bleiler does not submit to the male (or female) viewer but engages directly with him/her; she challenges the traditional male gaze by looking directly at the viewer and laughing. Nonetheless, mass media representations that emphasize female snowboarders' physical appearance promote responses that position female boarders as sex symbols. For example, after ogling Bleiler's *FHM* and *Maxim* spreads, one culturally naïve or satirical journalist wrote: 'Who knew snowboarders were as hot as America's Gretchen Bleiler? I thought they were all 5-foot tall Tomboys' ('Beyond Hollywood', 2006, para. 1).

Fashion magazines (e.g., *Seventeen, Glamour,* and *Cosmo*) also contribute to the 'distributing, organizing and classifying' of discourses of female snowboarding by depicting female models wearing boarding attire, posing with snowboards, or playing in the snow. By using flawlessly beautiful unathletic models, and placing them in static positions, magazines send the message that appearance rather than skill is the essential quality for judging women. This commonly promotes snowboarding as a fashion, rather than a fulfilling physical activity. *Transworld Snowboarding* journalist Tracey Fong (2000) expressed her distress at the appropriation of female snowboarding by 'mainstream money mongers' (para. 5) and complained of phone calls from fashion magazines and music, video, and art directors who 'want...the latest trends' and boarding clothes to show off in their layouts and shoots (para. 5). When Fong asked whether the girls would be snowboarding, she received the same predictable replies: 'No, we will have the girls wearing the clothes while playing in the snow looking cute' or 'We're going to have some really cool shots of the girls looking sexy and hanging out with some guys who just finished a hard day's work riding the mountain' (Ibid., para. 6). Some women's magazines also reinforce snowboarding as an activity best suited to the pursuit of heterosexual relationships rather than active participation. For example, an article featured in *CLEO* magazine (New Zealand) about journalist Tiffany Dunk's (2000) first snowboarding experience during a trip to the Canadian Rockies included the following comments: 'I knew I'd look cooler if I just stood around holding the board and smiling a lot' (p. 20); 'I may have had a few problems finding my feet during the day but I had no trouble getting the hang of things at night. Good food, buckets of wine, and lots of men to flirt with – perfect' (p. 21). Mass media representations of female snowboarders typically support prevailing assumptions that 'any girl on a board is either looking for a guy, there because her guy is, or trying to be one of the guys' (Blum, 1994, p. 9). In other words, the representation of female snowboarders and women's snowboarding in the mass media tends to promote a discourse of heterosexual femininity in which women's participation is based solely on consumption and the search for male approval.

Female boarding bodies in the niche media

In contrast to those in the mass media, the discourses of female snowboarders in the niche media are diverse. Discursive constructions of femininity in the snowboarding niche media range from respected female athletes and cultural participants to female models in sexually suggestive poses. Here I focus on the discourses of femininity in snowboarding niche magazines, particularly core snowboarding magazines and female-specific magazines. Contemporary snowboarding magazines tend to represent female snowboarders as respected participants in the boarding culture (see Wheaton, 2003a, for similar observations on the windsurfing culture). However, this has not always been the case. During the late 1980s and early 1990s, female boarders were subjected to the processes of exclusion (Foucault, 1981). As snowboarder and online zine journalist Alaina Martin (1994) recalls, 'with the exception of some occasional tits and ass, there weren't many girls [in the magazines], maybe a token girl here or there but basically nothing' (para. 6). In fact she 'felt so left out. I needed someone to look up to, something to let me know I wasn't the only one' (para. 6).

With the growth of the women's market during the late 1990s and early 2000s, advertisers and publishers increasingly embraced the female boarder, featuring her in more advertisements, editorials and photos (see Chapter 3). Jennifer Sherowski, senior contributing editor for *Transworld Snowboarding*, observed this trend: 'Most companies are keen to [access] the new (or expanding) market area that female snowboarding provides', hence 'we are making a really big effort to include women in our editorial, and that's including but not limited to, women's columns' (personal communication, November 2005). The 'Exposure-Meter' compiled annually by *Transworld Business* magazine, which calculates the total yearly editorial and advertising coverage in the two major snowboarding magazines (*Transworld Snowboarding* and *Snowboarder Magazine*) supports such claims. For the 2007/2008 winter season, Canadian snowboarder Leanne Pelosi ranked sixth in overall coverage, and second in advertising coverage; another six female snowboarders ranked in the top 50 (Lewis, December 2008); and in October 2009, Annie Boulanger gained the most media exposure of any snowboarder (Lewis, 2009). In contrast, no female skateboarders have ever ranked in the skating equivalent of these studies (summary of *Transworld Skateboarding*, *Skateboard Magazine*, *Skateboarder*, and *Thrasher Magazine*), and only three women have featured in the surfing 'Exposure-Meter' (summary of *Transworld Surf*, *Surfer*, and *Surfing Magazine*) also conducted by *Transworld Business* magazine.

The strength of the female market has created new space in niche magazines for a variety of representations of female snowboarders. When compared to advertisements featuring male boarders, images of female and male snowboarders often share similar styles of photography, such as camera angles, and design. Women often adopt similar poses to their male counterparts, with both sexes staring at the reader, challenging his/her gaze. Very rarely do female snowboarders appear in revealing clothing or sexually suggestive poses. Rather, many of the female snowboarders featuring in advertisements and editorials appear without make-up or other traditionally feminine markers. Furthermore, female snowboarders regularly feature in editorials and advertising in action photos that reinforce their physical prowess rather than physical appearances (see Figures 4.2 and 4.3). Journalists also tend to show greater respect to female boarders than they did during the 1990s, and are increasingly using gender-neutral language to describe their achievements, for example, 'Tara Dakides is the toughest and most fearless rider... right now' ('Tara-bly dangerous', 2000, para. 3); 'Juliane Bray has more focus and determination than any other snowboarder I know' (Butt, 2006, p. 58). Reporting on Boulanger's Exposure-Meter achievement,

Figure 4.2 This advertisement for Nikita Outerwear, a female-snowboard clothing company, is illustrative of the recent trend by some snowboarding companies and niche media to increasingly feature women solely in skill shots. Here, skill is privileged over gender such that the boarding body appears sex-less. The sex of the athlete, Vera Janssen, is marked primarily by the use of her name in small print at the bottom of the page. (image used with permission of Nikita Outerwear)

Figure 4.3 Female-specific board-sport magazines have traditionally privileged fashion and lifestyle. Recently, however, some magazines are emerging that target the committed female participant by prioritizing female athleticism and physical prowess (image used with permission of *Curl* magazine)

journalist Mike Lewis writes: 'Boulanger is one of the best snowboarders in the world. Notice that wasn't prefaced with "female", "girl", "woman", or any other adjective; Boulanger straight kills it on some of the biggest, steepest, gnarliest terrain out there' (2009b, para. 1). Representations of female boarders in snowboarding niche magazines are increasingly challenging traditional discourses of women as passive and heterosexually available to the male viewer.

'There is a lot more legit coverage of women riders now than there used to be, and more focus on seeing all snowboarders as just 'snowboarders,' not girl snowboarders and guy snowboarders,' stated Jennifer Sherowski. But increasing the coverage of women in core snowboarding magazines 'will always be a struggle,' she admitted (personal communication, November 2005). Despite huge market potential, female snowboarders still face a number of constraints. Coverage of female snowboarders continues to be limited in some niche magazines. Although Ste'en, editor of *New Zealand Snowboarder* magazine, 'keeps reminding the photographers to get good images of girls' he also acknowledges that most of them 'know from experience that a photo of a one foot air is not going to get picked [and paid for] over a 13 foot air' (personal communication, September 2005). Editor and photographer assumptions that women will typically perform at a lower standard (performing a one foot air) than their male counterparts (performing a 13 foot air), and thus are less deserving of photographic coverage, illustrate the constraints female snowboarders continue to face, that is, women should only be included in the niche media when they perform to male standards. Moreover, while many niche magazines do cover female snowboarders and are offering an alternative discourse of femininity based on active participation and cultural commitment, the same sources also reinforce traditional discourses of heterosexual femininity by including advertisements that feature female models (as distinct from female snowboarders) in sexually suggestive poses (also see Donnelly, 2003; Rinehart, 2005; Wheaton, 2003a). Furthermore, magazines and websites feature images of heterosexually appealing females in nonsnowboarding situations including bars, hot tubs, parties, or as fans of male boarders. Editors often insert humorous, yet demeaning, comments on the physical appearance and sexual desirability of these women. In contrast, the sexual status of men or male snowboarders is almost never compromised.

The strength of the women's snowboard and surf market has supported the emergence of female-specific boarding magazines.[3] These niche magazines provide important spaces for women to display their skills and voice their opinions. Yet many of the early female-specific magazines reinforced traditional discourses of femininity by privileging fashion, emphasizing the pursuit of heterosexual gender social relations, and relying on young, uniformly thin girls to model the board wear (Booth, 2002). Although these magazines proved popular among younger and less committed female participants, they became sites of some contention for many committed female boarders. According to some cultural commentators, the recent dissolution of *SG* (*Surfer Girl*) magazine, which ran from 2000 to 2006, can be attributed to its failure to cater to the diversity of the female board-sports market. 'The hardcore girl,' said Don Meek, president of Primedia Action Sports Group (ASG), is a 'niche of a niche' and would rather read the *'men's magazines'* such as *Transworld Snowboarding* or *Surfer* (cited in 'Fishing a wider', 2006, para. 6, emphasis added). On the other hand, 'the bulk of the market' constitutes those girls who go snowboarding once a year and read *'Cosmo Girl* or *ELLE girl* like they are the bible' (Randy Hild, Roxy senior vice president of marketing, cited in Ibid., para. 11). More recently, with the growing numbers of committed female board-sport participants, and new generations of young aspiring action-sport athletes, a few female lifestyle sport magazines have appeared that seem to be surviving (and, in some cases, thriving) by targeting *core* female participants. Examples include *Curl* – a New Zealand-produced magazine for female surfers, skateboarders, snowboarders and skiers, sold in New Zealand and Australia (see Figure 4.3) and *Cooler* – a U.K.-produced magazine for female surfers, skateboarders, snowboarders, skiers, and mountain-bikers, printed in English, French and German. While fashion and lifestyle continue to feature prominently in these magazines, they are making a strategic effort to prioritize female athleticism and physical prowess.

The mass and niche media help produce and reproduce numerous, even contradictory, discourses of female snowboarding. While the niche media provide space for a range of discursive constructions, including women as respected athletes and cultural participants, the mass media tends to focus on heterosexually attractive female boarders and promote snowboarding as a fashion for consumption. The key point here is that these discourses then help shape women's snowboarding practices and snowboarding bodies. The multiple discourses produced by the media systematically inform women's knowledge of snowboarding and play a role in governing their statements and perceptions of snowboarding and gender. It is important to note, however, that these discursive constructions of femininity do not bend all females into a coherent snowboarding femininity (see Foucault, 1977; Markula & Pringle, 2006). Rather, the multiple discourses of femininity communicated via the snowboarding media might be regarded as what Foucault (1977) called 'dividing practices' among female boarders. As Pringle and Markula (2005) explain, 'Foucault (1977) asserted that dividing practices were constructed via the use of particular discourses to justify social and, at times, spatial divisions between various categories of humans' (p. 477). The dividing practices in the snowboarding media justify the fragmentation of female boarders, and in so doing, support new niche markets essential for the continual economic growth of the boarding industry (see Chapter 3).

As well as influencing women's manifestations of cultural meaning, the mediated dialogues surrounding female snowboarders also influence the way 'we frame our cultural understandings of future actors walking onto the stage' (Sloop, 1997, cited in Andrews, 2000, p. 126). Foucault terms the process in which humans get tied to particular identities 'subjectivation', and as Markula and Pringle (2006) explain, 'he was particularly troubled with how being "known" or categorized can act to constrain and subject people to certain ends, identities and modes of behavior' (p. 8; see also Foucault, 1983, 1988a). Mediated discourses that promote snowboarding as a fashion for young women, for example, might work to limit some women's cultural membership to consumption rather than active participation. Some feminist scholars might reason that such discursive constructions of femininity in the media have a normalizing effect on female snowboarders, producing docile female bodies. However, I am wary of such interpretations. I believe it is necessary to question the extent to which discourses of femininity, and particularly discourses of sexism, in the snowboarding media, really do have a 'discursive effect'[4] on women's snowboarding experiences. How do men and women make meaning of discourses of femininity and sexism in the snowboarding media? How do such discourses influence gender relations in the snowboarding culture?

(Re)reading the media:
Foucault and the female boarding body

While some scholars argue that the sexualization and trivialization of women in the media reinforces male domination via the workings of ideology (Duncan & Messner, 1998; Messner, 2002), this interpretation sits at odds with a Foucauldian perspective. Foucault did not conceptualize discourses and relations of power as essentially positive or negative; thus, 'it is important not to preassign any practice as "liberating" or "oppressive" without a careful consideration of the cultural context where an individual woman's identity is formed' (Markula, 2003, p. 104). Indeed, adopting a Foucauldian approach, it would be erroneous for me to assume that sexualized images of women in the snowboarding media inherently repress female boarders. Rather, the 'effect' of these images depends upon the discursive lens through which men and women read them. Thus in order to understand the effect of mediated discursive constructions of women in the snowboarding culture, it is essential to consider the interpretations applied by boarders themselves.

In relation to the consumption of media texts, current thinking within media studies opposes the idea of mediated discourses having 'extensive unconscious powers' over audiences, spectators, or readers (Macdonald, 2003, p. 23). Most scholars agree that 'any study of meaning in the media' must incorporate 'audience or reader responses' (Ibid., p. 25). While the mediated cultural industries 'have the power to rework and reshape what they represent, and, by representation and selection, to impose and implant such definitions ... [that] ... fit more easily the descriptions of the dominant and preferred culture' (Hall, 1981, pp. 232–233), there are no guarantees that every individual will interpret such representations in the same manner. For example, while American snowboarder Jamie proclaimed that the overt sexualization of women in snowboarding advertisements 'kinda pisses me off' (personal communication, February 2005), New Zealand snowboarder Pamela was apathetic: 'it's like water off a duck's back, I barely register it' (personal communication, February 2005). If the media help to construct versions of reality for female boarders, then how do women, as subjects of discourse, decide their response? While all discourses communicate knowledge, argues Macdonald (2003), 'it is mistaken to elevate discourses to the position of being the sole originator of knowledge. We also arrive at knowledge through experience, through observation and through the evaluation of one discourse against another. Our experience is, of course, filtered through discourse but it is not contained by it.' (p. 37). Agents constantly make choices about competing versions of reality, and such choices involve the process of 'weighing up the competing (and incomplete) versions of reality on offer within our cultures' (Ibid., p. 24). This is certainly true for female snowboarders, many of whom demonstrate a critical awareness of the multiple discourses of femininity being produced by the media.

Foucault's early work, however, does not necessarily facilitate an explanation of how women make meaning of, or resist, these discourses. On the contrary, Foucault's understanding of individuals, principally in terms of the operations of power and discourse on the body, has the effect of keeping female snowboarders in the position of passive victims of the snowboarding media. The concerns raised here echo critiques aimed at Foucault's conceptualization of power more broadly. Some scholars contend that Foucault's understanding of power is deterministic and does not allow space for individuals to create change through resistance. Discursive power relations, they argue, dominate to the exclusion of agency, and Foucault has been charged with ignoring the role of the individual. 'The emphasis that Foucault places on the effects of power upon the body,' says McNay (1992), reduces 'social agents to passive bodies and does not explain how individuals may act in an autonomous fashion' (p. 3). Possibly in response to such criticisms, Foucault (1988b) acknowledged that he had not focused enough attention on how humans influence power relations. 'Perhaps I've insisted too much on the technology of domination and power,' pondered Foucault, adding that 'I am more and more interested in the interaction between oneself and others and in the technologies of individual domination, the history of how an individual acts upon himself, in the technologies of self' (cited in Pringle & Markula, 2005, p. 478). Therefore in Foucault's final work individuals are 'no longer conceived as docile bodies in the grip of an inexorable disciplinary power' but as 'self-determining agents who are capable of challenging and resisting the structures of domination in modern society' (McNay, 1992, p. 4). Foucault's understanding of how power relations influence the behavior of individuals underwent a significant methodological shift as he moved his focus from the 'constitution of subjectivity via the workings of discourse, to constitution via lived practices' within power relations (Markula & Pringle, 2006, p. 20). This shift introduced new tools for theorizing sport, 'notably sport as a space where technologies of the self and processes of subjectification are constantly at play' (Rail & Harvey, 1995, p. 169). Moreover, Foucault's conceptualization of 'technologies of self' has the potential to facilitate new understandings of snowboarding bodies within media power relations.

Technologies of self:
thinking critically about discourses of femininity in the media

In his later years, starting with the second volume of *The History of Sexuality* (1985), Foucault became particularly interested in the process by which individuals 'think about themselves, act for themselves, and transform themselves within power relations' (Rail & Harvey, 1995, p. 167). Foucault (1985) labels this process 'subjectification'. In the third volume of *The History of Sexuality* (1986), Foucault expanded on the notion of subjectification and how it can be realized through what he calls the 'technologies of self.' Such technologies

> permit individuals to effect by their own means or with the help of others a certain number of operations on their own bodies and souls, thoughts, conduct, and way of being, so as to transform themselves in order to attain a certain state of happiness, purity, wisdom, perfection, or immorality. (Foucault, 1988b, cited in Markula, 2003, p. 88)

Thus in contrast to the objectifying process Foucault described in relation to technologies of power, technologies of the self emerge in the process of subjectification, the forming of oneself as a subject within power relations.

Critical thought is at the core of Foucault's understanding of technologies of self. He was particularly interested in how people learn to problematize their identities by becoming more self-reflexive:

> Thought is not what inhibits a certain conduct and gives it its meaning; rather, it is what allows one to step back from this way of acting or reacting, to present it to oneself as an object of thought and question it as to its meaning, its conditions, and its goals. Thought is freedom in relation to what one does, the motion by which one detaches oneself from it, establishes it as an object, and reflects on it as a problem. (Foucault, 1984, p. 388)

The critically self-aware individual questions what seems natural and inevitable in his/her identity; through this interrogation of the limits of one's subjectivity emerges the 'possibility of transgression' and with it the 'potential for creating new types of subjective experiences' within existing power relations (Markula, 2003, p. 102).

Some snowboarders articulate conscious problematizations of the boundaries of the dominant female snowboarding identities promoted in the mass media and some niche magazines. Moriah, for example, complained:

> Women are sadly more models than anything else. Most ads do not show girls riding, even if the woman featured is a top rider. Most ads just show girls posing in cute clothes, and if they are riding, they are most likely doing [non-technical manoeuvres such as] a mute grab or a backside silly slide. (personal communication, October 2006)

An advertisement for a New Zealand ski resort featuring three young women with only snowboarding-related stickers covering their nipples dismayed Sophie to the extent that she refused to 'ever buy a season's pass there again' (personal communication, October 2006). While Jaime thought it was 'great to see lots of pics of tough snowboarder girls' in the magazines, 'chicks wearing make-up, tank-tops and posing with their snowboards' angered her (personal communication, September 2006).

Some male snowboarders also question the limitations of discursive feminine identities produced in the media. Ste'en explained that 'the purpose of advertising is to get your attention and have that attention associated with a product' and 'sexy images get the attention of most readers' (personal communication, October 2006). Continuing, he acknowledged the affective power of such images: 'When women are represented in a sexual way (in any form of media), yes, I can feel excited' (personal communication, October 2006; see Paasonen, 2007). However, when reading a snowboarding magazine Ste'en would rather see 'hard-core action shots', and when he sees sexual images of women in a boarding magazine his typical response is: 'Ho hum, flick the page' (personal communication, October 2006). Furthermore, when asked to comment on an advertisement in a snowboard magazine that featured a naked female taped to the floor with snowboarding stickers, Ste'en interpreted it as 'degrading' and would refuse to 'support the company' (personal communication, October 2006). Derek is also aware that 'lots of ads featuring women snowboarders are sexualized', but explained that 'these ads do not make me think less of female riders. There are many women who outperform the boys out there [on the mountain] and I recognize it, and I'm sure the other guys do too' (personal communication, October 2006). Perhaps, as Funnell (2010) suggests, some men are 'capable of consuming nude or seminude images of women in ways that are not inherently degrading to women' (p. 2).

Mediated images of female athletes that emphasize their sexuality tend to be interpreted differently by women (and men) from different social and cultural backgrounds and in different historical contexts. Women who view such images through a second-wave feminist discursive lens, for example, typically interpret them as 'diminishing women's power, trivializing their strength, and putting them in their sexual place' (Burstyn, 1999, p. 3). Many of today's young women, however, applaud such images as celebrating women's sexuality. Donna Burton Carpenter observes generational differences in young women's responses to the hyper-sexual, soft pornographic *Playboy* graphics featured on the Burton 'Love' snowboards: 'I have been around snowboarding's youth culture long enough to know that there is a real generational difference as to what constitutes pornography'; 'The young women that I speak to are not offended by these images at all. Actually, some women ... are buying these boards because they think the images are beautiful' (cited in Keck, 2008, para. 10). Many of the young female snowboarders interviewed for my research expressed a similar pro-sexuality attitude toward sexual images of female athletes in the media (Heywood & Dworkin, 2003; Keenan, 2008).

While young women (and men) are not united in their readings of the snowboarding media, many are interpreting the media through third-wave, rather than second-wave, feminist discourses; when combined with female athleticism, they embrace rather than shun women's sexuality. As Hana put it: 'If the magazines include a sexy shot of a pro woman snowboarder, then it's fine because it shows that she's a talented snowboarder – and cute too – so, one up on the boys I say' (personal communication, September 2006). Continuing, Hana claimed that images promoting female boarders as 'hot' are 'good for the sport'; they promote snowboarding as 'cool for chicks' and could even 'encourage young girls to try snowboarding' (personal communication, September 2006). Similarly, Mel applauded Tara Dakides and Gretchen Bleiler who featured on the February 2004 cover of *FHM* in body paint: 'Good on them! If you've got it, which they clearly do (how hot is Tara's lil' butt!), flaunt it I say. It certainly doesn't damage the industry or women's snowboarding in any way, so go nuts ladies!' (personal communication, February 2006). Olympic snowboarder Pamela also supported Bleiler's decision to pose for *FHM* and *Maxim* magazines: 'I have to say "good on her." She has a strong, fit and athletic body, so it's probably good for guys and other women to see that she is not a stick figure with balloon boobs' (personal communication, October 2006). Here Pamela demonstrates a critical awareness that Bleiler's 'athletic' body offers an alternative to discursive constructions that tend to celebrate the thin physique with large breasts as the contemporary feminine ideal. Pamela argued that such images do not undermine the snowboarding culture: male and female snowboarders 'often have fantastic bodies' of which they should be proud (personal communication, October 2006).

Nonetheless, as the following comments illustrate, some women are critical of discourses that caricature a particular form of femininity in both mainstream women's magazines and snowboarding magazines:

> Most women featured in fashion magazines are perfect pencil-thin, and perfectly made-up. But in snowboarding I think those things are frowned upon. I think snowboarding is more about being yourself, being natural, and having your own style, and I think the magazines sort of portray this. I like wearing hoodies, sneakers, hats and beanies. Yeah, I rock that look. But, I guess there is an ideal image of a 'shred Betty.' And I suppose I do kinda live my life under that shadow. I definitely feel pressure to look good and I do feel like I need to keep up and have the new gear every year. But I don't feel pressure to do anything except the things I want to. (Moriah, personal communication, October 2006)

> All girls grow up wondering why they didn't turn out like Barbie or the chicks in the magazines. Models constantly reinforce a thin image, which we all carry around in our heads but we all learn to deal with it in different ways. Self-confidence is [the] key, and this comes from age, independence, and finding something in life where you can excel and feel proud – for some girls, like me, this is snowboarding. There is a media image of the 'ideal' female snowboarder but it is definitely different from the models in most women's magazines. In snowboarding, there is a media image of a freestyle chick with long hair out of a beanie, matching snowboard outfit, a bit grungy, and riding hard with all the boys, etc. My specialty was racing and free riding, so I felt like I never matched this image. So I always felt like I was just doing my own thing but heaps of young girls appear to feel they need to conform to this snowboarder 'image' to fit in. (Pamela, personal communication, October 2006)

Some female snowboarders are aware of the limitations of discursive femininity in society and snowboarding culture more specifically, and consciously negotiate their own subjectivity within these discourses. However, the question is; where do women (and some men) gain this ability to critically evaluate the snowboarding media and their own identities within the culture?

Discourses are not the sole sources of knowledge. They are social constructions: thus 'we also arrive at knowledge through experience, through observation and through the evaluation of one discourse against another' (Macdonald, 2003, p. 37). Indeed, snowboarders constantly choose between competing versions of reality, and such choices involve 'weighing up the competing (and incomplete) versions of reality on offer within our cultures' (Ibid., p. 24). It seems that the more snowboarding experience and cultural knowledge an individual has, the more likely they will develop the ability to weigh up the competing versions of femininity and problematize some of these. Committed snowboarders tend to be more likely to observe inconsistencies between their experiences on the mountain as active cultural participants and the representations of women in the media as passive and sexualized subjects. Hana illustrated how some core boarders distinguish between images and advertisements of women in the media that they perceive as 'truthful' representations of their experiences as female boarders, and those that are not: 'I mostly only look at photos of REAL women' in snowboarding magazines, those 'female snowboarders doing sick moves'; 'as for the odd cheesy ad that sexualizes women, well, that doesn't really bother me...because *I know different*. At the end of the day, the only women snowboarders that get real respect are the ones that can ride well' (personal communication, September 2006, emphasis added). Similarly, Moriah explained: 'I don't really care about ads that show models in little or no clothing posing with a snowboard, because I ride and those 'babes' don't. These ads don't change the fact that I love snowboarding' (personal communication, October 2006). As these comments highlight, there is a discourse of authenticity pertaining to 'real' female snowboarders. While core female boarders tend to reject images that position women as passive and sexual beings, they celebrate those that show women as athletes in action. 'It is awesome to see women going hard. I love seeing women riding big, steep mountain terrain. It makes me want to seek out the big stuff,' said Sophie (personal communication, October 2006).

Clearly, some core female boarders negate the discursive effect of overtly sexual images by drawing upon 'reverse discourses' (Foucault, 1978, p. 101).[5] Committed female boarders differentiate themselves from the 'skanky,' 'slutty,' 'dirty' female models in the advertisements, who they reason are not 'real' female snowboarders. In so doing they are engaging in a technology of self that acts to transform each woman's sense of self to help her 'attain a certain state of happiness' (Foucault, 1988, cited in Markula & Pringle, 2005, p. 486). It appears that women who have experienced snowboarding as a fulfilling physical activity and view their bodies as powerful and athletic are the ones best able to problematize images in the boarding media. Committed female boarders tend to be the most likely to weigh up the competing discourses of femininity in the culture and to distinguish between those who are representative of their own snowboarding experiences and those who are not (the passive and sexualized). In so doing, these women are able to effectively negotiate discursive constructions of femininity that might otherwise limit their subjectivity. It seems that many of these women are drawing upon discursive resources from third-wave (rather than second-wave) feminism to critique these images (see Chapter 10).

However, while the majority of female participants interviewed for this book articulated a critical awareness of the representations of women in the snowboarding media, not all core boarders develop a critical consciousness.

Mel, for instance, is a passionate New Zealand boarder who has worked in the snowboarding industry for more than a decade. She admitted to reading snowboarding magazines 'almost every day' without ever noticing 'anything wrong' with the representation of women. Mel believed that if a female boarder 'doesn't like ads that sexualize women, then they probably should not get into snowboarding...if you can't deal with a couple of photos, there is no way you'll deal with the social scene that is snowboarding' (personal communication, October 2006). Implicit in this comment is an awareness of the maleness of the snowboarding culture, but rather than resisting discourses of sexism Mel employs an array of strategies to negotiate space within the hypermasculine snowboarding culture (see Chapter 6). The key point here, however, is that not all core female boarders adopt a critical awareness of the discursive constructions of femininity in the snowboarding media; some even internalize the attitudes held by many of their male colleagues. It is important to note that not all women with the opportunity to maneuver within power relations choose to do so. Critical awareness, and the likelihood of a female boarder developing such a consciousness is highly dependent upon both her life (education, parental and peer influences, generation, occupation and so on) and snowboarding experiences.

Through a conscious critique, some female (and male) boarders find the dominant discourses of femininity promoted in the snowboarding media problematic. However, mere critical thinking does not transform these discursive constructions of femininity. Thus it is also important to consider how this critique works in practice. While some of the boarders I interviewed articulated a critical awareness and problematization of discourses that sexualize women, the majority simply adopted 'coping mechanisms' (Markula, 2003, p. 103). In order to preserve their enjoyment of core snowboarding magazines they may 'ignore' problematic advertisements. Asked how she felt about seeing sexual exploitation of women in advertisements in snowboarding magazines, professional snowboarder Sondra Van Ert replied:

> I don't see it, because I choose not to see it. I don't purchase those magazines or contribute to that. The majority of these magazines are targeted at a certain populace of 17-year-old males. These advertisements keep perpetuating snowboarding's [hard-core, rebellious] reputation. And there's definitely a group that wants to hang on to that reputation. But there are a few magazines like *Snowboard Life* that cater to my targeted market, and that's what I buy. (cited in Murray, 2001, para. 5)

Some snowboarders, however, are more vocal in their critique. Male and female snowboarders, journalists, and editors frequently voice their discontent about advertisements that sexualize women. In 1994 *Flakezine*, a website dedicated to analyzing the snowboarding media, called an advertisement for Alpina goggles 'sexist.' The ad featured a large-breasted white woman in a black body suit, blue flannel, and Alpina Darksite goggles. According to *Flakezine*, Alpina's marketing director subscribed to the 'big boobs and beer' school of advertising encapsulated in the formula 'give 14-year-old boys a boner and they'll buy your product'. The website added 'while this style may work selling pay-per-view WrestleMania bouts to inbred white trash, it won't work here in the snowboard world, thank God' ('Sex rot', 1994, para. 17). At the same time as condemning sexism, *Flakezine* commended the shoe and snowboard boot company Airwalk, saying that 'it's nice to see that some companies appreciate the athletic abilities of the women in their ads' ('Women we', 1994, para. 21). Females such as Tory, a correspondent from Montana, United States, also remind editors that they will not accept overt or covert forms of sexism: 'What does a girl in a thong have to do with selling shoes?' (Mail 15.5, 2002). More recently, in an article featured in *Transworld Snowboarding* entitled 'Things not welcome in the 2006/2007 season' (April 2006), a group of young male journalists, 'the angry interns', warned advertisement executives against using bikini- or thong-clad women in the magazine: 'not only are you insulting the people you're trying to sell to by assuming they'll fall for your sophomoric crap but you falsely assume that snowboarders are a bunch of sex-crazed goons' (p. 170). These voices of cultural discontent appear to be persuading decision-makers in the media (editors and marketing directors), and images of this type continue to decline in frequency.

In sum, while they are the subjects of media discourses, snowboarders are not necessarily its victims. As illustrated in the case of representations of femininity in the snowboarding media, female boarders confront numerous and even contradictory discourses, but in everyday life they actively participate in deciding which discourses activate them; the act of doing this is a matter of individual agency. Simply put, the margin for resistance, and the tendency to engage in practices of freedom within existing power relations, varies depending on each individual boarder's lived experience (see Markula & Pringle, 2006; Thorpe, 2008). Thus adopting Foucault's unique conceptualization of power facilitates an account of the mundane and daily ways in which power is enacted and contested in the snowboarding culture, and allows an analysis that helps us appreciate the agency and autonomy of snowboarders 'without falling into idealist fantasies of sovereign subjects and pure, utopian freedom' (Maguire, 2002, p. 311).

Fresh questions with Foucault

Ultimately, the goal of this chapter was to embrace Foucault's challenge, 'to detach from established knowledge, ask fresh questions, make new connections, and understand why it is important to do so' (Cole et al., 2004, p. 207). Employing Foucault's concepts of power and discourse, this chapter illustrated how the snowboarding media, as a social institution, helps regulate the production and circulation of statements and perceptions of snowboarding bodies. However, the media is not simply a judicial mechanism that limits, obstructs, refuses, prohibits and censors. Rather, the media is only 'one terminal form power takes' (Foucault, 1978, p. 92) in the snowboarding culture. Drawing on Foucault's concept of technologies of self in the latter part of this chapter also helped reveal some of the diverse ways power operates within everyday relations between people (snowboarders) and institutions (the media), and facilitated my analysis of the complexities of the construction and negotiation of embodied knowledge and identities in snowboarding culture. Representations of snowboarding in the media are not inherently oppressive; some men and women are adopting critical and reflexive interpretations of various discursive constructions of snowboarding bodies in the mass, niche, and micro media. Moreover, some are actively engaging in an array of embodied and political strategies to challenge problematic representations, narratives and images of snowboarding bodies (see Thorpe, 2008). Building upon this discussion of the representation of multiple boarding bodies in the highly fragmented snowboarding media, in the next chapter I explore how snowboarding identities are learned, practiced, and performed, in physical and social settings. More specifically, I draw on the work of French social theorist Pierre Bourdieu to examine how distinctions among snowboarders, expressed as differences in embodied tastes and styles, contribute to their identities and ultimately what amounts to the social order in snowboarding culture.

5
Cultural Boarding Bodies: Status, Style, and Symbolic Capital

Board sports, for the most part, are about expressing individual-ity – that's what makes them cool. So the whole Olympic uniform thing, you know, it's a sensitive subject. The inspiration [for the 2010 US Olympic snowboard team uniform] was sort of that classic Americana look: the plaid blazer and old jeans. Yeah, it's a uniform, but it's also an anti-uniform at the same time. When these guys come out, it's going to be very different from what any other coun-try's team is wearing. (Greg Dacyshyn, creative director of Burton Snowboards, cited in Keh, 2009)

When people first get into snowboarding, the image becomes important, because they want to be recognized on the mountain as knowing what they are doing. But as you get better you either go one of two ways. You get swept up in the fashion/lifestyle aspect of it and make that as important as the riding itself; or you don't believe the hype and let your snowboarding do the talking. I know guys and gals that don't give a shit about how they look and abso-lutely kill it in the backcountry and big mountain riding. They don't bother with all the latest fashions, their riding says it all. (Colin, personal communication, August 2004)

The snowboarding body is a symbol of status, a system of social marking, and a site of distinctions. In snowboarding culture, the symbolic values attached to bodily forms are critical to many participants' sense of self. Bernard Rudofsky (1986) reminds us that many of these practices are not new; in fact different cultural or tribal groups have long inscribed their identities on their members' bodies. However, in contrast to premodern societies, where traditional signs marked the body in ritualized settings, today people treat the body as a phenomenon to be shaped, decorated and trained as an expression of both individual and group identity (Shilling, 1993). A host of theorists (Bourdieu, 1971, 1977, 1978, 1980, 1984, 1985, 1986, 1990a, b;

Harvey, 2001; Shilling, 1993, 2003, 2005; Turner, 1988; Veblen, 1970[1899])
point to these bodily differences as strategies for social distinction. Of particular interest here are the ideas of French sociologist Pierre Bourdieu. In
his theory of distinction, Bourdieu assigns a central place to the body, and
through a number of theoretical concepts provides insight into the distinctive bodily practices employed by individuals and groups within contemporary society. Complementing the results of this approach, Connell (1983,
p. 153) writes: '[Bourdieu] is one of the very few systematic social theorists to
have a way of talking about what living in the world is really like, its shadows and sunlight, its langours and teeth'.

In this chapter, I draw upon a selection of Bourdieu's concepts to explain
the significance of embodied practices for cultural distinction and identity
formation among snowboarders. The chapter consists of two main parts.
The first provides a critical overview of Bourdieu's theory of distinction and
a description of his major theoretical concepts, focusing particularly on how
they relate to the snowboarding body. The second examines the relational
nature of these concepts with a discussion of some of the distinctive cultural (e.g., dress, language) and physical (e.g., skill, courage) performances in
snowboarding. Adopting a Bourdieusian approach, this chapter illustrates
how distinctions among snowboarders, expressed as differences in embodied tastes and styles, contribute to their individual and group identities as
well as the structuring of the snowboarding culture.

Bourdieu and the snowboarding body

Undoubtedly the foremost social analyst of distinction, Bourdieu gives particular attention to this concept in *Distinction: a Social Critique of Judgement
of Taste* (1984). Bourdieu views what he calls social space, and the differences
that emerge within it, as functioning symbolically as a 'space of life-styles',
or as a set of groups characterized by different lifestyles. In his theory of
distinction, Bourdieu accords a central place to the body and embodied practices. He analyzes the formation and the reproduction of these practices and
explains their significance as subtle social markers. Bourdieu's insights into
embodied practices are inextricably intertwined with his concepts of capital,
field, class, taste, and habitus. These concepts remain deliberately vague and
malleable, encouraging their questioning and their adaptation to the specific
domain to which they are applied. These concepts are also relational in the
sense that they only function 'in relation to one another' (Wacquant, 1992,
p. 19). Attempting to illustrate the relationships between these major concepts, Bourdieu (1986) presents the generative formula: {(habitus) (capital)} +
field = practice. At first glance this equation mystifies more than it clarifies.
However, the equation becomes clearer when we examine these concepts
individually and in greater detail, before reflecting upon their relational
nature through a discussion of the cultural boarding body.

Habitus: embodying snowboarding culture

Habitus refers to a set of acquired schemes of dispositions, perceptions and appreciations, including tastes, which orient our practices and give them meaning (Bourdieu, 1992). The habitus is both a 'structured structure' – the effect of the actions of, and our interactions with, others – and a 'structuring structure' – it suggests and constrains our future actions (Bourdieu, 1990a, p. 53). Critically, the habitus is embodied, that is, 'located within the body and affects every aspect of human embodiment' (Shilling, 1993, p. 129). Bourdieu generally uses the term 'hexis' when referring to the embodied nature of the habitus. Hexis signifies 'deportment, the manner and style in which actors "carry themselves": stance, gait, gesture, etc' (Jenkins, 2002, p. 75). Bourdieu's concepts of habitus and hexis have the potential to help us to understand the ways in which embodied practices construct identity, difference and given social order in the snowboarding field.

All participants come to snowboarding with a habitus instilled from an early age and informed by a network of social positions (class, gender, race, sexuality, nationality, and region). Here, however, I am particularly interested in the snowboarding habitus which develops through practical engagement with, or rather socialization into, snowboarding culture. Socialization has been described as 'an active process of learning and social development that occurs as people interact with each other and become acquainted with the social world in which they live, and as they form ideas about who they are, and make decisions about their goals and behaviours' (Coakley, 1998, p. 88). The distinctive practices of a snowboarding habitus are imprinted and encoded in a socializing process that commences early during entry into snowboarding culture. In the past this was primarily through participation, but for many contemporary participants it often occurs through exposure to a variety of media sources, including snowboarding magazines, websites, video games, or television coverage of major snowboard events. It is during this socialization process that the 'practical transmission' of boarding 'knowledge' via instructors' and peers' comments, observation, and/or various media, becomes embodied (Ford & Brown, 2006, p. 123).

In contrast to the calculated performances of some novices, the habitus of core participants differs from imitation due to the 'lack of conscious effort involved in the reproduction of a gesture or action' (Ford & Brown, 2006, p. 125). According to Bourdieu (1992), 'what is "learned by the body" is not something that one has, like knowledge that can be brandished but something that one is' (cited in Ford & Brown, 2006, p. 125). Professional snowboarder Romain De Marchi identifies the habitus of core boarders: 'it's kind of a fashionable thing' to snowboard these days but 'the *real* snowboarders still have the passion and know the soul of snowboarding' (cited in Muzzey, 2003, p. 136, emphasis added). Richards (2003) agrees: 'Snowboarding is something you have to figure out. You have to earn it. You have to make it over different hurdles before it reveals its soul. And when that happens, its soul becomes part of you' (p. 281). The 'soul of snowboarding' constitutes what Bourdieu (1971) calls 'cultural unconscious' and it comes via 'attitudes, aptitudes, knowledge, themes and problems, in short the whole system of categories of perception and thought' acquired by a systematic social apprenticeship (p. 182). In snowboarding, the habitus or 'cultural unconscious' derives from a systematic cultural apprenticeship, and the longer one spends immersed in snowboarding culture the more ingrained this habitus becomes. For Ste'en, *New Zealand Snowboarder* magazine editor, the enculturation process is 'an all-consuming journey' that typically begins with the novice participant 'falling in love with snowboarding' and then becoming a 'cultural sponge', absorbing information from various sources, as well as learning from the occasional 'cultural faux pas'. After overcoming 'numerous hurdles' such as 'learning to snowboard on sheet ice, dealing with terrible equipment and sore feet', Ste'en proceeded to 'follow winter from mountain to mountain around the world...for more than a decade' (personal communication, July 2008). As Bourdieu (1986) explains, embodying cultural knowledge 'costs time' and time amounts to an investment (p. 222).

Habitus is 'both the internalization of the conditions of existence *and* the practice-generating principle of social agents' (Laberge & Sankoff, 1988, p. 270, emphasis added). For core boarders, the socially constructed habitus is a primary influence on their snowboarding practices; choices of equipment, clothing, terrain, and style of riding are made on the 'basis of practically oriented dispositions that have already been inscribed in the body and subsequently take place without overtly direct conscious awareness of the principles that guide them' (Ford & Brown, 2006, p. 126). As Ford and Brown (2006) write in their discussion of surfing, the 'practical logics' that sustain board-riding culture are, therefore, 'embedded in the body in the form of habitus' (p. 126). In other words, while the snowboarding habitus is typically unconscious, it informs core boarders' decisions regarding an array of embodied practices including dress, language, equipment, bodily deportment and gait, relationships, and lifestyle, as well as approaches to risk, pain, and pleasure. Snowboarding culture is, therefore, a productive locus of a particular habitus which gives rise to, as Bourdieu (1971, pp. 194–195) says, 'patterns of thought which organize reality by directing and organizing thinking about reality and makes what he thinks thinkable for him as such and in the particular form in which it is thought'.

The snowboarding habitus, internalized through years of participation, continues to be expressed in durable ways 'of standing, speaking, walking, and thereby of feeling and thinking' (Bourdieu, 1990a, p. 70) long after the objective conditions of its emergence have been dislodged. For example, Phillipa currently works as an architect in a large New Zealand city, but having 'snowboarded full-time for seven years', she feels the 'mountains and snowboarding will always be part of me' (personal communication, February 2005). Continuing, she describes how, ten years after her transition from semiprofessional athlete to 'weekend warrior', she still experiences physiological cravings for snowboarding: 'If I read a snowboarding magazine or think about the snow, my heart races, my blood pulses and I am overtaken by a desire to be back on the mountain' (personal communication, July 2008). Another ex-core New Zealand snowboarder notes that her body still 'shows all kinds of scars as a result of the asymmetric nature of snowboarding...the ACL reconstruction on my right knee has left me with problems in other joints on that side of my body, and my left knee is also ready to blow at any time' (personal communication, November 2008). Put simply, for some ex-core snowboarders, the snowboarding habitus continues to influence their everyday bodily experiences long after cultural retirement.

Habitus is a complex and multilayered concept, capturing both 'general notions of habitus at the level of society' and 'differentiated notions at the level of the individual' (Reay, 2004, p. 434). But Bourdieu is not always clear about the social or spatial boundaries of habitus formation – in other words, how we might identify the scale at which the habitus of a group or collective is defined. Bourdieu's unwillingness to specify the objective structures he believes generate a habitus can lead to problems in its operationalization (Reay, 1995). McRobbie (2009) admits finding analyses of the 'intersections and flows between and across so many fields and so many habituses' methodologically overwhelming (p. 142). Despite recognizing the virtue in Bourdieu's schema for 'bringing together' micrological analyses of particular fields with macrosociological analyses of wider social, cultural, and political fields, she warns of the tendency to 'get lost in a proliferation of fields' (p. 141). In the case of snowboarding, for example, is it the local (e.g., geography, climate, peer group) or global (e.g., media, transnational companies) conditions that most strongly influence the formation of an individual's snowboarding habitus? On the other hand, perhaps Bourdieu's argument that theory should provide 'thinking tools' to be deployed in empirical situations, rather than a clearly defined explanatory framework (Jenkins, 2002) ameliorates the confusion and leaves open a set of possibilities concerning the identification of habitus in a particular field. While there are many possible definitions of snowboarding groups and fields, in this chapter I focus on the 'collective' snowboarding field, or what some cultural commentators refer to as the 'global snowboarding culture' (Sherowski, 2004a, p. 106) to provide an introductory set of observations.

In the remainder of this discussion I focus on the collective or 'transnational habitus' (Kelly & Lusis, 2006) in snowboarding, that is, the cultural values, norms and styles shared and embodied by snowboarders across local, regional and national snowboarding fields (see Chapter 8). However, the interactions of local and global conditions in various social and physical geographies, and their influence on the development of the individual and collective snowboarding habitus, are significant and deserve further comment. Having traveled extensively during his snowboarding career,

Eric observed regional differences in the habitus of North American snowboarders:

> The personas of the riders vary according to the terrain they're exposed to. In the Pacific North West you find lots of long-board, hippy freeriders who shred powder all year. In southern California, you find a lot of teen-age kids wearing jeans and bandanas who slide rails in the sun. It's all snowboarding, but you just have to adapt to where you are and what you have and that affects the trends and styles of the snowboarders of those regions. (personal communication, November 2008)

Some snowboarders also identify national differences in the snowboarder habitus. Snowboarding athlete and coach Pamela, for example, 'can tell what country an athlete is from just by watching their riding style':

> Japanese snowboarders tend to ride low and smooth, with a really wide stance. Europeans are generally more physical and quite dynamic, and still quite heavily influenced by the alpine tradition, whereas the Americans are often the most technically correct and more freestyle-focused. (personal communication, December 2008)

Such differences in habitus might be attributed to a combination of social, cultural, and geographical factors, such as local and national media coverage, competition judging criteria, or instructional programs.

Styles of participation (e.g., big mountain snowboarding, alpine, half-pipe) also influence the snowboarding habitus. For example, while the dedicated big mountain boarder and the freestyle athlete exhibit similarities of habitus as a result of the physical and material inscription of snowboarding practice on the body, there are also significant differences (see also Ford & Brown, 2006). As a result of spending 'years learning about snow conditions and behavior, weather patterns, emergency techniques, and rock climbing', big mountain snowboarders or extreme riders are 'physically different than freestyle pros'; they tend to be 'four or five inches taller, with more bulk on them, so that they can ride a longer, stiffer type of board' (Howe, 1998, p. 140). The embodied cultural practices (e.g., hair styles, beverage preferences) of big mountain snowboarders are also distinctive. For example, in his autobiography, Todd Richards (2003) recalled meeting Alaskan snowboarders Jay Liska and Ritchie Fowler, whom he described as 'a couple of big, tough looking guys'; they were 'notorious big mountain snowboarders who rode big boards, wore their sideburns long, and drank whiskey like water' (p. 157). While local, regional, and national social, cultural, and geographical conditions, and styles of participation, influence the formation of an individual's snowboarding habitus, the discussion offered in this chapter focuses on the collective snowboarding habitus identifiable across social spaces. As a concept, habitus is highly nuanced and complex, and has been used in various ways in different research contexts. Here, however, I am particularly interested in the potential of habitus to help reveal how the snowboarding culture is embodied, and also how taken-for-granted social inequalities are embedded in everyday practices. Of course, habitus is a relational concept, and only makes sense when used in conjunction with capital and field.

Capital: power and privilege in the snowboarding culture

The concept of capital sits at the center of Bourdieu's (1985) construction of social space: 'The structure of the social world is defined at every moment by the structure and distribution of the capital and profits characteristic of the different particular fields' (p. 734), and thus it is important to work out the correct hierarchy 'of the different forms of capital' (p. 737). Capital refers to the different forms of power held by social agents. Bourdieu (1986) identifies various forms of capital (power), including economic (e.g., wealth), social (e.g., social connections), cultural (e.g., artistic taste), and symbolic (e.g., prestige). He also identifies linguistic (e.g., vocabulary and pronunciation), academic (e.g., tertiary qualifications), and corporeal (e.g., physical attractiveness) capital. These forms of power structure the social space and determine the position of social agents in the social hierarchy (Laberge, 1995). Of specific interest to this analysis are the concepts of cultural capital and symbolic capital as forms demarcating different groups of snowboarders.

Bourdieu argues that cultural capital exists in three irreducible forms, the objectified state (e.g., pictures and books which are the traces or realization of theories and bodies of knowledge), the institutionalized state (e.g., as academic qualifications conferred on those who reach a certain level of education), and the embodied state (e.g., in the form of long-lasting dispositions of the body and mind) (see Shilling, 1993). In snowboarding, cultural capital in the objectified state refers to snowboarding magazines, films, instructional manuals and DVDs, and books, such as cultural histories of snowboarding and autobiographies of athletes or pioneers, which are producers of cultural knowledge (see also Chapters 2 and 4). Cultural capital in the institutionalized state refers to roles obtained in the sport or industry through either formal qualifications, such as certified snowboard instructor or competition judge, or informal cultural apprenticeships, such as snowboard journalist or photographer. Institutionalized cultural capital also refers to prizes and accolades received within the sport (e.g., National champion or U.S. Open champion). For many core snowboarders, events more closely aligned with snowboarding traditions and cultural values, such as the Mt Baker Banked Slalom (Washington) and the Arctic Challenge (Norway), hold the most cultural gravitas.

Clarifying the embodied state, Bourdieu (1986) notes that 'most of the properties of cultural capital can be deduced from the fact that, in its fundamental state, it is linked to the body and presupposes embodiment' (p. 244). Bourdieu (1978) also refers to this embodied form of cultural capital as physical or corporeal capital, which he treats as a form of capital in its own right. During the late 1990s and early 2000s, for example, 'goggle tans' were a popular form of embodied cultural or physical capital in the snowboarding culture. Goggle tans were perceived as visual demonstrations of an individual's cultural commitment. According to *Snowboard Magazine*, 'a sure-fire way to tell the local from the yokel is the goggle tan' (Scott, 2009, para. 1), and the magazine even held a competition inviting readers to submit photos of their goggle tans, with the most dramatic 'raccoon eyes' winning a new pair of goggles. Shilling (1993) views physical or corporeal capital as a particularly useful conceptualization that shares an important relationship with 'all other varieties of capital' (p. 149). Indeed, corporeal capital is one of the key concepts employed in the second part of this chapter to provide insight into distinctive snowboarding bodies, with a particular focus on clothing practices.

Symbolic capital is another name for distinction. It is a 'unique form of motivation – a resource, a reward' (Booth & Loy, 1999, p. 4) closely tied up with the concepts of status, lifestyle, honor, and prestige. Symbolic capital is highly valued within the snowboarding field; participants gain prestige or symbolic capital through displays of physical prowess, risk-taking, and commitment. For example, the number of years or 'back-to-back' seasons (following the winter between hemispheres) participating in the snowboarding culture signifies an individual's commitment to the activity and boarders receive symbolic capital for such demonstrations (see also Beal & Weidman, 2003; Wheaton, 2000a, 2003b; Wheaton & Beal, 2003). In sum, capital, in its various forms, refers to the different forms of power held by social agents. These forms of power structure social space, or 'field' in Bourdieu's terminology, and determine the relative social positioning of agents.

Field: the snowboarding hierarchy

Field refers to a structured system of social positions occupied by either individuals or institutions engaged in the same activity (Tomlinson, 2002). Fields are structured internally in terms of power relations. 'In order for field to function,' said Bourdieu (1993), 'there have to be stakes and people prepared to play the game, endowed with the habitus that implies knowledge and recognition of the immanent laws of the field, the stakes, and so on' (p. 72). Within each field, individuals and groups (or classes) struggle to transform or preserve the configuration of power. Importantly, social fields often have unique valuation systems privileging different forms of capital, as well as distinct practices and strategies for accessing capital.

As Bourdieu (1984) explains, a range of classes occupies each field. A class is a group of people whose 'similar conditions of existence produce similar habituses and similar access to goods and power' (Jenkins, 2002, p. 140).

According to Bourdieu, every class and its factions have distinct tastes or preferences for cultural goods and consumption. Taste, Bourdieu (1984) observes, 'unites and separates' these classes or groups:

> It unites all those who are the product of similar conditions while distinguishing them from others. And it distinguishes in an essential way, since taste is the basis of all that one has – people and things – and all that one is for others, whereby one classifies oneself and is classified by others. (p. 56)

In short, taste is one of the key signifiers and elements of social identity (Jenkins, 2002). For Bourdieu, taste is the source of distinctive features of each social space and an 'expression of a particular class of conditions of existence, i.e., as a distinctive lifestyle' (cited in Booth & Loy, 1999, p. 5). Turner (1988) also identifies taste, the practical dimension of lifestyle, as a primary means of separating groups. He sees social groups distinguishing themselves from their competitors by adopting certain bodily gestures, speech, and deportment that are embodied tastes that not only play an important role in identifying social groups but also function to accommodate and reinforce the existing structure of the social space or field.

Bourdieu (1977) refers to the 'sport field' as a site that defines sport with respect to the allocation of rewards, system of rules, and the social identity of participants. As a site of struggles, the sport field represents a context for the 'monopolistic capacity to impose the legitimate definition of sporting practice and of the legitimate function of sporting activity' (Bourdieu, 1978, p. 826). The alpine snow field has traditionally consisted of two main groups, skiers and snowboarders. Although these groups share the same mountain space and comply with the same set of rules, for example, ski resort etiquette, they each have their own institutions (associations, media, and so on), cultural rules, knowledge, practices and people. Over the past four decades, numerous power struggles developed between these two groups as they fought for territory and preeminence (see Humphreys, 1996; Thorpe, 2004). As I explain in the second part of this chapter, however, while snowboarders employed various embodied tastes, such as clothing or language, to clearly distinguish themselves from skiers during the 1980s and 1990s, in some local fields and among some groups (e.g., freestyle skiers and snowboarders; big mountain skiers and snowboarders) these divisions are dissolving. In the contemporary snow field, however, various groups of snow users (e.g., freestyle, alpine, backcountry) continue to struggle over access to space, capital and resources.

The contemporary snowboarding field is highly fragmented; various subgroups include competitive athletes, big mountain riders or extreme snowboarders, jibbers or freestyle riders, alpine boarders, weekend warriors, novices and poseurs (see Figures 5.1a–c). Participants from these groups

Figure 5.1 The contemporary snowboarding field consists of various sub-groups including (a) alpine, (b) jibbers, and (c) freeriders. (Figure 5.1a: Rider: Blair Davidson; Image used with permission of photographer Greg Michat); (Figure 5.1b: Rider: Gabby Maiden; Image used with permission of Nikita Outerwear); (Figure 5.1c: Image used with permission of Johanna Fridheim)

engage in an array of embodied practices in their attempts to preserve, nego-tiate, and transform the legitimate tastes, styles, and allocation of capital, and meanings of the snowboarding body. With individuals and groups reg-ularly engaging in embodied struggles over status and access to capital, the structure of the snowboarding field is in a constant state of negotiation. To paraphrase Ford and Brown (2006), the precise degree of value or symbolic capital that a big mountain boarder, half-pipe athlete, or any other kind of snowboarder, possesses will differ according to the position they occupy within a particular group in the snowboarding field, and the current value of the group tastes and styles in relation to the dominant legitimate norm of the social period in question (p. 127). New Zealand snowboard judge and magazine editor Ste'en has observed 'all forms of snowboarding... going through in and out stages', and notes, 'slope-style is in focus now, jibbing has taken a bit of a backseat, and alpine seems to be struggling' (personal communication, October 2005). Indeed, the alpine racer tends to receive very little symbolic capital in the current generation where freestyle is the most prized form of participation. In an article entitled 'The Outsiders', for example, alpine racers are described critically as wearing 'skin-tight speed suits and helmets, and ride boards that hardly resemble anything you'd find on the racks at your local snowboard shop. They wear ski boots for crying out loud' (Berkley, 1998, cited in Heino, 2000, p. 183). New Zealand snow-boarder Andrew Morrison also demonstrated the lack of symbolic capital allocated to alpine racing when he defined a participant as 'someone... [who] carves, carves, carves and carves and carves', adding 'I don't have much respect for those guys' (cited in Humphreys 1996, p. 17).

Various 'other' groups also negotiate space on the margins of the field (e.g., older, gay, disabled, or nonwhite snowboarders). For example, Lance, a 55-year-old black American, describes feeling like 'a duck out of water' while on a snowboarding trip with a group of colleagues because he didn't have the right equipment or the embodied knowledge that would enable him to contribute to conversations about snow conditions and so on (cited in Hua, 2006, para. 9). Similarly, on a blog called 'Stuff white people like: #31 snowboarding', Adisa recalled taking a snowboarding lesson with a group of black friends where 'the white instructor... frustrated by how slowly we were picking up the basics... said (I kid you not): "Come on guys! You people are natural athletes. This should be easy!" We laughed about it then, as we do now' (Stuff white, 2008, para. 3). Some 'other' marginal participants find pleasure in disrupting stereotypes of snowboarders as young, white, hetero-sexual males. Marcia, a 58-year-old Canadian snowboarder, for example, has been boarding for more than 12 years and enjoys 'surprising people when I take off my helmet and show my long silver hair' (personal commu-nication, February 2004) (see also Chapters 6 and 7).

Marginal participants often have limited access to capital accumulation within the snowboarding field, yet many find the support they need to enjoy their snowboarding experience by forming social groups (e.g., Black Avalanche), creating websites (e.g., www.graysontrays.com), and establishing specialized instructional programs (e.g., adaptive snowboarding programs are available for individuals with various disabilities at many ski resorts), teams (e.g., First Nations Snowboard Team, a Canadian organization that supports Aboriginal competitive snowboarders and qualified instructors) and organizations (e.g., Alpino, an organization founded in Colorado that strives to get more people of color to the mountains for both recreation and work). To support the participation of gay snowboarders, some have formed clubs and websites, such as Outryders (www.outryders.org) and OutBoard (www.outboard.org). The latter has almost 4000 members in 50 American states and 27 countries. The key point here, however, is that the field of snowboarding is comprised of a number of groups, all of which give value to the practiced, boarding body in different ways. These groups have distinct styles, practices, institutions and practitioners with subtle, but important, distinctions in their habitus that command different degrees of capital conversion. In the second part of this chapter I explore some of the distinctive tastes and styles embodied by participants from various positions within the field in their attempts to preserve, negotiate or resist the configuration of power.

Practice: the cultural boarding body in action

As Bourdieu's formula implies, the three-way relationship of habitus, capital and field generates practices. According to Wacquant (1993), 'it is out of this perpetual and multileveled dialectic of field and habitus, position and disposition, social structures and mental structures that practices emerge that (re) make the world which makes them' (p. 4). These practical logics only make complete sense, however, in relation to the field of activity that produces and gives them value. Therefore, to paraphrase Ford and Brown (2006), the social logic of snowboarding revolves around snowboarding practices that, over time, inscribe or condition the body (habitus) in ways that then have social (relating to social institutions), cultural (relating to ways of living), economic (relating to material wealth) and symbolic (relating to something that is invisible) exchange value in a cultural economy of groups of people that share a common interest in these practices (the field) (p. 122). Put simply, boarding practices, bodies and their relative values only make 'real' sense in practical relation to others within the snow field (Ford & Brown, 2006). In this way, it is through participation in social practices (which are determined by a snowboarding habitus) that snowboarding culture is embodied and the structure of the snowboarding field is reproduced. Of particular concern to Bourdieu are those practices that involve struggle among social groups trying to maintain or change their social position.[1] These cultural practices are subtle markers of the different positions in social space; they manifest 'a vision and a division of the world', and bear particular symbolic value (Laberge & Kay, 2002, p. 243).

The remainder of this chapter draws on Bourdieu's relational concepts – habitus, capital, field and practice – to shed light on the snowboarding body, as a 'mnemonic device in cultural coding and as an effective vehicle for the less-than-conscious communication or expression of these codes' (Jenkins, 2002, p. 179). In so doing, it illustrates how snowboarders employ an array of embodied and bodily practices to distinguish themselves from nonsnowboarders, marginal participants, and each other, and ultimately reinforce (or resist) the structure of the snowboarding field.

The snowboarding body: a site of distinction

Bourdieu's concepts of field, habitus, capital, style, and taste facilitate insights into snowboarding bodies as possessors of power, and the struggles over the legitimate use and meaning of the body. This section analyzes embodied dress and language practices, as well as physical competence, in snowboarding culture, and their contributions to the social construction and classification of group identities within the alpine snow field. This discussion is divided into three main parts. First, I examine the early embodiment of inter-group divisions between skiers and snowboarders. Second, I consider the horizontal internal structuring of the contemporary snowboarding field with a particular emphasis on the intra-group conflicts between different groups of snowboarders. Third, I discuss how core boarders distribute symbolic capital for displays of commitment, physical prowess and risk-taking. Ultimately, this discussion reveals a multidimensional picture of the snowboarding field where an array of boarding bodies struggle to negotiate various forms of capital and navigate cultural positions.

Embodied inter-group divisions in the snow field

Skiers and snowboarders share the same social space, from car parks to chairlifts to slopes. However, since the beginning, the two groups have been separated by age, fashion, etiquette, lingo and per capita income (Williams et al., 1994). As one journalist commented, the skier and the snowboarder typically 'ride up the mountain together in chilly silence' (Wulf, 1996, p. 69). According to Bourdieu (1991), when two groups occupy the same social space, it is more likely that members will establish collective identities to distinguish themselves. This was certainly the case in the alpine snow field during the 1980s and 1990s. Emerging in opposition to the then dominant ski culture, snowboarders, as the newcomers to the slopes, sought 'difference, discontinuity and revolution' and employed a variety of 'strategies to create space for themselves and displace the established' (Featherstone, 1991, p. 92). Fights between skiers and snowboarders occasionally occurred as the two groups fought for territory and eminence. Labeling skiers the 'enemy' and 'slope scum', some snowboarders called on their peers to use 'violence and discrimination' to 'end the reign of the skier' ('The snowboard', no date, para. 2). Tom Burt, CEO of Sims Sports, remembers artists sending him 'graphics with snowboarders stabbing skiers' and spraying 'blood everywhere' (cited in Howe, 1998, p. 96). These overt displays of physical, verbal and symbolic violence clearly distinguished the two groups, but faced with the very real risk of losing access to mountain facilities, many snowboarders abated their unruly behavior, opting instead for embodied practices to emphasize their distinctiveness, the most obvious of which was clothing.

Dressing for distinction: snowboarders versus skiers

Clothing constitutes an important symbolic marker of group membership. Bryan Turner (1988) theorizes that, 'dress symbolizes and states one's wealth and political power by indicating one's superior sense of taste and distinction' (p. 68). Similarly, Barnes and Eicher (1992) note that 'dress serves as a sign that the individual belongs to a certain group but simultaneously differentiates the same individual from all others: it includes and excludes' (p. 1). As snowboarding Olympian and clothing company owner Pamela explained: 'Personal style in snowboarding is so important. You can read a person by what they're wearing, before they even strap in [to their board]. Everything in snowboarding is a full expression of who you are...that's why we wear clothes' (personal communication, September 2005) (see Figure 5.2). Over the past four decades, snowboard clothing has gone from 'garish to grunge to gorgeous, from incredibly impractical to highly technical, from something for the outlandish few to the standard for the majority of snow sliders' ('Snow sports industries', 2003–2004, para. 1). Here I will examine the significance of dress practices for distinguishing snowboarders from skiers, and how different meanings have been bestowed on these embodied practices at different historical junctures.

During the late 1970s and early 1980s, snowboarders were only concerned with their clothing as far as it kept them dry. Trevor, an early snowboarder, recalled getting 'on the bus in Utica, New York to go to the ski hill, wearing wetsuits' (Howe, 1998, p. 24). It wasn't long, however, until snowboarders began adopting clothing styles to distinguish themselves from skiers. One early reporter described 'conservative skiers in dull blue and red outfits clutch[ing] their poles and watch[ing] aghast' (Hughes, 1988, para. 1) as two boarders rode past, one wearing a 'green leopard-spot bodysuit' and another wearing a 'lilac snow jacket, red pants and neon-green glasses' (Ibid., para 3). Male and female snowboarders both readily adopted this dress style. The early clothing practices of wearing bright and mismatched colors helped unite this marginal group of snowboarders and clearly distinguish them from skiers.

The first signs of division among boarders emerged in the early 1990s: 'There were the experienced alpine snowboarders...and there were the scrub skater guys...who wanted to get as much air as possible, mimicking skating heroes of the day' (Richards, 2003, p. 64). The majority of snowboarders

Figure 5.2 The clothed and accessorized snowboarding body is an important site of distinction. For many core participants, the snowboard also carries important symbolic meaning. As seen in this image, the 'top sheet' of the board is often used for creative and personal displays of identity (e.g., art, sticker placement, political slogans) (also see Figure 7.3) (Photograph taken by author)

adopted the 'skater' look, which sharply distinguished them from skiers. Rebelling against the ski industry, boarders wore 'giant cut off jeans covered in ice, huge chain wallets, big hooded sweatshirts, backwards baseball caps, and windbreakers' (Troy Bush, cited in Howe, 1998, p. 85). In addition, snowboarders in the early 1990s often exhibited stoicism and strength by wearing clothing that offered no protection from the snow and cold temperatures. Holly, a participant in an early study, remembers snowboarders 'wearing pants that sag down to their knees and flannels...covered in snow...they care more about the way they look than if they are freezing their butts off' (Anderson, 1999, p. 63).

Male snowboarders embodied elements of the masculine images of skateboarders, gangsters (e.g., baggy clothing, low riding pants with exposed boxer shorts, gold chains) and punks (e.g., Mohawks, body piercings, studded belts, brightly colored hair), and manipulated these into the stereotypical snowboarder style of the mid- to late 1990s. The appropriation of clothing styles from the male-dominated gangster and punk cultures clearly distinguished snowboarders from skiers; it also contributed to the marginalization of some female participants (Anderson, 1999). As a young skier during this period, Marie found the masculine image of the early snowboarders intimidating:

> When I was 10–12 years old, the people that would snowboard past you were 15- to 25- year-old males. They were really hard-core, even my parents were freaked out by them. I don't remember seeing girls...There was the odd time when you'd see a chick, and you'd think, 'oh, that's kinda cool.' But a lot of the time, these girls weren't the most feminine girls, they wore guys' clothes and were all hanging out with boys, and that's kinda why I thought snowboarding was a guys' thing. (personal communication, November 2005)

As this comment suggests, these styles discouraged some female participants, but they definitely did not discourage all. Some early committed female riders mirrored their snowboarding 'brothers' by wearing baggy pants and jackets, studded belts and bandanas. The masculine snowboarding style offered some women a refreshing alternative to emphasized femininity dominant in other fields, such as other sports and school (see also Chapter 6).

By aligning themselves with the styles of the historical and contemporary underclass, the mostly white and privileged snowboarders attempted to authenticate their claim to being marginal, deviant and poor and, most importantly, different from the upper-class skier (see Kusz, 2007a). While historically the middle classes have 'differentiated themselves sharply' from the lower classes and have mimicked upper-class style (Jenkins, 2002, p. 139), snowboarders in the 1990s preferred to emulate lower-class styles. Kyle Kusz (2007a) argues that extreme sports, such as snowboarding, were popularized during the 1990s at a particular historical conjuncture when cultural diversity and white privilege were made visible to white America. According to Kusz (2007a) white people developed a number of ways to disavow their investment or connection to white privilege during this period. He explains that many white people frequently downplayed the security or comfort of their economic position, or they claimed working-class, poor, or 'white trash' roots. For Kusz (2007b), 'extreme sports served as a cultural means through which white dominance could be restored ironically through the promotion of stories and ideas which implicitly denied and disavowed the existence of social and economic white privilege' (p. 361). The 'white trash' identity was certainly embraced by many privileged snowboarders during this period, as were the punk, skateboarder, and urban gangster identities. While Kusz's argument is insightful in relation to snowboarding in North America, it is less relevant for explaining the emulation of underclass styles by privileged snowboarding youth in Europe, Australia, New Zealand, and Asia, where snowboarding developed in different social, cultural, and racial contexts. Of course, the tastes and styles of snowboarders in other social contexts are informed by the predominantly American-produced and internationally distributed niche media (e.g. snowboard magazines and films). My key argument here, however, is that snowboarders' alignment with the styles of underclass groups is more a reflection of youth rebellion against skiers and against their parents' generation, rather than a class (or race) issue.

Skiers and snowboarders have long struggled to preserve and/or transform the configuration of power on the slopes, and in various other social and physical spaces, such as car parks, restaurants, and liftlines. The dynamics between the two groups are in a constant state of negotiation and change. Skiing held the dominant position for many years, but in the late 1990s and early 2000s snowboarding increasingly gained power to allocate rewards, and to define the systems of rules and the social identity of participants in the field. Ski resorts that once banned snowboarders began investing heavily in personnel, equipment, and marketing to attract boarders. With the configuration of power and the cultural dynamics in the snow field shifting in favor of snowboarders, many young skiers began drawing inspiration from the styles of participation, technologies, jargon, and fashion of snowboarders. A snowboarding journalist describes the long-standing 'feud' between skiers and snowboarders 'fading':

> The boom in freestyle snowboarding attracted more skiers to the terrain park areas. Skiers began sliding rails, riding switch and performing huge aerial spins, which served to attract new, young recruits to the skiing crowd. Skiing, like boarding, was once again super cool and a symbiotic relationship was born, with both sports influencing, inspiring, and benefiting from one another. (Baldwin, 2006, para. 16)

Figure 5.3 The contemporary alpine snow field no longer consists of two clear groups – skiers and snowboarders. Today, many skiers and snowboarders enjoy sharing the mountain experience together (image used with permission of Johanna Fridheim)

Although these cultural shifts are occurring predominantly at the core level of the snow field – that is, among the most committed, and typically younger, snowboarders and skiers – this trend is filtering into the broader alpine snow culture, and relations between the majority of skiers and snowboarders are becoming more amicable. The contemporary snow field no longer consists of two clearly opposing groups, skiers and snowboarders. Rather, the alpine snow field is increasingly being divided into styles of participation (i.e., freestyle, big mountain, alpine) with each group sharing terrain as well as styles of talk and dress, training methods and so on (see Figure 5.3). It is important to note, however, that this is not the case in all snow fields; the divisions between skiers and snowboarders are still very much in existence in local, regional, and national fields where skiing has had a particularly long tradition of dominance, for example in some regions of France, Italy, and Switzerland.

Embodied intra-group divisions in the snowboarding field

In contrast to its united beginnings, the rapid commercialization and popularization of snowboarding during the late 1990s and early 2000s fueled many divisions within the culture. Andy Blumberg, editor of *Transworld Snowboarding* magazine, observed this trend:

> Snowboarding is not so cool that riders should act like the educated do among the ignorant, the rich among the poor. It's not so tough that people need to represent it like hoods on a corner, disrespecting anyone on the mountain outside their little crew. Once united we seem today divided, excluding and ignoring those not hip to what's the new hype this season. It almost pains some snowboarders to acknowledge others on the chair next to them; they stare forward, through their goggles up the hill, consciously silent. They clown style, equipment, and ability. (Blumberg, 2002, p. 16)

While the most obvious division in the contemporary snowboarding culture is between insiders and newcomers, various identities also exist within the group of core participants. Numerous qualities underscore the social hierarchy in snowboarding, for example, geographical divisions, commitment, equipment, ability, and age. Yet bodily disposition, personal style, and clothing are critical markers. In the remainder of this section I examine how clothing and language practices reinforce the position of 'established' groups and the marginal status of 'outsider' groups within the contemporary snowboarding field.

Dressing for distinction: pros versus poseurs

Initially, the distinctive clothing styles of the gangster and punk clearly distinguished core snowboarders from skiers and nonparticipants. Yet during the late 1990s, this alternative snowboarder look became fashionable among the scores of new participants. No longer did these clothing styles perform the function of producing and reproducing clear social boundaries between insiders, newcomers, and outsiders. Graham, a New Zealand snowboard shop owner, witnessed this cultural shift:

> In the early days, it was lots of surfers because they weren't interested in skiing. So, for a number of years we had a surf culture mentality. But today, lots of people just go out and shop. We see the poseurs getting out of their cars in the car park [across from the snowboard shop], they pull down their pants to get the baggy look going on, put their goggles back on and tilt them to the side ... then start walking down the road ... looking as *cool* as possible. We watch them from the shop and just laugh. (personal communication, September 2005)

Another New Zealand snowboarder described this trend:

> I will never forget coming back from Whistler [in the mid- to late 1990s] and walking round town and thinking, 'Oh cool, all these people are snowboarders, or they must be because they're all dressed like snowboarders', and then working out that no one snowboarded, they just dressed like this because suddenly snowboarding was cool, and I remember thinking, 'you fake-asses, what are you doing, this is *our* sport'. (Pamela, personal communication, September 2005)

As a core participant, Pamela's distinctive snowboarding identity was threatened by newcomers who did not demonstrate commitment to the activity itself but rather embodied what Beal and Weidman (2003) call a 'prefabricated version' of a boarding identity, by consciously displaying brand-name clothing and equipment (p. 340; see also Wheaton, 2000a).

In an effort to regain authenticity, it is ironic that many core snowboarders moved away from the traditional 'rebellions' of piercing and tattooing and toward a more conservative and mainstream stance, with less visual signification and more technically functional clothing (Howe, 1998). 'There is no set snowboarder look anymore,' said Graham; 'clothing is a lot mellower ... but there is a cult following with some brands' (personal communication, September 2005). Certainly a central issue in the contemporary snow field is branding. Today, more than a hundred companies provide snowboarding-specific clothing in an abundance of styles. Snowboard clothing carries status based on understanding the nuances of the culture. To the initiated member, decoding a combination of clothing and equipment graphics and other visual signifiers is an automatic process. For example, while Volcom Stone's distinctive fashions may appeal to 'alternative' youth, more conservative, older snowboarders might prefer the quality of Helly Hansen outerwear. According to Ford and Brown (2006), concern with authenticity of various boarding clothing brands may be viewed as a response not only to the increasing levels of participation in board sports but, more importantly, to the global appropriation of boarding fashion by mass youth culture. As discussed in Chapter 3, the owners and managers of these companies are very aware of this concern among core participants and work hard to maintain an 'authentic' corporate image.

With the increasing number of participants, turnover rates in fashion trends have accelerated. According to Mike Featherstone (1991), 'the constant supply of new, fashionably desirable goods' has produced a 'paperchase effect in which those above will have to invest in new (informational) goods in order to reestablish the original social distance' (p. 18). Having worked in the snowboarding industry for many years, American snowboarder Moriah is acutely aware of the importance of the latest fashions among core boarders: 'if you're not wearing the coolest gear, or what the top riders are, or rocking the newest bindings and board, then you're wack [uncool]' (personal communication, November 2005). In this context, knowledge of the snowboarding culture becomes critical; cultural insiders need knowledge of new goods, their social and cultural value and how to use them appropriately. Snowboarding magazines, websites, and videos play key roles in communicating these new culturally and socially valuable styles and tastes. Indeed, the snowboarding media are important bearers of embodied snowboarding style (see Chapter 4). For example, it was *Transworld Snowboarding* that informed readers: 'goggle tans are no longer considered a status symbol in snowboarding' (Sherowski, 2003c, p. 58).

Ironically, the homogeneity of the contemporary snowboarder's appearance, especially among the young, core, and elite, is conspicuous in any snowboard magazine and at most mountain resorts. As noted by the editor of *Transworld Snowboarding*, 'everyone looks the same in snowboard clothing' (Coyle, 2002, p. 128). *Snowboarder Magazine* also reported 'up on the hill there are few things that distinguish the hard-core rippers from the weekend warriors. It used to be clothes, it used to be style and it used to be easy. But now, with everyone looking the part ... you are forced to use more nontraditional means' (Scott, no date, para. 1). For many core members this meant once again appropriating unconventional clothing to reinforce difference. During the early and mid-2000s, for example, tight jeans (inspired by the punk and emo cultures) were a popular fashion. However, professional U.S. snowboarder J. P. Solberg questions this trend, asking: 'Why would anybody go snowboarding in jeans so tight they don't even come over your boots?' ('What sucks', 2004, p. 48). Symbolic struggles over the power to produce and impose 'legitimate' dispositions continue unabated in the contemporary snowboarding field.

A good example of the struggles over defining tastes and styles, and meanings of the snowboarding body, occurred in the lead-up to the 2010 Winter Olympic Games in Vancouver. Boardercross is officially a speed event: the first rider to cross the finish line wins the race. However, the discipline has historically been more closely linked to freestyle than to racing styles of participation. In contrast to alpine racers, who wear speed suits, hard boots and focus solely on speed, boardercross snowboarders have traditionally worn baggy outerwear and soft boots, and occasionally perform stylistic maneuvers on various terrain and obstacles. As snowboarding became increasingly competitive, particularly during the lead-up to the Olympics, some performance-focused athletes began arriving at competitions wearing speed suits. Critically aware of the significance of clothing and style for accessing both symbolic and economic capital in the contemporary snowboarding field, some freestyle-focused athletes actively resisted this trend:

> I think there is a need for a rule [against snowboarders wearing speed suits]. The image is what's at stake…. I like to wear stuff that consumers can buy at stores. And they're not going to buy a speed suit at a store that I'm wearing during a race…. I've seen other riders get heated up on it. There definitely is a backlash if you show up with something tight. If someone is showing up to [boardercross] races in tight clothes, we wouldn't recommend that person for a spot [at the X Games]. (Nate Holland, five-time X-Games gold medallist and member of the selection committee, cited in Higgins, 2010b)

The International Ski Federation ruled that suits worn at World Cup events and the Olympics must be two-piece and speed suits are not allowed, but there is no ruling on the 'tightness' of a uniform. Thus, some freestyle-oriented athletes drew on their own cultural and symbolic capital (e.g., as selection committee members) to regulate meanings of the legitimate boardercross body, and actively police their fellow competitors. As the comments from Holland suggest, athletes who chose to wear speed suits were excluded from peer-selected invitational events (e.g., X-Games). Another competitor confirms: 'If somebody shows up with a race suit, they'll get laughed at and [sometimes] won't be allowed to compete' (Daron Rahlves, cited in Higgins, 2010b, para. 17). This example clearly illustrates how the work of producing and imposing meaning is carried on in and through the everyday struggles within the snowboarding field.

Not all snowboarders align with specific groups or subscribe to the latest fashions. While snowboarding may be associated with a certain 'cool' style by some members of the wider society and mass youth culture, the ways that such an appeal has been used in the commodification and commercialization of snowboarding culture are regarded with considerable ambivalence and even distain by some snowboarders. Some snowboarders lodge concerns with *Transworld Snowboarding*:

> I was cut off and laughed at, clowned, and left to ride the lift alone by those who wouldn't ride with just anybody. It seems it's no longer about

riding but how tight [fashionable] your button-up looks with your bandana hanging off your tattered jeans. I've been riding for six years and have never felt such dismay. (Cody, cited in 'Sensitive in', 2002, p. 28)

I get pretty pissed when [friends] are always dissn' on my old Kemper 165 and neon-green and purple jacket. Gone are the days when people were cool to one another because they were all snowboarders. Judge people by how they ride, not how they look. (Charlie, cited in 'Antifashion', 2002, p. 30)

Although many marginal participants, and some core participants, refuse to buy into the snowboarding fashions, they are acutely aware of the implications of such decisions for their status within the field. One occasional participant admitted feeling 'like a muppet when I wear trackies with waterproof hiking over-trou[sers] over the top and sunnies, oh, plus my ripped up mitts. But then again, the rest of that stuff is so damned expensive that I just don't care' (James, personal communication, May 2004). Relatively older participants, who presumably have other identities beyond snowboarding, tend to express such attitudes more frequently. Another marginal participant explained: 'I'm one of those geeks who wears old geeky stuff, and just wants to have fun. I don't think image matters if you are comfortable with who you are' (Dan, personal communication, May 2004). However, it seems that even those unconcerned about the latest snowboarding fashions and their marginal position in the snowboarding field are aware that clothing styles influence their cultural positioning (e.g., 'I feel like a muppet'; 'I'm one of those geeks'). As Turner (1988) explains, social status involves 'practices which emphasize and exhibit cultural distinctions and differences which are a crucial feature of all social stratification' (p. 66). Clothing is one such practice that has always been a crucial feature of social stratification in the snowboarding field; the distinctive use of snowboarding-specific language or 'lingo' is another.

Snowboarding lingo

Snowboarders not only mark their group identity with the embodiment of visible symbols (clothing, goggle tans, creative 'sticker jobs' on their boards and so on), they also embody less visible aspects of style such as language. Snowboarding lingo is identifiable and distinct from both mainstream and other sports cultures, especially skiing. Snowboarders have their own argot to describe the snowboarding experience as well as equipment and techniques. *Transworld Snowboarding*'s website defines hundreds of these terms in their 'lexicon of snowboarding language'. Some common terms include: Fakie – A term for riding backwards; Hucker – One who throws himself/herself wildly through the air and does not land on his/her feet; Cheesewedge, Hip, Booter, Spine – All types of snowboard jumps. Snowboarders have also incorporated the lexicon and slang from various other board-sports (e.g., surfing, stateboarding), as well as youth and popular cultures, including American gangster culture. The snowboarding media blatantly appropriate this gangster lingo, writing texts in the colloquial language and terminology that only core snowboarders, and those well versed in contemporary popular culture, understand. For example, *Transworld Snowboarding* writes to 'all you fresh-ass mofos out there' (Letters 13.4, 1999, para. 1). Much of the jargon in the culture also uses violent metaphors such 'killing', 'slashing', 'tearing', and 'destroying' to describe high performance.

The extensive technical vocabulary, as well as violent and gangster language and slang, distinguishes the insiders from the outsiders. However, popularization of snowboarding has brought about a more widespread use of the basic lingo. One correspondent to *Snowboarder Magazine* expresses his irritation:

> It just pisses me off when I come to school and hear 'fags anonymous' talk about how 'the boss' was 'doing awesome stuff in the pipe'. Before that [Olympics, X-Games, corporate sponsorships] they had probably never even seen snowboarding before and if I ask them now, I guarantee that they would have no idea who the hell Danny Kass or Ross Powers were. 'Huh? What's a Kasserroll?' ('Sold out', 2003, p. 44)

The use of snowboarding lingo as an existing symbolic marker by outsider groups contributes to the 'paper-chase effect' (Featherstone, 1991, p. 18), and snowboarding language is becoming increasingly technical and obscure. While cultural identity can be imitated, only those with high cultural knowledge recognize the difference between a 'Kasserroll', a 'switch ally-oop mc-twist' and a 'corked backside five'. The widespread use of a distinctive lexicon within the snowboarding field contributes to the production and reproduction of snowboarders as a social group. However, the increasing complexity of the lingo also helps support the structuring of the social order, or cultural hierarchy, within the snowboarding field.

Defining snowboarding style: a matter of power, position and privilege

Snowboarding culture produces never-ending symbolic struggles over the power to produce and impose legitimate styles and tastes. With the growing differentiation of the snowboarding culture, individuals and groups increasingly clash over the meaning of their social identity, and the legitimate use of the body. In the struggle to impose legitimate forms of embodiment, agents wield power in proportion to their position in the field. In an increasingly mediatized culture, professional snowboarders are iconic; they hold the highest position within the field, and thus they have the most power to define the latest snowboarding styles. According to Zane, professional snowboarders have a 'ridiculous influence on the kids': 'A couple of days ago we went up to Brighton [Salt Lake City, Utah] and you could tell who each little kid's favorite pro rider was because of what they were wearing, some even had the same haircut as their favorite pros, it was that easy to tell' (personal communication, November 2005). Typically, it is male professional snowboarders who define snowboarding's styles of dress and participation. More specifically, it is predominantly North American (or at least Western) male snowboarders who give rise to many of the styles infiltrating the global snowboarding field. For example, despite witnessing a 'thriving snowboard culture in Japan', *Transworld Snowboarding* journalist Chris Coyle observed 'droves of chain-smoking kids ... dressed just like [North American-based professional snowboarders] Jamie Lynn and Terje Haakonsen' (February 2005, p. 154). As in other realms of physical culture, professional male snowboarders become 'agents of transmission and reconstruction of practice, style and valued forms of capital to the next generation' (Ford & Brown, 2006, p. 130). Some of the more distinctive tastes and styles legitimized by professional male snowboarders even have the potential to cross local, regional, and national fields, and become part of the collective snowboarding habitus. It is important to note, however, that as the position of women within the culture has improved, they too have gained access, albeit limited, to define their own snowboarding styles (see also Chapter 6).

In this section I have explored some of the ways core snowboarders embody and display their cultural affiliation through the choice of symbolic goods and their subsequent customizing, and using sport-specific argot. Clothing and language provide the 'small number of distinctive features which, functioning as a system of difference ... allows the most fundamental differences to be expressed' (Bourdieu, 1984, p. 226). The snowboarding 'field' has increasingly become a structured system of social positions, and the embodiment of distinctive snowboarding tastes and styles, and the allocation of cultural capital, help reinforce the position of 'established' groups and the marginal status of 'outsider' groups. However, which type of capital is the most relevant varies according to one's position in the snowboarding field. While many novices and marginal boarders privilege style and taste, physical ability is most highly valued among core boarders. In the final part of this chapter I focus on the physical experience and its function in the distribution of symbolic capital. Here I describe less visible characteristics, such as displays of commitment, physical prowess and risk-taking, as highly valued among core snowboarders and particularly important for gaining respect and cultural status from one's peers.

Symbolic capital: 'Let your snowboarding do the talking'

Social status in the snowboarding culture derives from the accumulation of symbolic capital. Although taste and style play an important part in constructing a distinctive snowboarding identity, members cannot buy their way into the core of the culture. As *New Zealand Snowboarder* put it, respect has 'to be earned, usually with a lot of blood, sweat and tears' ('Onset: Respect',

1995, p. 9). In snowboarding, the only usable and effective capital – symbolic capital – is 'prestige' or 'authority,' and, as Bourdieu (1980) argues more generally, the 'only legitimate accumulation consists of making a name for oneself, a known, recognized name' (p. 262). Among core participants – as distinct from novices, poseurs, and outsiders – less visible characteristics are more important in building cultural status. While the fashion and stylistic attributes of snowboarding are an important aspect of the culture, they are epiphenomena to the experience of snowboarding itself; the pursuit of boarding experience and competence is at the core of the snowboarding value system (see Ford & Brown, 2006; Wheaton, 2000a, 2003b). While core snowboarders can still clearly demarcate themselves from the popular tastes and cultural practices of outsiders, marginal participants, and poseurs, they can only enhance their status (symbolic capital) by performing for their peers (Honneth, 1986).

Prestige is shaped partly by appearing in the snowboarding media and films, and by success in contests. But in contrast to more explicitly competitive sports, symbolic capital is assessed more subjectively by snowboarders in terms of style, commitment to snowboarding, capability on challenging terrain, and difficulty and range of maneuvers able to be performed in various found (e.g., cliffs, cornices) and constructed (e.g., jumps, half-pipes) snowy spaces (see also Ford & Brown, 2006; Wheaton, 2003b). Only one's peers confer prestige and honor in the snowboarding culture (Midol, 1993). In his autobiography, Olympic snowboarder Todd Richards (2003) identified the importance of peer recognition as a form of symbolic capital. 'Gaining respect from my friends', he said, is 'way more important than the prize money or the trophy' (p. 166). Snowboarders compete amongst themselves, via the symbolic practices of physical prowess, commitment, skill, courage, and risk-taking, for marks of 'distinction' (Bourdieu, 1984). In the words of one male participant, snowboarders earn respect by going 'bigger and fatter than everybody'[2] (cited in Anderson, 1999, p. 55). These are, of course, practices exclusive to only the most committed boarders.

Snowboarders earn prestige and respect from their peers through displays of physical prowess, which include finely-honed combinations of skill, muscular strength, aggression, toughness and, above all, courage (Morford & Clarke, 1976). *Transworld Snowboarding*'s introduction to professional boarder Roman De Marchi highlighted the value of such practices and performances for gaining cultural status:

> How many people do you know who live life like there's no tomorrow? He'll look at something and say, 'I'm gonna do that. Get out your camera.' And everyone else will be like, 'are you f–king nuts? Shit that doesn't look doable,' he'll stomp it nine out of ten times … his riding is going bigger, harder, and gnarlier then everybody else's. (Muzzey, 2003, p. 126)

As with many sporting cultures, engaging in risk and injury proves dedication and toughness, and snowboarders who perform while injured gain 'kudos within peer groups' (Nixon, 1993; Young et al., 1994, p. 176). The glorification of injuries is prevalent in the snowboarding culture. The media regularly endorse the physical prowess and risk-taking embodied by professional boarders. Interviews in magazines usually include 'worst injury' questions with replies reported in detail. The snowboarding media insist on revealing the gory details, prompting riders for the particulars of their injuries. For example, 'So did they rip it straight out of you?' 'They just stuck it back on?' 'It took off the cartilage?' 'You cut off your tongue as well?' 'Did you pass out?' (Coyle, 2002, p. 134). In another representative example, *Transworld Snowboarding* narrated the injury of professional rider Scotty Wittlake:

> A brutal knee to face contact completely shattered his cheekbone. Apparently, Scotty's eye was so distended that doctors had to come up with a temporary fix to hold it in until the swelling went down. His eyelid became so swollen it turned inside out and oozed pus. ('Yellow snow', 2002, p. 206)

The article bestowed symbolic status on Wittlake, praising his commitment to snowboarding: 'Just a few weeks after the surgery, Scotty headed up to Oregon to help Whitey film using his one good eye. Now *that's* punk' ('Yellow snow', 2002, p. 206). These mediated accounts construct professional riders as heroes for risking physical injury and tolerating pain. The act of riding while injured and resuming full participation quickly provides symbolic evidence of a professional rider's dedication to snowboarding, and thus their deserving of cultural capital.

Like their male counterparts, many committed female snowboarders also embody the cultural values of courage, physical prowess, and risk-taking; they experience their share of injuries, and often embrace short-range views on participation. For example, professional female snowboarder Annie Boulanger explains that she plans to continue snowboarding 'until Advil [painkillers] in the morning doesn't do it anymore' (cited in Thorpe, 2004, p. 194). Phillipa claimed: 'I've broken stuff in my back and I've broken my ankle, and bad strains and I've blown my knee out. But I have been quite lucky. I've been injury free, really' (personal communication, September 2005). As I explain in Chapter 6, among committed snowboarders an individual's relative position in the snowboarding field is based primarily on their ability and commitment to the activity, rather than their sex. The key point here is that symbolic practices of physical prowess, courage, and risk-taking, and the media representation of these practices, reinforce the snowboarding hierarchy, and clearly distinguish pros from poseurs.

Converting symbolic capital into economic capital

Snowboarders gain cultural status through exhibiting commitment, physical prowess, and risk-taking; some convert this symbolic capital into economic capital. The relationship between economic capital and cultural capital, however, is more complex than a direct exchange (Bourdieu, 1984). With larger-than-life snowboarding personalities, professionals including Gretchen Bleiler, Torah Bright, Tara Dakides, Romain DeMarchi, Marc Frank Montoya, J. P. Walker, and Shaun White, have been labeled cultural 'superstars' by both the mainstream and snowboarding-specific media ('Is snowboarding', 2002, para. 3). Bourdieu (1980) notes that to 'make one's name' means 'making one's *mark*, achieving recognition (in both senses) of one's differences from others...' (p. 289). Professional snowboarders attempt to make their name through a combination of physical prowess and distinctive and marketable identities. Although physical prowess plays a key role in determining the symbolic capital possessed by a snowboarder, image is also crucial for converting their symbolic capital into economic capital; gender and race appear to be implicated in some instances. Indeed, many top male snowboarders work hard to create distinctive identities based on hypermasculine (or fratriarchal) characteristics such as hedonistic lifestyles, or in the words of one participant, 'shitty attitudes' and 'booze and drugs' (Kelsey, personal communication, September 2004). In an interview with *Snowboarder* magazine, professional snowboarder Romain DeMarchi reveals that he has a 'bad boy image' for being 'a hard-core partier' and admits he has been arrested four times. Interestingly, DeMarchi is very aware of the economic value of a distinctly hypermasculine image: 'People say, "Ah, Romain's the wild guy, he's going to go out and rage his ass off and be a f—ker and a dickhead!" But you know, who cares if these things are said? People label me as crazy, and it's good for me. It sells, so the sponsors use it and the magazines use it' (Bridges 2004, p. 101).

As suggested in Chapter 4, in a field dominated by white participants, racial difference can also be a sign of distinction and thus a potential source of capital for a select few athletes. The following exchange between Marc Frank Montoya, the first Mexican American professional snowboarder, and a snowboarding journalist is insightful:

Transworld Snowboarding: Most snowboarders, back in the day, were white kids. Did people accept you back then?

Montoya: I didn't really notice. Everybody was cool with me, I think. Sticking out that way, if anything, made people want to hook me up [offer financial and product sponsorship]. I think it was because I came from the streets–you know, Denver–and they liked the fact that I was trying to do my thing in the mountains. Maybe that worked a little bit to my advantage. (Montoya, 2001, para. 5)

Drawing on practices, styles and tastes from other fields (e.g., hip hop, urban gangster, Latino culture), Montoya combined his cultural capital with symbolic capital – gained via demonstrations of physical prowess and courage – to create a distinctive hybrid snowboarding identity that appealed to the desires of young, white, male snowboarders, as well as snowboarders from 'other' groups, such as Mexican or New Zealand Maori snowboarders (see Brayton, 2005; Kusz, 2007a). As one action sports website writes: 'Montoya embraces his urban roots which many deem refreshing in a sport generally ruled by young suburbanites' ('Athlete Bio', no date, para. 1). While the snowboarding field remains largely dominated by young, white males who continue to dictate tastes, styles, and legitimate uses of the boarding body, the intersection between race, masculinity, and capital is interesting and deserves further attention. As I explain further in Chapter 6, some professional female snowboarders are also drawing on their femininity as a unique source of capital in their efforts to construct marketable identities. In sum, for a few top snowboarders, particularly those, like DeMarchi and Montoya, who recognize, and are prepared to capitalize on, their characteristics of distinction, the accumulation of symbolic capital and cultural capital merges with the accumulation of economic capital.

Bourdieu and the boarding body: some final thoughts

In sum, Bourdieu's conceptual schema enables an examination of the intricate cultural details surrounding the meaning and use of the body in the snowboarding culture, and how such practices influence the everyday experiences of participants from different groups and positions within the field. Snowboarders dress, speak, and behave in distinctive ways. The values attached to these practices have changed during snowboarding's short history; participants from different groups continue to struggle to preserve or transform meanings of the cultural snowboarding body. Indeed, the distinctive tastes and styles in the snowboarding culture conceal differences in power. The embodied practices of male and female snowboarders act as mechanisms that control access to the culture by selecting and rejecting new members according to both overt criteria, such as owning the latest snowboard equipment or wearing clothing from 'authentic' snowboarding brands, and covert criteria, such as demonstrations of cultural commitment and physical prowess. Simply put, the snowboarding body is a cultural and social phenomenon; it is a possessor of power, a form of status, a bearer of symbolic value, and a form of *cultural, physical* and *symbolic* capital. The symbolic values attached to these bodily forms, and the cultural legitimacy of particular forms of capital, remain crucial to many snowboarders' sense of self.

Although Bourdieu never wrote about snowboarding, his concepts are 'good to think with' (Jenkins, 2002, p. 176) and offer useful and suggestive insights into how socially competent behavior is achieved within contemporary sport and physical cultures. It is Bourdieu's proposal that key areas of culture are embodied, rather than simply 'in the mind', that is the most challenging and relevant to analyses of physical cultures such as snowboarding. As Rojek (2000) acknowledges, 'Bourdieu does succeed in revealing the complexity of performative culture in contemporary society' (p. 88). Bourdieu's conceptual schema proved useful for explaining how snowboarding culture is embodied, yet his concepts remain under-developed in a number of key areas, including understandings of lived experience, masculine and feminine identities and embodied gender relations, and the significance of space. Scholars from various disciplines, including cultural geography, sociology, youth cultural studies, education, and feminism, however, are critically (re)engaging with Bourdieu's original work, and deploying, rethinking, and developing his conceptual schema for their own ends. In the next two chapters I draw upon recent feminist engagements with some of Bourdieu's key concepts to offer fresh insights into the gendered snowboarding body. Arguably, such an approach has the potential to help us explore the hierarchies among men, and among women, as well as the relations between men and women, in the snowboarding field.

6
Female Boarding Bodies:
Betties, Babes, and Bad-Asses

Women are growing in the sport – and fast. They're out there riding hard and sacrificing their bodies to challenge and progress snowboarding. They're in videos, getting interviews, winning contests... Not to mention the fact that they're busy spending tons of money on both boards and accessories. (Chrissy Coffinger, Drake Bindings marketing manager, cited in Sherowski, 2005a, p. 54)

Of all the sports that I am aware of, snowboarding is the one where girls can compete on a level with the men. So the excuse is gone, you can't say we are all on different levels, because I've seen girls snowboard better than guys. A lot of snowboarding is about strength but it's also about balance and flexibility and state-of-mind, things that girls can excel at over boys. In many ways, snowboarding is a gender-neutral sport. (Ste'en, Olympic snowboard judge and magazine editor, personal communication, October 2005)

I see girls doing almost everything the boys are doing now. But I think girls will always be a step behind the boys. Girls are never going to be leading the sport, never. The big difference is testosterone. In order to ride the stuff these guys are riding you need to be a man, and guess what, we don't have a ball-sack... To be a really good snowboarder I don't know if you can really be a lady, it's not a ladies' sport. Even though we are really pushing it and trying to make it a ladies' sport, it's a man's sport... we are the minority. (Monique, committed US snowboarder, personal communication, November 2005)

The female snowboarder is a recent social phenomenon. Unlike many modern and some alternative sports, women participated in the early forms of snowboarding (see Anderson, 1999; Thorpe, 2005). Although fewer in number than men, women participated alongside their male counterparts, in such a way that the activity was not 'burdened with the years of entrenched

sexism that plagues most sports' (Robinson, 2002, p. 4). Since its emergence
in the late 1970s, women have progressively negotiated new space within
the male-dominated sport, culture, and industry, such that today they are
participating in an array of snowboarding styles at various levels (novice,
weekend warrior, core, and professional) with a sense of enthusiasm and
entitlement unknown to most of their mothers and grandmothers. In the
United States, the number of female snowboarders has more than doubled
in the past decade (NGSA, 2005a). In 1994 only 20 percent of snowboarders
were female; by 2003 women made up approximately 34.3 percent (Ibid.).
A study completed by Label Networks in 2005 showed three times as many
young American women wanting to learn to snowboard in the next five
years as young men. Other market analysts have identified the women's
market as the 'fastest growing aspect of snowboarding' ('Women's market',
2001, para. 4). Women also increasingly hold positions of responsibility in
the industry as manufacturers, CEOs, filmmakers, publishers, journalists,
and event organizers.

Not only are female snowboarders increasingly receiving their share of
the substantial prize monies, but the inclusion of professional female snowboarders in globally televised events including the X-Games and Olympics,
and video games, such as *Cool Boarders*, and blockbuster movies, such as
First Descent (2005), has added to the visibility and legitimization of female
boarders. Indeed, professional female snowboarders, including Gretchen
Bleiler, Torah Bright, Kelly Clark, Tara Dakides, Lindsey Jacobellis, and
Hannah Teter, have achieved superstar status within the culture, attracting
corporate sponsors including Nike, Mountain Dew, Campbell's Soup, Visa,
and Boost Mobile. Some earn seven-figure salaries (Settimi, 2010). Clearly
women are a visible feature of contemporary snowboarding and popular
culture. Yet women's snowboarding is a complicated and multidimensional
phenomenon interwoven with numerous political, cultural, biological,
social, and economic events and processes. In light of such complexities,
some challenging questions arise. How do we make meaning of young
women's experiences of opportunity and constraint within sport and physical cultures in the early twenty-first century? How can we explain the various ways in which gender is practiced, embodied, reinforced, challenged
and negotiated, in contemporary physical cultures such as snowboarding?
Before I attempt to answer these questions, it is necessary to briefly contextualize this discussion within the broader field of feminist scholarship on
gender and the body.

Feminism, gender, and the body

Prior to the emergence of second-wave feminism in the late 1960s and
1970s, most scholars assumed that gender was a 'natural' phenomenon that
did not require explanation (Waters, 2000).[1] Thus for much of the history

of sociological theory, gender remained under-analyzed. Second-wave feminist scholars, however, put gender on the map of social theorizing. They argued that gender could no longer be explained purely in biological terms, but needed to be located within social relations, institutions, and practices (Howson, 2005). While gender-specific bodily experiences, such as reproduction and sexuality, 'exert powerful forces in shaping the individual's self-conception and position in the social world', no experience is strictly 'limited to biology' (Krais, 2006, p. 127). Feminist scholarship during this period revealed understandings of the feminine (and masculine) body as intimately shaped by the 'symbolic order of gender' – that is, 'body ideals, a sense of one's place in a society's patterns of subordination and domination, a sense of honour and shame, [and] ways of presenting the body in terms of what is revealed and what is hidden' (Krais, 2006, p. 128) – and always localized in a particular place and time. Put simply, feminists placed on the agenda the project of 'reexploring, re-examining, notions of female corporeality' (Grosz, 1994, p. 14). In so doing, they opened up the relationships between biology, culture and society, body and mind, and sex and gender, for critical scrutiny, interrogation, and debate. Their work has been widely acknowledged as making a 'significant contribution to the flourishing and diverse interest in the body' (Shilling, 2005, p. 2).

Feminist scholars from an array of fields, including sociology, history, geography, anthropology, and cultural studies, continue to contribute to debates about the relations between gender, the body, and masculinity and femininity (Grosz, 1994; Howson, 2005). Feminist scholarship on gender and the body ranges from the level of experience and concern with body politics, such as women's health projects, sexual violence, and pornography, to problems of bodily regulation and discipline. Speaking from and across various disciplines, feminist scholars draw on an array of methodological and theoretical perspectives to address key issues relating to women's (and men's) social, cultural, political, lived, interacting and/or gendered bodies in different sociocultural-political contexts. It is beyond the scope of this chapter to summarize all of these developments, or the wide-reaching effects of feminist scholarship on the 'corporeal turn' in the social sciences and humanities; a number of excellent resources have achieved these tasks (see Davis, 1997; Howson, 2005; McNay, 2000). Rather, here I am particularly interested in recent feminist engagements with the work of Pierre Bourdieu.

In this chapter I consider the potential of a gendered (re)reading of Bourdieu's original work for extending theorizing of the gendered body in sport and physical culture, and answering complex questions about women's experiences of agency and constraint in the early twenty-first century.[2] The following discussion consists of two parts. First, I draw upon feminist engagements with Bourdieu's concepts of capital, field and habitus, respectively, to offer insights into some of the complexities of gender and embodiment in the snowboarding culture. Second, I consider how the gender-habitus-field complex can illustrate the 'synchronous nature of constraint and freedom' (McNay, 2000, p. 61) for women in contemporary physical cultures such as snowboarding. Here I explain how crossing within and across various fields prompts gender reflexivity among some women. The resulting discussion reveals that, while there needs to be much more sustained attention to the gendered dimensions of his conceptual schema, theoretical syntheses between feminism and Bourdieu offer new ways to productively reconceptualize the relationship between gender, power, structure, agency, reflexivity, culture, and embodiment in sport and physical culture.

Bourdieu, feminism, and female boarding bodies: gendering capital, field, and habitus

For many years, Pierre Bourdieu had little to say about women or gender, with most of his writings framed predominantly in class. In the article 'La Domination Masculine' (1990b), however, Bourdieu draws upon his ethnographic research into the Kabyle of North Africa to show how 'masculine domination assumes a natural, self-evident status through its inscription in the objective structures of the social world', which is then embodied and reproduced in the habitus of individuals (McNay, 2000, p. 37). Although Kabyle is a peasant culture and his data were gathered during the 1960s, Bourdieu claims it exemplifies the ways in which gender hierarchies are maintained in modern industrial society. The publication of 'Masculine Domination' drew almost no reaction from feminist sociologists. It was only when the book version was released in 2001 that Bourdieu's analysis was noticed. However, it evoked strong criticisms from feminist scholars who argued that it presents an ahistorical, androcentric worldview and is 'largely restricted to analyzing the structural constraints of masculine domination' (Fowler, 2003, p. 479). According to McLeod (2005), Bourdieu 'writes defensively' in *Masculine Domination*, and 'appears somewhat oblivious to the diverse range of important feminist work that has historicized gender division. Moreover, his insights into gender reproduce standard binaries of masculine domination and female subordination as if these structures are unitary, coherent and unchanged by and in contemporary social life.' (p. 53).

Despite such criticisms, some feminist scholars, including Adkins (2003), Fowler (1997), Krais (2006), Lovell (2000), McCall (1992), McLeod (2005), McNay (1999, 2000), Moi (1991) and Skeggs (1997, 2004), recognized the potential in Bourdieu's social theory for 'deepening and developing' (Walby, 2005, p. 376) feminist theorizing, and set about deploying, rethinking, and critically developing his conceptual schema. In the remainder of this chapter I introduce some of the recent arguments offered by these scholars and explore the potential of their critical engagements with Bourdieu's original work for extending theorizing of gender and the body in sport and physical culture. More specifically, I adopt a gendered reading of Bourdieu's concepts of capital, field, and habitus, respectively, to examine women's snowboarding experiences, focusing particularly on some of the subtle negotiations of gendered power relations within the snowboarding culture.

Capital and gender

For Bourdieu (1986), the power of an agent to accumulate various forms of capital (economic, social, cultural, symbolic, linguistic, academic, and corporeal) and to define those forms as legitimate, is proportionate to their position in social space. While Bourdieu allocates much space in his work to exploring the various forms of capital and the embodied strategies and struggles over such resources, he does not recognize women as typically capital-accumulating subjects. Rather, they are 'capital bearing objects' whose value accrues to the primary groups to which they belong (e.g., husband, family) (Lovell, 2000; Skeggs, 2004). Feminist scholars, however, maintain that many women do pursue capital-accumulating strategies (see, for example, Moi, 1991; Skeggs, 1997). Similar observations can be made in the snowboarding culture where core female boarders are increasingly gaining symbolic capital from their snowboarding abilities and commitment to the sport.

Symbolic capital and the female boarding body

Snowboarders assess symbolic capital in terms of style, commitment, ability on challenging terrain, and difficulty and range of maneuvers able to be performed (see Chapter 5). For many years, only the most committed males enjoyed access to symbolic capital. During the mid-1990s and 2000s, however, male boarders began to recognize and praise their female counterparts for displays of physical prowess and courage. Recalling his first experience riding with Amy Howitt, professional boarder Todd Richards (2003) admitted his expectations were 'pretty low', but he quickly conceded that she 'hit big jumps and grabbed airs: rocket airs, mutes, methods' and most importantly 'earned my respect' (p. 64). After performing a 720-degree spin maneuver at the 1998 Winter X-Games, Tina Basich (2003) remembers a few male pro snowboarders 'telling me that they couldn't yet do that trick. They looked at me a little differently – they were truly impressed' (p. 134). It should be added here that the criteria upon which female snowboarders are judged by males and females alike often differ from those of male boarders. Displays of high performance by a female snowboarder are often met with surprise: 'whoa, you're a girl? That's amazing' (Moriah, personal communication, November 2005).

Female boarders who embody the legitimate traits of physical prowess, skill, risk-taking, and courage can earn symbolic capital in the snowboarding culture. Yet my analysis reveals some gender disparities in the distribution and transferability of symbolic capital. In the contemporary snowboarding culture, the distribution of capital remains limited and largely determined by a male valuation system. Arguably, Bourdieu's theories of symbolic violence and misrecognition help explain the subordination of women's activity (Krais, 1993; McRobbie, 2004), and the subsequent unequal distribution of symbolic capital in the snowboarding culture. According to Bourdieu, symbolic violence is the imposition of systems of symbolism and meaning upon groups or classes in such a way that they are experienced as legitimate (Jenkins, 2002b). This has been achieved through a process Bourdieu calls 'misrecognition', whereby 'power relations are perceived not for what they objectively are but in a form which renders them legitimate in the eyes of the beholder' (Bourdieu & Passerson, 1977, cited in Jenkins, 2002b, p. 104).

As the following comments from Moriah illustrate, some women accept the biological explanations offered for their 'inferior' performances, even when there is no validity for such explanations: 'Boys are always stronger than girls...no matter what, and to be a really good snowboarder you need to be strong...strong girls are never going to be as strong as the top guys. Jana Meyhen, she's the raddest girl snowboarder there is. For us girls, we are like "wow she can do that?" But to the boys, she ain't shit. I mean she's good for a girl but there is no girl that boys can think "wow she's as good as I am"' (personal communication, November 2005). Phillipa also identifies biological differences in risk-taking and physical prowess in snowboarding: 'If I think about the whole girl/boy thing, the only thing I find most frustrating is the physical element...not pushing yourself or going to the same limits as boys. I always admired how boys could have less fear. Girls have so much more self-preservation' (personal communication, September 2005). Even though some female snowboarders, such as Olympians and professionals, display particular combinations of force and skill much more effectively than many male boarders, the persistence of beliefs in 'normal' differences in physical ability reinforces males' ability to accumulate symbolic capital and undermines women's participation in snowboarding.

Symbolic violence in the snowboarding culture not only reinforces the assumption that male boarders are more deserving of symbolic capital, but also their ability to convert symbolic to economic capital. For example, when *Transworld Snowboarding* recently asked readers to respond to the question 'should female riders get paid as much as the dudes [male snowboarders]?', most correspondents emphasized male superiority: 'guys can throw bigger tricks, so why not pay them more' (Chelsea, Ontario); 'If the girls are as good as the guys, then yes. But if they're not, then to hell with this equality crap' (Sean, Florida) ('In your', 2005, p. 54). Bourdieu's notion of symbolic violence thus helps shed light on snowboarding as a male-dominated sport in which male views tend to have the most power to construct experiences and opportunities. Yet female snowboarders are not passive in these processes; some actively negotiate space within the snowboarding field using an array of embodied practices and strategies. Some women, for example, are drawing upon their gender and femininity as a unique source of capital.

Gender capital

While symbolic, cultural, and economic capital are central to the structuring of Bourdieu's conception of social space, gender does not appear in his fundamental structuring principles. Bourdieu (1986) briefly acknowledges that 'certain women derive occupational profit from their charm(s), and that beauty thus acquires a value on the labour market' (p. 245). Yet he paid little attention to the relationship between gender and capital, and generally did not consider gender to be a form of capital. For Kay and Laberge (2002), Bourdieu's (1984) treatment of gender as a 'secondary' constituent of social division contradicts claims elsewhere in his work that gender is a major principle of social stratification. Since the early 1990s, however, a number of feminist scholars have argued that women not only accumulate capital, but also possess their own *feminine* forms of capital (Huppatz, 2009; Lovell, 2000; McCall, 1992; Skeggs, 1997, 2004). According to Skeggs (1997), femininity is embodied, but it is also a learned competency and thus may operate as a form of capital.[3] Femininity, as cultural capital, is 'the discursive position available through gender relations that women are encouraged to inhabit and use. Its use will be informed by the network of social positions of class, gender, sexuality, region, age and race which ensure that it will be taken up (and resisted) in different ways' (Skeggs, 1997, p. 10). Also arguing for a positive engagement between Bourdieu's social theory and contemporary feminist theory, Lovell (2000) believes femininity as a form of cultural capital has increasing currency in the contemporary labor market.

Building upon earlier feminist work, Huppatz (2009) recently distinguished between *female* capital – the gender advantage derived from being perceived to have a female (but not necessarily feminine) body – and *feminine* capital – the gender advantage derived from a disposition or skill set learned via socialization, or simply when members of a particular field recognize one's body as feminine – and described women capitalizing on their femaleness and femininity within particular occupations (e.g., paid caring work) to gain an income. It is important to note, however, that while the traditional feminine ideal continues to be encouraged and venerated in certain fields, notions of culturally valuable forms of femininity are constantly evolving and differ within and across fields; women wield femininity and femaleness as forms of capital in an array of innovative ways within different social fields (family, workforce, education, and sport). The gender norms, identities, and behaviors available to female snowboarders differ from those in other social fields. For example, Tina Basich describes the snowboarding field in the late 1980s as offering her group of female snowboarding friends a liberating alternative to the emphasized femininity celebrated at their local high school: 'we were the misfits of the misfits – the anticheerleaders.

We didn't fit in [at high school]. Snowboarding was a savior to us' (Basich, 2003, p. xi).

The snowboarding field offers space for some women to embrace alternative female identities and gender norms. Yet abundant evidence also demonstrates traditionally defined heterosexual femininity as a potential form of cultural capital in the snowboarding field. For example, professional boarder Michele Taggart remembered female snowboarders in the late 1980s and early 1990s being 'included [in media coverage] because of their cuteness and their beautiful hair' (cited in Howe, 1998, p. 64). Femininities, like masculinities, are assets in the snowboarding market, tradable for economic if not symbolic capital (Lovell, 2000). Committed Australian boarder Colin's response to the question 'what qualities does a female snowboarder need to become a professional?' is enlightening here:

> Determination and the ability to huck it with the boys. Looks help... However, Janna Meyen has got to the top of the game without relying on looks, by showing as much balls and determination, throwing down on the rails and slope-style course as any guy. (personal communication, August 2004)

As this comment suggests, not all female snowboarders have access to femininity as a form of cultural capital. Moreover, within the contemporary snowboarding field, different groups of females privilege different forms of cultural investment. Whereas some female boarders, such as Janna Meyen, acquire symbolic capital by demonstrating the traditionally defined 'masculine' traits of physical prowess, risk, and commitment, others overtly employ their femininity as a form of capital (see also Kelly et al., 2005; Wheaton & Tomlinson, 1998).

A great deal has been written about women's investments in their bodies as gendered and sexual. As previous research has revealed, different women take different views of gender capital and their opinions are often shaped by context (Moi, 1991; Skeggs, 1997). In the contemporary snowboarding culture, women's capital investment and accumulation strategies differ depending on their position within the snowboarding field (professional, core, weekend warrior, novice, or poseur), and other social fields (class, race, nationality, education, family, other sports, and workplace). Observing the investment strategies of less committed female participants, Jackie noted: 'I always see girls in the bathrooms on the hill putting on more make-up and shit. Maybe they will take a couple of runs during the day, but they are really just there to hang out in the lodge, look cute and either wait for their boyfriends or find a boyfriend' (personal communication, June, 2003). In contrast to marginal female participants who tend to be unfamiliar with the unique capital valuation system within the snowboarding field, many core female snowboarders learn through the process of enculturation that symbolic capital (not gender or feminine capital) is the most legitimate and highly valued form of capital in the contemporary snowboarding field. This cultural knowledge informs their capital-accumulating decisions and investment strategies. Core New Zealand snowboarder Phillipa, for example, prefers 'to be recognized for my skills and style, not my looks' and thus actively avoids adopting traditionally defined 'feminine' traits on the mountain, such as 'applying lipstick and batting my mascara-covered eyelashes at everyone on the chairlift' (personal communication, February 2005). American core snowboarder Jamie described herself as 'a big tomboy': 'there is nothing feminine about me on the mountain. I like to be aggressive, wear big baggy outerwear and don't care what I look like' (personal communication, February 2005). Similarly, Tara Dakides describes herself on the mountain, as 'probably the furthest thing from feminine...when I get frustrated and mad, I can't help but throw mini tantrums or yell...aggressive sports call for a little aggression at times' (Ulmer & Straus, 2002, para. 5). Dakides confesses that although she tried to conform to gendered expectations and 'be nice', it 'always felt forced', so eventually accepted 'I just had to be me' (Elliot, 2001, para. 13).

An important issue here, however, is that in the male-defined symbolic structure of snowboarding, whatever form of capital female snowboarders possess in one respect, they often lose in others. For example, women choosing to privilege feminine capital are often written off as 'snow bunnies' uncommitted to the activity itself, while those who prioritize traditionally defined masculine capital and position themselves in opposition to the culturally valued discourse of stereotypical femininity may experience ideological constraints, (e.g., accusations of being 'butch lesbians' (Field notes, 2005), and/or difficulty converting their symbolic capital into economic capital, such as sponsorship or media coverage. In other cases, the embrace of stereotypical 'feminine' traits tends to distract the attention of male boarders and the snowboarding media away from female boarders' physical skills and towards their physical appearance. For example, *Transworld Snowboarding* admitted, 'Torah is so cute it's easy to overlook her talent on the snowboard' ('Check out', February, 2005, p. 101). According to Bourdieu (2001), it is common for women to experience a 'double bind' when attempting to access power: 'if they behave like men, they risk losing the obligatory attributes of "femininity" and call into question the natural right of men to the positions of power; if they behave like women, they appear incapable and unfit for the job' (p. 67).

In the contemporary snowboarding field, however, some women appear to be overcoming this quandary by blurring the boundaries that divide the two. Some of the female participants demonstrate a traditional 'masculine' capacity for aggression and dominance, and have simultaneously mastered the 'feminine' arts of image management. For example, professional boarder Victoria Jealouse described 'jumping off roofs and out of trees since I was a little kid' but, as far as she is concerned, this 'doesn't mean I'm not feminine. I love being a woman' (Ulmer & Straus, 2001, para. 6). U.S. Olympic silver medalist Lindsey Jacobellis also claims: 'I'm not just a hard-core athlete. I'm a girly-girl too' (Berra, 2006, para. 11). Opportunities to convert cultural and symbolic capital into economic capital currently abound for a select few women who are able (and willing) to accumulate both symbolic capital *and* feminine capital.

According to Gill (2008), the 'fun, fearless, young, attractive, heterosexual woman who knowingly and deliberately plays with her sexual power' became a dominant figure in advertising during the mid- and late-1990s (p. 41); Owen et al. (2007) describe similar trends in the representation of young women in film and television programming. Combining a courageous and powerful riding style with 'a rad SoCal style, gnarly fashion sense, lovely looks, and sense of humour', professional U.S. snowboarder Tara Dakides became snowboarding's archetypal 'sexy bad girl' during this period (Athlete Bios, 2002, p. 1). A journalist describes the commercial appeal of Dakides' alternative femininity as 'a knockout combo of skill, swagger and sex appeal', adding 'it helps that she's beautiful: deep green eyes, toothpaste-ad grin, a hyperathletic body, biceps bulging and abs rippling...pierced nostril and belly button, and an intriguing tattoo' (Elliot, 2001, para. 2). Similarly, Reed (2005) writes: 'though she may ride (and cuss and spit) like a guy on the snow, that's where it ends. There's no question, she's sexy with a capital X. Indeed, her unique combination of skill and sex appeal helped to cross yet another threshold – that of mainstream pop-culture' (p. 164). Dakides achieved broader celebrity status featuring in *Rolling Stone, Sports Illustrated, Maxim, FHM,* and *Sports Illustrated for Women;* the latter named her 'The Coolest Sports Woman in 2001'. Embodying a unique combination of physicality, femininity and sexuality, Dakides has garnered more media coverage and corporate sponsorships than any female snowboarder before her. The extensive mass and niche media coverage of Dakides has provided a much needed source of inspiration for many female boarders. According to one core female snowboarder, 'I was never really inspired by girls until Tara Dakides in 1998. I really looked up to Tara, not only did she rip, but she was also a gorgeous girl. I think it's important to be able to step it up on the hill and still have a bit of femininity too' (Moriah, personal communication, July 2008). Yet Gill (2008) cautions against 'too easy' celebrations of 'empowered sexual agency' as seen in the representations of popular cultural icons such as Dakides and other 'midriff advertising', arguing that such representations exclude 'any woman who is unable to live up to increasingly narrow standards of female beauty and sex appeal that are normatively required' (p. 44).

In the contemporary snowboarding field, a few women are profiting from their investments in femininity. However, a number of feminist scholars warn that feminine capital is a limited currency and 'always operates within constraints' (Huppatz, 2009, p. 61). But it is not always easy to 'distinguish the difference between women's "capital accumulating strategies" and the use of women by others as bearers of capital value' (Lovell, 2000, p. 25). While female snowboarders' investments in feminine capital may appear to be no more than another example of 'women functioning to produce and reproduce social capital, creating ties between men which serve men's interests' (Ibid.) – and this may be one of the things it does – we should be cautious of overlooking or misinterpreting practices in which women are active agents with stakes in the field, and which are in large part self-interested. Professional boarder Gretchen Bleiler, for example, understands that 'times are tough, and it's crucially important to seize every opportunity in order to make the most of your career', adding 'trust me, I know ... I was featured dressed up in body paint on the cover of *FHM*' (Bleiler, January 2005, p. 60; see Chapter 4). In another interview she demanded that sponsors 'whip out your chequebooks' and 'show me the money' (cited in Sherowski, 2004b, p. 48).

Clearly, some of the younger generation of professional female snowboarders understand well the cultural valuation systems of the distinct, but overlapping, fields of snowboarding and the sport and physical culture industries. Drawing on this knowledge, they employ an array of gender and symbolic capital-accumulating strategies to negotiate space for themselves within and between these fields. Many of the female athletes who embrace their sexuality to boost their public profile and image, and reap the financial benefits, have embodied neo-liberal discourses of individualism and entrepreneurialism (see Gill, 2008; Heywood, 2006), and tend to show limited awareness of the unintended broader consequences of their actions. These young women exist, as Baumgardner and Richards (2000) put it, in a state of 'pre-consciousness' and they 'haven't yet had the opportunity to examine the politics of their own lives' (p. 84). However, some women do deliberate the broader implications of their actions. On receiving an offer to pose in a *Playboy* feature on women in extreme sports, Tina Basich's first reaction was 'Hell no!' but she admits that 'curiosity led me to call them back' (Basich, 2003, pp. 191–192). She gave the offer serious consideration but, following discussions with her parents and analyzing the content of *Playboy*, concluded that she did not belong in the magazine. Importantly, the opinions of female participants regarding appropriate strategies (i.e., the ownership and celebration of feminine dispositions) for gaining space and access to resources within the snowboarding field and broader sports and popular cultural industries, are also informed by their position and experiences in other social fields, including generation, sexuality, and religion. For example, despite numerous offers, Australian professional snowboarder Torah Bright refuses to feature in any '*FHM*-style' photo-shoots because of her 'religion' ('Questions for', 2005, para. 7). In her own words, 'I'm Mormon, so I personally would not do it. We are taught that our bodies are our most sacred things. I definitely would never do anything like that to better my career, but each to their own' (Ibid.).

Perhaps Bourdieu had difficulty explaining women's capital preferences and accumulating abilities because, despite recognizing that women play a significant role in the processes of the gendered accumulation of capital, he rarely considered women as subjects with capital-accumulating strategies of their own. Drawing on the work of feminist scholars, however, we are encouraged to (re)consider the kinds of 'investment strategies' women follow in particular circumstances. Here I have suggested that women's understanding of the cultural valuation system, and thus their interpretive and capital-calculating and -accumulating strategies, differ depending on their position within the snowboarding field (professional, core, weekend warrior, novice), as well as their experiences in other social fields (religion, nationality, race, sexuality, generation, class, education, family, other sports and leisure activities). In the second part of this chapter I build on this discussion by employing a feminist interpretation of Bourdieu's habitus-field nexus and, in so doing, recognize agency and reflexivity as central to understanding both young women's capital-accumulating strategies, and how they negotiate their gendered habitus across different fields.

While there needs to be much more sustained attention to the gendered dimensions of Bourdieu's notion of capital, I believe it has the potential to offer a powerful resource for theorizing relations of power and privilege in contemporary society and physical cultures. Any questions regarding the 'capitals' possessed by women, the composition of those capitals, their trajectory over time, and the control of their deployment, however, must be related to historical and cultural contexts and to the positions occupied by women within particular fields (Lovell, 2000; Skeggs, 1997, 2004).

Field and gender

Bourdieu failed to consider the full implications of the concept of field in his work on gender. However, other theorists claim that field has the potential to illuminate some of the 'complexity and multilayeredness' of relations between the sexes in contemporary social life (Mottier, 2002, p. 355). Krais (2006), for example, argues that gender does not constitute a specific social field as it is sometimes assumed, but 'enters into the "game" of different social fields in ways specific to each field' (p. 128). Rather than a specific, autonomous field, gender is far better conceptualized as 'part of a field' because, according to Adkins (2004), gender is 'extraordinarily relational, with a chameleon-like flexibility, shifting in importance, value and effects from context to context or from field to field' (p. 6). Thus, while all fields contain and enforce a set of gender rules, some of these rules may be common to many other fields, whereas others may be specific to that field (Chambers, 2005). For example, the field of snowboarding overlaps strongly with the surfing and skateboarding fields and thus shares some similar cultural value systems, including some common gender rules (e.g., female surf, skate and snow boarders who demonstrate considerable physical prowess and cultural commitment typically have access to symbolic capital from their peers). Yet these fields are not identical. As Wheaton (2004) has explained, action sports such as surfing, skateboarding and snowboarding also have distinctive histories, environments, geographies, identities, and development patterns, as well as gender norms. Thus the opportunities for a female boarder to convert symbolic capital into economic capital differ vastly between the snow, surf and skate fields, with female skateboarders typically having the least potential to do so within the hypermasculine symbolic structure of skateboarding (see Atencio et al., 2009; Beal, 1996; Thorpe, 2006; see also Laurendeau & Sharara, 2008).

In Chapter 5, I described the contemporary snowboarding culture as highly fragmented. Geography, commitment, equipment, ability, bodily disposition, and clothing styles, reinforce the position of 'established' groups and marginal 'outsider' groups. Importantly, gender is not the primary principle of division in the snowboarding field. Rather, female boarders hold distinctive positions in each of the groups that make up the snowboarding field (professionals, core, weekend warriors, and poseurs). The legitimate forms of femininity (and masculinity) differ between these groups. The influx of female participants during the late 1990s and 2000s, for example, saw individuals and groups increasingly clash over the meaning of their social identity, the legitimate use of the female boarding body, and the cultural value attributed to various forms of capital, both gender and symbolic. In particular, ideological differences caused divisions between committed female boarders and recreational boarders, and those whose participation is based on fashion, social status, and heterosexual pursuits. Jenni indicates the hostility: 'Girls who do things like stare at boys and sit in the pipe and on the sidelines of the park are just f**king poseurs. They need to get a life and go have a sleepover in their thongs' ('Girls and', 2003). Importantly, such comments allude not only to the divisions between groups of female boarders but also to a division between core and noncore boarders with the former demonstrating a commitment to the activity itself and thereby bearing an 'authentic' cultural identity. This division is far more important than gender.

It is also important to note that gender relations are not produced in an invariant way across the snowboarding field. In Bourdieu's (1984) own words: 'Sexual properties are as inseparable from class properties as the yellowness of a lemon is from its acidity: a class is defined in an essential respect by the place and value it gives to the two sexes and to their socially constituted dispositions' (p. 107). Put simply, class and gender are always intimately connected.[4] This is why, in a highly fragmented snowboarding field, 'there are as many ways of realizing femininity as there are classes and class fractions' (Ibid., p. 109). The interactions between men and women, and the most valued types of capital, vary between and within different classes or groups, such as core, weekend warriors, novices, and pro-hos, in the contemporary snowboarding field.

Core female boarders typically participate alongside their male peers. Hana, a top New Zealand snowboarder who rides, lives, works, and travels with a group of 'guys', negotiated space within the group by riding fast, keeping up with the boys, and dismissing 'boy talk' that sexualizes and degrades other women (personal communication, April 2006). By demonstrating physical prowess and commitment, and ignoring symbolic violence (e.g., boy talk), Hana earned symbolic and cultural capital, and thus a place among her male peers. Yet she was conscious that other women are excluded from this group: 'They treat me like one of the boys but I've seen them treat their girlfriends much worse' (personal communication, April 2006). Similarly, core female snowboarder Moriah described her experiences within an all-male group:

> We go out, and there will be 10 of us, and I'll be the only girl. ... Sometimes I'm even better than some of those guys. We are all just out there to have fun ... all of my snowboarder friends are supportive of one another. If you fall, no big deal, that's part of the fun ... but you have to get up fast, otherwise you'll be left behind. ... I'm definitely the only girl. Most of my snowboarder guy friends know to leave their girlfriends at home or in the café if they will slow us down. (personal communication, November, 2005)

Many core male snowboarders also enjoy sharing the snowboarding experience with their committed and proficient female friends. As one core male boarder explained: 'I love riding with girls with good skills. I think it's great when we can all ride together. There aren't many sports or pastimes where you can do that and have that much fun' (Nick, personal communication, April 2006).

In contrast, the following narrative from a novice Canadian female snowboarder highlights how some less skilled women experience and explain their exclusion from groups of recreational male boarders:

> I went snowboarding with [my boyfriend] and a couple of his buddies. This was one of the worst experiences for me. He went riding with his friends, and I rode alone for the day. I really don't think it was a gender thing, they are really nice guys and if I'd been a better snowboarder, I think I would have been *allowed* to ride with them. ... But they always expect me to not be as tough as them. If I get frostbite or are bummed out about something they are sensitive: 'Are you too cold, honey?' 'Do you want to go inside for a bit?' But they are much harder on each other. Them treating me that way, sort of babying me, I think, unconsciously gives them a sense of 'ok, girls are still not at our level, this is still something

I'm doing with the guys'. (personal communication, November 2005, emphasis added)

Pro-hos (snowboarding's equivalent of groupies) are the least respected in the snowboarding field, as illustrated in the coarse words of the following male boarder: 'Pro-hos just hang around with pro riders because they think it will make them cool-by-association and help them get into the good parties…Most of them don't even snowboard. All a pro-ho is good for is a suck-off' (Tom, personal communication, August 2004).[5]

The key point here is that female boarders experience gender differently, depending on their position within the snowboarding field. It is also important to note, however, that women's positions within the snowboarding field are dynamic, and their motives can change over time. The following comments from long-time core snowboarder Melissa are revealing here: 'I started snowboarding in 1997 because…I don't want to say, this is embarrassing, this is not why I snowboard now…Well, the first boy I ever loved was a snowboarder. He moved to the mountains…and I followed…' (personal communication, November 2005). Thus, while many women enter the snowboarding field as 'girlfriends' of male snowboarders (or as 'poseurs' or 'pro-hos'), some continue to become active, highly proficient and committed participants. Moreover, as young committed female snowboarders move out of the core of the snowboarding field and embrace more adult responsibilities, such as motherhood, full-time employment, mortgages, marriage and so on, their participation within the field also tends to change (see also Chapter 8). For example, Pamela, an ex-professional snowboarder and instructor, explained that 'with motherhood and my Masters study, snowboarding is no longer my main priority' (personal communication, July 2008). Continuing, however, she describes looking forward to returning to the mountains as 'a family' and enjoying new forms of participation: 'the next person I teach will be my daughter…this is something I am just so excited about, words fail me' (personal communication, July 2008). As Spowart et al. (2008) explain, while the snowboarding experience changes for many women (and men) when they become parents, some snowboarding mothers employ an array of creative strategies, such as use of childcare, sharing parental responsibilities on the mountain with their partner, and support from other snowboarding mothers, to continue participation and negotiate new space within the snowboarding field.

In conclusion, this examination of the interaction of gender and social group distinction in the snowboarding field supports Bourdieu's claim that gender is a secondary principle of division. The embodied practices of snowboarders suggest that an individual's initial capital is gender-neutral, being fundamentally defined by their relative position in the structure based on their ability, commitment to the activity, and lifestyle. But, as illustrated by the 'core' female boarders, 'novices', 'girlies', and 'pro-hos', the legitimate forms of snowboarding femininity, preferred forms of capital (e.g., symbolic, gender), and gender relations, differ between groups. Of the various groups, it seems that core females have the most space to define and redefine cultural meanings pertaining to the female boarding body within the contemporary snowboarding field. Yet the rules structuring the snowboarding culture, and the gender relations within it, are not fixed but inherently contested by those within the field. Moreover, these struggles are not solely between men and women, but also between women (and between men) occupying different spaces within the field.

Habitus, gender, and female boarding bodies

Throughout his work, Bourdieu took cognizance of the fact that men and women use and manage their bodies in very different ways in most cultures. Yet it was not until late in his career that he attempted to explain how this type of learning, which affects men's and women's perceptions of their bodies and selves, does not occur at the cognitive level but at the bodily level (Burkitt, 1999). In other words, Bourdieu was concerned with how gendered norms, and particularly gender inequality, become embodied. The concept of habitus is central here. Gendered habitus broadly refers to the 'social construction of masculinity and femininity that shapes the body, defines how the body is perceived, forms the body's habits and possibilities for expression, and thus determines the individual's identity – via the body – as masculine or feminine' (Krais, 2006, p. 121). According to Bourdieu (1997), gender is an 'absolutely fundamental dimension of the habitus that, like the sharps and clefs in music, modifies all the social qualities that are connected to the fundamental social factors' (translated by Krais, 2006, p. 128). Put slightly differently, the gender-specificity of habitus is among the fundamental elements of a person's identity primarily because it 'touches the individual in an aspect of his/her self that is generally seen as "pure nature": the body' (Krais, 2006, p. 121). Indeed, it is with this bodily reference that gender differentiation becomes 'deeply and firmly' anchored in the habitus (Ibid.).

Since a central element of Bourdieu's work is his argument that habitus develops in response to field, it seems logical to ask which field is responsible for the development of a gendered habitus (Chambers, 2005). For Bourdieu (1992), the habitus, which 'at every moment, structures new experiences in accordance with the structures produced by past experiences' is 'modified by new experiences... [to] bring about a unique integration' (p. 60). Early experiences, however, have particular weight because the habitus 'tends to ensure its own constancy and its defense against change through the selection it makes within new information by rejecting information capable of calling into question its accumulated information' (Ibid., p. 60). He views the dispositions, which make up gendered habitus, as the products of opportunities and constraints framing the individual's earlier life experiences. They are 'durably inculcated by the possibilities and impossibilities, freedoms and necessities, opportunities and prohibitions inscribed in the objective conditions' (Ibid., p. 54).

The confusion here, however, occurs when we try to understand how this gendered habitus, instilled from an early age, intersects with the snowboarding habitus, embodied later in life by many core female boarders via enculturation into the snowboarding field. As the following comments from Moriah suggest, the weight of past experiences or, rather, the gendered habitus instilled from childhood, continues to influence the way some female snowboarders think about their bodies:

> We are girls... we still have that feminine aspect. I think it's really hard to overcome that, and you feel like you still have to be a lady. But in order to ride this stuff, you need to have serious balls. When I can't do something, I say that it's 'cos I'm not a boy but, really, fuck that, there should be no difference between girls and boys, right? We are capable of doing anything we wanna do, right? But sometimes it's just so hard to get over that negative way of thinking... sometimes you just can't do it. (personal communication, November 2005)

Here, Moriah voices confusion in mediating the new social messages about the potential of the female body ('girls can do anything') and her deeply entrenched gendered habitus ('I can't do something...cos I'm not a boy'). But Moriah adds an interesting caveat:

> The young ten-year-old girls aren't going to be thinking like this. They've grown up with way more role models and stuff. These are the girls that are gonna be fucken doing it, and we are going to be the old ladies that will be like...'Yeah, we wanted to do it but it was just so hard'. (personal communication, November 2005)

As this comment implies, habitus is context-specific. Women will inevitably experience snowboarding in diverse ways based on the gendered habitus instilled during childhood in different historical periods and in different social, cultural, and political contexts.

A particular strength of habitus is that it introduces a temporal dimension to an understanding of the body that is 'missing in many accounts of gender' (McNay, 1999, p. 102). However, while the 'praxeological notion of time embedded in the concept of habitus' highlights the 'uncertainties inherent in even the most routine act of reproduction', it also 'underscores the entrenched nature of normative social identity' (Ibid., p. 103). As Moriah's comments above suggest, gendered habitus comprises a 'layer of embodied experience that is not immediately amenable to self-fashioning' (Ibid.). The concept of habitus draws our attention to the ways in which gendered values and expectations are imprinted on our bodies, but there is little room for change, or resisting gender norms, in Bourdieu's original work. In *Masculine Domination*, he describes women 'condemned' to participate in symbolic violence of gender and compelled to adhere to structures and agents of domination (Bourdieu, 2001, p. 30). The common criticism of Bourdieu's work, that is, its implications of determinism, seems particularly relevant in the context of his discussion of habitus and gender.

It is frequently argued that Bourdieu's conceptual schema reveals an 'impoverished, two-dimensional model of individuals and agency' (Jenkins, 2002b, p. 93). The emphasis on social reproduction in Bourdieu's work affects the degree to which people are able to exercise agency. Arguably, this leads him inexorably into deterministic explanations. In Bourdieu's (1985) own words

> The social world is, to a large extent, what the agents make of it, at each moment; but they have no chance of unmaking it and re-making it except on the basis of realistic knowledge of what it is and what they can do from the position they occupy within it. (p. 728)

This is a social world 'where behaviour has its causes but actors are not allowed their reasons' (Jenkins, 2002b, p. 97). While the deterministic nature of Bourdieu's social theory troubles many (e.g., Jenkins, 2002b; Shilling, 2004), McNay (1999) sees virtue in the generative nature of habitus, arguing that it helps explain the persistence of reasonably entrenched gender identities. For McNay (1999), the very value in Bourdieu's work is that it demonstrates the difficulty of change: it 'provides a corrective to certain theories of reflexive transformation which overestimate the extent to which individuals living in post-traditional order are able to shape identity' (p. 113).

Certainly, while *some* female snowboarders are able to negotiate space within the snowboarding field and accumulate capital (symbolic, gender and both), their gender identities remain limited and determined by a male valuation system (see Anderson, 1999; Thorpe, 2005). Olympic New Zealand snowboarder Pamela Bell, for example, complained of 'unfair expectations of girls' abilities, as if there is only one scale of judgment – the boys' scale' (cited in Webster, 1996, p. 43). Professional American boarder Roberta Rodgers also declared snowboarding 'a male-dominated sport – on the slopes, in the magazines, and in the management of every snowboard company' (cited in Rodgers, 2001, para. 4). The notion of habitus illuminates the 'entrenched dimensions' of embodied experiences and, in particular, male and female snowboarders' 'deep-seated, often unconscious investments in conventional images of masculinity and femininity which cannot easily be reshaped' (McNay, 1999, p. 103).

It is important to bear in mind, however, that some female snowboarders, like Pamela and Roberta, are critically aware of such gender inequalities and are creating new social, cultural, and financial opportunities for themselves within the snowboarding field (see Thorpe, 2005, 2008). But the reasons a female snowboarder gives for her embodied and reflexive practices would be of little concern to Bourdieu. For him, the actors' own explanations of their practices tend to be an illusion; the true explanation of behavior exists in the habitus. McCall (1992) argues that Bourdieu 'stops short of realizing the potential of gendered dispositions because he considers female gender status imbued only with uncontested symbolic violence' (p. 845). Some female snowboarders actively resist the male bodily hexis and make attempts to redefine the female snowboarding body. But with Bourdieu's concept of habitus, it is difficult to understand the source of such impulses. Thus a key question facing feminists is whether Bourdieu's work gives any chance for explaining agency and reflexive awareness. As a response to this question, the final part of this chapter examines the potential of the habitus-field complex for understanding gender reflexivity in contemporary sport and physical culture, focusing particularly on the opportunities available to some female snowboarders to reflect critically on gender and cultural dimensions of their habitus, as well as problematic norms and practices within the snowboarding field.

Habitus, field, and reflexive female boarding bodies

While most criticisms of habitus invoke determinism, some of Bourdieu's texts provide more space for agency and reflexivity than others. In particular, in some of his later work, especially *State Nobility* (1998), Bourdieu suggests that moments of disalignment and tension between habitus and field may give rise to increased reflexive awareness. For Bourdieu, habitus operates at an unconscious level unless individuals with a well-developed habitus find themselves moving across new, unfamiliar fields. It is in such moments that an individual's habitus may become 'divided against itself, in constant negotiation with itself and its ambivalences', resulting in 'a kind of duplication, to a double perception of the self' (Bourdieu, 1999, cited in Reay, 2004, p. 436). This becomes what Bourdieu (2003) has termed a habitus clivé, a 'split habitus' (cited in Krais, 2006, p. 130). For Bourdieu, reflexive awareness arises from the 'negotiation of discrepancies by individuals in their movement within and across fields of social action' (McNay, 1999, p. 110; see also Powell, 2008). Bourdieu was careful to emphasize, however, that despite a proliferation of fields and an increasingly mobile population, such disjunctions between habitus and field are not common occurrences. Chambers (2005) notes that 'most people tend to remain within compatible fields most of the time', thus there is usually a fit between field and habitus (p. 340). In such circumstances, the habitus tends to be reinforced rather than challenged. Therefore Bourdieu shows how reflexivity is not an inherently universal capacity of subjects, rather, it is a 'piecemeal, discontinuous affair' (McNay, 1999, p. 110), uneven in its application, emerging only with its experience of dissonance.

Although Bourdieu acknowledges the 'destabilizing and potentially sub-versive effects that might arise from movement across fields', he ignores what this might imply for an understanding of modern gender identity (McNay, 1999, p. 107). In *Masculine Domination* he fails to fully integrate the notion of habitus with his work on the concept of field. This is prob-lematic because, in contrast to traditional societies, such as the Kabyle, modern society is marked by the 'complexity of its structures, criteria and social differentiations' and the experiences of individuals in general, and women in particular, are heterogeneous and contradictory, 'encompass-ing not only practices of subordination to masculine domination, but also practices in which women assert independence and receive recognition for their work' (Krais, 2006, p. 131). According to McNay (1999), while Bourdieu is 'undoubtedly right to stress the ingrained nature of gender norms', his lack of a sustained consideration of gendered habitus in relation to the field means he 'significantly underestimates the ambiguities and dissonances that exist in the way that men and women occupy masculine and feminine positions' in contemporary society (p. 107). In so doing, he is inattentive to the 'internally complex nature of subjectivity' (McNay, 2000, p. 72), as well as the impact of particular social changes on how women 'inhabit, experience, move across, change and are changed by new and emerging social fields, as well as by gender relations within existing fields' (Kenway & McLeod, 2005, p. 535).

Despite such oversights, some feminist scholars have identified poten-tial in the concepts of field and habitus for understanding how reflexive awareness might arise with regard to gender identity. In particular, McNay (1999) has drawn out these implications to show that gender reflexivity, or the questioning of conventional notions of femininity, does not arise from exposure to, and identification with, a greater array of alternative images of femininity, but rather from 'tensions inherent in the concrete negotia-tion of increasing conflictual female roles' which occur when women move between various social fields, such as family, work, and sport (p. 111; see also Adams, 2006; Hills, 2006; McNay, 2000). Thus, feminist syntheses of gen-der, habitus, and the relational concept of field, yield 'a framework in which to conceptualize the uneven and nonsystematic ways in which subordina-tion and autonomy are realized in women's lives' (McNay, 1999, p. 113), including their sport, physical cultural, and snowboarding experiences.

Field crossing and gender reflexivity among female snowboarders

On entering the snowboarding field, some (not all) women experience a dis-junction between habitus and field as they are (temporarily) distanced from constitutive structures, such as family, workplace, or other sports fields. For some women, this movement across fields leads to empowering experiences, and sometimes gender reflexivity. For example, Amy Spence, a beginner snowboarder, describes entering the snowboarding field as helping her reflect upon everyday domestic and familial gender constraints:

> I'm on chairlift #8 at Mount Snow in Vermont, a borrowed snowboard dangling from my left foot, the bright April sun's warmth helping me temporarily forget my sore, wet body... For a moment, I forget my age, my gender, my responsibilities as a mother and wife. ... [With] my blonde hair stuffed in under a hat, my face hidden under Oakley's, my body disguised by my baggy coat and pants... I could be any age, any gender. But I'm not. Here I am, a 29-year-old-woman who, only after three days, is ready to trade in her world for the flight on the board. (cited in Carlson, 1999, p. 3)

Movement across the fields of work and snowboarding also encourages Marie, a Canadian recreational snowboarder, to reflect upon differing feminine ideals and gendered norms in these two fields:

> I wear mascara and heeled shoes every day to work. But when we go to the mountain in the weekend I get to be less feminine and I really like that. I can, what I call, 'get dirty,' wear no make-up, maybe not shower in the morning, get sweaty, and hang out with my friends. I'll have a burger and fries at lunch, which I wouldn't do when I'm off the mountain. When you put on a snowboard jacket and several layers, you can feel fun and cool and sexy, and no one can tell if you're ten pounds overweight... so there aren't as many body image worries as in my day-to-day city life. (personal communication, November 2005)

When top New Zealand snowboarder Hayley Holt was asked why she quit competitive ballroom dancing and chose to focus on a snowboarding career, she replied, 'snowboarding was more my thing, I didn't have to *pretend* to be a lady anymore' (cited in Catsburg, 2005, p. 110, emphasis added). Arguably, Holt's movement *between* the sports fields of ballroom dancing and snowboarding prompted her to critically reflect on gendered aspects of her habitus instilled from early (and prolonged) socialization into ballroom dancing culture.

Furthermore, as *some* female snowboarders move between overlapping but distinct groups *within* the field of snowboarding (e.g., competitive sport, industry), they become critically aware that, while 'all fields embody gender rules, and some gender rules apply in all fields', gender norms are not identical across all fields or even groups within fields (Chambers, 2005, p. 333). For example, when pregnancy compelled professional snowboarder and 1998 Olympic half-pipe bronze medalist Shannon Dunn to take a step back from the field of competitive snowboarding, it enabled her to look at women's snowboarding from a different perspective (Stravers, 2004). Observing significant gender inequalities in the media coverage of female boarders for the first time, Dunn vowed to initiate change and she set about organizing the 'P-Jamma Party', a four-day, all female, noncompetitive event with the aim of maximizing female exposure through editorial photos and TV/video coverage. Similarly, moving between the related fields of snowboarding culture and the sports film industry on a daily basis, Tiffany Sabol became critically aware of company personnel simply ignoring an 'abundance' of film that captured female talent (cited in Berkley, 1999, para. 2). For Sabol, women's invisibility in the snowboarding films being produced by her employer was inconsistent with her own experiences in the snowboarding culture and, more specifically, women's visibility on the mountain (Berkley, 1999). This critical consciousness led her to a transformational practice: she cofounded the first women's snowboard film company, Misty – later renamed XX Productions – and coproduced *Empress* (1999), *Our Turn* (2000), and *Hardly Angels* (2001).

For some core female snowboarders, moving out of the snowboarding field (either temporarily or permanently) can prompt critical reflection on some of the norms and behaviors regarding physical and social risk, cultural commitment, and lifestyle that have been internalized during their prolonged socialization into the snowboarding culture. For example, it was only when Phillipa left the snowboarding field that she began to critically reflect on some of the unquestioned cultural assumptions regarding physical risk celebrated in the snowboarding field: 'if I had my snowboarding time again I would...not rush back into the sport after each injury, I would allow more healing time' (personal communication, November 2008). For semiprofessional snowboarder Kumara Kelley, moving into and (temporarily) out of the snowboarding field prompted introspection and reflection on some of the risks taken, and mistakes made, as a fledgling athlete in the highly competitive snowboarding industry:

> I wanted to 'go pro' so badly...But I didn't know how to do it...I guessed from videos that you partied, met the right people, moved to Mammoth [California] and then boom – you're pro....I was really young, wildly insecure and lacked discipline...Moving to Mammoth at 18 and diving deep into the industry proved a hard hit for me. I ended up partying more than competing or filming...Eventually I hit bottom, my party-antics had gotten out of hand. (cited in Lipton, 2009, para. 3)

Taking an extended 'time out' from snowboarding culture, Kelley proceeded to move into and out of various fields (acting, modeling, Buddhism, yoga, martial arts, and tertiary education). According to Kelley, her experiences in these new social fields not only helped her reflect critically upon some of the self-destructive behaviors engaged in during her early years as a professional snowboarder, but also enabled her to return to the snowboard-ing field with a heightened awareness of the politics and risks involved in the industry. In her own words,

> Moving home, working through some tough life shit and exploring spir-ituality with yoga has helped me feel okay with myself.... Coming at this [professional snowboarding] a second time around, I know this is a busi-ness. I know they [new sponsors] will be looking out for their interests and I will have to do the same. One thing is for certain, I am not looking to get strung along by sponsors... I'm dedicated and doing it [for myself], with or without [them]. (cited in Lipton, 2009, para. 23)

Similarly, when serious injury (broken fibula, torn anterior cruciate liga-ment, sprained ankle, spinal compression fracture, and eight stitches in her head) forced Tara Dakides to withdraw from the field of professional snow-boarding, she began to reflect on past and present lifestyle choices:

> During the time I was injured I started asking all these big questions... It's no wonder that I couldn't have a successful relationship or get close to people or have that connection, because I'd never done the work. I just ran away from it [parental divorce] and put it all in snowboarding... During that time I learned that there was more to life than snowboarding. (cited in Landan, 2008, scene. 14)

As these brief examples suggest, for some female snowboarders, moving into and out of the snowboarding field and across other social fields can prompt critical reflection on various risky or self-destructive behavior engaged in during participation in the snowboarding field. To date, young women's experiences of risk and pleasure in youth-dominated physical cultures, such as snowboarding, have received very little academic attention. Arguably, recent feminist appropriations of Bourdieu's habitus-field complex may offer a potentially fruitful way forward for scholars seeking to better understand women's experiences of agency and constraint, and reflexivity, in physical cultures.

Female snowboarders, field crossing, and privileged reflexivity

As women increasingly move across various fields (the home, family, workplace, different sport cultures, the ski resort, different countries), and positions within fields (novice, weekend warrior, athlete, event organizer, film-maker), they are exposed to different concepts of order and ways of behaving that may generate 'questions as to the "naturalness" of established gender practices' (Krais, 2006, p. 131). Experiencing the tensions between different fields can, according to Adams (2006), 'create dissonance and an awareness of "objective" gender relations in these fields': the 'lucidity of the excluded' can in turn generate resistance and negotiation (Ibid., p. 518). Bourdieu makes a similar argument when not discussing gender: 'It is difficult to control the first inclination of habitus, but reflexive analysis, which teaches that we are the ones who endow the situation with part of the potency it has over us, allows us to alter our perception of the situation and thereby our reaction to it' (Bourdieu & Wacquant, 1992, p. 136).

With only some women critically reflecting upon gendered and cultural dimensions of their habitus, and only a select few attempting to initiate changes in the sport, culture, and industry of snowboarding, it is necessary to consider who is likely to do so. The ability to reflexively analyze gender norms in snowboarding culture tends to depend on the individual's gendered habitus instilled during childhood, their lived experiences and position in the snowboarding field, and the opportunities available for them to move across the social fields of work, education, home, sport, and leisure. For example, it appears that young 'core' female snowboarders – whose work, accommodation, friendships and intimate relationships, and travel experiences, are typically organized around snowboarding – tend to do the least amount of field crossing, which may help explain why they often demonstrate limited critical reflection in relation to gender inequalities in the snowboarding field. But, as the Shannon Dunn example above demonstrates, on leaving the 'core' group (whether this is due to the pursuit of professional or educational opportunities, injury, marriage, pregnancy, or any other reason) and entering other fields (e.g., work, sport, leisure, family), some women reflect differently on the gender and sexual politics of their experiences in the male-defined snowboarding field; observing gender disparities, a select few become inspired to improve conditions for the next generation (see Chapter 10). It is important to note, however, that mobility within and between fields, and in regard to gender styles, is a privileged position (Adkins, 2002). Perhaps it is worth while considering, then, whether the increased opportunities for young middle- and upper-class women – notably this is the background of most female snowboarders – to move across multiple fields, and enter spheres that were previously closed to them, such as workplaces and sports traditionally defined as masculine, have increased their potential for reflexivity. If this is the case, one way of encouraging further reflexivity and changes in gendered habitus may be, as Chambers (2005) suggests, to encourage more 'interaction between fields, between communities or ways of life, so that individuals become aware of new options' (p. 340).

Of course, the presence of reflexivity does not automatically translate into identity transformation. As highlighted in Moriah's comments above, in some circumstances 'our capacity for reflexive thought can leave us recognizing but unable to do anything about our lack of freedom' (Craib, 1992, p. 150). Even when women experience a disjunction between habitus and field leading to gender reflexivity, these alterations do not necessarily work to 'undermine gender, or masculine domination' (Chambers, 2005, p. 343). As women enter into new fields certain aspects of gender relations may be destabilized, yet other aspects may be further entrenched (McNay, 1999). Indeed, as women enter male-dominated fields, many make adaptations and adopt strategies to 'manage the masculine culture into which they are entering' (Chambers, 2005, p. 342). This also seems true of many women in snowboarding culture, particularly core female boarders who engage in prolonged periods of enculturation into, and sustained participation within, the snowboarding field, and thus have most fully embodied the (masculine) snowboarding habitus. Mel, for instance, a passionate New Zealand boarder who has worked successfully in the snowboarding industry for more than a decade and continues to hold a dominant position in the field as a competition judge, insists that women in the snowboarding culture 'have to have a very open mind and accept a lot of things that you may not agree with' (personal communication, October 2006). The 'cultural inculcation' of symbolic violence in the snowboarding field continues to be 'exercised with the complicity' of many female boarders (McRobbie, 2009, p. 140; see also Krais, 1993; McNay, 1999, 2000).

The contemporary snowboarding field is a contradictory social context of ongoing sexism *and* greater opportunities for women (Thorpe, 2005). It would be a mistake, however, to assume that core female boarders passively embody the masculine snowboarding habitus during their participation within the field, and only begin to critically reflect on their gendered experiences upon exiting, or moving to a different position (e.g., weekend warrior), within the field. Rather, core female snowboarders frequently encounter differences and problems *within* the field, which encourage them to engage in day-to-day negotiations of gender identity. In theorizing critical reflexivity and gender identity transformation, then, we need to recognize that there is a continuum from relatively minor daily conflicts *within* fields, to more serious experiences of dissonance as individuals cross and enter new fields (Brooks & Wee, 2008). In other words, we need a way of conceptualizing the habitus that 'recognizes its potential for ambivalence, while acknowledging that this potential resides in relatively mundane conflicts as well as in more dramatic habitus-field mismatches' (Brooks & Wee, 2008, p. 516; see also Mouzelis, 2007). Arguably, Bourdieu's (1991) notion of 'regulated liberties' – small exercises of power that arise in the context of the existing social order, but which resignify it in some way – has the potential to help us capture some of the ambiguities, dissonances, and subtle negotiations of power experienced by women within contemporary sport and physical cultural fields such as snowboarding.

'Regulated liberties' in the snowboarding field

As with many contemporary social fields, the snowboarding field is a 'changeable, albeit constrained, world of gender relations' (Powell, 2008,

p. 171), within which some women experience tensions and express feelings of conflict regarding the practices associated with femininity and physicality. As the following quote from professional snowboarder Tina Basich's (2003) autobiography illustrates, during the late 1980s and early 1990s, some early female boarders found it difficult to demonstrate traditionally defined masculine practices of physical prowess and risk, *and* maintain their perceptions of femininity:

> I felt like I had to at least do everything the guys were doing... Not only did I have to get big air jumping cliffs and ride fast and hang with the guys but be cool, pretty and feminine. I liked riding with my ponytail flying behind me so there was no question of my femininity. I was so proud to be a snowboarder girl. But the balance between being a great rider and a girl was schizophrenic. (Basich, 2003, p. 70)

In 1994, frustrated by the lack of space for female snowboarding bodies within the male-defined snowboarding field, Basich and fellow professional Shannon Dunn openly defied the decision by organizers of the Air and Style Big Air snowboarding contest in Innsbruck (Austria), to exclude female participants. Dressed in pink Prom outfits and pigtails, they hiked up the scaffolding and, with the large crowd rowdily cheering them, they proceeded to jump the gap on their snowboards (Basich, 2003; Howe, 1998). In so doing, Basich and Dunn actively challenged assumptions within the field regarding the legitimate use of the female boarding body. Pamela, a professional New Zealand snowboarder during the late 1990s, also took delight in 'shocking' her interviewers and expanding limited definitions of the female boarding body:

> I would turn up and be really organized and wouldn't dress like a snowboarder. They would be like 'oh, we wanted you to have pink hair and heaps of piercings in your eyebrows and stuff'. And I was like, 'sorry to disappoint you but I'm really boring'. There's this crazy misconception of what a female snowboarder is, and I used to kind of delight in not being that just to really piss them off. (personal communication, September 2005)

Some contemporary female snowboarders also deploy fluid and hybrid identities and engage in active self-fashioning to produce sites of contestation over the meanings of the female snowboarding body. For example, U.S. Olympic silver medalist Lindsey Jacobellis consciously disrupts stereotypes of snowboarders as 'pot smoking punks' by 'play[ing] piano, speak[ing] in complete sentences, and avoid[ing] saying "like" or "dude" during interviews' (Swift, 2006, p. 63).

In the current cultural moment, core female snowboarders embody subtle practices to create a distinctive space within the snowboarding culture and further distinguish their own taste from what has increasingly become the mass snowboarding taste. For example, core female boarders are reinterpreting and feminizing the images of the gangster and punk, which were originally an attempt to preserve snowboarding as a masculine activity distinctly different from skiing (see Chapter 5; Anderson, 1999). While many male snowboarders imitate the urban gangster by wearing bandanas on their heads, some female snowboarders make and wear crocheted headbands. Underneath their head-bands, bandanas, and beanies, many females wear their hair long as another subtle marker of femininity. Although the punk-inspired studded belt was a standardized accessory among male snowboarders during the late 1990s and early 2000s, female snowboarders feminized this style, wearing bright pink studded belts. While many female boarders wore the same baggy pants and exposed boxer shorts as their male counterparts, some added feminine flair by wearing a shorter top exposing a pierced or tattooed midriff. By reappro-priating these styles in different ways to men, female boarders are creating hybrid identities based on the mixing and movement of cultures. The result-ing fusion or creolization of femininity with the punk and gangster styles is not the assimilation of one culture or cultural tradition by another but the production of something new, a distinctly female snowboarding identity (see Figure 6.1). In so doing, women are establishing their own space within the snowboarding field. Simply put, some core female boarders engage in 'reg-ulated liberties' – small exercises of power that subtly resignify the female snowboarding body from *within* the field.

The key point here is that women's embodied practices 'can not be under-stood through binaries of domination and resistance, but rather involve more complex processes of investment and negotiation' (McNay, 2000, p. 58). While the various 'regulated liberties' performed by female snow-boarders, such as demonstrations of physical prowess and cultural commit-ment, or defining their own styles and tastes, may suggest gender instability within the snowboarding field, they do not guarantee reflexivity or gender identity transformation. In sum, a feminist turn to Bourdieu suggests that gender reflexivity in physical cultures such as snowboarding is 'uneven and discontinuous', potentially arising as a result of mobility *between* social fields and, to a lesser extent, as a result of the requirements to reconcile the dissonant experiences that this invokes *within* fields (regulated liberties) (Kenway & McLeod, 2005; McNay, 1999, 2000).

Gender reflexivity and change

According to Bourdieu, an individual's conscious awareness does not lead to fundamental social change by itself. As Krais (2006) explains, Bourdieu vehemently argued against the 'intellectualist illusion' – and in particu-lar the position of Judith Butler – that simply performing individual acts of 'deviant behaviour' would be enough to overthrow dominating social structures (p. 131). For Bourdieu (2001), performativity and other regulated

Figure 6.1   A professional female snowboarder performing a 'jibbing' maneuver on a rubbish bin. As well as demonstrating physical prowess and creativity in her use of space, this rider also draws upon symbols from various youth cultures (e.g., hip hop, skateboarding) to produce a distinctive, hybrid female snowboarding identity (Rider: Gabby Maiden) (image used with permission of Nikita Outerwear)

liberties fail to offer genuine opportunities for emancipation from structures of domination, for two main reasons. Firstly, regulated liberties are 'performed by individuals', and so lack the 'cohesive, collective character required for wide-ranging social change' and political mobilization necessary for effective resistance (Chambers, 2005, p. 339). Secondly, regulated liberties take place from '*within* the dominant context and corresponding habitus' and thus 'do not really subvert those structures' (Ibid.). He claimed that practices often hailed as 'resistant' may have an impact only on the relatively superficial 'effective' relations of a field rather than its deeper structural relations (Bourdieu, 1992, cited in McNay, 1999, p. 105). Certainly, while some individual female boarders are critically aware of the gendered nature of their habitus, and are trying to create new social, cultural, and financial opportunities for themselves (and others) within the sport, culture, and industry of snowboarding, their efforts are often (though not always) limited to various dimensions of the snowboarding field (see Thorpe, 2005, 2008, 2009).

Feminist scholars, including Chambers (2005) and Adkins (2003), add some interesting caveats to Bourdieu's thoughts on reflexivity and change. Chambers (2005), for example, argues that the strategies Bourdieu proposes for change – principally a disjunction between field and habitus, and the regulated liberties – are 'not best suited to changes in gender systems' because 'gender operates across fields' and 'regulated liberties concerning gender are often reactionary' (p. 326). In her view, because gendered habitus tends to be reinforced in all fields it 'cannot be significantly undermined by mobility across fields' (p. 343), and thus may be 'even less susceptible to change than is the habitus more generally' (p. 323). Similarly, Adkins (2002) suggests that women might be regarded as 'reflexivity losers' due to relative lack of mobility within and between fields, and the extent to which some forms of femininity have become naturalized across fields (p. 6). In a subsequent publication, Adkins (2003) suggests that the presence of critical reflexivity may not be sufficient to warrant any discussion of identity transformation, since it may be the case that, in the contemporary cultural moment, 'reflexive practices are so habituated that they are part of the very norms, rules and expectations that govern gender in late modernity, even as they ostensibly appear to challenge these very notions' (p. 35). Making a similar point more broadly, Sweetman (2003) also argues that a flexible or *reflexive habitus* is increasingly common in late, high, or reflexive modernity due to various economic, social, and cultural shifts, which have led to 'a more or less permanent disruption of social positions, or a more or less constant disjunction between habitus and field' (p. 541). In this context, reflexivity 'itself becomes habitual' such that certain contemporary individuals or groups 'may easily and largely unquestioningly engage in reflexive projects of self (re)construction as a matter of course' (Ibid., p. 542). Sweetman (2003) adds that those displaying a reflexive habitus, 'whilst at a

potential advantage in certain respects may also face considerable difficulties "being themselves"' (p. 528).

While I prefer the slightly more sanguine interpretation of the gender-
habitus-field complex offered by McNay (1999, 2000), the issues raised by
Chambers (2005), Adkins (2002, 2003), and Sweetman (2003) may invigor-
ate theoretical debates surrounding how best to understand and explain
gender, identity, agency, and social change in sporting cultures in the early
twenty-first century. Clearly, there are many possible interpretations of
Bourdieu's habitus-field nexus. Here, however, I have attempted to illustrate
the potential of recent feminist extensions of Bourdieu's work for revealing
both 'change *and* continuity, intervention *and* repetition' (McLeod, 2005,
p. 24) in gender identities and embodied practices in contemporary physical
cultures such as snowboarding.

Final thoughts on gendering Bourdieu

In this chapter I have examined the recent feminist critiques of, and engagements with, Bourdieu's conceptual schema via a case study of female snowboarding bodies. In so doing, I have highlighted some of the possibilities
offered by Bourdieu's conceptual schema for revealing more nuanced conceptualizations of gendered subjectivity, power relations, and transformations in contemporary physical cultures. Arguably, a particular virtue of
feminist syntheses with Bourdieu's relational concepts of capital, field, and
habitus is that they have the potential to highlight the 'uneven and discontinuous' nature of changes in the gender identities of young women in
contemporary society and physical culture per se (McNay, 1999, p. 109).
Bourdieu's original work glossed over the 'ambiguities and dissonances'
existing in the occupation of 'feminine subject positions' within and across
particular fields, but an array of feminist scholars are 'highlighting the
importance of these subtle disidentifications in conceptualizing change
and agency' (Hills, 2006, p. 553). Thus gendered readings of capital, field,
and habitus have the potential to offer fresh insight into how the feminine
subject is 'synchronically produced as the object of regulatory norms by
phallocentric symbolic systems and formed as a subject or agent who may
resist these norms' (McNay, 1999, p. 105). In other words, gender identity
in physical cultures, such as snowboarding, is 'not a mechanistically determining structure but an open system of dispositions – regulated liberties –
that are "durable but not eternal"' (Ibid., p. 105). While research examining
the gendered dimensions of Bourdieu's conceptual schema is still relatively
new, most of it has focused on the embodied gender experiences of women.
In the next chapter I argue that a gendered (re)reading of Pierre Bourdieu's
conceptual schema also has the potential to shed new light on men and
masculine identities in snowboarding culture.

7
Male Boarding Bodies: Pleasure, Pain, and Performance

Football requires tons of training and big muscles – snowboarding, well, doesn't. It's more a means to express your creativity, an added bonus being that if you're a skinny, scrawny person, you might do even better than that guy with big muscles. (Bleiler, March 2005, p. 58)

Scotty Wittlake rides with a determination to take snowboarding to a not-yet-defined level, with complete disregard for what the snowboarding world is doing, and with no thought to what pain and abuse his body goes through. He searches out terrain that others steer clear of. Jumps with nightmare take-offs and punishing landings aren't obstacles but challenges to Wittlake, who has broken teeth, ribs, both ankles, his nose, collapsed a lung, cracked a femur, and crushed bones in his cheek resulting in the loss of sight in his right eye during his quest to stick the scariest of landings. (Blehm, 2003, p. 115)

All of my mates knew me as the guy that would hit the big jumps first and fast...But now I regret the inch diameter mass of bone growing on my shoulder...the twinge in my neck I get if I stay in a certain position for too long...the headaches from one too many smacks on the brain. When I go to the mountain these days, I am much more contemplative about risk. I don't feel like I have to prove myself to anyone. Now I prefer to take it easy and enjoy being out of the city and in the mountains with friends. (Andy, personal communication, November 2006)

In the public imagination, snowboarding has traditionally been viewed as an activity best suited to young, white, hedonistic, rebellious males. Early perceptions were that the activity was for '13–18 year olds with raging hormones' who liked skateboarding and surfing (Hughes, 1988). The distinctive personalities and styles of early male snowboarders certainly contributed to the general public's perception of the activity and subsequent 'extreme' labeling. During the late 1980s and early 1990s, snowboarders such as Damian Sanders and Shaun Palmer epitomized the hypermasculine, rebellious image of snowboarding. According to snowboarding historian Susanna Howe (1998), Damian Sanders was the most 'visible poster boy of snowboarding's radical, extreme image': 'He embodied this with everything from clothing to riding style. Spiky hair and Day-Glo head bands; every flashy mutation of the board garb was "extreme". Huge cliffs, over-extended postures, gritted teeth and clenched fists were signs of aggression and in vogue...' (p. 70). Continuing, Howe describes Palmer as snowboarding's archetypal 'bad boy', he was foul-mouthed and 'would drink and do drugs all night, and win half-pipe contests in the morning' (Ibid., p. 78). While the hypermasculine image of snowboarding repelled many, the representations of hedonistic and aggressive behavior and idyllic lifestyles (travel to exotic snowboarding destinations, financial independence, partying, heterosexual prowess) of early professional male snowboarders combined to create a cultural ideal that appealed to many adolescent males seeking a distinctive masculine identity.

Today, with more than 75 percent of snowboarders under the age of 24, and between 60 and 70 percent of all participants being male, young men in their late teens and early twenties continue to constitute a dominant force at the core of the snowboarding culture (NGSA, 2005a). A young hypermasculinity continues to be celebrated within this group, yet cultural demographics are changing; not only do women increasingly occupy a physical presence in the sport, culture, and industry (see Chapter 6), but men from different ages, ethnicities, nationalities, and sexual orientations are also participating in a variety of styles and engaging in an array of embodied cultural practices. Ways of talking, thinking, representing and practicing masculine identities in the contemporary snowboarding culture are plural and in a constant state of flux. But how might we begin to understand the multiplicity, fluidity and dynamicism of masculinities, and the relationships between masculinities and femininities, in the contemporary snowboarding culture?

Gender, masculinity, and the male body

Before the 1980s, men undertook most social science research that, not surprisingly, focused on their worlds; yet rarely did men investigate masculinity. Since the late 1980s, however, there has been a surge of theorizing about masculine precepts, identity, behavior, and relationships. Some theoretical frameworks and conceptual schemas have been more fully utilized than others. The work of R. W. Connell, for example, has been particularly influential in theorizing about masculinity in many disciplines, including sports studies (see, for example, Messner and Sabo, 1990; Pronger, 1990).[1]

Connell's work on gender and masculinity came to prominence at a distinct historical moment involving the rise of second-wave feminism and the reaction of men to heightened gender politics. During this period, Connell, in collaboration with colleagues, popularized the concept of 'hegemonic masculinity' which has been defined as 'the configuration of gender practice which embodies the currently accepted answer to the problem of the legitimacy of patriarchy, which guarantees (or is taken to guarantee) the dominant position of men and the subordination of women' (Connell, 1995, p. 77; see also Carrigan et al., 1987; Connell, 1987, 2002). Hegemonic masculinity is regarded as a state or condition of the workings of ideology. In other words, male power is a 'hegemonic project' (Connell, 1995), a specific strategy for the subordination of women that is embedded in ideological and material structures. Another key feature of Connell's conceptual schema is the 'gender order', which, while further extrapolating on the gender relations between men and women, also highlights the relations of dominance and subordination between groups of males. At any given historical moment there are 'competing and co-existing masculinities, some hegemonic, some marginalized, and some stigmatized' (Messner & Sabo, 1990, p. 12).

Despite its continued wide application in many fields, generational shifts in gender relations since the 1980s have called into question much of Connell's work. A debate has recently emerged between supporters of the concept of hegemonic masculinity, and a new wave of gender scholars, as to how best to explain the dynamic and fluid relationships between men, and men and women, in the early twenty-first century. Many of the latter are critical of any conceptual schema that locates all masculinities (and femininities) in terms of a single pattern of power – the 'global dominance' of men over women (Connell, 1987, p. 183). More specific criticisms include the ambiguity of the hegemonic masculinity concept, its over-emphasis on structure and dualistic model of hegemonic power, a tendency to focus on men and ignore women, a lack of attention to the relational aspects of gender, the privileging of negative aspects of masculinity, and the narrow representation of men's subjectivities (see Donaldson, 1993; Edley & Weatherell, 1995; Miller, 1998; Pringle, 2005; Seidler, 2006; Speer, 2001; Star, 1999; Weatherell & Edley, 1999; Whitehead, 1998, 2002). Summing up the thrust of recent critiques, Seidler (2006) asserts we can no longer assume the viability of a theoretical framework that emerged during the era of second-wave feminism:

> We need to be aware of how gender relations have transformed within patriarchal cultures...This does not imply that patriarchal relationships have disappeared or that violence against women and gays has lessened, but such relationships do not carry the same legitimacy for young people who have often grown up within very different gender and sexual

orders. They do not have the same concerns as previous generations; nor do young women and men identify the centrality of their relationships with feminism. (p. 3).

Similarly, Whitehead (1998) sees critical writing on masculinity 'locked in an unproductive, sterile and incestuous relationship with concepts that, while useful, have little more to tell us about men – and even less to tell us about multiple masculinities as ways of being, now apparent in late or post-modernity' (p. 61). Thus, for those of us seeking to 'relate to different generations and cultural experiences of masculinities' and femininities, it might be argued that the time has come to 'break with some of the inherited frameworks and ask new kinds of questions' (Seidler, 2006, p. xxvi).[2]

In this chapter I concur with many of Connell's critics, and suggest that a feminist reading of Bourdieu's original conceptual schema – field, capital, habitus, practice – may facilitate fresh insights into the multiplicity, dynamicism and fluidity of masculinities and gender relations in contemporary sport and physical cultures such as snowboarding. Building on previous literature on masculinities in sport, youth culture, and alternative or lifestyle sports (e.g., Beal, 1996; Evers, 2004, 2009; Ford & Brown, 2006; Henderson, 2001; Kusz, 2007a; Robinson, 2008; Waitt, 2008; Waitt & Warren, 2008; Wellard, 2009; Wheaton, 2000b, 2003a), and extending feminist engagements with Bourdieu's conceptual schema, this chapter consists of two main parts.[3] First, I offer a description of some of the practices and performances of three different masculinities identifiable across the global snowboarding field – 'The Grommets', 'The Bros', and 'The Old Guys' – and the power relations between these groups.[4] Here I also discuss some of the reciprocal relationships between men and women in this mixed-gender snowboarding environment. Second, I consider the potential of the gender-habitus-field complex for explaining how some male snowboarders come to critically reflect upon problematic aspects of the hypermasculine snowboarding habitus. Ultimately, this chapter not only offers a discussion of the masculine identities and interactions in the snowboarding field, but also contributes to recent debates about how best to explain different generations and cultural experiences of masculinities.

Bourdieu and masculinities in the snowboarding field

Bourdieu failed to consider the full implications of the concept of field in his work on gender. A number of feminist scholars, however, have engaged with field, and particularly the field-habitus complex, to illustrate the 'synchronous nature of constraint and freedom' (McNay, 2000, p. 61) for women in contemporary society. Feminist scholars from various disciplines, such as education, youth studies, and women's studies, have worked with the concept of field to explain how gender norms and practices, and interactions between men and women, vary between and within different classes or groups in social fields (see, for example, Allard, 2005; Hills, 2006; Huppatz, 2009). In so doing, they highlight the potential of a gendered (re)reading of the field concept to illuminate some of the 'complexity and multilayered-ness' of relations between the sexes in contemporary social life (Mottier, 2002, p. 355). According to McNay (1999), the result of introducing such a notion of differentiation into an understanding of the social construction of gender identities is that 'masculinity and femininity can be seen as imbricated in complex ways rather than as opposed and separate categories' (p. 112). Thus, it might be argued that, in contrast to R. W. Connell's theory of social stratification (i.e., gender order), Bourdieu's conceptual schema helps us move beyond gender hierarchy.

Despite a growing body of feminist literature that suggests the potential of field for illuminating the multiplicity and fluidity of femininities and masculinities in various social spaces and places, the concept of field has been largely overlooked by scholars interested in men and masculinities. The work of Coles (2009) is a notable exception. Combining Bourdieu's concept of field with Connell's notion of hegemonic masculinity, Coles explores the possibility of multiple dominant masculinities operating simultaneously within various subfields bound by a 'field of masculinity' (p. 30) According to Coles, within the 'field of masculinity' there are 'sites of domination and subordination, orthodoxy (maintaining the status quo) and heterodoxy (seeking change), submission and usurpation' (p. 36). Continuing, he describes individuals, groups and organizations struggling to 'lay claim to the legitimacy of specific capital within the field of masculinity' (Ibid., p. 36). While Cole's idiosyncratic interpretation of Bourdieu's conceptual schema certainly offers some interesting possibilities for thinking differently about multiple masculinities in and across various social spaces, I find his discussion of a 'field of masculinity' problematic, primarily because it presents gender, and masculinity in particular, as a separate field.

In Chapter 6 I drew upon the work of feminist Bourdieusian scholars to argue that, rather than a specific, autonomous field, gender is far better conceptualized as 'part of a field' because gender is 'extraordinarily relational, with a chameleon-like flexibility, shifting in importance, value and effects from context to context or from field to field' (Adkins, 2004, p. 6; see also Chambers, 2005, and Krais, 2002). While all fields contain and enforce a set of gender rules, some of these rules may be common to many other fields, whereas others may be specific to that field (Chambers, 2005). As explained in Chapter 6, while the snowboarding field overlaps with other sport fields, such as surfing, skateboarding, freestyle skiing, and big mountain skiing, and youth cultural fields, such as music and fashion, such that they share some similar cultural values and common gender rules, they are certainly not identical. Surfing, skateboarding, and snowboarding each have distinctive histories, environments, geographies, identities, development patterns, equipment, and physical requirements

(Wheaton, 2004), and thus masculine and feminine identities, and gender relations (see Anderson, 1999; Beal, 1996; Booth, 2002; Thorpe, 2005). Thus, rather than conceptualizing snowboarding culture as a separate 'field of masculinity' or as a subfield bound by a 'field of masculinity', the following analysis focuses on masculinities in the 'field of snowboarding' (Thorpe, 2010b).

Many different masculine practices, performances and identities can be observed in and across the field of snowboarding. Indeed, in the highly fragmented snowboarding field, there are almost as many ways of realizing masculinity as there are groups and styles of participation (Wheaton, 2000b). Global flows of media, patterns of consumption, and participants, however, communicate cultural values and styles across local, regional, and national fields, such that many of the elements of the youthful, hyper-masculine snowboarding identity are observable in most locations where groups of young male snowboarders congregate. While cultural differences in and across various local, regional, and national snowboarding fields are observable,[5] here the focus is on masculinities in the global, particularly Western, snowboarding field.

Male snowboarders' gendered identities are not only multiple, they are also dynamic. The configuration of power and the cultural dynamics in the snowboarding field are in a constant state of flux, and groups and individuals continue to struggle to preserve or transform the configuration of power, or rather the legitimate use and meaning of male (and female) snowboarding bodies. Moreover, some male snowboarders practice and perform different masculine identities as they move across different fields in their everyday lives, including school, family, work, snowboarding culture, organized sports teams (e.g., soccer, rugby, basketball), other sport and leisure activities (e.g., skateboarding, online gaming), and youth fashion or music cultures (e.g., punk, hip hop, emo). As Coles (2009) explains, the masculine behaviors practiced by men often depend on the field, their location within the field, their knowledge of the rules and stakes structuring the field, as well as 'the resources they have available at their disposal in the way of capital' within these fields (p. 42). One of the participants in my research, for example, identified different cultural norms and gender expectations regarding legitimate masculine practices, (e.g., physical confrontations), at school and the ski resort, and described performing different masculine identities in these two distinct fields:

> To be honest, in all the days I have spent on the mountain, I have never thrown a single punch, let alone seen a fight. In contrast, at high school, where I spent a comparable number of days in my life, I was suspended three times, and involved in well over 20 fights. (Adam, personal communication, November 2006)

The key issue here is that, although the snowboarding field is a central site for the creation of masculine identities, it is not the only domain: 'masculinities are fluid, and learned and negotiated in a variety of [fields] such as the family and work environments' (Wheaton, 2000b, p. 445), as well broader social, cultural and national contexts. Male snowboarders do not embody a youthful hypermasculine identity at all times. Rather, they position themselves in multiple ways, depending on the context, such that they can seem 'both hegemonic and non-hegemonic...at the same time' (Weatherell & Edley, 1999, p. 343). Simply put, (some) men embody multidimensional masculine identities which they practice differently in and across various fields. Yet to date, many studies have focused on masculinity at the structural level 'with little consideration given to the strategies men use to negotiate masculinities in their everyday lives' (Coles, 2009, p. 30). Arguably, Bourdieu's conceptual schema can help us account for the variety of masculinities present within and across fields at any given time, and 'describe how masculinities operate in and over men's lives' (Ibid., p. 31).

Unlike hegemonic masculinity or masculine domination, a feminist interpretation of field encourages us to move beyond conceptions of men as the bearers of power, and question the tendency in previous studies to dichotomize the experiences of men and women. Adopting a gendered reading of field, our attention is drawn to relational issues, particularly the connections between, and hierarchies among, men, as well as the interactions between men and women.[6] This is an important contribution to contemporary theorizing on gender because, as Brod (1994) accurately observes, there has been a tendency in men's studies to presume 'separate spheres' and proceed as if women were not relevant to the analysis (cited in Connell & Messerschmidt, 2005, p. 837). According to Connell and Messerschmidt, the exclusion of women from research into men and masculinities is regrettable because 'gender is always relational' and 'patterns of masculinity are socially defined in contradistinction from some model (whether real or imaginary) of femininity' (Ibid., p. 848).

In the remainder of this section, I describe three snowboarding masculinities identifiable across the global snowboarding field: 'The Grommets' (pre and early adolescent boys), 'The Bros' (young men), and 'The Old Guys' (thirties and beyond) – categories used by the participants themselves. As the discussion reveals, the legitimate forms of masculinity, valued forms of capital, and gender relations, differ between these groups. In addition to describing some of the masculine practices and performances of these groups, the following discussion also examines some of the reciprocal relationships between men and women in the mixed-sex snowboarding field.

Grommets: learning masculinities

'Grommet' is a name typically given to pre and early pubescent male snowboarders. Grommets tend to experience snowboarding in different ways to their older peers. They take snowboarding very seriously; as one young male boarder wrote, 'I eat, breathe, and sleep snowboarding. It takes all of my thought away from me during school and while I'm at home. I almost get breathless watching snowboarding on television' (retrieved from www. snowboard.com, February 16, 2005). For these young males, snowboarding is an important site for constructing a distinctive 'snowboarder identity' that has links to masculinity. As with many other sports and physical cultures, physical prowess seems to be, and is seen as, a 'rite of passage' to manhood, the 'completion of a young boy's masculinity' (Whannel, 1992, cited in Macdonald, 2001, p. 106; see also Young, 1965). Especially among young male snowboarders, for whom 'other sources of recognized masculine authority (earning power, sexual relations, fatherhood) are some way off, the development of body appearance and body language that are suggestive of force and skill is experienced as an urgent task' (Whitson, 1990, p. 23). Indeed, many grommets approach snowboarding with full gusto and, having yet to experience or understand the full consequences of serious injury, often appear fearless. According to Pamela, a New Zealand snowboarding coach, 'being naïve is the most valuable thing and you see that with the young guys, before they have their first big accident, they are just mad, they have so much youthful enthusiasm and energy' (personal communication, September 2005). Many older male boarders are more cautious: 'Grommets seem out of control...always trying to progress too fast and end up endangering us all. Plus they seem so over-done with the current fashions, music and catch phrases. They look and act like dickheads sometimes' (Nick, personal communication, April 2006).

Older male snowboarders often see it as their responsibility to actively patrol boys' behavior on and off the mountain. According to Gavin, a more senior core boarder: 'Grommets are the best, they are the future of the sport and it's good to see them ripping. But it's important to pull them up when they get out of line and start getting too cocky, or too smart, for their own good' (personal communication, March 2006). Grommets occasionally experience aggressive and demeaning 'initiation' rituals from older male boarders who believe this is an important part of 'becoming a real snowboarder.' As one male snowboarder declares:

> Grommets these days lack respect, they are cocky, and will get to a stage in their lives where they will realize they should have shut their gobs and learned from those older and wiser. It is these smart-ass grommets with no respect that get their nuts shaved and glued onto their legs. (Andrew, personal communication, March 2006)

Despite (or perhaps because of) having experienced similar initiation practices in his early snowboarding career, Gavin accepts it as 'a rite of passage that we all experience' (personal communication, March 2006).

Most frequently, grommets, like other young males, congregate with peers of similar age and ability, who become their audience and an important source of validation (Messner, 1987). In fact, peer approval seems to be the most important motive for these boys (see also Wheaton, 2000b). These groups are hierarchically organized based on snowboarding ability, and the boys are often highly competitive with one another for positions within this hierarchy. As Kimmel (1994) writes, masculinity depends upon comparison; it 'must be proved, and no sooner is it proved than it is again questioned and must be proven again' (p. 122). Grommets are often so focused on proving themselves to their peers and older males that they give little attention, or respect, to female snowboarders. While largely oblivious to the talents of female snowboarders, grommets tend to hero-worship professional male snowboarders. For example, writing about his years as a grommet in the snowboarding field, Todd Richards (2003) described his adoration of an early professional male snowboarder: 'in my mind the theme song from *Chariots of Fire* came on as he slid slow motion toward the giant kicker and floated the most stylish, gigantic method air... smooth, effortless, and god-like... from that moment forward, I wanted to be Terry Kidwell' (p. 66). This excerpt is representative of many grommets' cultural idolization of professional male snowboarders who demonstrate significant physical prowess.

Furthermore, the transition from grommet to one of The Bros can be an exciting experience for young male boarders particularly when it is based on recognition of their physical prowess, and thus 'manliness'. Richards (2003) recalled two occasions in which he first started gaining acceptance into the snowboarding fratriarchy:

> This session was 'just for fun' but I still felt the *pressure to perform*. I waited for a gap in the action, dropped in, snapped into an Andrecht [hand-plant] on that little wall, stalled the living shit out of it, and then casually laid it down. I looked around and noticed Tucker and Kidwell were staring at me. Kidwell said, 'Dude, that's messed up!' and Tucker followed with, 'How did you do that?' Nothing compares to that moment...when Terry Kidwell and the Tahoe crew paid me a compliment for my riding. (p. 89, emphasis added)

> I showed up [to the 1990 US Open] a couple days early to practice. The pipe had just been built by a legendary pipe cutter... I was allowed to session the pipe early by Burton police, along with *proven competitors* like Mike Jacoby, Craig Kelly, Kelly Jo Legaz and others. Normally, the *newer kids* had to wait and practice with the other open-class riders but *I was invited inside the fence* when they saw me watching. *I had graduated from the minors*, even though I still felt like [a] boy. (p. 98, emphasis added)

As these comments illustrate, for young male snowboarders to gain acceptance into the snowboarding fratriarchy, it is not simply enough to *be*: 'A [young] man must do, display and prove' (Miles, 1991, cited in Macdonald, 2001, p. 103). Making claim to a masculine snowboarding identity also 'depends upon public acceptance of that claim and social support for expressing that claim' (Emler & Reicher, 1995, p. 229).

The Bros: fratriarchal masculinities

A fratriarchy is a group of young men who compete for prestige through demonstrations of physical prowess, courage and gameness. Fratriarchy is the 'rule of the brother-[hood]s' (Remy, 1990, cited in Loy, 1995, p. 265). Remy (1990) notes that fratriarchy: (i) 'is a mode of male domination which is concerned with a quite different set of values from those of patriarchy'; (ii) 'is based simply on the self-interest of the association of men itself'; (iii) 'reflects the demand of a group of lads to have the "freedom" to do as they please, to have a good time'; and (iv) 'implies primarily the domination of the *age set*... of young men who have not taken on family responsibilities' (cited in Loy, 1995, p. 265). Across the social world, young men engage in action situations in which they display, test, and subject their behavior to social evaluation. This fratriarchal behavior is also apparent in snowboarding, particularly at the core of the culture. Indeed, young men in their late teens and early twenties, sometimes referred to as the 'brotherhood' or The Bros (Field notes, 2003, 2004, 2005), have always constituted a dominant force in the snowboarding field.

The *Whiskey* videos produced by core Canadian boarders Sean Kearns and Sean Johnson in the mid- to late-1990s epitomized the snowboarding fratriarchy. They featured young male snowboarders, many of whom were also skateboarders, consuming excessive amounts of alcohol, vomiting, performing violent acts against themselves and others (e.g., smashing empty beer bottles over their own heads or over their friends' heads, often repeatedly), and engaging in destructive behavior (e.g., smashing windows). The only images of women were in the style of soft pornography. The low-budget *Whiskey* videos were the first to document this aspect of the snowboarding lifestyle. 'In those days, *Whiskey* was the dope shit,' recalled Sean Kearns, 'fuckin' smash, break and crash – that was it' (cited in LeFebvre, 2005, para. 9). In the first *Whiskey* video, a conversation between snowboarder Kris Markovick (who is seen vomiting violently) and the unknown camera operator reveals the criteria for inclusion into this fratriarchal group:

> Kris: Someone told me the only way to get into the Whiskey videos was to throw up.
>
> Camera operator: It's either that or you smash a bottle over your head. You chose the easier way [vomiting from excessive alcohol consumption].
>
> Kris: Oh I'll do the bottle later. (*Whiskey The Movie*, 1994)

The men in these videos show a complete disregard for their own, and their friends', safety and health. Moreover, the following excerpt from Richards'

(2003) autobiography highlights the excessive alcohol consumption and juvenile humor and pranks at the core of the snowboarding fratriarchy during this period:

> The secret was to pick the *weakest* animal in the herd and then patiently wait for him to drink himself to oblivion. After he passed out, someone would generally say a prayer to the effect of 'God help him'. Then we would move in like hyenas, with magic markers, honey, duct tape, and anything else that was handy. It would begin innocently enough, with a large 'idiot' written on the forehead. A moustache would be added then a big red penis on the side of the cheek with the business end aimed right at the ol' kisser. Empty beer cans and beer bottles would be shoved ceremoniously down the victim's pants, honey massaged into his hair, and by the time we'd finished, his entire face, eyebrows, neck, and other exposed skin would be covered in 'non-toxic' ink. (p. 176)

This comment also identifies strong elements of the hierarchy (the 'weakest animal') that is characteristic of the snowboarding fratriarchy.

Despite the increasing professionalism in snowboarding, many contemporary professional male snowboarders do, in various ways, continue to express widespread hypermasculine ideals, fantasies and desires. Physical prowess, risk-taking, and a 'hard-core' 'bad boy' image (e.g., hedonistic and party lifestyle, disregard for authority, heterosexual pursuits, and high jinks), are all important aspects of the fratriarchal masculinity embodied by many professional male boarders, and endorsed by the media (see Figure 7.1). A reckless, short-term approach to the body also continues to be celebrated by the snowboarding fratriarchy. In an increasingly mediatized culture, professional male snowboarders are iconic; they hold the highest position within the field and thus they have the most power to define the latest snowboarding tastes and styles (see Chapter 4). Observing the influence of such cultural exemplars on the actions of other male boarders, particularly younger males, professional female snowboarder Morgan Lafonte asked: 'Why do boys worship men so much? All the men in snowboarding look the same, have the same mannerisms, talk the same and ride the same ... I can't tell the difference and I'm inside the sport' (cited in Howe, 1998, p. 118). The commercial promotion and cultural celebration of snowboarding's fratriarchal exemplars is illustrative of how the structure of the snowboarding field is maintained.

Much like the stars of the early *Whiskey* videos, and contemporary professional male snowboarders featured in mass (television and newspapers) and niche (snowboarding magazines and films) media, many young male snowboarders accept injury and risk-taking as part of the snowboarding experience. The following comments, shared with me proudly by a core

Figure 7.1   A male snowboarder embodies the 'bad boy' image celebrated within the snowboarding fratriarchy (image used with permission of photographer Gavin Key)

male snowboarder during an interview, are illustrative of the reckless relationships many young men have with their bodies:

> In the 2002 X-Games at Whakapapa, I was competing. I came down to the medical bay; I had 4 cracked ribs and a twisted knee and I was the least injured guy there; fractured skulls, massive back injuries, guys with their calves ripped open, you name it. It was crazy. I was just like, 'give me my two Panadols [painkillers] and I'll be on my way.' *Accidents happen aye.* (Hamish, personal communication, September 2005, emphasis added)

Not dissimilar to proving hypermasculinity by smashing a bottle over your own head (as seen in the *Whiskey* videos), experiencing serious injury and demonstrating stoical courage in the endurance of pain is portrayed as simply part of the achievement of manhood and confirms particular forms of superiority in relation to other men and women (see Seidler, 2006; Whitehead, 2002). As one male snowboarder notes, somewhat sarcastically, 'catching an edge on hard pack [ice] will put hair on your chest. I'm a man!' (cited in Curtes et al., 2001, p. 6).

The importance of male bonding as an exclusionary practice, or of the extreme desire of fratriarchal groups to differentiate themselves from women, should not be underestimated. Loy (1995) notes that the presence of women as objects of ridicule, humiliation, and abuse helps strengthen fraternal bonds and reinforce male domination. While blatant abuse on snowboard fields is rare, some young men continue to ridicule and humiliate women to further 'encourage the exclusion of women from the brotherhood' (Whitson, 1990, p. 25; see also Laurendeau, 2004; Wheaton, 2000b). While completing fieldwork in Whistler in November 2005, I overheard an interesting conversation that sheds light on how some young men encourage male bonding and successfully discourage relationships with women that might ultimately threaten the brotherhood. A group of young males sitting at a local bus stop were chatting about a group of girls they had met the previous night. When one member of the group declared the girls 'just a bunch of snow bunnies,' the others nodded and leered in agreement. But when one young man disagreed and admitted he was 'interested in "Nancy" and might call her back', his friends immediately tried to dissuade him. They proclaimed loudly: 'She would just be a distraction from your snowboarding, man, and that's what we are here to do, snowboard every day. Come on bro, we made a pact, no girlfriends, remember? She will just get in the way. Bros before hos!' (field notes, November 2005). Mark Stranger (1998) found similar sexist attitudes among male surfers where women seeking genuine companionship and shared relationships quickly discovered their expectations 'clashed starkly with the pattern of a surfer's life that prioritized the search for surf over virtually all else' (cited in Booth, 2002, p. 7). Like surfing, the fraternal structure of snowboarding culture devalues women as part of a process to help men define their masculinity.

While some women (e.g., pro-hos, poseurs) passively accept their marginalization, and in so doing support the snowboarding fratriarchy, others refuse to be excluded and successfully negotiate spaces for themselves within the snowboarding fratriarchy. By demonstrating physical prowess and commitment, and ignoring various forms of symbolic violence, some women earn symbolic and cultural capital, and thus a place among their male peers (see also Chapter 6). For some core female snowboarders, being treated like 'one of the boys' and accepted into fratriarchal groups is seen as a clear sign of achievement. But, as the following comments from one long-time core U.S. female snowboarder suggest, some women are critically aware of the fratriarchal and homo-social practices of young men in the snowboarding field:

Guys wanna hump guys. Boys love themselves and other boys. Really, boys don't want to be with girls that snowboard. If you're a girl that *really* snowboards or skateboards then you are competition to them, and they don't want competition. That's why all these rumors are coming out about X being a bit kinky in her sex life and Y being a lesbian. They like girls who pretend to snowboard but if you're a girl that actually skateboards and snowboards you're kind of a threat to them...I think boys are intimidated by a girl that can actually do it. (personal communication, November 2005)

While some women make adaptations and adopt strategies to 'manage the masculine culture into which they are entering' (Chambers, 2005, p. 342), others act in ways to undercut these. The following case of an unknown woman deflating a known male snowboarder's ego, for example, highlights the agency (or 'regulated liberties') of female snowboarders within the snowboarding fratriarchy, and its effect on male subjectivities:

> The mandatory post-contest party was held at someone's house in nearby Donner (California). Swierz and I were getting pushed around in this sea of people, when some girl asked us, 'So, who are you guys?' Swierz said, 'I'm Kris,' and I said, 'I'm Todd Richards.' She flattened me with one fell swoop. 'Do you always introduce yourself with your full name?' she asked. I was a stuttering idiot at that point but she went on. 'Why do you have to introduce yourself as Todd Richards? Do you think I'll recognize your name or something? I don't care if you are some pro, so get over yourself.' This wouldn't have been so horrible if she hadn't been so right on. Truth be told, I knew there was a little bit of a buzz going on about me, and I wanted to impress her. Being a pro had been my biggest goal, and I flaunted it a bit. Boy, that girl chopped my ego in half. (Richards, 2003, p. 93)

Other female snowboarders respond to the maleness of the culture by creating more alternative spaces for women within the snowboarding field, such as female-only snowboard camps, competitions, magazines, and websites (see also Chapters 3 and 4).

The snowboarding fratriarchy not only excludes women, it also marginalizes 'other' men. As the following comment illustrates, the hypermasculine practices adopted by young male snowboarders frustrate some men, particularly older men and novices, who do not experience snowboarding in the same way:

> There is always gonna be rudeness in any context that involves predominantly 18–25-year-old males. Young males on the mountain tend to act like pack animals, constantly attempting to reassert their dominance. ...Sometimes it really annoys me, especially when they do stupid stuff that puts others at risk. (Andrew, personal communication, March 2006)

As well as excluding older and less skilled males, the snowboarding fratriarchy also has the potential to be violently homophobic. 'I hate to think what the young hard-core boarders would do to a homosexual rider,' said Nick 'I'm reasonably sure it would be abusive' (personal communication, April 2006; see Kimmel, 1994). Despite the prevalence of homophobia among men (and women) in the snowboarding fratriarchy, many gay men (and women) enjoy snowboarding. While most participate on the margins of the culture, as novices or weekend warriors, some gay snowboarders are actively negotiating new space within the field. For example, in 2002, American snowboard racer Ryan Miller became the first professional snowboarder to declare his homosexual status. After many years of 'making excuses' and 'putting up' with the hyper-heterosexuality of his peers, Miller responded to an invite from team-mates to visit a local strip club by stating matter-of-factly, 'I'm not into that... I'm gay'. According to Miller, the initial response from team-mates and the industry was 'colder than a Canadian winter'; 'invitations to social events dried up, the camaraderie ended' and he was 'basically shunned' by both his peers and snowboarding companies 'not eager to be associated with an openly gay snowboarder' (cited in Buzinski, 2002, para. 10). Despite experiencing marginalization from some of his peers, Miller is 'out and proud' and clearly displays stickers from a variety of gay organizations (e.g., Outboard, a gay and lesbian snowboarding group; Team Flame, an organization for gay elite athletes) on his snowboard.

Fratriarchal cultures exclude women and some men, and can encourage aggressive, sexist and homophobic behavior. But, according to John Loy (1995), such modern tribal groups can also provide young men with comradeship, a sense of community, adventure and excitement, and a release of youthful aggression. Indeed, friendships between male snowboarders are an essential aspect of the fratriarchy. Professional Canadian snowboarder Devun Walsh described the infamous 'Wildcats' team as 'just a crew of friends. You don't have to do some crazy trick to be on our team. We ride together and just support each other. The main theme of the Wildcats is fun and friendship. No one's trying to outshine one another. [We] fail, fall, and overcome together' (cited in Dresser, 2003, para. 12). Friendships within the fraternal structure of snowboarding culture are based on sharing mountain experiences as well as the lifestyle. Nonetheless, while the snowboarding fratriarchy provides some young men with friendship and a sense of community, it also fosters male domination in at least three ways: it brings young men together, keeps young men together, and often works to put women down or to exclude them. In short, the snowboarding fratriarchy, like all fratriarchies, works to 'develop male bonding, maintain sex segregation, and generate an ideology of male supremacy' (Loy, 1995, p. 267). Young men in the snowboarding fratriarchy continue to adopt a variety of covert and overt strategies to exclude and marginalize women and 'other' men, and reinforce their dominant position in the hierarchical structure of the snowboarding field (see Figure 7.2).

Figure 7.2 A group of young male snowboarders building a jump in the Whistler backcountry. With only a select few highly skilled women (occasionally) invited to join these day-long excursions, 'backcountry booter sessions' are often sites of homo-social fratriarchal bonding (image used with permission of photographer Gavin Key)

The old guys: masculinities in transition

As men take on more social responsibilities (marriage, children, mortgages, long-term employment), it is inevitable that their snowboarding experiences also change. No longer is snowboarding culture a site for proving their manhood. In the words of one ex-core snowboarder, 'as you get older you become more comfortable and confident in your own skin. Proving yourself becomes less important but it still happens for some poor sons of bitches' (Nick, personal communication, April 2006). As male boarders grow older, many tend to abandon fratriarchal groups and adopt a more individualistic approach to snowboarding. Many older male snowboarders are also more cautious in terms of their bodies and risk-taking. As 'one of the old guys', Gavin, a 35-year-old snowboarder, described himself as 'a real wimp on the mountain these days' (personal communication, March 2006). Moreover, as they gain adult responsibilities, the importance of snowboarding in their lives often tends to wane. Snowboarding is still important to me,' said Nick, 'but I find it increasingly hard to get to the slopes nowadays, with work and stuff. We are also saving to buy a house next year, so no spare cash... I just can't justify spending so much time and money on snowboarding any more' (personal communication, April 2006).

For many, the focus shifts towards sharing the snowboarding experience with their partner. Many ex-core male snowboarders actively encourage their nonsnowboarding girlfriends to take up the activity by buying them equipment and/or trying to teach them themselves. Participating with a partner, however, has the potential to introduce new gender dynamics to the snowboarding experience. According to Nick, 'I love snowboarding with Carissa. She is so stoked, and I love her energy', but he noted that, in general, girlfriends have the tendency to 'get quite grumpy when things don't go right, especially when they are learning. And generally girls get hurt more and bruise easier, and then they pack it in...there are always a few tears on icy days' (personal communication, April 2006).

The gender dynamics can become even more complicated when both partners are core or ex-core boarders. 'Snowboarding is something that we can enjoy and do together,' said Jamie but she admitted that 'sometimes I don't want to hear his [boyfriend's] criticism and it can turn into bickering' (personal communication, February 2005). Another ex-core female snowboarder enjoys riding with her boyfriend at the weekends but acknowledged 'there is always a bit of competition going on between us' (personal communication, March 2005). Some women demonstrate more physical prowess than their partners and, in so doing, challenge traditional gender power relations where males are assumed to be 'naturally' physically superior. For example, when professional snowboarder Tina Basich dated David Grohl, member of the band the *Foo Fighters* and novice snowboarder, she felt she had to 'pretend to look the other way when he would catch an edge and fall' to save him from embarrassment (Basich, 2003, p. 146). For some snowboarding couples, traditional gender roles are nullified, while for others they are reinforced. When snowboarding with his girlfriend, Nick admitted, 'I'm kinda the protector...if some idiot smashes into her I'm going to wring his scrawny neck' (personal communication, April 2006). Interestingly, as male snowboarders transition out of the fratriarchy and begin participating in different ways, some are prompted to reflect critically on aspects of the hypermasculine snowboarding habitus. Arguably, a gendered reading of Bourdieu's habitus-field complex has the potential to shed new light on men's multiple and dynamic subjectivities, and potential for gender reflexivity.

Habitus, field, and reflexive masculinities

In Chapter 6 I employed a feminist appropriation of Bourdieu's notion of habitus-field to explain how some female snowboarders come to critically reflect upon gendered dimensions of their habitus. Arguably, as men move across social fields, they too can be alerted to variations in norms and practices in different fields which, in some cases, can lead to increased critical reflexivity regarding gender behaviors and values in particular fields, and/or problematic aspects of their own masculine habitus. My research on snowboarding reveals that, as men move between various fields (snowboarding, home and family, education, workforce, different sport cultures), and change positions within fields (grommet, core boarder, professional, retired athlete, ex-core participant, weekend warrior; son, brother, husband, father), some experience conflicts between different concepts of order and ways of behaving that generate 'questions as to the "naturalness" of established gender practices' (Krais, 2006, p. 131).

As male snowboarders transition out of the snowboarding fratriarchy and adopt new positions – often with more adult responsibilities – in other fields with different gender norms and expectations, *some* reflect critically upon elements of the hypermasculine habitus embodied by young men (and some women) during their participation in the snowboarding fratriarchy (such as abusive behavior, reckless and short-term approaches to risk, pain and injury, hyper-heterosexuality, sexism, and homophobia). Canadian ex-core snowboarder Kelsey, for example, described how he was 'obsessed with all things snowboarding' during his teenage years, but on graduating from university and getting a full-time job in an urban metropolis, his snowboarding experiences changed:

> Now I live and work in the city...and can only get to the mountains in the weekends...but I'm always struck by how rude and obnoxious some of the young guys are. I hate it when I see the young guys who think they're too cool...to wear a helmet...to apologize to an older man or woman whose skis they just ran over...not to spit on people from chairs...to ride an older board that's not a brand name, too cool...geez, I could go on....I know the punky, rebellious, 'I don't give a damn' attitude has been around since day one, but now I really hate it. (personal communication, September 2004)

Moreover, as the following comment illustrates, when ex-core male boarders start experiencing the physical consequences of their previous snowboarding participation, some begin questioning the fratriarchal value system that rewards risk-taking, and pain and injury tolerance:

> My body bears the signs of years of snowboarding and that's a bit unfortunate....Sometimes I wish I hadn't been quite so reckless with my body, but it was just the way we did things. You know, the whole 'go hard or go home' mentality. I don't think like that anymore, but all the young guys still seem to be living and riding by that philosophy. (Nick, personal communication, March 2008)

Similarly, when injury forced professional snowboarder Todd Richards to take a step back from the field of competitive snowboarding for the first time in 15 years, it enabled him to look differently at his priorities and motivations for snowboarding. Prior to his injury he was driven to 'make more money' and 'stay ahead of the other guys', but through a long rehabilitation process and many months away from the sport, he 'began to understand how important my family was in a whole new way' (Richards, 2003, p. 277). For some professional and core male snowboarders, adopting new positions in the field of the family (e.g., husband, father) prompts critical reflection on fratriarchal norms and values regarding priorities (e.g., time, money) and approaches to risk, as well as their relationships with friends, women and family members (e.g., dismissal of the 'bros before hos' mentality dominant within the fratriarchy). For example, when asked to offer some advice to other 'rad dads', that is 'young dads who still want to get their shred on', professional snowboarder and father of twin girls, Louie Fountain, stated matter-of-factly: 'Put your family first. Snowboarding will fade and die away' (Huffman, 2006, para. 3).

For some snowboarders, movement out of the core of the snowboarding field and into other social fields, such as the workplace, can also prompt critical reflection on practices of marginalization and degradation observed within the fratriarchy, as well as their role in such situations:

> Snowboarders seem to think of themselves as open-minded and accepting of difference, but in my experience there is a staunchness towards anything that doesn't comply with the stereotypical snowboarder who is a hyper-active, heterosexual, amateur stuntman, fashion conscious, party boy. I'll admit...I used to buy into this image...There were heaps of situations where other guys said really rude stuff to women, or guys that looked gay...and I didn't try to stop them. But now I try to speak up more...there is no way that sort of behavior would be accepted at my workplace, so why should it be okay on the mountain? (Nick, personal communication, March 2008)

Some ex-core male snowboarders also explain how riding with their partners and female friends has alerted them to some of the cultural and societal gender norms limiting female participation:

> I enjoy riding [with my girlfriend], and sharing the whole experience. I try to be supportive and listen to her when she wants to head in a different direction, or take a break...But I see more competitive males, particularly some of the young guys, giving their girlfriends grief for not keeping up, in both appearances and literally. (Dave, personal communication, November 2006)

As these brief examples suggest, on leaving the 'fratriarchal' group – either temporarily or permanently due to the pursuit of professional or educational opportunities, injury, marriage, parenthood, or any other reason – and entering 'other' fields (e.g., work, higher education, sport, leisure, parenthood, long-term relationship), some men are prompted to reflect critically on various aspects of the hypermasculine snowboarding identity (e.g., celebration of risk and injury, marginalization of women and 'other' men) which, in some instances, leads to behavioral changes (e.g., 'I try to be supportive and listen to her') and subtle practices of resistance (e.g., 'Now I try to speak up more'). Of course, the presence of reflexivity does not automatically translate into masculine identity transformation. As previously suggested, in some circumstances 'our capacity for reflexive thought can leave us recognizing but unable to do anything about our lack of freedom' (Craib, 1992, p. 150; see also Adams, 2006; Brooks & Wee, 2008). Even when men experience a disjunction between habitus and field leading to gender reflexivity, these alterations do not necessarily work to 'undermine gender, or masculine domination' (Chambers, 2005, p. 343). Moreover, as men leave the snowboarding fratriarchy and enter into new fields and adopt new social roles, certain aspects of gender relations may be destabilized, yet other aspects may be further entrenched (McNay, 1999).

Male snowboarders, reflexivity, and 'regulated liberties'

The contemporary snowboarding field simultaneously celebrates and reinforces a hypermasculine fratriarchal snowboarding identity *and* provides space for alternative masculinities; it is a contradictory social context of ongoing sexism *and* greater opportunities for men and women to share the snowboarding experience and lifestyle. It would be a mistake, however, to assume that young male boarders passively embody the hypermasculine snowboarding habitus during their enculturation into the field and only begin to critically reflect on their gendered experiences upon exiting, or moving to a different position (e.g., weekend warrior, 'rad dad'), within the field. Not dissimilar from their female counterparts, core male snowboarders frequently encounter differences and problems *within* the field, which encourage some of them to engage in day-to-day negotiations of gender identity and sexual politics. Some core male boarders perform 'regulated liberties' (Bourdieu, 1991) by engaging in subtle practices that challenge the legitimate meaning and use of the male (and female) snowboarding body from *within* the field. For example, during the early 2000s, some core male snowboarders wore outerwear, clothing, and equipment in traditionally 'feminine' colors, such as pastel pinks and blues, or bright pink, and in so doing were subtly playing with traditional notions of masculinity and femininity, and assumed heterosexuality (see Figure 7.3). In the words of a

Figure 7.3 This image, featured in the September 2002 issue of *Transworld Snowboarding* magazine, illustrates how some fratriarchal male snowboarders are playing with traditional notions of masculinity. This particular (heterosexual) male snowboarder's equipment is pink and purple, traditionally 'feminine' colours, he sports extensive tattooing on his arms, and he wears a T-shirt that reads: 'Don't assume I'm straight' (image used with permission of photographer Embry Rucker, www.embryrucker.com)

committed female snowboarder, 'it is really acceptable for boys to be "super feminine" these days. I mean...all my snowboarder boy friends are way more gossipy than me. They are wearing pink and fur, and they love going shopping too' (Moriah, personal communication, 2005; see also Anderson, 2009; Wheaton, 2000a, 2000b).

Some core male snowboarders also challenge the male valuation system within the field by expressing feminist sentiments in support of their female peers, and occasionally publicly question their exclusion from magazines, videos, events, and the industry. For example, one male correspondent wrote to *Transworld Snowboarding* complaining about the lack of attention given to women in snowboarding: 'And why the hell hasn't Forum put a woman on their team? I am offended when people discriminate against women' (September 2002, p. 28). Danny Burrows, editor of *OnBoard European Snowboarding Magazine* and self-proclaimed 'manimist/feminist', also publicly protested against gender disparities in the snowboarding culture:

> Sponsorship deals for girls are minimal in comparison to those of guys. They always draw the short straw when it comes to combined-contests – either having to ride in the dark or once the boys have trashed everything. And even when all goes in their favor and they are riding well, they're served up the ultimate sexist insult: 'Damn, you ride like a guy.' We boys might think this is a compliment, but in reality it suggests that all boys ride better than most girls, which is just not true. There are...a hell of a lot of girls who have nuts of nickel whether that be on the rails, in the pipe or getting face shots [powder] in the backcountry. See, even the expression for being brave or good, 'having balls' is sexist. (December 2005, p. 15)

Some men are actively challenging assumptions regarding the position of women within the snowboarding field. Such questioning seems particularly strong among those men who have witnessed their daughters, sisters, girl-friends, and friends experiencing sexism (in its various guises) in the snow-boarding field, and those who have learned different gender norms, value, and expectations in other social fields, such as family or education.

The key point here is that men's embodied practices 'cannot be under-stood through binaries of domination and resistance, but rather involve more complex processes of investment and negotiation' (McNay, 2000, p. 58). While the various 'regulated liberties' performed by male snowboard-ers may suggest gender instability within the snowboarding field, they do not guarantee reflexivity or gender identity transformation. Moreover, while the habitus-field complex draws our attention to interesting examples of male snowboarders' agency and reflexivity, it is important to reiterate that such experiences are rare and not shared by all men in the snowboarding field. The concept of habitus reminds us that the 'entrenched dimensions' of embodied experiences, as well as individuals' and groups' 'deep-seated, often unconscious investments in conventional images of masculinity and femininity [*sic*] cannot easily be reshaped' (McNay, 1999, p. 103). In sum, a feminist turn to Bourdieu suggests that masculine reflexivity in physical cultures, such as snowboarding, is 'uneven and discontinuous', potentially arising as a result of mobility *between* social fields and, to a lesser extent, as a result of the requirements to reconcile the dissonant experiences that this invokes *within* fields (regulated liberties) (Kenway & McLeod, 2005; McNay, 1999, 2000; Thorpe, 2009, 2010).

Understanding male boarding bodies: some final thoughts

In this chapter I have argued that, in contrast to R. W. Connell's outdated concepts of hegemonic masculinity and gender order, recent feminist engagements with Bourdieu's conceptual schema may help us 'ask new questions' about men and masculinities in sport and physical cultures in the early twenty-first century. Adopting a gendered reading of Bourdieu's concept of field, I described three different masculinities – 'The Grommets', 'The Bros', and 'The Old Guys' – within the global snowboarding field. The legitimate masculine practices and performances, valued forms of capital, and gender relations, differ between these groups. 'The Bros' – typically young, white, middle- and upper-class males – continue to hold a dominant position at the core of the culture, and thus have the most power to define the latest snowboarding styles and tastes. But the snowboarding field is a site of struggles where various agents (e.g., Grommets, 'Old Guys', gay boarders, and women) attempt to negotiate, transform, and preserve the legitimate meanings and use of the boarding body. Simply put, the rules structuring the snowboarding culture, and the gender relations within it, are not fixed but inherently contested by those within the field.

Masculinities in the contemporary snowboarding culture are multiple and dynamic; they differ over space, time, and context, and are rooted in the cultural and social moment. The concept of field, in conjunction with habitus and capital, can help explain how men experience snowboarding differently depending on their positions within the field, their (explicit and tacit) knowledge of the rules and stakes within the field, and their ability (and willingness) to accrue culturally valued forms of capital (symbolic, physical, social, cultural, or hypermasculine capital). Moreover, men's snowboarding identities, behaviors and interactions (with other men and women) often change as they age and enter new life stages and gain (or lose) access to particular forms of capital, such as physical, symbolic, masculine, or economic capital. The movement of male snowboarders between and within overlapping social fields, and from different generational milieu, further complicates gender relations in the snowboarding field. In the next chapter I build on the theoretical arguments offered in Chapters 6 and 7 to explore male and female participants' movement across and within local, national, and virtual snowboarding fields. In so doing, I shed light on how snowboarders' experiences of travel and lifestyle sport migration influence their sense of cultural, national, and gender identity and reflexivity.

8
Transnational Boarding Bodies: Travel, Tourism, and Lifestyle Sport Migration

Travelling is an integral part of snowboarding for me. Stepping off the beaten track and leaving familiarity behind can add an entirely different dimension to a snowboard trip. Experiencing new environments and different ways of living brings rewards all of its own. The most important thing that snowboarding has given me has been the opportunity to expand my horizons. It's hard to forget the feeling of cranking a turn in bottomless powder, but when I'm too old to strap in anymore, the memories that I'll hold tightest will be the places I've been and the people I've met along the way. (James McPhail, snowboard photographer, cited in Barr et al., 2006, p. 92)

As a snowboarder the 'Big OE' [overseas experience] is a bit different from your good old traditional 'going to London and getting a job at a pub' or 'backpacking around Europe on the smell of any oily rag'. It's more a pilgrimage, a mission of intent to ride as much as possible, to experience previously unknown depths of snow, and conquer the peaks and parks that you've seen so many times in DVDs and magazines. (Westcot, 2006, p. 63)

Approaching the sport from a position of privilege, many snowboarders travel extensively – locally, nationally, internationally, and virtually – in pursuit of new terrain, fresh snow, and social interactions and cultural connections. According to the authors of *Snowboarding the World*, 'Snowboarders are, by definition, travellers. Unless you're lucky enough to live at the foot of a mountain, the typical snowboarding trip means planning an overseas journey' (Barr et al., 2006, p. 3). A recent online survey of more than 2000 snowboarders from around the world showed approximately 43 percent of correspondents had snowboarded at least once in a foreign country ('Poll results', 2006).

According to *Transworld Snowboarding* journalist Jennifer Sherowski (2004a), 'when it comes to seeing the world, snowboarders are lucky':

> we don't have to vacantly watch it pass by outside the tour-bus window or through the camcorder scope like most people. Nope, the emptiness of 'tourism' is not for us, because we belong to a *planet-wide culture* that makes journeying to the remotest places the equivalent of visiting a pack of friends for a day of slashing it. You shred a place, you live it, you know it – you don't just buy the postcard at the airport. (p. 106, emphasis added)

Glossing over local, regional, and national differences, as well as the logistical complexities and privileged nature of such travel opportunities, Sherowski (2004a) continues to wax lyrical: snowboarding is a 'global culture' that 'transcends borders and language barriers' (p. 106). Professional Norwegian snowboarder Terje Haakonsen also believes that 'with people travelling and having friends all over the world...nationalism [has become] a really backwards-looking concept' (cited in Benedek, 2009, para. 12).[1] In this chapter I draw on literature from the burgeoning field of transnational migration and mobility studies to explore how these global connections are being experienced by snowboarders in and across different local, national, and virtual spaces.

Transnationalism and the 'sociology of mobilities'

Transnationalism broadly refers to 'multiple ties and interactions linking people or institutions across the borders of nation-states' (Vertovec, 1999, p. 447). Transnationalism is not a new phenomenon, yet it has been argued that technological developments (especially telecommunications) have contributed to the intensification of systems of ties, interactions, exchange, and mobility, such that they are spreading throughout the world with increasing speed and efficacy (Ibid.). According to transnational theorist Ulf Hannerz (1992), 'it must now be more difficult than ever, or at least more unreasonable, to see the world...as a cultural mosaic, of separate pieces with hard, well-defined edges. Cultural interconnections increasingly reach across the world' (cited in Crang et al., 2003, p. 439). Indeed, it is now widely accepted that 'social and cultural processes regularly exceed the boundaries of individual nation states, sketching "transnational" cartographies of cultural circulation, identification and action' (Crang et al., 2003, p. 439).

Scholars from various disciplines are increasingly drawing on an array of theories, concepts and methods to examine the different social, economic and political characteristics of transnationalism. The result, however, has been 'much conceptual muddling' (Vertovec, 1999, p. 448). Attempting to 'disentangle' the term, Vertovec identifies six interrelated conceptual premises of work concerned with transnationalism. These include studies of transnationalism as social morphology (or social formations and networks spanning borders), as a type of consciousness, as a mode of cultural repro- duction, as an avenue of capital, as a site of political engagement, and as a (re)construction of 'place' or locality. In this chapter, I am particularly inter- ested in how a high degree of *human mobility* contributes to a 'transnational imaginary' (Wilson & Dissanayake, 1996) in contemporary snowboarding and how these transnational experiences contribute to 'new subjectivities in the global arena' (Nonini & Ong, 1997). Focusing on the mobilities of various groups of snowboarders, this chapter aims to reveal fresh insights into the lived transnationalism and global migration of contemporary youth facilitated by the 'extreme', 'alternative' or 'lifestyle' sports economy (Wheaton, 2004).

According to Rojek and Urry (1997) 'a major reason for the actual and met- aphorical significance of mobility' in the social sciences is because 'cultures travel as well as people' (Ibid., p. 11). Continuing, they explain that 'know- ing a culture involves work, of memory, interpretation and reconstruction', and 'almost always involves travel' (Ibid., p. 12). In their efforts to 'know' cultures and social groups in the early twenty-first century, anthropolo- gists, sociologists, and human geographers are critically engaging with an array of theoretical approaches to explain some of the profound changes in travel, mobility, migration, flow, and displacement. Of particular relevance for this study of snowboarders' transnational travel, tourism, and lifestyle sport migration experiences, is John Urry's recent 'sociology of mobilities' paradigm:

> Some of the diverse mobilities that are materially transforming the 'social as society' into the 'social as mobility' include imaginative travel, move- ments of images and information, virtual travel, object travel and corpo- real travel. The consequence of such diverse mobilities is to produce what Beck terms the growth of 'inner mobility' for which coming and going, being both here and there at the same time, has become much more glo- bally normal. (Urry, 2000, p. 185)

According to Urry (2000), various global 'networks and flows' are 'criss- crossing societal borders in new temporal-spatial patterns' such that 'a novel agenda for sociology' concerned with 'the diverse mobilities of peo- ples, objects, images, information' and of the 'complex interdependencies between, and social consequences of, these diverse mobilities' is required (p. 185). For Urry (2007), the 'sociology of mobilities' paradigm broadly refers to the project of establishing a 'movement driven social science' where mobility (or immobility) is conceptualized as consisting of a wide range of social, political, and economic practices and processes (p. 43). To rec- ognize the 'exceptional levels of global interdependence' and the 'fluidity and malleability' of contemporary social phenomena, 'more mobile theorizing' and greater 'academic mobility' across disciplinary borders is necessary (Urry, 2000, p. 186). Thus in this chapter I cross disciplinary borders (youth cultural studies, social and cultural geography, tourism studies, migration studies, sociology of sport, and physical cultural studies) and draw on an array of transnational ethnographic methods (see Chapter 1) to examine the networks, and flows and mobilities of various groups of snowboarders for the purpose of sport, leisure, work, and lifestyle.

This chapter consists of three parts. In the first part I draw on Urry's (2000) 'sociology of mobilities' paradigm to offer a description of the various corporeal mobilities in the snowboarding culture. More specifically, I examine travel patterns of snow-sport tourists, professional athletes, and core participants, respectively. In the second part I focus on lifestyle sport migrants' lived experiences of transnationalism. Here I engage recent work by human geographers, and Pierre Bourdieu's key concepts of field, capital, and habitus, to enhance understandings of privileged youth's lifestyle sport migration experiences, and the influence of these mobilities on their identity construction and 'transnational consciousness.' Lastly, I briefly 'ground' my study of snowboarding mobilities in a discussion of mountain resort destinations as transnational physical cultural spaces, and offer some insights into the complex interactions and dynamics between snowboarders in these unique geographies.

Transnational mobilities and snow border crossings

The contemporary snowboarding field is highly fragmented – participants include professional athletes, devoted or 'lifestyle' participants, less committed newcomers and novices, marginal participants (e.g., poseurs, weekend warriors), and various subgroups. With such cultural diversity, it is perhaps not surprising that snowboarders' travel patterns are diverse, ranging from budget to luxury national and international holidays, in the case of marginal participants, ex-core participants, or retired athletes, to cyclic seasonal migration between the hemispheres, for core participants working in the sport or tourism industry, to brief international adventures to remote and exotic destinations for competitions, events, or as part of media or contractual obligations, for professional athletes. Here I build upon existing research on youth and travel more broadly (for example, Skelton & Valentine, 1998; Vogt, 1976; Wearing et al., 2010) to offer a discussion of the corporeal mobilities and migratory practices of snowboarding tourists, professionals, and core participants, respectively.[2] It is important to keep in mind, however, that while travel practices and patterns vary considerably among tourists, professionals, and lifestyle sport migrants, snowboarders typically share a middle- or upper-class habitus. For many snowboarders, travel – real, virtual and imagined – is a highly valued, yet often taken-for-granted, part of their social location. In other words, many snowboarders approach the sport with attitudes to travel already 'durably inculcated by the possibilities and impossibilities, freedoms and necessities, opportunities and prohibitions inscribed in the objective conditions' of a relatively privileged upbringing (Bourdieu, 1992, p. 54). Put simply, snowboarders are often able to imagine opportunities for snow-related travel or lifestyle sport migration unavailable to those from less privileged social fields.

Snowboarding tourism: from hitchhikers to helicopters

For many years, snow-related travel was an expensive and privileged activity limited to upper-class skiers (Coleman, 2004). Recent changes in the ski industry and international travel, however, have contributed to shifts in the social demographics of snow-sport tourists. During the 1990s and early 2000s, ski-fields and mountain resort destinations recognized snowboarding as offering the industry a new youth market and potential for ongoing economic prosperity. Attempting to further attract regional, national, and international snowboarding patrons, many (not all) resort destinations began offering cheaper travel and accommodation options for the typically younger and less affluent (though still privileged) snowboarder, as well as developing unique events for niche groups, such as snowboarding competitions for university students, women's snowboarding clinics, or gay ski and snowboard weeks. Many travel companies also realized the economic potential in snowboarding tourism and began offering a wide range of snow-sport travel options, such as budget or backpacker specials, long-weekend student deals, and all-inclusive family packages. Some airlines also retooled to better service the influx of snow-sport tourists. For example, in 2007 low-cost carrier Ryanair announced a new winter schedule 'designed with skiers and snowboarders in mind' (cited in Ski Tourism, 2007, para. 5). Nonetheless, while international snow-related travel has become more accessible to (some) families, younger participants, and budget travelers, other experiences (e.g., helicopter snowboarding), and locations (e.g., Aspen, Colorado), remain remote, costly, and exclusive.

Despite steady economic growth during the 1990s and early 2000s, international winter sport tourism in many countries experienced a considerable downturn during the global recession of the late 2000s. As Ralf Garrison, author of the Mountain Travel Research report, explains: 'economic conditions had a significant impact on the long-distance, multi-day visitor' (cited in Lewis, 2009, para. 3). Due to the rising cost of jet fuel, many airlines are also imposing baggage charges which are directly impacting snow-travelers' 'decisions of where to travel and what to bring' (Lewis, 2008a, para. 4). The irony here, of course, is that despite growing diversity in the cultural demographics of snow-sport tourists over the past two decades, in the current socioeconomic climate international snow-sport travel may once again become an activity afforded by only the most privileged.

Professional snowboarders: 'living the dream'

The life of the contemporary professional snowboarder is indeed a privileged one, typically consisting of extensive national and international travel for competitions and events. Not dissimilar from professional golfers or tennis players, competitive snowboarders following the International Ski Federation (FIS) Snowboard World Cup circuit compete at ski resorts in countries including Argentina, Austria, Canada, France, Germany, Italy, Japan, Korea, New Zealand, Russia, Spain, Sweden, Switzerland, and the United States. As a competitive athlete on the World Cup tour during the mid- and late 1990s, Pamela reflects upon her hypermobility as follows:

> I can't remember all the places I have travelled to for snowboarding…Obviously some places are not so memorable – but each is connected by that sense of newness, adventure and trepidation. But travelling for competitions is pretty nerve-wracking, so you don't get much of a chance to soak up the place and *be a tourist* – you are preoccupied and focused on the competition preparation and trying to have an optimal competition experience. (personal communication, July 2008, emphasis added)

Not all professional snowboarders, however, follow a strict international competition circuit. Some make a living from sponsorships with snowboarding companies who pay salaries based primarily on niche media coverage (e.g., interviews and photos in snowboarding magazines and websites, segments in snowboard videos). Some of these athletes are paid to travel to exotic and remote locations to pioneer new spaces in destinations such as Alaska, Japan, or New Zealand; their exploits are then covered in snowboard magazines, films, and websites. The representations of idyllic transnational lifestyles of professional male (and some female) snowboarders, promoted by snowboarding companies and media (through, for example, advertisements and videos), then work to create a compelling mythology for many cultural participants (see also Frohlick, 2005; Kay & Laberge, 2003). According to Chris Sanders, CEO of Avalanche Snowboards,

> The dream is basically what the kids see when they look in the magazines and see Damian [Sanders] or Terje [Haakonsen]. They are great lifestyle icons. They have it great. It looks like their lives are 24-hour-a-day adventure. You get handed these plane tickets, you hang out with cool photographers, dye your hair however you want to, and you're making money so your parents have no say in your life. It's all sex, action, and glamour. To an 18-year-old snowboarder, this is the dream. (cited in Howe, 1998, p. 68)

Snowboarding companies and media invest heavily in the transnational hypermobility of professional snowboarders because it enhances global connections, and promotes youth cultural consumption of discourses, images, product, and travel.

Not all professional snowboarders, however, receive the same levels of support from their sponsors; some struggle for many years to subsidize their own transnational snowboarding career and lifestyle. Professional snowboarder and editor of *New Zealand Snowboarder* Dylan Butt offers readers a more sobering perspective:

> Becoming a professional 'Extreme Athlete' has gotta be the best career in the world. Getting paid huge amounts of money to do what you enjoy, living the 'rock star' lifestyle, rolling around in pimped-out wagons, groupies hangin' off each arm, non-stop parties and travelling the world to the most luxurious of destinations... You better pinch yourself because you're dreaming... (Butt, 2005, p. 88)

While most of the media and snowboarding companies work hard to (re)create the 'dream' of the transnational snowboarding lifestyle with extensive coverage and sponsorship of traveling professionals, in reality such opportunities are only afforded a select few. In pursuit of this 'dream' lifestyle, however, many others (e.g., core boarders, semiprofessional snowboarders) invest heavily (financially, physically, and in time) in their own snowboarding journeys, and in so doing, support the global snowboarding economy.

Core snowboarders as 'lifestyle sport migrants'

Typically in their late teens and early twenties, many core participants have yet to take on the adult responsibilities of marriage, children, mortgages, long-term employment, and so on, and their commitment to snowboarding is such that it organizes their whole lives (see also Wheaton & Tomlinson, 1998). Many core snowboarders are nomadic, traveling nationally and internationally to experience new terrain, meet new people, or 'live the dream' of the endless winter. At the end of high school or tertiary education (or during a leave of absence from education or work), many committed snowboarders migrate to mountain towns where they find accommodation and employment, and spend several months to many years practicing, playing and performing in the various physical spaces (mountains) and social places (bars, cafes, and shops). Core snowboarders typically begin their lifestyle migration by moving to snowy destinations within their country of origin. For example, many Canadian snowboarders living on the east coast relocate to larger resorts in Alberta, such as Banff, and British Columbia, such as Whistler; passionate New Zealand snowboarders living in the North Island often move to mountain towns in the South Island, such as Queenstown and Wanaka, which host a thriving international snowboarding scene during the winter months. Observing the lifestyle migration of core snowboarders, Sherowski (2005b) writes:

> Not everyone who rides a snowboard is a snowboarder but for those who do bear this illustrious title, it's an undeniable *way of life*. High school ends, and the road starts calling – off to mountain towns and the assimilation into weird, transient tribes full of people who work night jobs cleaning toilets or handing you your coffee in the early mornings, all so they can shove a fistful of tips in their pocket and ride, their real motives betrayed by goggle tans or chins scuffed by Gore-Tex. In this world, people don't ask what you 'do,' they ask you where you work – knowing that what you do is snowboard, just like them, and any job you might have is simply a means for it. (p. 160)

Some of the more fervent snowboarders follow the winter between hemispheres, thus becoming what Maguire (1996) termed 'nomadic cosmopolitans' (p. 339) and I refer to as 'seasonal lifestyle sport migrants' (see also Thorpe, 2010c; Wheaton, 2004). To facilitate (and prolong) their transnational snowboarding lifestyles, many pursue further training and education to obtain skilled employment in the snow-sport industry as, for example, an instructor, coach, journalist, photographer, or judge. It is important to reiterate, however, that despite the skilled nature of many of these jobs, the majority are not highly paid; they tend to be held by passionate snowboarders committed to the lifestyle rather than the economic rewards. In the words of top snowboarding photographer Trevor Graves: 'If you're shooting to maintain the lifestyle, it's worth it. That's all you can do with the time constraints anyway. It's not a huge cash-maker, like fashion or rock photography. It's really about travelling the world and living snowboarding' (cited in Howe, 1998, p. 107).

While committed snowboarders are traveling within and across many Western – and some Eastern (e.g., China, Japan, Taiwan, and South Korea) – countries, the transnational flows of youth cultural participants are stronger in some directions than others. Some salient flows of seasonal lifestyle sport migrants observed during my fieldwork include Australian, British, New Zealand, and Japanese snowboarders to Canada – particularly Alberta (i.e., Banff) and British Columbia (i.e., Whistler) – and the United States – particularly California (i.e., Mammoth), Colorado (i.e., Breckenridge) and Utah (i.e., Salt Lake City); American, Australian, British, Canadian, European, and Japanese snowboarders to New Zealand (i.e., Queenstown, Wanaka); and British snowboarders to France (i.e., Chamonix).

Importantly, the transnational mobility of snowboarding 'lifestyle migrants' is facilitated (and constrained) by various factors, including work and travel visas, travel and accommodation costs, employment opportunities and wages, languages, and exchange rates. For example, the availability

of temporary youth work visas among the Commonwealth countries facilitates the mobility of Australian, British, Canadian, and New Zealand snowboarders, and J1 visas enable tertiary students from an array of countries to
spend five months working in ski towns in the United States during their
university holidays. A plethora of commercial services have been established
to facilitate (and profit from) the growing number of students wanting to
experience an international 'working holiday' at a ski resort (e.g., Work USA,
Work Canada; see Duncan, 2008). In contrast to the mobilities available to
tertiary education students, a recent quota on the number of H-2B visas
(which permit internationals with the support of a U.S. sponsor to work
temporarily in the United States) has significantly impacted the seasonal
migration of skilled ski industry employees – many of whom have invested
heavily in their 'careers' in the U.S. snow-sport industry.[3] As this example
illustrates, the mobilities of both transnational lifestyle sport migrants and
less privileged migrants are inextricably linked to the changing conditions
of global capitalism, as well as the continuing power of nation-states.

Transnational experiences of lifestyle sport migrants

In the second part of this chapter I draw on recent scholarship in transnational migration and cultural geography, as well as Pierre Bourdieu's habitus-
field complex, to further explore lifestyle sport migrants' lived experiences
of transnationalism. In so doing, I discuss some of the social, physical, and
affective experiences of seasonal sport migration, and consider some of the
potential effects of the hypermobile snowboarding lifestyle on snowboarders' sense of identity (national, cultural, and gender), belonging, and transnational reflexivity.

(Un)settling experiences of lifestyle sport migration

For many first-time lifestyle sport migrants, negotiating space within mountain towns and ski resort destinations can pose a number of practical, social,
and financial challenges. The authors of *Snowboarding the World* offer potential 'seasonnaires' the following sage advice: 'save up during the summer',
'live throughout the winter on a strict budget', and 'fin[d] an apartment or
chalet (the internet can help, but nothing beats visiting your chosen resort
in late summer to check the local agencies and supermarket corkboards),
then fill it with double the amount of people it was intended for and hav[e]
the time of your lives' (Barr et al., 2006, p. 78). Recalling the difficulties of
finding (and affording) accommodation during his first season in an expensive New Zealand ski town, Thomas explained:

> I was sleeping in my snowboard bag beside a guy's bed. I barely knew the
> guy but for $40 a week I could sleep there…. It was in a basement and it
> was known as 'the dungeon'. It didn't bother me that it was cold; I just

slept in a beanie. ... I was one hell-of-a moocher... bounding from couch to couch, thumbing rides, squeezing every penny. (personal communication, July 2008)

Snowboarders arriving in a mountain town for their first season will typically be at the bottom of the 'pecking order' in terms of available accommodation and employment. But due to the transient nature of most ski town populations, opportunities for employment and accommodation typically expand with each consecutive season. Those snowboarders who stay for the summer months, or return for subsequent winters, gain cultural and social capital within the local community and thus access to the more desirable, and highly sought after, forms of accommodation (warm, affordable, close to facilities) and employment (flexible work hours, higher wages).

Typically from the middle- and upper-classes, many snowboarders approach the travel and migration experience with a sense of confidence and entitlement unknown to those from less privileged social positions. Nonetheless, it would be remiss to ignore the considerable social, financial, and emotional investments they make in pursuit of the transnational snowboarding lifestyle: 'The long hours of work to save enough money... The calls, emails and random hook-ups through friends of friends... Dragging bags off planes onto trains and buses, through cities, small towns and villages...' (Butt, 2006, p. 16). For many core snowboarders, lifestyle sport migration requires careful saving and extensive social networking and organization skills, which are often acquired during the enculturation process. As Pamela explains:

If you really enjoy something and work really hard at it, you will find a way to financially survive... I've learnt heaps of really good skills about saving and living cheaply. I've learnt lots of things from different snowboarders over the years, because there is quite a creative, scamming element, about how to get by. In Whistler, Paul and Tony [early New Zealand snowboarding migrants] would live in a van, and Tony would wake up with a frozen beard, and all their peanut butter would be frozen. They'd collect aluminium cans and cash them in to get a subway for dinner. (personal communication, September 2005)

Further commenting on the 'creative and entrepreneurial' efforts of her fellow lifestyle sport migrants, Pamela declared: 'everyone was progressively forging and making their own careers and jobs. It was such a young sport, there was no-one to follow, you had to make it up as you went along. Many of the early guys and girls went on to become really successful business owners in snowboarding and other industries' (personal communication September 2005). As this comment suggests, for some lifestyle sport migrants, participation encourages the development of highly creative, entrepreneurial, financial, and organizational skills, which in some cases transfer into social fields outside snowboarding. To fund her own snow-boarding career and transnational lifestyle, Pamela founded her own snow-board clothing company.

With access to critical material conditions – space, encouragement, and legislation – unknown to previous generations and women from less privileged social positions, many young women are pursuing careers in the international snow-sport industry (as, for example, instructors, coaches, photographers, journalists, athletes, and/or company owners) with enthusiasm and a sense of entitlement (see Figure 8.1; also see Chapter 3). Research on young women's travel and tourism practices suggest that independent solo travel can provide some women with 'opportunities to push the boundaries of constraint', 'find sources of inspiration, empowerment and self-development', and 'generate feelings of independence, freedom, self-reliance and confidence' (Harris & Wilson, 2007, p. 244). Many female lifestyle sport migrants express similar sentiments. New Zealand snowboarder Abby, for example, proclaims the positive social and psychological benefits of her career in the international snowboarding industry: 'I've made so many amazing friends

Figure 8.1 Young, privileged women are increasingly traveling independently and pursuing the transnational snow-sport lifestyle with a sense of confidence and entitlement. To support their nomadic lifestyle, Johanna (left) and Nadja (right) founded NAJO – a homemade beanie company – in 2005 and brought a van from which they travel throughout Europe skiing and snowboarding during the winter, and surfing in the summer, producing and selling their headwear at various events and locations along the way (image used with permission of Johanna Fridheim)

all over the world. Snowboarding has taken me to the place in life where I wanna be. Who knows where else it will take me, snowboarding makes me shine and the sky is the limit!' (cited in Butt, 2006, p. 38). Continuing, Abby attributes to snowboarding the confidence to travel to Canada, America, and Japan, and to become a Snow Girls coach at the women-only snowboard camps at Snow Park, Wanaka New Zealand (Butt, 2006).

Despite the new-found opportunities for international travel and professional careers in the snow-sport industry, many female lifestyle sport migrants 'retire' from the 'back-to-back' lifestyle earlier than their male colleagues. A conversation with Erin, Kim, and Lisa – three highly esteemed New Zealand snowboard instructors who have been doing consecutive winters between New Zealand and North America since the early 2000s – revealed some of the difficulties experienced by female lifestyle sport migrants:

> It is quite hard to stay in the industry for a long time, whether it's because you're sick of travelling, or sick of being broke, or you're ready to settle down. While doing back-to-back winters is awesome, it can take a lot out of you; you are always living out of a bag...you definitely can't have 15 pairs of shoes like city girls [laughing]. (Erin, personal communication, August 2008)

> I think my success in the industry is partly due to the fact that I've never had a boyfriend that I would be prepared to stop traveling for. I'm very selfish, but that's because I am so self-motivated. My career is my priority right now, not boys. ... I've seen so many awesome female instructors stop doing back-to-backs when they fall in love. I think that's partly why the industry is so male-dominated at the senior level. (Kim, personal communication, August 2008)

> Another big thing with doing lots of back-to-back winters would be 6-month friendships. You meet the coolest, like-minded people who have travelled and love, love, love snowboarding, and you have these intense friendships, then at the end of the winter you all go your different ways. It can be really hard, emotionally, sometimes. (Lisa, personal communication, August 2008)

Pamela also describes the financial and physical difficulties and personal sacrifices she made as a semiprofessional athlete and lifestyle sport migrant during the 1990s:

> 'Living the lifestyle' meant a small bag, not many possessions, all funds funneled into travelling to the next competition. I used to come home and think I could have had a street lined with cars, but I'd spent all that money on snowboarding, and I guess, my 'life education'...I was riding up to 200 days a year; I had chill-blains, constant aches and pains, and colds and flus that would last for months. My body never got to recover

or get strong between seasons...Doing back-to-back winters also puts a
lot of strain on your relationships. It's hard to maintain a long-term relationship when you are constantly on the move. (personal communication, February 2008)

Continuing, however, Pamela declared that through her transnational
snowboarding experiences she developed 'a sense of confidence that is
priceless': 'I now know,' she adds, 'that I can do things that other people
think are impossible' (personal communication, February 2005). Clearly, for
many female (and male) lifestyle sport migrants, 'burdens are borne alongside opportunities, in different ways in different times, places and social
locations' (Pratt & Yeoh, 2003, p. 160; see also Mahler & Pessar, 2001).

Seasonal migration, narratives of transformation, and reflexivity

Lifestyle sport migrants and traveling snowboarders alike frequently
recount dramatic and exciting stories of their journeys to snowy destinations. While these travel narratives take various forms (such as verbal
story-telling, written and photographic blogs, poems and short stories on
snowboarding websites or in snowboarding magazines, home-made videos), they often reveal complex and fluid temporal-spatial patterns (e.g.,
'one year turned into seven pretty fast'; 'those winters seemed to blur').
As transnational lifestyle sport migrants become embedded in the global
processes and flows of the snowboarding culture and snow-sport industry,
many experience similar 'time-space rhythms' (Burawoy, 2000, p. 4). They
become highly attuned to weather and seasonal patterns, such that they
often narrate their journeys in terms of winters, storms, and total number
of days 'on snow' per season.

Not dissimilar from the travel narratives of other young budget travelers, many snowboarders also describe journeys of self-growth and personal
transformation (Noy, 2004). For example, reflecting upon his previous lifestyle sport migration experiences, one New Zealand snowboarder claims:

Looking back, the years when I was immersed in snowboarding had a
huge impact on me. I think I gained a lot of confidence out of my experiences, and self belief. There is something about moving to a ski town
without a job or a place to live. If you can sort all that out, survive and
have a great time, then you can do anything. It puts a lot of stuff in
perspective. It made me think 'if I can do this, what else can I do?' It
changed the future I saw for myself. (Nick, personal communication,
November 2008)

Arguably, for some participants, transnational migration can prompt self-
growth and, in some cases, lead to greater personal and social reflexivity.

For privileged lifestyle sport migrants, crossing local, regional, and national 'fields' with different cultural, social, and gender values, norms, and rules has the potential to lead to moments of dissonance and tension, and thus a 'more reflexive account of one's location and habitus' (Kenway & McLeod, 2004, p. 525). As the comments below from Mel, Pamela, and Adam suggest, international travel across local, regional, and national fields, and interactions with snowboarders from different nationalities, prompts some participants to reflect on various aspects of their own habitus, including national identity, social privilege, and gender and race relations within their host and home countries. Committed New Zealand snowboarder, Mel, for example, credits her snowboarding travel experiences with helping her reflect on her privileged upbringing and position in society:

> [Snowboarding] helped me push myself to places there's no way I would've gone otherwise, and I'm not just talking about cliff drops, rails and booters [terrain features upon which snowboarding maneuvers are performed]. I'm talking about people, places, and major attitude adjustments. It's helped me become a much better person in so many ways. I grew up on the Northshore, sheltered as, basically a snob. But through the places snowboarding's taken me, here and overseas, the people I've met, it's made me a much more open and accepting person. (personal communication, February 2005)

During her transnational snowboarding experiences, Pamela witnessed a 'really strong Japan-Canada-New Zealand triangle', which prompted her to reflect on national and cultural differences in group dynamics and social support, and gender expectations and opportunities:

> During the 1990s, I spent a lot of time hiking the half-pipe at Cardrona [New Zealand ski resort] when it was just me – a little white-European girl – and the rest were Japanese. I really noticed how positive and supportive they were of each other. If one of them falls they would just say good stuff. I used to think how different this was to western culture, where we seem to be pretty good at tearing each other down. Trying new things is much more difficult if you think people are going to laugh and criticize you.
>
> I always loved talking to the Japanese snowboarding girls. At that time, it was a huge thing for them to be travelling alone and to 'be snowboarders'. A lot of them were a bit older too. It was so less expected for Japanese girls to travel than Kiwi girls, which kind of showed a lot more spirit for them to pursue the snowboarding lifestyle around the world. (personal communication, September 2005)

During his second season working at a ski resort in America, core New Zealand snowboarder Adam became aware of class and ethnic inequalities in his workplace that encouraged him to question race relations in his home country:

> I liked working in the Food and Beverages department. It gave me an interesting insight into all the stuff that goes on 'behind the scenes' of ski resorts. It was pretty much me and all the Mexican guys, which was awesome. They weren't there for the same reasons as me, you know, the free season pass and to snowboard as much as possible, but we had lots of fun working together. Those guys really get treated like crap though … they get all the worst jobs and get paid the least …. When I went home I saw similar things happening for Maori in our country which I hadn't really noticed before. (personal communication, November 2006)

While anecdotal evidence points to some lifestyle sport migrants experiencing perceptions of self-change, identity transformation, and enhanced reflexivity, I am wary of romanticizing the effects of such transnationalism. Not dissimilar from other young budget travelers, many lifestyle sport migrants appear to have developed 'specific, well-stylized forms of narrating their travel experiences' (Noy, 2004, p. 79). In recounting their travel narratives, snowboarders often gloss over less than savory aspects of their journeys, such as homesickness, experiencing injuries without adequate insurance, poor living conditions, low pay rates, tensions between colleagues, housemates or with local residents, and zealously endorse popular discourses of travel as facilitating self-growth and personal empowerment.

Moreover, while some lifestyle sport migrants consciously negotiate their class, national and/or gender habitus across different fields, reflexivity is not an inherently universal capacity; some travelers are oblivious to local, regional, and national differences. Young Australian male snowboarders, for example, are particularly notorious for their distinctive larrikin behavior which they perform across all fields, often to the chagrin of local residents, other traveling snowboarders, and some fellow Australian snowboarders. For example, a recent article in *Australian/New Zealand Snowboarding* entitled 'Aussies behaving badly: Global thugs?' vilifies the behavior of young (predominantly male) Australians while overseas:

> A mob of Aussies overseas can be heavy. When one swallows you, you truly feel like part of a team. A team on a mission to spread Australianness. Indestructible. … From the days of yore, Australians have bravely used alcohol to increase their Australianness. [But] when the smoke clears, and all the local women have been hit on, and the local men beaten and affronted, and the cranky Australasian mob tear off to the next town, there is only one thing that the locals can be sure of – that another wave is not far away. … Essentially – whether it's from too much bravado, or too much booze, or just too many of us period – we may be ruining it for

ourselves. That tired old adage of: 'Go hard or go home' will win us no friends. (Costios, 2005, p. 15)

The article concludes with the firm message: 'Respect your hosts' (Costios, 2005, p. 15). The following comments from Todd Richards (2003) offer another example of traveling snowboarders disrespecting local peoples and cultures:

Japanese skiers and snowboarders made their way down [the slopes of a ski resort in Hokkaido, Japan] in an orderly fashion, staying inside the ropes like cattle. ... The visiting snowboarders, on the other hand, ducked under (or aired over) the ropes and rode the amazing powder between the runs. It was paradise. The ski patrol tried to stand between us and the closed powder fields. They'd blow whistles, wave their arms, and point at the rope saying, 'No!' We'd just dodge them, yelling, 'I'm American!' (p. 142).

An older and somewhat more reflexive Richards (2003) concludes: 'We were blatant assholes, and I feel bad about it now, but that's how we were. It was mob mentality. One person did it, and everybody followed. These days, I have a greater respect for the Japanese people and their culture; if I have to break the rules, I do it very discreetly'. (p. 142) Clearly, there is 'nothing inherently transgressive or emancipatory about transnationalism. Rather, the effects are contradictory and complex, and must be assessed within specific times and places' (Pratt & Yeoh, 2003, p. 159).

Lifestyle sport migration and affective home comings

Thus far, I have focused on the experiences of core snowboarders going 'away' to snowy places, but for some lifestyle sport migrants the formation and metamorphoses of their transnational consciousness and national and cultural identities are intimately connected with conceptualizations of 'home'. Far from a fixed and bounded location, 'home' – as symbolic meaning, as social relationship, as developed rhythms, and as physical place – is a 'multi-layered, interactive and productive process' (Wiles, 2008, p. 123). For some scholars, transnational flows and mobilities are further complicating understandings of 'home' (see, for example, Morley, 2000; Vertovec, 1999). Certainly for many lifestyle sport migrants, coming or going 'home' – either temporarily or permanently – can prompt them to 'renegotiate their entwined understandings of place and subjectivity' (Knowles, 1999; McKay, 2005, p. 75; Wiles, 2008).

For some lifestyle sport migrants, understandings of 'home' become much more complex as their lives become increasingly transnational. As the following comments from Lisa suggest, for some lifestyle sport migrants the familiarity of cultural norms, values, and relationships within the global snowboarding culture offer a symbolic and social 'home' while 'away' from their physical or spatial 'home':

> I've done 15 winters in a row, between here [New Zealand], Australia, the US and Canada...all of them instructing. I usually go *home* for a week between winters. My parents kind of know the deal now. I arrive, unpack my bags, sleep for a couple of days, do my washing, get organized, see all my family, eat some good food, pack my bags, and then head off again...back to my *other home* in the mountains with my snowboarding family. (personal communication, August 2008, emphasis added)

'Returning' home from a snowboarding journey can also be a highly affective experience, as one New Zealand snowboarding migrant and journalist writes:

> There's nothing quite like returning to New Zealand after a winter overseas, and on the plane home emotions can be mixed. You might be dreading coming back after living it up in North America or Europe and having what can only be described as the 'best time of your life'. On the other hand you're probably looking forward to getting back to good food, friends and family.... You may be returning home battered and bruised, dosed up on codeine with a broken wrist, tweaked shoulder or torn ACL, and facing the daunting task of rehab before the next season. Whatever the case...you can't help but feel some kinda 'butterflies in the stomach' when you look down and see the Southern Alps, Mt Ruapehu or Mt Taranaki. (Westcot, 2006, p. 18)

For core Canadian snowboarder Eric, temporarily returning 'home' can be a 'frustrating' experience:

> I've spent 12 years riding in Whistler and five winters living there full-time...I've also travelled throughout most of Canada and the United States, as well as several countries in Europe, Japan, India, and South America for snowboarding. For so long I've lived in the mountains, and I've dedicated a huge part of my life to snowboarding. But when I go home at Christmas to visit my family, I'll often run into old friends or seldom seen relatives and it's like we live on different planets...Sometimes I am so relieved to get back to Whistler where people understand snowboarding, and my friends get me. (personal communication, July 2008)

Other transnational lifestyle sport migrants describe the 'home' visit as prompting some reflection on lifestyle choices:

> Coming back from a winter overseas and going home to [small New Zealand town] on my way down south was always a weird reality

check...Many of my mates from home hadn't been overseas; in fact they had gone straight from school to work. They had nice houses, long-term girlfriends or wives, and some had kids. There was always a little part of me that would briefly wonder if I was doing the wrong thing. I always thought that it must be nice to have some money. I was living on a couch, borrowing blankets, eating Weetbix for lunch, cutting my own hair. But many of my old friends, particularly the ones who still lived in [name of home town] and were married with kids, were really interested in my snowboarding stories...I even felt there was some jealousy there too. (Nathan, personal communication, November 2008)

For some transnational lifestyle sport migrants, coming 'home' from a winter overseas can evoke affective and cognitive responses, and questions regarding national identity, lifestyle and career decisions, and social relationships with family and friends.

'Time to settle down and get a real job': lifestyle sport retirement and (im)mobility

In contrast to temporary homecomings in which lifestyle sport migrants are still 'moving', retiring from a transnational career in the snow-sport industry and adopting a less mobile lifestyle can raise different practical and emotional issues. The careers of many (not all) lifestyle sport migrants are short-lived and, whatever the cause of 'retirement' (injury, social pressures to 'grow up and get a real job', or adoption of more social responsibilities such as marriage, children, mortgage and so on), reemplacement can be an emotional experience. Indeed, some lifestyle sport migrants describe experiencing physiological and sociopsychological difficulties transitioning out of the hypermobile transnational snowboarding lifestyle and into a more permanent and/or structured existence:

When I stopped snowboarding it was really hard, but it was less the snowboarding and more the people I missed the most....Going back to university after snowboarding more than 200 days per year for seven years was incredibly difficult. I was always looking for a window to open. I couldn't handle being inside all day, everyday...I had horrendous headaches. (Phillipa, personal communication, February 2005)

Everything I did was for snowboarding, whether it was saving money to head south for winter, or organizing university papers...Snowboarding was my whole life and everything I owned fit into my car....In later years, this was a really tough mind-set to break. I felt really uncomfortable buying a bed or furniture because, in my mind, I couldn't take it with me. Settling down, and even staying in one place for more than a few months, was really difficult at the beginning. (Nathan, personal communication, November 2008)

While older or injured participants may no longer be able, or willing, to organize their whole lives around the transnational snowboarding lifestyle, many proceed to enjoy regular trips to local ski resorts, or family holidays to national and international ski resorts, or save up for short luxury snowboarding adventures with groups of friends (e.g., a helicopter-accessed snowboarding trip).

To facilitate their transition out of a career as a lifestyle sport migrant, many ex-core participants use new media, such as websites and live webcams, to access information and maintain their 'connection' with the transnational snowboarding culture. As Nick, a recently retired lifestyle sport migrant, explains:

> The homepages on my laptop are still set to display the local snow reports because, in winter, that's the first thing I want to know in the morning...The websites sort of give me the 'fix' that I need...If I know it's crap on the mountain I can settle down and get on with my day, but if I know it's good and I'm not up there, I really struggle. I feel kind of itchy and agitated all day. My first winter away from the mountain was the worst...it's definitely getting easier. (personal communication, March 2008)

Continuing, Nick describes how his snowboarding media consumption changed with shifts in his lifestyle: 'While I was snowboarding and traveling a lot, my focus was keeping up with what was happening internationally, mostly America. Now I buy the New Zealand snowboard mags and go on the local websites...I think because I want to stay connected to the local scene' (personal communication, March 2008). As Cohen (1996) explains, transnational identities 'no longer have to be cemented by migration or by exclusive territorial claims': 'in the age of cyberspace, a diaspora can, to some degree, be held together or re-created through the mind, through cultural artifacts and through a shared imagination' (p. 516, cited in Vertovec, 1999, p. 450). Indeed, many current and ex-lifestyle sport migrants use new forms of electronic communication, such as Facebook, email, and Skype, as well as cultural artifacts like snowboarding magazines, websites, and films, to maintain – real, virtual, and imaginary – connections with local and global snowboarding cultures (see Chapter 4). While 'complex transnational flows of media images and messages' facilitate and sustain connections within the transnational snowboarding community, 'microelectronic transnationalism' (Spivak, 1989) also has the potential to create 'disjunctures for diasporic populations' since 'the politics of desire and imagination are always in contest with the politics of heritage and nostalgia' (Appadurai & Breckenridge, 1989, p. iii; see Chapter 2).

Even for those long retired from the transnational snowboarding lifestyle, memories and stories of places traveled and experiences shared with close friends often remain in heavy – verbal, virtual, and cognitive – circulation (e.g., 'I will spend much of the day at work dreaming of the snow and thinking back to the old days...'), and continue to influence their sense of identity and personal history for many years (see Robertson et al., 1994). According to Appadurai and Breckenridge (1989), diasporas always leave a trail of 'fractured memories' about 'another place and time' which can 'create new maps of desire and of attachment' (p. i). Moreover, when combined with an awareness of multilocality, such memories can result in 'a refusal of fixity often serving as a valuable resource for resisting repressive local or global situations' (Vertovec, 1999, p. 451). For example, after more than a decade 'following winter from mountain to mountain around the world', Ste'en no longer organizes his life around snowboarding, yet he believes 'snowboarding will always be part of who I am...The freedom of the lifestyle and individual expression in snowboarding is residual and it remains a defining feature in the way I live my life' (personal communication, July 2008).

Through prolonged participation, some retired lifestyle sport migrants have 'some sort of connection to a way of belonging, through memory, nostalgia or imagination' such that 'they can enter the social field when and if they choose to do so' (Levitt & Schiller, 2004, p. 1011). As these enduring transnational connections suggest, for lifestyle sport migrants 'movement and attachment is not linear or sequential but capable of rotating back and forth and changing direction over time...and depending on the context' (Ibid.). Of course, lifestyle sport migrants manage reemplacement and the incorporation back into the homeland in different ways, but new media, (such as magazines and websites), and media of memory (e.g., museums, autobiographies, and films) appear to help some participants maintain transnational connections and 'ways of belonging' (Ibid., p. 1010) even when they are no longer 'there', that is, on the mountain and immersed in the hyper-mobile snowboarding lifestyle.

Lifestyle sport migration and the transnational snowboarding habitus

While the transnational acts and behaviors of snowboarders are 'essentially individualistic, composed of an abstract awareness of one's self, diaspora and multiple belonging' (Ghosh & Wang, 2003, p. 278), many lifestyle sport migrants share similar experiences of transnational mobility (e.g., creative entrepreneurial and frugal practices, pressures to 'get a real job', time-space-seasonal rhythms) which produces a 'common consciousness' or an 'imaginary coherence' (Vertovec, 1999, p. 450). As Vertovec (1999) explains, for many contemporary migrants 'the awareness of multi-locality stimulates the desire to connect oneself with others, both "here" and "there" who share the same "routes" and "roots"' (p. 450). In addition to personal transformations of national, gender, and/or cultural identity, memory, reflexivity, and other modes of consciousness, for some participants collective meanings and perspectives of lifestyle sport migration result in a 'transnational imaginary' (Wilson & Dissanayake, 1996) that 'criss-crosses [sic] societal borders in new temporal-spatial patterns' (Urry, 2000, p. 186). Indeed, many life-style sport migrants share a set of acquired schemes of dispositions, percep-tions, and appreciations, including tastes, for travel and lifestyle, and thus a 'transnational habitus' of sorts (Guarnizo, 1997). The longer one spends immersed in the hypermobile transnational snowboarding lifestyle the more ingrained this transnational habitus becomes. For some participants, moving out of the field of lifestyle sport migration and returning 'home', or to a less mobile lifestyle, can prompt highly affective experiences, thus pointing to an interesting nexus between habitus, emotions, and embodied experiences of place, culture, and movement (McKay, 2005).

Mountain resorts as transnational physical cultural 'hot spots'

In recent years there has been a growing recognition that research on tran-snational migration and mobilities needs to encompass *both* the 'large scale movement of people, objects, capital, and information across the world', and 'the more local processes of daily transportation, movement through public space, and the travel of material things within everyday life' (cited in Burns & Novelli, 2008, p. xxi). According to Levitt and Glick Schiller (2004), our analytical lens must 'broaden *and* deepen' because migrants are 'often embedded in multi-layered, multi-sited transnational social fields, encom-passing those who move and those who stay behind' (p. 1003, emphasis added). For Jackson et al. (2004), while borders and boundaries are, in some places and for some people, becoming 'increasingly porous', we 'must not let the often elite ideology of transnationalism blind us to the practi-cal and emotional importance of attachments to and in place' (p. 7). Thus the remainder of this chapter responds to recent calls for the 'geographi-cal "grounding" of transnational discourse' (Crang et al., 2003, p. 440) by offering a brief discussion of some of the mobilities within transnational mountain resort destinations as 'complex, multi-dimensional and multiply inhabited' places (Jackson et al., 2003, p. 3).

Once the exclusive domain of upper-class skiers, ski resorts and mountain destinations are increasingly being shared by skiers and snowboarders from the middle- and upper-classes, and various nationalities and age groups, and from different positions within these physical cultures (such as professional athletes, core cultural participants, tourists, novices, and poseurs). As a result, the interactions between individuals and groups in ski towns are becoming increasingly complex. This is particularly true for some key locations (e.g., Chamonix, France; Queenstown, New Zealand; Whistler, Canada) which host such strong flows of physical cultural enthusiasts (skiers, snowboarders, climb-ers, mountain-bikers, kayakers, skateboarders, sky-divers, and hang-gliders) that they have become what I refer to as transnational physical cultural 'hot spots'. According to Reed (2005), these places are among 'snowboarding's great cathedrals... places of pilgrimage, where likeminded devotees from all over the world congregate during the holy season of winter' (p. 184). Indeed, every year hundreds of thousands of young men and women make the journey to these snowboarding 'Meccas' where they proceed to 'play' in the mountains for days, weeks, months, and sometimes, many years. While many are drawn to these sites by the desire to experience new, more challenging, or culturally infamous, terrain, others are attracted by the opportunities for social interactions with like-minded snow-sport enthusiasts. Arguably, what distinguishes these transnational destinations from other popular national and regional winter locales, is that they each offer a unique combination of social (e.g., quality restaurants, cafes and nightlife) *and* physical geographies (e.g., snow conditions, weather and mountain terrain), as well as established infrastructure (e.g., relatively easily accessible via international airports and regional transport, accommodation, user-friendly village design, etc). Importantly, these destinations also tend to be *privileged* places of play, pleasure, and performance (Frohlick, 2003; Sheller & Urry, 2004). Compared to the average populations of their respective countries, the resident populations of transnational destinations such as Whistler, Chamonix, and Queenstown, contain a higher proportion of educated, white, young, men, with higher than average household incomes. The majority of those traveling to, and temporarily residing in, these transnational physical cultural spaces also come from positions of social privilege.

Of course, the global and local flows of tourists, and physical cultural enthusiasts, are unique to each transnational social space, facilitated (and constrained) by various factors, including weather and snow quality, availability of transport and accommodation, exchange rates, media coverage of the destination, work and travel visas, language barriers, global and national economic conditions, and so on. The multiple mobilities within these transnational mountain destinations, however, raise some common questions: Whose place is this? Who has access to social and physical resources? How do different individuals and groups negotiate space in these fields? How do individuals elaborate or conceal some markers (e.g., nationality, gender, race, class) within these spaces in attempts to preserve or create status within the local transnational community?

Tensions regularly develop as individuals and groups struggle for territory and eminence within hierarchically structured transnational physical cultural fields. As the following three brief examples suggest, the configuration of power within these mountain resort destinations is site-specific and influenced by various factors, including the sociocultural-political-historical relations between nations, as well as local migratory politics. The first example illustrates the tensions between British and New Zealand lifestyle sport migrants in Queenstown:

> I've lived and worked in Queenstown for three seasons now, and I love it. I don't mind all of the tourists. I mean, they can be annoying, but in

the end, if they weren't here, I wouldn't have a job, so I shouldn't complain. But I can't stand all of the Poms [English] that come here for the winter and spend the whole time complaining. They come in hoards and take up all the accommodation and all of the jobs. Lots of them are rich kids on their Gap years with mommy and daddy sending them money throughout the winter. Half way through the season their accents really start to drive me crazy, you just can't seem to escape them. (Adam, personal communication, November 2006)

A key division in Chamonix is between local French residents and English migrants. In the early 2000s local newspapers reported on the 'English invasion' – with the British having purchased up to two-thirds of the local property, many French residents could no longer afford to live in Chamonix. According to the director of the Chamonix Tourist Board, Bernard Prud'homme, 'It's making everyone jealous and developing tensions between locals and foreigners' (cited in Packard, 2006, para. 4). A long-time Chamonix resident of British origin also explained: 'Some of the Brits come here and throw their money around. They've been buying up all the housing, so there is a real anti-English thing going on these days. On the odd occasion, Brits have had glue put in the locks of their cars' (personal communication, March 2010). In Whistler, tensions between local residents and Australian lifestyle sport migrants come to the fore on January 26, Australia Day. The following comments from an Australian lifestyle sport migrant's personal blog are revealing:

Still blind drunk from the night before, the beers started cracking again at 6am on Australia Day. All the Aussie gear came out... surf lifesavers, kangaroos, mullets, zinc, vegemite moustaches, cork hats... and everyone was getting ready for the Longhorns pub opening at 9am at the base of the ski run. The atmosphere [in the Longhorns pub] was unreal; they imported VB (crap I know but better than Canadian beer) and meat pies... Everyone was dressed up... At one stage, full of drinks and bullet proof, I head up the hill with my Aussie flag as a cape and started to tackle the skiers as they came down the hill... admittedly, this probably wasn't the brightest idea I've had. The Aussie's completely took over Whistler and there weren't many Canadians out at all. Most of the Canadians I work with say it's the craziest day of the year, so they all stay home. ('The Aussie's take over', 2009, para. 1)

Arguably, in their celebration of Australia Day, Australian lifestyle sport migrants in Whistler are creating what Tweed (1999) calls 'trans-temporal and trans-locative space'. Despite the author's awareness of the inappropriateness of his own aggressive and drunken behavior, and his Canadian colleagues' disapproval, he embraces an 'Aussie' identity on this day and in this space because it enables him (and others) to recover or recreate a sense of national identity and imaginary transnational connections while away from home.

Distinctions between 'local' and 'tourist' identities are often blurred (and hotly contested) within mountain resort destinations with highly transient populations. Thus local residents, tourists and lifestyle sport migrants employ an array of embodied practices to establish notions of self and the group, and a sense of belonging, and demarcate who belongs and who is excluded in these unique mountain resort destinations. Local residents and core snow-sport participants often become highly efficient at reading the body and all its national, cultural, and gender symbols. For example, having observed new participants in the early stages of socialization into the Whistler snowboarding culture, Marie commented that

> There are lots of guys here for their first season, they are wearing Volcom hats for the first time, you can see it in their faces...they are so pumped. They are spending, spending, spending, to buy all the gear. They get on the bus with a new board, boots, etc, and they have an Aussie accent, then they start talking so big, about all the jumps they are going to hit and all the videos they have watched. I don't think they realize how hard it actually is and how many years of practice and hard work that it requires. They come here and spend thousands of dollars on gear, they will learn to snowboard but they will never learn how to make it a part of their life. (personal communication, November 2005)

For Sherowski (2005b), local Whistler residents and committed snow-sport participants can be distinguished from tourists by their 'goggle tans and chins scuffed by Gore-Tex' (p. 160). In Chamonix, the 'archetypal figure' has been described as a 'hard-core mountain man' typically 'under 30 [years old] and kitted out in such a way that you immediately know he's an aggressive backcountry animal who'll snarl if you mess with his powder': 'The helmet, Gore-Tex clothing, ice-axe, harness and transceiver all have a double role. On the mountain, they may save his life; in the bars they announce his toughness to impressed intermediates who wish to God they were like him' (Murphy, 2006, para. 7). While clothing and equipment constitute important symbolic markers of group membership in most mountain resort destinations (see Chapter 5), other cultural practices and embodied symbols also help distinguish the bodies of 'local' and committed residents from tourists. A local Queenstown resident, for example, described the symbolic significance of material objects: 'I can look at people's cars and instantly know if they are locals or tourists...I can tell a lot by the stickers...and the state of their car – the tires, the dust, the mud' (personal communication, July 2006). Snowboarding bodies are performed and read differently by individuals and groups from various positions within local transnational physical cultural 'hot spots'. Of course, key to reading these symbols and practices, and making meaning of physical cultural bodies and material objects within local fields, is the tacit knowledge – or 'nexus of competences' (Vertovec, 2009, p. 47) – embodied by the resident, migrant, or tourist during their past or present local and/or transnational experiences.

Cultural hierarchies are contested, negotiated, and reinforced in various locations (e.g., buses, bars, and cafes) in transnational physical cultural 'hot spots' such as Chamonix, Queenstown, and Whistler. In contrast to tourists and newcomers, many local residents develop an intimate understanding of the unique valuation system and the subtle (and not so subtle) 'rules' structuring the transnational physical cultural field. It is typically during the process of enculturation into the local community that lifestyle sport migrants learn the norms, values, and 'rules' of the local field, and the 'consequences' of breaking these rules (e.g., physical or verbal confrontations, or social exclusion), as well as the identities of individuals or groups who reinforce the valuation system and cultural hierarchy. The unique cultural value system within local fields is important because it determines who gets access and priority when natural (e.g., fresh powder) and socioeconomic (e.g., accommodation, jobs) resources are limited. With such stakes on offer, it is perhaps not surprising that some groups and individuals engage in an array of overt and covert practices to regulate the allocation of capital (symbolic, cultural, economic, social, linguistic, national, and gender) within local fields.

Unfortunately, it is beyond the scope of this chapter to discuss in detail how individuals and groups 'experience multiple loci and layers of power and are shaped by them' or 'act back upon them' in transnational physical cultural spaces (Levitt & Schiller, 2004, p. 1013). However, it is hoped that these brief comments point to some of the diverse, dynamic, and complex embodied practices and symbolic strategies employed by (permanent and temporary) residents and lifestyle sport migrants as they simultaneously maintain and shed cultural repertoires and identities, and interact in transnational physical cultural 'hot spots' within unique sociocultural, economic, political and temporal contexts (see Thorpe, In Press). Focusing on the everyday interactions among a variety of actors, such as snowboarders, skiers, local residents, lifestyle sport migrants, and tourists, within physical cultural destinations can help shed new light on the 'complexity and multiple inhabitation' (Crang et al., 2003, p. 449) and unequal 'power geometries' (Massey, 1994) that characterize these unique transnational locations.

Moving on

Drawing inspiration from the sociology of mobilities paradigm, this chapter offered an examination of the multiple corporeal mobilities within the transnational snowboarding culture, and revealed 'a wide variety of actors' with 'varying investments in, experiences of and expressions of transna-tionalism' (Crang et al., 2003, p. 449). In the latter part, I explained that, while there are many ways of 'being transnational' (Smith, 2002) in the global snowboarding field, these experiences are always intimately linked to place. Snowboarders' transnational experiences, acts and behaviors 'work through – not over or apart from – locally embedded social relations' (Pratt & Yeoh, 2003, p. 163). In other words, their diasporic experiences are 'inextricably entangled with the material and social relations' (Crang et al., 2003, p. 45) in local places. Here I argued that paying closer attention to the interactions and micro-mobilities within various transnational physical cultural 'hot spots' such as Whistler, Chamonix, and Queenstown, can help us reveal some of the complex relationships and networks of power within particular destinations, as well as some of the wider cultural connections in the global snowboarding field. In the next chapter I build on this discussion of snowboarding macro- and micro-mobilities to explore the affective and sensual experiences of moving snowboarding bodies in particular social and physical geographies.

9
Sensual Snowboarding Bodies in Affective Spaces

Big mountain riding is scary. It can result in the most memorable experiences of your life or it can result in a horrible death by suffocation or bloodied trauma buried under hundreds of tons of moving snow. Snowboarders can reach speeds of over 150km/h as they race down rocky faces, over cliffs, crevasses and outrun avalanches. Snowboarding down mountains in places like Alaska, that are so steep you cannot see more than 10 meters in front of you...takes amazing snowboarding ability and a super heightened awareness of the mountain....Unlike freestyle riding, which is heavily visual, big mountain riding relies on feeling, being in the moment and experiencing everything that is around you; the snow, the mountain, the trees, the speed, the wind, the airtime. (Holt, 2005, p. 91)

Shannon and I took the gondola up to the very top [of Cortina Resort, Italy]. We scouted out a run that was untracked powder. We had to traverse on our boards around this cliff range to get to it. We kept going around the mountain and at one point I looked up and thought, 'Oh my God!' I told Shannon to stop and look up. We couldn't believe the mountain and this cliff we were standing under – it was about 600 feet above us and we were right underneath it so the view was breathtaking. Down below looked like the perfect run...wide, open, diamonds of powder. We thought, let's do this run together – we'll do doubles instead of going down one at a time. Fresh powder turns that were perfect, snow flying in plumes with each turn, and we were yelling to each other the whole way down. At the bottom, we high-fived and hugged each other and were crying. We were so wrapped up in this feeling of a powder day in a beautiful place with friends. It was incredibly emotional. (Basich, 2003, p. 118)

Given the richness and cultural significance of the images, narratives, representations, and meanings so powerfully associated with snowboarding as

218

a cultural form, it is sometimes 'easy to forget that these are all epiphenomena' (Ford & Brown, 2006, p. 149). Boarders frequently reiterate that
the embodied and immediate experience of snowboarding is the key to the
cultural practice and words cannot articulate the experience. According to
one cultural commentator,

> Trying to talk about it is like trying to explain why you like your favourite
> song. It feels good. It makes you happy. To snowboarders, snowboard-
> ing is not a book. It's not a symbol or a fashion or an attitude either. It's
> an awesome, personal experience that's better left unarticulated. (Howe,
> 1998, pp. ix–x)

When asked why he keeps returning to the slopes, professional Norwegian
snowboarder Terje Haakonsen replied, 'It's just a joy, the joy of...playing'
(cited in Galbraith & Marcopoulos, 2004, p. 83). Clearly, the lived experience is integral to snowboarding, but social scientists have traditionally sub-
ordinated issues of lived experience beneath a concern for the determining
power of social structures (Howson & Inglis, 2001). We need to find new
ways to integrate the sensual and affective dimensions of physical cultural
experiences into our research.

Sensual relations in space and place

In recent years, scholars from an array of disciplines within the social sciences
and humanities, including cultural geography, sociology, philosophy, cultural
studies, critical studies of sport, and physical culture, have expressed concerns
that experience is too often reduced to language or discourse or representation,
and more traditionally neglected in favor of politics. Despite the recent corporeal turn, it has been argued that the emphasis remains on the disciplined,
exploited, and controlled body, that is, the body which serves as a 'screen for
the social' (Evers, 2006, p. 233). Similarly, Howson and Inglis (2001) observe
that while sociology may have done much to illuminate the *Körper* – the structural objectified body – it has yet to come to grips fully with the *Leib* – living, feeling, sensing, perceiving, and emotional body subject (cited in Ford &
Brown, 2006, p. 146). If embodied meaning is to be found primarily in 'modes
of action or ways of life' (Kirmayer, 1992, p. 380), researchers need to 'rethink
some of the basic notions of what a body is and does as an acting, perceiving, thinking, feeling thing' (Massumi, 2002, p. 90). For Howes (2003), this is
particularly important because 'sensation is not just a matter of physiological
response and personal experience.... Every domain of sensory experience is
also an arena for structuring social roles and interactions. We learn social divisions, distinctions of gender, class and race, through our senses' (p. xi).

Increasingly, however, scholars are acknowledging the experiential dimensions of embodied life (see Ford & Brown, 2006; Hargreaves & Vertinsky,

2007; Howson & Inglis, 2001) and valorizing the emotional, sensual, and aesthetic sense of embodiment (see, for example, Burkitt, 1999; Shilling, 2005). Observing these trends, some argue that there has been a 'sensual revolution in the humanities and social sciences', such that the emerging focus on the 'social life of the senses' is 'rapidly supplanting older paradigms of cultural interpretation (e.g., cultures as "texts" or "discourses", as "world-views" or "pictures"), and challenging conventional theories of representation' (Bull et al., 2006, p. 5). Numerous attempts are being made to counterpose approaches to the discursive body that have 'subtracted movement from the picture' (Massumi, 2002, p. 3; see also Ankersmidt, 2005; Denison & Markula, 2003; Duncan, 2007; Stoller, 1997). Some scholars are adopting an array of methodological and theoretical approaches to examine the affective dimensions of the moving body (see, for example, Booth, 2009; Evers, 2006; Hockey & Collinson, 2007; Klugman, 2009; Laviolette, 2010; Pringle, 2009; Saville, 2008). Put simply, there has been an affective turn in the social sciences and humanities whereby scholars are increasingly interested in the 'properties, competencies, modalities, energies, attunements, arrangements and intensities of differing texture, temporality, velocity and spatiality, that act on bodies, are produced through bodies and transmitted by bodies' (Lorimer, 2008, p. 552; see also Blackman & Venn, 2010). While the conceptual definition (like the theoretical explanations) of affect continues to be hotly contested, Probyn (2004) sees affect emerging from the space where bodies, psyche and memory interact, producing bodily knowledge and separating the internal from the external world. Certainly, the sensual and affective turns have produced a whole host of fruitful research directions that could facilitate understandings of the unique movements and lived interactions and experiences of snowboarders. Here, however, I am particularly interested in recent efforts by sociologists, anthropologists and human geographers to explore the 'sensual relations' of social life within various geographies (Howes, 2003; Rodaway, 1994; Rojek & Urry, 1997).

This chapter is located at the intersection of the affective, sensual *and* spatial turns in the social sciences and humanities. According to Rodaway (1994), 'the sensuous – the experience of the senses – is the ground base on which a wider geographical understanding can be constructed' (p. 3). Similarly, Rojek and Urry (1997) prompt social geographers to consider the senses involved in the 'perceptions, interpretation, appreciation and denigration' of spaces, how senses work across space, and 'hierarchies of value between the different senses' (p. 5). Snowboarding bodies practice, play and perform in various snowy spaces and social places. The senses – the sights, smells, sounds, tastes, and tactile feelings – in each of these locations are rich, multifarious, and dynamic, each contributing in different ways to the lived snowboarding experience. In this chapter I examine the sensual experiences of participants within various physical and social spaces, focusing particularly on three distinct geographies – snowboard terrain parks, the backcountry, and the après-snow culture.

Unlike the approach adopted in earlier chapters, my analysis here is not framed by social theory. As Ankersmit (2005) suggests, experience is moving some scholars away from theory:

> Meaning now tends to weaken its ties with 'theory,' that is, with the theoretical instruments we traditionally relied on to courageously expand the scope of cultural, narrative, textual meaning; it now preferably draws its content from how the world is given to us in experience. 'Theory' and meaning no longer travel in the same direction, meaning has now found a new and more promising travel companion in experience. (p. 2)

Indeed, some researchers are moving away from theory and toward more embodied forms of research in their attempts to better understand and explain the sensual dimensions of social life. Evers (2006), in his recent study of surfing culture, highlights the affective turn for researching gendered performances and physical experiences. For research to 'begin to get across what it actually feels like to [engage physically] and do masculinity', we need to conduct more research at the 'embodied level', suggests Evers (2006, p. 239). According to Evers, 'sensual research', in which the researching body is 'penetrated by and feels the field it is investigating', can be a 'productive, contagious, and affective exchange' and a 'move away from the sovereign researching body' (Evers, 2006, p. 239; see also Pink, 2010). Some scholars write critical auto-ethnographies and ethnographic fiction to shed light on their own and others lived and embodied sport and exercise experiences (see, for example, Denison & Markula, 2003; Denison & Rinehart, 2000; Evers, 2006). Nonrepresentational theorist Nigel Thrift (2008), is also excited by such scholarship that is able to make objects and practices more personally affective and affecting.

In the remainder of this chapter, I draw inspiration from three emerging bodies of literature, including cultural geography, auto-ethnography, and affective and sensuous scholarship. In so doing, I hope to shed light on some of the somatic, multisensual, and affective experiences of snowboarding in different spaces by experimenting with alternative ways of presenting my research. Each case begins with a description of some of the politics and practices, and sensual experiences, involved in the production and consumption of these distinct geographies, and concludes with a brief auto-ethnographic tale to help bring the snowboarding experience a little 'closer to our skin' (Thrift, 2008, p. 5). Rather than following the 'divide and rank' tradition apparent in much writing about the senses, these narratives illustrate that, while some senses are more important in some snowy geographies than others, they cannot be separated. For Michel Serres, French philosopher and author of *The Five Senses: A Philosophy of*

Mingled Bodies (2008), 'the senses are not islands, or channels, that keep themselves to themselves. They do not operate on different frequencies, in different parts of the waveband, but are subject to interference – they are even interference itself' (Connor, 2008, p. 7). Attempting to capture some of the 'folds, tangles, pleats and knots' of the senses as 'a means to knowledge' (Sankey & Cowley, 2008, p. vii), Serres 'declines the rules of engagement that govern academic theory' (Connor, 2008, p. 7), opting instead for a poetic approach that privileges 'unfolding rather than analysis' (Ibid., p. 5). Drawing inspiration from Serres, the following discussion seeks to 'unfold' some of the affective messiness of snowboarding bodies in different snowy places and landscapes. Put slightly differently, I hope to reveal the sensuous snowboarding experience as 'nothing but the mixing of the body, the principal means whereby the body mingles with the world and with itself, overflows its borders' (Ibid., p. 3).

The bigger the better:
terrain parks as places of play and performance

Freestyle riding is currently the most popular form of participation among young snowboarders. This style rests on creative and technical maneuvers, such as spins, grabs, and inverts, many of which have their roots in skateboarding. In response to this trend, some ski resorts have invested heavily in equipment and personnel to create and maintain artificially constructed playgrounds such as terrain parks and half-pipes. An advertisement for Heavenly Resort (Lake Tahoe, California) featured in *Transworld Snowboarding* magazine, for example, boasted '$200 million in improvements' including 'three new terrain parks with 29 rails, 20 tables [jumps], 13 fun-boxes and sick designs like the Dual C Boxes and Wall Ride' (Resort Guide, 2005, pp. 48–49). Two other Californian resorts, Mammoth Mountain and Big Bear Mountain, also employ 20 and 35 full-time 'park staff' respectively, to build and maintain their extensive terrain park facilities. A recent trend in freestyle snowboarding is the development of freestyle-focused resorts. Snow Park (New Zealand), for example, caters specifically for young, core freestyle snowboarders and skiers. The resort offers just one chairlift that provides access to an extensive array of well maintained artificial freestyle features, including a superpipe, a quarterpipe, and numerous jumps and rails; the resort regularly features live DJs who deliver music over the entire terrain park via a 5000-watt sound system. Described as 'more like a skate park than a snowboarding resort', and offering a 'video-game-like spectacle', Snow Park attracts freestyle snowboarders and skiers from around the world (Barr et al., 2006, p. 231). In the words of professional snowboarder Tim Warwood, 'this one lift freestyle hotspot is the dream of every snowboard park monkey worldwide ... jumps, rails and the best pipe in the southern hemisphere. It's perfect!' (cited in Ibid., p. 230). For some experienced snowboarders and skiers, highly technical terrain parks, such as Snow Park, offer exciting opportunities to test their skills and perform in front of their peers; for others, these highly visible and exhibitionist spaces are sources of much intimidation, fear and anxiety (also see Laurendeau and Sharara, 2008). Phillipa, for example, comments:

> Terrain parks are getting so big these days. At Blackcomb the park is enormous! It's so big I wouldn't even want to ride in it. It's a little bit frightening, it's dividing people up and it's taking the fun element out a little bit. And the people who can do it have less patience for those who can't, that get in your way, and things get more aggressive. (personal communication, September 2005)

Another direct consequence of this trend is the increasing severity of injuries. Ste'en observed that the 'consequences of pushing your limits have changed ... we never used to do jumps that could kill you ... people are dying now' (personal communication, October 2005).

As terrain parks have grown and become increasingly technical, the severity and rate of injuries have also increased. A number of highly controversial legal cases involving skiers and snowboarders injured in terrain parks have prompted some resorts to rethink the management of these spaces. In particular, in 2007, a jury awarded a snowboarder paralyzed from a fall in a terrain park at Snoqualmie Ski Area in Washington State US$14 million, marking the largest jury award levied against a U.S. ski resort (Blevins, 2007). The verdict sent shockwaves throughout the ski resort industry. Attempting to minimize terrain park injuries and avoid expensive liability claims, some resorts proceeded to limit the size of jumps and difficulty of obstacles, many made helmets mandatory, and some are employing various media to better educate users about terrain park safety practices and etiquette. Terrain park development manager for Boyne Resorts (New Hampshire, United States) Jay Scambio reveals some of the financial and managerial considerations for ski resorts attempting to attract younger patrons:

> You have to build a place that is attractive to teens, which means it has to be perceived as something just for them and away from the mainstream. Then you have to say, 'O.K., but there are rules here'. It can be a little tricky. You really want this age group because they are the biggest growth sector, but you can't just let them do whatever they want in your parks. (cited in Pennington, 2010, para. 6)

In an effort to protect themselves from expensive personal injury and fatality-related lawsuits, many ski resorts in North America have introduced release waivers to be signed by patrons before entering terrain parks. For example, access to the Whistler-Blackcomb 'highest level terrain park' in Canada is restricted to 'advanced and expert riders' who must produce a valid 'highest level pass' at the entrance. The passes costs CAD$15 and require the participant to sign a waiver that states: 'I freely accept and fully assume all risks, dangers and hazards associated with using the terrain park and the possibility of loss, personal injury or death resulting there from'. Adopting an even more radical approach, the Resorts of the Canadian Rockies Inc. (RCR), undertook a self-proclaimed 'industry-leading initiative' by 'eliminating all man-made snow jumps' from all six of its ski resorts across Canada. According to senior director of business development for RCR Matt Mosteller, 'We believe we have a strong moral obligation to not compromise the safety of our guests' (cited in Press release, 2007, para. 2). Snowboarders, however, interpret this decision differently. 'What a "we got our asses sued" piece of bullshit!' proclaimed one online user (cited in Press release, 2007, para. 9). Others actively challenged the decision by creating petitions, writing letters to local newspapers, and organizing groups of snowboarders to boycott the resorts. The key point here is that, within the current hyperlegal milieu, terrain parks (particularly in North America) are becoming increasingly regulated and controlled. In this context, terrain parks and half-pipes are becoming highly political spaces in terms of construction, maintenance, management and consumption. To further reveal some of the affective experiences involved in the production and everyday use of terrain parks, I offer a narrative based on my participant-observations in a terrain park at a North American ski resort:

8:30 am, 28 February 2009: I inhale deeply. My nostrils tingle with the crisp morning air mixed with the grease from the chairlift cables overhead. My board weighs heavy from my left foot, I wriggle my toes inside my boots to keep the blood flowing. As soon as the chair passes over the snowy knoll, I forget the chill. Eagerly leaning forward, over the metal safety bar, I scan the snowy sculptures below – twenty foot jump, followed by a thirty, forty, rainbow rail, kink rail, huge spine, jump, jump, quarter pipe. I am filled with anticipation. How much 'kick' will the take-offs give? How soft are the landings? How much speed will I need to clear the third jump? As I am calculating angles, distances, snow quality, I see the first group of riders approach the park. They stand behind the red rope. Inside the rope, a 'parkie' wearing a baggy blue uniform checks his watch; when he points in the direction of the third jump, the largest of the lot, I see the young guys nodding enthusiastically. As the 'parkie' reaches for the rope, the group slides forward in anticipation.

Approaching the drop-in zone, my stomach churns. As I take a spot in the line-up, I feel the eyes upon me, but I direct my attention to the rider at the front of the cue. He stands boldly, adjusts his pants so that they hang from his narrow hips, yells 'dropping', and proceeds to flow effortlessly through the various obstacles. His run appears carefully choreographed, linking the jumps and rails with the perfect amount of speed. Others follow, but are more tentative and fearful; their arms and legs bending, extending, reaching and twisting too quickly or too slowly, wobbling, out-of-time. The snowboarder sitting to my left gestures for me to proceed, it is my turn. I take a deep breath, ready my legs, and then purposefully point the nose of my board toward the first jump. As I begin to slide, the butterflies in my stomach disappear. The groomed snow massages the base of my board and I feel the edges hold on the frozen corduroy. I gain confidence. As I proceed toward the jump I gather velocity and resist the desire to control my speed with another turn – my thighs explode as I pop off the lip of the jump, my left arm reaches out for the grab, I extend my back leg into a 'method' manoeuvre regaining balance just in time for the snowy touch-down – I land with speed, but in control, so I spot the next jump and refocus. Hearing hooting from the chairlift overhead, I smile to myself. I am relieved, my body remembers...

Many hours later, I sit on a bench at the base of the mountain, my feet ache, my legs are fatigued, and my right shoulder throbs from a fall around mid-afternoon. The skin on my face is hot, raw, and tight. As I wait for my interviewee to arrive, I watch the final skiers and snowboarders sliding down the mountain, unbuckling their bindings and shaking out their legs. As families and friends regroup, I overhear bits of animated stories – hidden stashes of powder, near collisions, slushy snow conditions.

Jeremy – the 'park groomer' – arrives on-time and introduces himself briefly before leading me to his 'cat'. Standing on the metal teethed treads, he opens the door. A little tentatively, I climb up and into the cab. I am surprised by the plush interior, and only have time to note a stack of CDs and a bag of chips before the beast roars into life. Picking up his radio, Jeremy chats briefly to other drivers spread across the mountain – I catch snippets of information about locations, tasks, times, and snow conditions. As he works systematically through the terrain park digging, grooming, and shaping take-offs and landings, Jeremy speaks candidly about his career as a 'park groomer'. He complains about the new rules and regulations. 'No jump can be over 40 feet this season...it's ridiculous, and management aren't budging either. The riders are pissed, some of the top guys are even moving back to California. There's just no room for creativity. I'm just another grooming robot.' Then, with more than a hint of pleasure in his voice, he confesses to discovering a 'loop-hole in the system': 'on paper they don't look big, but well designed hips and spine jumps allow the rider to go as big as they want'. Jeremy begins to hum an unfamiliar tune as he pushes and pulls at the various levers and twists about his waist to get a better view of his snowy canvas.

The sun set quickly, and now the mountain seems disconcertingly dark. The groomer casts strange shadows as it proceeds to shape icy mounds. I imagine the long night-shifts, alone on the mountain, inside the belly of this mechanical monster, and I shudder. As I do, I am blinded by the bright lights of another snow cat heading in our direction. I am to change vehicles now. Climbing out into the darkness and up into the second machine, I am surprised to see a petite young woman, no more than 20 years old, with long dark hair falling straight from her beanie, sitting behind the controls. Perhaps noting the surprise on my face, she pushes her boot down on the accelerator with vigor and we start climbing up the backside of the second jump; the cabin is on a steep angle and gravity forces me into the back of my chair. Calm and in control, she lowers the bucket at the front of the groomer, tearing apart and then flattening the landing. 'Sandra' introduces herself and begins chatting casually. As the conversation continues we share experiences and observations, quickly developing a sense of rapport. But I sense there is something missing from Sandra's story. I probe a little deeper and then worry that perhaps I shouldn't have.

Sandra takes a deep breath, and then sighs heavily. Not sure how to respond, I gaze out into the night, watching the trees swaying gently, and the shadows dancing across the snow. Despite the roar outside the cabin, inside we are quiet. Time seems to slow. I am curious, yes, but concerned not to force the conversation. I wait while Sandra concentrates on jump construction. She then proceeds to tell me the tragic story of how she came to be a groomer at this resort. Even as tears well in her eyes, Sandra continues to drive meaningfully, pushing snow, shaping snowy pyramids.

A little over two years ago, her boyfriend had been a well-known and respected groomer driver and terrain park designer at this resort. Sandra smiles as she describes spending many evenings with him as he crafted the jumps, and taught her how to drive. But, one afternoon, after building a large jump specifically for a photo shoot featuring a group of top freestyle skiers, he made a mistake. He agreed to give the group a ride up to the top of the park on the back of the tray. But as they traveled up the mountain, one of the young skiers lost his grip, falling under the metal treads. An up-and-coming local skiing star, his death devastated the community. Many questions were asked, and Sandra's boyfriend lost his job. After this incident, the previously informal rules for snow-cat etiquette were strictly enforced.

Sandra's voice becomes shaky as she describes the emotional turmoil preceding the incident. Her partner was devastated; he lost his career, identity and income, and subsequently suffered many months of grief, guilt, and depression. When his job was advertised, Sandra never considered applying. How could she possibly work in the terrain park where all of this pain had happened? Despite her doubts, her boyfriend and friends at the resort strongly encouraged her to apply. 'You are a talented driver Sandra, go for it,' they enthused. She admits that the first few months were incredibly difficult; she struggled emotionally and with some of the technical aspects of the job. She often became frustrated with the maleness of the culture and the impatience of some of her colleagues. But she persevered, and now gets immense pride and satisfaction from constructing a perfect jump; 'The architecture of a good jump is so beautiful. After building a sweet jump, I love looking at it and imagining how it will perform.'

A male voice booms through the radio, startling us both; Sandra is instructed to make her way over to another part of the mountain to help prepare a difficult slope for a skiing competition tomorrow. Before heading over, she drops me at the base of the mountain. We say our quick farewells, and stepping out into the darkness, I turn to look back up at the young woman sitting high in the cabin of this huge machine. I am filled with admiration and respect.

As I begin the cold walk home, I look forward to returning to the terrain park tomorrow and feeling the freshly groomed snow purring under the base of my board. But I know that I will do so with a different appreciation. Not only is this a place of play and performance, it is also a lovingly crafted space of art and dedicated work. As well as a site of pleasure, the terrain park is a place where lives are lived and lost – it is also a site of risk, pain, guilt, darkness, memories, and redemption.

Many boys and girls, and young men and women, spend a lot of time snowboarding in terrain parks and half-pipes. As well as highly exhilarating and exhibitionist spaces where individuals learn, practice and perform technical maneuvers on various obstacles (jumps, rails, quarterpipes, half-pipes), terrain parks are also social spaces where participants engage in various interactions with friends, resort employees ('parkies'), as well as other park users. While sight is often a dominant sense in these spaces, the sounds (such as music; cheering from chairlifts and/or peers alongside the half-pipe or at the top or bottom of the terrain park; the 'grind' of snowboard along a metal rail; the 'stomp' of the board on snow upon successfully landing a jump; or the 'crack' of the body as it 'slams' into the icy walls of the half-pipe), smells (such as grease from chairlifts overhead; sausages cooking on a barbeque; fumes from snowmobiles) and feelings (such as the 'pop' of the board upon take-off; the sense of 'soaring' while in flight (see Figure 9.1); the firm edge of the snowboard between the glove-covered fingertips while performing a 'grab') are also unique. Attempting to articulate his experiences of performing highly technical maneuvers in the half-pipe, Olympic snowboarder Shaun White waxes lyrical: 'Doing these tricks is the most vertiginous feeling you can ever get, especially during the day, when the snow matches the sky. You're up there spinning, like, "Where am I?" and your life depends on finding the blue line marking the pipe' (cited in 'Shaun White', 2010, p. 43) (see Figure 9.2). While serious injury can, and does, occur in these artificially constructed playgrounds, for the majority of participants (as distinct from elite-level athletes such as White), risk tends to be perceived rather than real. Terrain parks and

Figure 9.1   Embodied research: The author playing/performing on a jump in a New Zealand terrain park

Figure 9.2   Terrain parks and half-pipes are architecturally designed spaces of play and performance. Increasingly, they are also political sites, with various agents attempting to control and regulate snowboarding bodies. The construction of the 2010 Olympic superpipe (centre of image) and the boardercross course (right) on Cypress Mountain, Vancouver, was particularly controversial due to lack of natural snow and the huge expense of transporting snow from surrounding mountains via helicopter (Image taken by Author)

half-pipes are carefully constructed and maintained by trained professionals, they are positioned within ski resort boundaries, rules and regulations are signposted and policed by resort employees, and, if injury should occur, the ski-patrol and medical facilities are only minutes away. In comparison, the risk involved in big mountain riding is very much a reality.

Snowboarding out of bounds: peak experiences in the backcountry

It is in relation to riding big mountain terrain that the term 'extreme' has relevance in snowboarding. In the words of cultural commentator Susanna Howe (1998), 'big mountain riding is downright dangerous. Avalanches, sluffs, helicopter crashes, crevasses, rocks, and exposure to the elements take their toll on those who aren't prepared or aren't lucky' (p. 143). Indeed, big mountain snowboarding requires a different set of physical, social, psychological, and technical skills, thus offering (typically) older and more advanced snowboarders a very different affective and sensual experience.

Alaska, 'the fabled North Shore of snowboarding', is the home of big mountain snowboarding and offers some of the most celebrated terrain in the world (Reed, 2005, p. 66). According to Israel Valenzuela, senior editor of *Heckler*, there are 'cliffs that dot the landscape that are as big as the biggest ski resort in Tahoe and they are merely part of the terrain'. Professional snowboarder Tina Basich (2003) describes Alaska as 'so intimidating', because 'unlike a ski resort, there are no boundaries or clearly marked trails and warnings about cliffs and crevasses or shallow snow. It's up to you to learn the mountain you're riding. Alaska is mother-nature at her most extreme – the weather changes quickly, snow conditions can change within one run – it's vast and steep and bigger than all of us'. The following narrative from Tina Basich's (2003) biography further highlights some of the perils of snowboarding in Alaska:

> The helicopter dropped us off and we crouched down with our gear and waited for it to lift off. Right after the heli[copter] started to rise our radios exploded with the voice of the helicopter pilot, 'it's gone, it's gone! The whole thing is gone!' About seven feet away from where we were standing there was a fracture line going across the entire mountain. The entire mountain had avalanched. The pressure from the heli[copter] landing had released this fracture, called a climax fracture, which means it cracked off all the snow all the way down to the dirt, rock and ice, sending the entire side of the mountain sliding all the way across the entire bowl. The avalanche had gone 3,500 feet down to the glacier below. We were all very quiet and just waited for the helicopter to come back and pick us up. It was a freaky feeling because if any of us had dropped into that bowl, it would have released and we would not have survived. (p. 174)

Elsewhere she describes some of the pleasures offered by the Alaskan backcountry:

> The feeling of the untracked powder under my board as I was flying down the run was amazing. The glittering snowflakes flew in plumes off the side of my board as I made my turns. I was so small riding down this huge mountain and had to keep turning, remembering to look back every couple of seconds to see if any snow was moving with me. When I got to the bottom, I sighed with relief that I'd made it down, and what an accomplishment! I named the mountain 'T-top'. I looked back up at my turns and the run I had just come down and could barely believe it. I couldn't tell if I was going to cry or laugh, so I just kept smiling. (p. 173)

Cultural commentator Rob Reed (2005) accurately describes Alaska as 'a place where mythic lines and narrow escapes give way to snowboarding legend' (p. 66).[1]

Many participants lacking the financial or social resources needed to travel to remote and expensive destinations, such as Alaska, hike or use snowmobiles (or sleds) to access backcountry terrain within their local regions (see Figure 9.3). Others ride the lifts at ski resorts and then 'duck the ropes' to

Figure 9.3 Three snowboarders following a well-laid trail to access backcountry terrain at a New Zealand resort (image used with permission of photographer Greg Michat)

go 'out of bounds' in search of fresh snow and more challenging terrain. Ski resorts in different countries and regions, however, police their boundaries in various ways. For example French resorts often celebrate a hiking 'earn your turn' philosophy and adopt a 'user beware' attitude; many resorts in the United States strictly prohibit backcountry access, often confiscating ski passes and threatening legal action against offenders; and in Japan 'ducking the ropes' to access stashes of powder hidden in the trees is strictly forbidden due to spiritual meanings attached to these spaces. While accessing the backcountry via helicopter, hiking, snowmobiling, or 'ducking the ropes' each carries a slightly different set of physical and social risks, some risks are common to all backcountry snowboarding experiences. As revealed in the following comments from Eric, a professional Canadian snowboarder and experienced backcountry rider, avalanches are a very real source of anxiety:

> For me, avalanches are the scariest part of snowboarding. I have seen some massive slides and known people who have died in their tracks. I've been buried once and was dug out within minutes by my friends who were there. Avalanches put you in your place and remind you about how strong and dangerous the mountains can be. Safety and proper equipment is an absolute must whenever you're in avalanche potential territory. You have to trust the awareness and abilities of everyone you're with because your life is literally in their hands and theirs in yours. (personal communication, February 2008)

Despite such dangers, the backcountry environment has the potential to offer such affective and sensual experiences that it becomes a highly alluring space for many participants (see Figure 9.4).

Backcountry and big mountain snowboarders often describe riding powder on natural terrain as offering opportunities for 'optimal' physical and psychological experiences, or what Csikszentmihalyi (1990) refers to as 'flow'. Capturing some of the hypersensual dimensions of big mountain snowboarding, Reed (2005) writes:

> No matter how one accesses the backcountry, be it by helicopter, snowmobile, or a long hike, the journey inevitably culminates in a cathartic descent down a mountainside covered in the snowy white stuff that dreams are made of. It's the fresh snow that echoes a most intense and irresistible siren song. Powder begets joy and speed and flight. To surf powder is to exist in a state somewhere between weightlessness and suspended animation, a Twilight Zone where boundaries are only in one's perception. (p. 184)

Indeed, big mountain snowboarding can evoke 'transcendental' experiences for some snowboarders (Celsi, 1992). Craig Kelly, the quintessential

Figure 9.4　A snowboarder enjoys the highly sensual experience of snowboarding in fresh powder (image used with permission of rider Gavin Key)

soul-boarder, for example, describes snowboarding in the backcountry as transcending both the physical and mental realms:

> When I go into the backcountry, I sort of feel this elation at being out there and the purity and the freedom that comes with the experience. It sort of lends itself to believing that there is another dimension to everything we do. It doesn't have to have anything to do with God necessarily – for a lot of people it would – or have anything to do with self-actualization. But there's a feeling you get from certain things you do in life that just kind of feels pure and independent of what's actually, physically going on. All of a sudden you have this feeling of clarity. (cited in Reed, 2005, p. 59)

According to Thrift (2000), body practices that 'amplify passions, provide mystical experiences', and stress sensory appreciation through a more complete control of the body have the potential to 'provide more harmonious relations with the environment' (p. 42). Indeed, Kelly's philosophy toward risk and pleasure in the backcountry environment reflects such a harmonious relationship. He told Jeff Galbraith, founding editor of *Frequency*, that he sought not 'the most dangerous line but the one that feels the best – the grooviest' (cited in Reed, 2005, p. 57). According to Reed (2005), Kelly's signature style embodied this 'groovy-ness'; he 'flowed with the terrain like equal forces at odds and in perfect harmony' (p. 57). Peak experiences and/or transcendental moments in the backcountry, however, are not available to all snowboarders; experience, education, skill, and courage cannot be feigned in this environment. As the quote at the head of this chapter suggests, big mountain snowboarding not only requires high-level physical and psychological skills and snow science knowledge, it also requires 'a super heightened awareness of the mountain': 'Big mountain riding relies on feeling, being in the moment and experiencing everything that is around you; the snow, the mountain, the trees, the speed, the wind, the airtime' (Holt, 2005, p. 91). Put simply, big mountain snowboarding draws upon the 'metasense', or what Aristotle called the *sensus communis* – the combination of the other five senses – to produce a 'heightened being in the body' (Connor, 2008, p. 3).

Big mountain riding not only 'separates the novices from those who have been around much longer', it also provides a space for 'real men' to 'prove their worth on the steeps' (Howe, 1998, p. 143). Big mountain snowboarding ideologically separates the men from the 'grommets' and the 'bros' (see Chapter 7). The following comments from Shaun White (one of the world's top terrain park and half-pipe snowboarders) regarding his first experience of snowboarding in Alaska reveal his discomfort in this new 'masculine' environment:

> This is going to sound really bad but I hated it. ... Everything seems to be about dying out there. 'Oh man, you go over the falls there and you're dead.' 'Don't set that off, or you're dead.' 'You're gonna die here.' 'Oh, that's death for sure.' Even getting ready to go up the mountain is sketchy. I'm wearing peeps [avalanche transceiver], I have their gnarly backpack survival kit with a shovel and probes and all this stuff in it, and then I'm wearing a harness. I'm like, 'why do I need a harness?' They go, 'Dude, if you fall in a hole and you're dead we have to use it to drag you out.' What? I don't want to deal with that! Are you kidding me? I thought knee surgery was bad; I don't want to die. (cited in Bridges, 2005, p. 88)

Older men (and some women), more confident in their abilities and knowledge, however, are excited by the challenges of big mountain riding. 'There's always a chance to die but you don't go out and try to kill yourself,' says Tom Burt; 'to say that what I do is the most dangerous aspect of snowboarding... well, it's a relative thing because of ability, training, and experience' (cited in Reed, 2005, p. 79).

But even the most experienced snowboarders do not always avoid death. On January 21, 2003, Craig Kelly – four-time World Champion snowboarder, legendary big mountain rider, and backcountry guide – was tragically killed by an avalanche while working with Selkirk Mountain Experience (SME), a backcountry ski-touring business based in Revelstoke, British Columbia. News of his death sent shock waves around the global snowboarding community. 'To the world of snowboarding, losing Craig Kelly was like the passing of a Pope or the untimely death of Princess Diana, resonating with immeasurable grief', says Reed (2005, p. 62). Snowboarding pioneer Tom Sims also grieves: 'My eyes well up when I think about him...how in tune he was with himself, how in tune he was with nature. This guy was a Zen snowboarder, and it was a sacred experience for him, the backcountry. He sacrificed material wealth to seek oneness with his riding and the backcountry' (cited in Reed, 2005, p. 62). For many core snowboarders, the death of Craig Kelly reinforced the extreme dangers inherent in this environment, and prompted some to reconsider (if only briefly) the severity of consequences of backcountry snowboarding.

While the activity continues to be dominated by older, highly experienced, and typically white, male snowboarders (see Frohlick, 2005; Stoddart, 2010), some women have become celebrated big mountain riders through demonstrations of exceptional physical prowess, courage, and experience (e.g., Victoria Jealouse, Tina Basich, Annie Boulanger, Karleen Jefferey, and Julie Zell). Backcountry snowboarding remains a masculine terrain, yet the following narrative reveals some of the highly affective and aesthetic aspects of snowboarding 'out of bounds', regardless of gender[2]:

> *3:30 pm, 18 January 2002*: The snow crunches under my heavy footsteps. I can barely lift my legs but I must go on. The boys are further ahead, and they don't seem to be slowing. I must keep up. But with each step up this steep mountain face, I know I am getting further and further away from the safety of the resort. No one, except the three guys in front of me, knows I am out here hiking deeper into the Canadian backcountry; the snow is three feet deep, and the terrain is steep and unpredictable. We ducked the red rope over 45 minutes ago and we are now miles from anywhere and surrounded by looming mountains, I feel very small. My life suddenly appears before me in a new perspective...
>
> A thunder-like boom echoes across the valley, and jolts me from my daydreaming. One of the local guys who is hiking ahead of me stops, turns, and states matter-of-factly, 'Oh, that's just an avalanche, don't sweat it.' Perhaps noticing the fear in my eyes, he then asks me how I am holding-up. Gulping for air, and desperately trying to swallow the unsavoury mix of adrenaline and fear that churns even more violently in my stomach, I manage to smile, 'I'm fine, cheers.' He nods, wipes the sweat from his forehead, and continues hiking. Within minutes, another of the locals exclaims loudly: 'We are only half an hour from the sweetest powder run of our entire lives guys. Yeahaa, bring it on!' A chorus of hooting and hollering ensues.
>
> At the conclusion of our hike, we gather. I am not alone in my exhaustion. Sweat is trickling down faces, lungs are heaving, and bodies are slumped. I notice one of the locals pull up his shirt to wipe his face. In

doing so, he reveals an avalanche transceiver strapped to his chest. A lump forms in my throat as I become very aware that I am out of my league. I am without an avalanche transceiver in avalanche country. I am unprepared and vulnerable in this raw environment. I swear that I will never allow myself to get in such a position again; for a brief moment I consider taking the exit route. But there isn't one.

Dave defogs his goggles and I can see the anticipation in his face. Not wanting to appear overly anxious, I take a deep breath before casually asking him what I need to do to make it out of here alive. The tone of his reply is a confused mix of caution and exuberance: 'Just make sure you keep up with us, and don't stop, whatever you do. It's going to be super steep and the snow is going to be really deep. The trees are going to be tight too. Just keep up, or you might get lost out here, ok? It's going to be insane!' One of the locals interrupts Dave: 'I'm going for it,' he declares. Pushing off, he rides into the trees. Plumes of powder engulf his shadowy figure and he quickly disappears from sight.

The foul mixture of fear and adrenaline has crept up into the back of my throat. My heart pounds violently in my chest. I can barely breathe. Dave pats me on the shoulder, and declares, 'I'm off too, see you at the bottom,' as he points his board and takes off in the same direction as the others. For a brief moment, I am alone at the top of this Canadian peak, surrounded by majestic beauty. Snowflakes glisten in the day's last rays of sunlight, and I am momentarily overwhelmed by the silence and still-ness of this environment. It's now or never, I tell myself, and forcefully push off into the unknown.

I gather speed and weave in and out of the trees. The snow that whis-pers beneath my board is light; I feel as if I'm floating, flying, soaring down this mountainside. It's all happening so fast. The trees blur and the snow heaves. The adrenaline rushes through me when I see a small rock drop ahead of me; I grit my teeth and launch off it. I fill with relief as I stomp the landing and then flow out into the endless powder for a few more turns. An uncontrollable holler of exhilaration escapes my lips. The snow flying all around me quickly fills my mouth and I can't help but snort and laugh aloud. I am part of a beautiful surreal moment and I don't want it to end, ever. But, a few more blissful powder slashes later and I see the guys gathered at the bottom; I point my board in their direction. As I ride toward the group, I notice they are all grinning from ear-to-ear. I too cannot stop smiling. Hiking back towards the resort, we chatter excitedly and animatedly describe our every turn.

Upon entering the ski resort bar, we are greeted by another group of locals. Slinging his arm casually over my shoulder, one of my new riding buddies introduces me to this group and proudly declares that I have just been riding 'out west' with 'the boys'. We share knowing looks, and they nod in approval. Another of the local guys buys me a beer and slaps me on the back: 'You were awesome out there girl. I could tell you were pretty scared, aye, but you put some killer lines in. I could hear you laughing all the way.' I am buzzing with pride and joy. Not only did I face my fears and experience the most amazing run of my life, I also proved to myself and my peers that I can keep pace with the locals, and as a result I am now being warmly embraced as 'one of the boys.'

As this narrative suggests, big mountain snowboarding is a unique social, physical, and psychological experience. While the danger in this environment raises many political issues in terms of safety, trust, communication, access, and responsibility among group members, it also offers a richly evocative, sensual, and alluring experience. As well as the sights (snowflakes glittering, transceivers strapped to chests, sunlit mountain peaks), sounds (avalanche echoing across the valley, crunch of snow under boots), textures (feathery snow under board), smells (sweat, or the fumes of a helicopter or snowmobile) and tastes (snow melting in the mouth) unique to this snowy geography, the 'supplementary senses' of heat, effort, lightness, weight, and speed, are other 'important components or symptoms of the metasense of enjoyment, or heightened being in the body' (Connor, 2008, p. 3). According to Michel Serres, this metasense of joy opens opportunities for the body to be 'transfigured in its entirety by new forms of knowledge and communication' (Ibid.). Indeed, for some participants, the metasensual experience of big mountain or backcountry snowboarding offers access to new forms of embodied knowledge: 'To me, the feeling of shredding deep powder is better than any high you can get artificially. And yes – I was addicted after my very first powder turn. Riding deep powder gives you that special feeling; it's like your eyes are blind, but you can see' (Gagnon, 2008, para. 3). Interestingly, in their attempts to articulate the backcountry snowboarding experience, many participants blur the boundaries between physical and social sensation seeking; one committed male snowboarder, for example, describes riding 'deep powder' as 'better than sex' (Fieldnotes, December 2007).

Sex, drugs, and pleasure in après-snow culture

Since the late 1980s, the relationship between sensation-seeking personalities, extreme sports, and risk-taking in physical geographies, such as mountains, oceans, and rivers, has increasingly gained attention from psychologists and social scientists (see, for example, Diehm & Armatas, 2004; Self et al., 2007; Wagner & Houlihan, 1994). Somewhat surprisingly, however, the sensation-seeking behaviors of participants in social places, such as bars and nightclubs, have been largely ignored (cf. Evers, 2010; Laurendeau, 2004). Although rarely discussed in the literature, many alternative, extreme, or action sport cultures, such as skateboarding, surfing, and snowboarding, have long been, and continue to be, organized around highly festive social gatherings where the consumption of alcohol and recreational drugs is often widespread.

In the remainder of this chapter I offer an exposé of the après-snow culture, focusing particularly on the party lifestyle, alcohol and drug consumption, and hypersexuality in the mountain town nightscape. As the following comments suggest, these are important dimensions of the snowboarding experience, particularly for young core participants:

> Snowboarder's party, that's a fact. When you think about it, it's composed of a counter culture of alternative people who tend to resist social norms. At certain snowboarding events and contests, all these people are grouped together and the wheels fall off. Some of the wildest parties I've been to have been at the SIA tradeshows in Las Vegas, and major contests in Europe and Japan. There's something about being in a scenario with your common social group on foreign territory and behaving inappropriately. Sometimes things get broken, sometimes you forget to sleep, and sometimes you're forced to sleep in jail. (Eric, core snowboarder, personal communication, February 2008)

> For many people, snowboarding is associated with letting your hair down, going away to the mountains, to a foreign country, and trying something new…. Boarders often get drunk and naked and then climb trees in places like Whistler. I've seen people running around naked, trying to see how many hot tubs they can get into without getting busted. (Jenny Jones, British Olympic snowboarder, cited in Thompson, 2006)

Since its inception in the 1970s, the physical act of snowboarding has typically been enjoyed alongside social gatherings and events at ski resorts, in local cafes, bars, and nightclubs, in the homes of participants, and at competitions, prize-giving events, and video premiers, where alcohol and recreational drugs are often (though not always) present. Reflecting on the festive nature of early snowboarding competitions in New Zealand during the late 1980s, Phillipa recalled:

> Partying after competitions was always a highlight – the video clip and music of the event made the whole day seem larger than life. We always got drunk, it was pretty easy after the mental and physical exertion of the day – and we were always amongst great friends. Everyone took it to different levels – but the common thread was that of 'riding hard – partying hard'. (personal communication, February 2008)

As well as demonstrating physical prowess, commitment and courage on the mountain, committed male *and* female snowboarders were also expected to 'rage equally hard at bars and parties' (Richards, 2003, p. 98). Participation in the hedonistic lifestyle continues to be intimately connected to notions of cultural commitment and authenticity, identity, and belonging.[3]

While early snowboarding competitions were organized primarily for the enjoyment of participants, many contemporary competitions are designed as spectator events for young consumers. Blurring the boundaries between music festival and sporting event, many snowboard competitions offer a 'sense of carnival' for both spectators and athletes (Rinehart, 2008, p. 184). Posters for the 2006 U.K. National Championships held in Laax (Switzerland), for example, read: 'Snow-loving, Freestyle Junkies with Party Streak Wanted'. In particular, many Big Air competitions are held at night on purposefully built jumps in urban environments – either in a mountain town or urban metropolis – and accompanied by live music and various other forms of entertainment (e.g., fashion shows, dancers); such events often attract thousands of (often highly intoxicated) spectators. Interestingly, even the snowboarding events at the 2010 Winter Olympics embraced the 'sense of carnival' by including live graffiti art displays, break-dancers and beat-boxers performing in the stands, live DJs and bands during breaks in competition, interviews with snowboarding pioneers, as well as Olympic snowboarding video game competitions between audience members (see Thorpe and Wheaton, In Press).

The excessive alcohol consumption of young snow-sport tourists (many of whom are snowboarders) has increasingly gained the attention of local councils, national agencies, ski resort organizations, and the mass media, as well as insurance companies. A recent study by the British Foreign Office, for example, estimated that at least one-third of skiers and snowboarders under the age of 25 had experienced problems abroad linked to a mixture of altitude, adrenaline and alcohol (see Bradley, 2010). A poll conducted by insurance company 'More Than Travel' also found that British winter sports enthusiasts have on average seven units of alcohol still in their bloodstream when they arrive on the slopes in the morning (this is the equivalent of being almost twice over the legal drink-drive limit in the United Kingdom). An Australian study, conducted by the New South Wales Health Service, found that of the 1084 young adult snowfield resort visitors surveyed, 56 percent had consumed 11 or more standard alcoholic drinks on the previous night, 65 percent reported having less than four hours' sleep, and 77 percent had used psycho-stimulants in the previous 24 hours (see Sherker et al., 2006).

It is perhaps not surprising then that the après-snow culture carries risks with potentially serious consequences (e.g., criminal charges, serious injury, death) for some snow-sport tourists, core snowboarders and professional athletes. For example, Jeff Anderson – a talented 22-year-old professional U.S. snowboarder – died from head injuries sustained during a late night stunt after a competition in Nagano (Japan). Staying at the same hotel with Anderson when the incident occurred, Todd Richards (2003) recalls: 'He was out with his buddies, drinking, having a good time .... Jeff had been doing what all of us have done at some time in our lives: sliding down the hotel's exterior stair banister on his butt. But lost his balance and fell over backward four storeys to the ground below....The grief was so close and so overwhelming...' (p. 278). Continuing, he reflects criti-cally upon the dangers faced by young snowboarders in the après-snow culture: 'I thought about the things I'd done when I was just screwing around [at] twenty-two [years old]. I got away with crazy things, but I was lucky' (p. 278). In response to an increasing number of accidents involv-ing young skiers and snowboarders under the 'strong influence of alcohol', the British Consulate-General in Geneva launched a campaign in a range of snow-resort destinations in France, Italy, and Switzerland to educate 'young British nationals who perhaps are not fully aware of the effects of low temperatures and how the body reacts to alcohol at altitude' (Bradley, 2010, para. 5). The campaign was a co-ordinated attempt by local and UK authorities to discourage the 'let's get pissed on the piste' attitude preva-lent among many snowboard enthusiasts.

'Riding high': the cultural politics of drug use for pleasure and performance

While the alcohol consumption of snow-sport tourists has recently attracted the attention of the mass media and various social agents, the relationship between snowboarders and recreational drug use is more firmly etched in the public imagination. According to an ESPN journalist, 'From decriminal-ization of marijuana in [some] mountain towns, to positive drug tests at the Winter Olympics, to the Grenade Games festival held each year on April 20 – the unofficial National Pot Smoking Day – snowboarding seems to embrace stoner sensibilities' (Higgins, 2010a, para. 2). Editor of *Snowboarder Magazine* Pat Bridges confirms: 'Marijuana is a part of snowboarding culture' (cited in Ibid., para. 3). While most snowboarders accept the prevalence of marijuana within the après-snow culture, they are divided as to their opinions on the use of the drug while on the mountain. According to one male Canadian snowboard instructor: 'Smoking a bowl [of marijuana] before riding puts me in the zone and I like the sensation of cruising when I'm stoned. I feel more confident, spin smoother and it just feels good' (cited in Baldwin, 2006, para. 9). Professional U.S. snowboarder Nate Bozung also openly admits: 'If I'm sitting there getting ready to hit a rail, my mind goes crazy if I'm not stoned. It makes you relax and get into the groove. I won't even go snow-boarding if I'm not stoned. I get bored with it' (cited in Higgins, 2010, para. 33). For many others, however, snowboarding under the influence of mari-juana compromises both safety and the overall psycho-physical experience: 'I've tried snowboarding after smoking weed, but I prefer to ride with a clear head. I like to be totally aware of my surroundings and weed makes me feel blinkered. The last time I smoked a joint on a chair lift I ended up sitting in the snow outside a lodge and falling asleep' (Whistler lifestyle migrant, cited in Baldwin, 2006, para. 13). Such debates continue to be hotly contested on website forums, in magazine editorial sections, and in everyday conversations between boarders.

Interviews with core snowboarders for this project not only confirmed my observations regarding the use of marijuana by snowboarders both on and off the mountain, but also pointed to the prevalence of other recreational drugs in the après-snow culture, as well as a 'pain-killer culture' among core snowboarders:

> There is a fair amount of marijuana in surfing, skating, and snowboard-ing. That just goes with the territory, I guess. It's a popular drug with people who are creative. All mountain tourist towns usually have their share of party drugs too…ecstasy, speed, cocaine…But I found the whole pain-killer culture much harder to understand. I used to see a lot of Japanese riders washing down a few [painkillers] at the start of each day. (New Zealand male snowboarder, personal communication, February 2008)

> When I was training and competing in the early 1990s I knew a few guys who relied on smoking pot every day during training (in the trees) in order to function at their 'optimum'. That was their deal – not for me, I was hopeless at riding stoned. I tried it once and it was just a complete joke. Other guys were basically addicted to Ibuprofen, anti-inflammatory drugs, for various ailments. (Ex-professional female snowboarder, personal communication, February 2008)

The second quote alludes to another heavily contested topic within the snowboarding culture and snow-sport industry, as well as antidoping agencies, that is, the 'performance-enhancing capabilities of giggle smoke' for elite athletes (Richards, 2003, p. 208).

When Canadian snowboarder Ross Rebagliati – the first Olympic snow-boarding gold medalist – tested positive for marijuana during the 1998 Winter Olympics in Nagano (Japan), the IOC (temporarily) revoked his medal. Not surprisingly, the incident grabbed headlines around the world. To explain a reading of 17.8 nanograms of marijuana per milliliter (the World Skiing Federation permits a limit of 15 nanograms per milliliter), Rebagliati argued that he must have inhaled second-hand smoke at a pre-Olympic Games party in Whistler. Rebagliati's medal was only returned when his lawyers found a loophole – marijuana was not on the IOC's list of banned substances. For many, the scandal was the source of much humor, for others it confirmed snowboarding culture's antiauthoritarian and countercultural roots, and offered support for arguments – from snow-boarders as well as many mainstream commentators – that snowboarding was not ready to become an Olympic sport (see Humphreys, 2003; Thorpe & Wheaton, 2011). In his recent autobiography, Rebagliati (2009) presents a frank discussion of the incident and the use of performance-enhancing drugs more generally:

> Although boarders want to win, we don't want to win badly enough to wreck our livers with anabolic steroids or ruin our hearts with metham-phetamines. We care, but we don't care *that* much. Our drive is tempered by a certain slacker-ish undercurrent, and marijuana embodies that ethic. Of the hundred guys on tour in the early nineties, I'd say about half used marijuana more or less regularly...I smoked weed on tour because it relaxed me...it also helped with extreme jet lag...Basically, it reduced the pressures of competing at an elite level, day, after day, after day. (p. 131)

More than a decade after this incident, however, snowboarding is a highly institutionalized and professional sport, and athletes competing at the World Cup or training for the Olympics are very familiar with the rules and regulations regarding drugs, and particularly the frustrations with manda-tory drug testing (Thomas, 2009). As Bob Klein, a former professional snow-boarder and current snowboard agent, observes, 'it's gotten a lot more serious in recent years...there's a lot less [athletes] smoking weed' (cited in Higgins, February 2010, para. 15). The coach of the British Olympic snowboarding team concurs: 'People think snowboarders smoke a lot of dope, party all the time and are always drinking in bars. But the actual professionals aren't doing that at all' (cited in Thompson, 2006, para. 6). Pat Bridges, however, laments the political shift among professional snowboarders and within the culture more broadly: 'As you see corporate sponsors get involved, it's defi-nitely drifting further and further – to put it in political terms – to the right, whereas we started out so far to the left' (cited in Higgins, 2010, para. 43). Yet there are still instances where the hedonistic ethos at the core of the snowboarding culture occasionally clashes with the strict, hierarchical, and disciplinary regimes of traditional sports organizations such as the FIS and IOC (see Thorpe & Wheaton, 2011). For example, when risqué photos of U.S. 2010 Olympic half-pipe bronze medalist Scotty Lago posing with a female fan at a postevent party appeared on a snowboarding website, the general public and mass media criticized Lago's actions as unprofessional and decid-edly un-Olympic. Many core snowboarders, however, celebrated his behav-ior as evidence of the sport's continued connection with its countercultural and antiauthoritarian roots. 'If you invite the naughty kids to the party don't be shocked when someone pisses in the punch. Snowboarders are not the typical Olympians, for better or worse,' proclaimed Todd Richards (cited in Lipton, 2010, para. 2).

'Sex on the slopes': physical prowess and sexuality in the snowboarding culture

The relationship between physical, social, and sexual risk-taking and pleasure-seeking in youthful physical cultures, such as snowboarding, cannot be separated. 'Snowboarding does have a "rock-n-roll" stigma to it, where sex, drugs and partying tend to accompany it,' claimed one committed Canadian male snowboarder (personal communication, February 2008). Similarly, a female snowboarder from New Zealand confirmed: 'Snowboarding is a sport with lots of young people and an emphasis on the nightlife – it is already overtly sexual – so to deny that would be lying' (personal communication, February 2008). Many bars and nightclubs in snowsport destinations become sites where tourists, lifestyle sport migrants, and residents seek short-term social and physical pleasure. According to one young male lifestyle sport migrant, some bars and nightclubs are 'meatmarkets' where locals and tourists go to 'get some loving' (personal communication, February 2008). For a Canadian male snowboarder, 'casual sex and snowboarding go together like tea and crumpets... Whistler is nicknamed "Club Bed" and Banff is the "STD capital of Canada"'. Continuing, he acknowledges the risks inherent in such interactions: 'I lived up in Whistler for a few seasons and did a season in Banff.... Most of my hook-ups were alcohol induced, but luckily I was smart enough to wrap it up [wear a condom], but some of my friends caught the clap [Chlamydia]' (Bakesale, 2009).

Interestingly, a number of other interviewees also acknowledged the relationship between snowboarding physical prowess and risk-taking, and sexual desirability. For one Canadian male snowboarder, female snowboarders demonstrating skill and courage on the mountain gain 'extra hot points in my book' (personal communication, December 2007). Similarly, a committed New Zealand male snowboarder stated:

> I think a woman who can ride a snowboard well is very sexy... well, what I mean is an attractive girl becomes even sexier if she can ride at an advanced level. It's something about the courage, focus, and disregard for safety... Personally I like women that are self-confident and strong... and I just love the way women look in snow gear. (personal communication, February 2008)

Concurring with these sentiments, a core New Zealand female snowboarder claimed:

> Snowboarders are hot, physical prowess is hot, demonstrating finesse and grace and style is hot, hot, hot! It is all part of the allure, the adrenaline, the addiction. The most attractive aspect of a snowboarder is in their unique snowboarding style and how this is manifested in their riding. It is possible to find it alluring and sensual and satisfying to look at, without wanting to have sex with them. (personal communication, October 2006)

Interestingly, some of the young women I interviewed, confident in both their sexuality and physical prowess, described gaining pleasure from being (active) objects of the male gaze. As one New Zealand snowboarder put it: 'Guys are always checking out girls on the hill, and I like checking out the boys. I think it's nice to be good to look at' (Abby, personal communication, October 2006). Another female boarder also welcomed the male gaze: 'Yeah boys, you can peep this. Go right ahead' (Moriah, personal communication, October 2006). Similarly, Monique, a core American boarder, declared: 'to be honest, I love boys, and I really like it when I know they are checking me out on the mountain' (personal communication, October 2006). She described drawing the attention of 'cute boys' with displays of physical prowess: 'I love it when I ride up and [jump] over them. That makes it even better. Then they *really* like what they see' (personal communication, October 2006). To further reveal some of the complex and dynamic interactions and sensual experiences in the après-snow culture, I offer a narrative of my experiences in the nightscape of a popular French mountain village:

5 pm, 14 December 2007: I find my bunk bed, unload my backpack and board-bag, and say a quick 'bonsoir' to my roommate – a female English climber in her mid-20s here on a work trip for a climbing equipment company. Interested to observe the interactions in this British-owned backpacker hostel, I wander down stairs and take a seat in the bar. A Canadian guy in his early 30s enters a few minutes after me, pulls up a seat, and promptly introduces himself as 'Chris'. He then proceeds to rave about the snow conditions. Chris is travelling home from Dubai where he has been working for over six months; he describes his 'unbearable frustration' of knowing it was 'dumping' on his home mountain in British Columbia while being 'trapped in the desert'. He tells me he is in France 'just to warm my legs up' before heading home for a week of backcountry riding with a group of old high-school buddies. During our conversation I notice a steady flow of British 'locals' entering the bar; some appear to have come straight from the mountain – their hair is tousled and their snow-proof pants scuff loudly along the floor – others wear overalls and hard-capped work boots covered in snow-crust, so I assume the latter have come directly from work at a local construction site. They order pints and relax into what appear to be their 'usual' seats, all the while chatting animatedly about the day-to-day goings on in the village.

Outside the bar, dusk has descended into darkness – the snow-capped mountains, luminous in the moonlight, mark the physical boundaries of this mountain village. Inside, the temperature steadily climbs as the bar continues to fill with migrants – mostly English – seeking the warmth of familiar faces, accents and stories. A live football game is now playing on a large television screen and an open fire roars in the corner. A bell rings loudly and the group of young snowboarders, skiers, and climbers gathered behind me seems to surge spontaneously in the direction of the bar. As I scan my eyes across the room, I witness a game of bodily Tetris begin. Eager for a final drink, I watch thirsty patrons ducking and driving their shoulders and elbows around human obstacles, creating space, weaving through the crowd.

As I step backwards to allow one mover through, my body bumps against another. I turn to see a young man with a stubbly-beard and a distinctive goggle tan regaining his balance. Our eyes meet, and we instinctively laugh. The brief collision, however, was not without consequence. His jug is now half-empty, he sports a large stain on his shirt, and I feel beer soaking through my shoes and into my socks. After a quick apology, he continues on his way, navigating his broad shoulders through the crowd. As he goes, I pick up the subtle scent of his deodorant and note his casual gait, skate-brand shoes and the symbol on his cap – somehow I instinctively know that he is a proficient snowboarder. The local residents are now sculling the last of their pints, and pulling their jackets from the hooks, replacing their beanies, and wrapping their scarves in preparation for the cold walk home; some of my fellow backpackers are debating their next move. I am invited to join a motley crew – an Australian (Sam), a couple of English guys (James and Steve), Chris the Canadian, a South African (Garth) and a Greek guy (Jimmy) supposedly straight out of the army – to 'Brazil Night' at an infamous local bar.

After a brisk walk, we arrive at our destination. Pushing open the heavy wooden door, I step into a warm, smoky, dimly-lit bar. Groups of youth dressed in the latest snowboarding attire sit around tables, lean against the grimy walls, and gather at the bar. A DJ is mixing records, blending layers of Brazilian-style beats and electro-pop. A few young women dressed casually in jeans, skate-shoes, and colourful fitted t-shirts, sway their hips, flick their hair, and lean flirtatiously into conversations with a group of nonchalant male snowboarders holding the majority of the stools at the bar. A snowboarding video plays on a screen next to the glowing wall of liquor bottles. Our group attempts to navigate space among the throng at the bar. Garth reaches the front first and orders a round of drinks in English with a few French words tossed in. I cringe as I notice a few steely glares from the room; the French bartender offers merely a grunt in our vague direction. Feeling a little uneasy, our group retreats to a pool table in the furthest corner of the room.

Another hour or so has passed when our third game of pool is abruptly interrupted. The music stops and the French DJ begins yelling violently at us from his booth. I feel a room of unfriendly eyes upon us. Unable to understand the French tirade, I quickly make my way for the door. As I step out onto the snowy street I turn immediately to Chris desperate for his translation. Before he has a chance to respond, we witness four of the guys stumbling out the door, and Steve being thrown forcefully into the street. Picking himself up from the cobbled pavement and brushing the stones and ice from his jeans, I see rage in his eyes. Luckily, I am not the only one to notice this and two of the guys grab his shoulders and start walking him away from the door. 'What was all of that about?' I inquire. 'The dude was telling us to fuck off. He was angry because we were speaking English. This is a local bar and we should be speaking the local language, but he said it was ok for the girl to stay', explains Chris. I'm confused by the last statement. 'Why did he say it was ok for me to stay?' I query. Chris laughs, 'Haven't you noticed? This town is a total sausage-party. So any girl, even an English-speaking one, is ok. More "meat" on the barbie, as you Kiwis might say'. I don't have time to respond, the group seems to have forgotten the scuffle already; an icy rock has become a makeshift puck and a game of street hockey is under-way. By the time we stumble across our final destination my toes are throbbing and I have lost all feeling in four of my fingers.

As we approach the next bar I notice condensation streaking the win-dows. Inside throngs of intoxicated tourists sway, twist, and bend on the dance floor. The top-of-the-pops style music rattles through my chest cavity. Here it doesn't matter what language or accent you have, the music is so loud that conversation is impossible; the bouncing, grind-ing, sweating, groping bodies seem to be speaking an infra-language of their own. Within minutes, Chris and Garth are dancing with a group of young women wearing short skirts, sparkly tank-tops, and glittery lips. Desperate to avoid this situation, I make my way to the bathroom where I find water-logged toilet-rolls littering the floor and doors covered in scribbled graffiti. Two young women in tight black leggings and high-heeled shoes lean into the mirror, reapplying eyeliner, mascara and lip-stick. Their conversation's fast, high-pitched, and in an unidentifiable foreign language. On my way out, I notice two small plastic zip-lock bags strewn near the rubbish bin, on the other side of the doorway a con-dom dispenser glows on the wall. As I push my way through the wobbly crowd, I feel a hand firmly clasp my left buttock; automatically my elbow drives backwards sharply, connecting with flesh. I don't turn to see the perpetrator and instead make a beeline for the door through a maze of stumbling, blurry bodies. The bouncers step aside and I gasp at the fresh mountain air.

As I begin my weary walk home, I will the cold darkness to wash me clean of the spilt beer, the clammy hands, and the drunken slurs. As I look skyward, I am excited to see heavy clouds hugging the surrounding mountaintops; the forecasted front has arrived. Sensing snow, my body begins to ache in anticipation for a powder filled morning. I pick up my pace.

Passing a dark alley, I hear muffled murmurs and turn to see two shad-owy figures entwined in a moment of drunken passion. I extend my stride further across the cobbled pavement and feel my chilled quadriceps stretching inside my frozen jeans. Crossing a bridge, I hear stifled laughter over the babble of the mountain stream and catch a waft of a distinctly aromatic smoke. Glancing down the side street, I see a beanie- and baggy jacket-clad group huddled under an awning, passing a glowing ember; as one draws the light to his lips, the others converse in hushed tones.

Upon arrival at the backpackers', I am smiling to myself. Despite being miles from home, the sights, smells, sounds, tastes, and textures of this nightscape are so familiar. As I tiptoe up the dark stairs of the backpackers', my sensual knowledge and embodied memories of mountain towns from other times and places comfort me, temporarily. My smile quickly disappears when, upon opening the door to my bunkroom, I am overwhelmed by the pungent smell of drying snowboard boots and sweaty gloves. As I shift uncomfortably on the thin slat-bed, kept awake by a chorus of snoring strangers, I conclude that there are some sensual memories from the snowboarding culture that I could probably do without.

As this narrative suggests, the après-snowboarding culture offers a plethora of opportunities for highly sensual and affective experiences in various cafes, bars, nightclubs, as well as streets and alleyways. While the group dynamics and interactions, and sensual and affective dimensions, are unique to each mountain resort, and indeed to each venue, some commonalities can typically be observed across many of these places (e.g., alcohol consumption, recreational drug use, live music, dancing, and hyper-heterosexual interactions). The hedonistic après-snow culture is particularly visible in transnational physical cultural 'hot spots' such as Chamonix, Queenstown, and Whistler (see Chapter 8). This narrative also reveals some of the physical and social risks involved in conducting research in transnational physical cultural social settings. As explained in Chapter 1, the physical cultural ethnographer should be prepared to navigate and negotiate socially and physically dangerous situations and interactions based on the dynamics of the social, cultural, and physical environment. Drawing upon all of the senses can certainly facilitate the art of practicing 'situated ethics' in transnational physical cultural geographies. However, as this narrative illustrates, the ethnographer should also be prepared for the element of (sometimes unwelcome) surprise. While sometimes highly distressing, 'research moments' such as the groping incident described above, can also prompt the reflexive ethnographer to (re)discover the significance of their own and/or others' 'intuition as thinking-in-movement' (Thrift, 2008, p. 14), as well as 'precognitive triggers, practical skills, affective intensities, enduring urges, unexceptional interactions and sensuous dispositions' (Lorimer, 2005, p. 84), in unexpected places and spaces. Such experiences can also raise challenging ethical questions for ethnographers negotiating multiple roles in the field (i.e., feminist, researcher, snowboarder) and prompt further reflection regarding our embodied research practices and politics in sensuous geographies.

Summarizing the sensuous snowboarding body

In sum, the boundaries between play and performance, risk and pleasure, drugs and alcohol, and sociability and sexuality, are blurred in snowboarding culture. The social interactions and sensual experiences are unique to different spaces and places within ski resorts (e.g., terrain parks, cafes, bars, gondolas and chairlifts, 'smoke shacks' in the trees), the après-snow scene (e.g., bars designed for tourists and/or local residents), snowboarding events and competitions (e.g., local snowboard competition held on the mountain, international Big Air event held downtown in the mountain village), and various other places within the local community (e.g., backpackers' hostel, local residents' accommodation) and natural environment (e.g., backcountry terrain). Yet the interactions within various physical and social geographies cannot be artificially separated for analysis; participants often move through many of these locations within hours, days, weeks, months, and years. As the narratives above suggest, the individual and group dynamics and affective experiences in these social and physical locations are further complicated by issues regarding nationality, gender, sexuality, age, physical prowess, language, cultural commitment, bodily deportment, clothing, and personal style. In this chapter I offered three autoethnographic tales in an attempt to present an alternative approach to representing critical social research on the body, as well as to reveal some of the 'messiness' of the social interactions and sensual experiences of snowboarders in and across various physical and social geographies. It is also hoped that these narratives raised critical issues regarding some of the perils, pleasures, politics and ethics of doing ethnographic fieldwork in various sensous spaces and places. In the next chapter I expand on this discussion to examine some of the affective politics employed by snowboarders who have been moved to action by the injustices they observe in the social and physical world around them. In so doing, I explore the potential of nonrepresentational theory and third-wave feminism for explaining the alternative body politics being employed by reflexive and socially conscious snowboarders to initiate change in local, national, virtual, and global contexts.

10
Body Politics, Social Change, and the Future of Physical Cultural Studies

> I think we are powerful, positive and able to effect change in our sport – we just have to go out there and make those changes ourselves and create the difference by working together and using all the resources we have available to us. (Pamela, Olympic snowboarder, personal communication, February 2005)

> In post-industrial societies, the younger generations...have become less willing than their parents and grandparents to channel their political energies through traditional agencies...and more likely to express themselves through a variety of ad hoc, contextual, and specific activities of choice, increasingly via new social movements, internet activism, and transnational policy networks...they are becoming more actively engaged via alternative means of expression. (Norris, 2002, p. 222)

The snowboarding body is a multidimensional and dynamic social, historical, economic, material, mediated, cultural, gendered, moving, and sensual phenomenon. While the preceding chapters each explored different dimensions of the snowboarding body, some key themes and sociological concepts weave through these discussions, including structure, agency, culture, power, subjectivity, reflexivity, gender, media, time, and social change. In this chapter I draw some of these strands together with a discussion of alternative body politics in contemporary youth-dominated physical cultures. For Parkins (2000), 'we cannot think of political agency in abstraction from embodiment' (p. 60). Similarly, any critical discussion of the body in contemporary sport and physical culture would be incomplete without considering its potential for initiating social change. This final chapter consists of two main parts. In the first part, I draw upon two theoretical approaches – nonrepresentational theory and third-wave feminism – to reveal some of the creative and embodied approaches employed by contemporary youth to produce new forms of passionate and affective politics in local and global contexts. Second,

I offer some concluding comments about the opportunities and challenges for theorizing the body and researching physical cultures, and particularly youth-dominated action sport cultures, into the twenty-first century, and possibilities for the 'strategic dissemination of potentially empowering forms of knowledge and understanding' (Andrews, 2008, p. 54).

Physical culture, social change, and body politics

Sport-related social movements have been attempting to draw attention to key political, social, and cultural issues (e.g., the women's sport movement, the African-American anti-racism movement, the antiapartheid movement, and efforts to eliminate Native American mascots), and to initiate social change at local, national, and global levels, at least since the 1960s (see, for example, Davis-Delano & Crosset, 2008). In the early twenty-first century, however, sport-related social movements appear to be more prolific, creative, and variegated than ever before. Many of these new sport-related social movements – including non-governmental organizations, not-for-profit organizations, and commercial organizations – are drawing upon an array of new technologies such as Facebook, YouTube, Twitter, Skype, and personal blogs, to produce political demonstrations quickly, with very little infrastructure, and often from a distance. While a number of sociologists have produced detailed examinations of an array of 'new' sport-related social movements (e.g., Harvey & Houle, 1994; Sugden, 2008; Wilson, 2007), here I am particularly interested in the recent proliferation of alternative sports-related social movements.

Since the mid- and late 1990s, alternative sport participants have established nonprofit organizations and movements relating to an array of social issues, including health (e.g., Boarding for Breast Cancer; Surf Aid International), education (e.g., Chill – providing underprivileged youth with opportunities to learn to snowboard, skate, and surf; Skateistan – coeducational skateboarding schooling in Afghanistan), environment (e.g., Protect Our Winters (POW); Surfers Environmental Alliance (SEA); Surfers Against Sewage (SAS); see Heywood & Montgomery, 2008; Laviolette, 2006; Wheaton, 2007), and antiviolence (e.g., Surfers for Peace – an informal organization aimed at bridging cultural and political barriers between surfers in the Middle East). Indeed, many of the organizations are employing an array of creative strategies to produce new forms of passionate politics in local and global contexts. Some are gaining recognition from mainstream social justice and humanitarian organizations for their innovative efforts. For example, Surf Aid International – a nonprofit humanitarian organization dedicated to 'improving the health and well-being of people living in isolated regions connected to us through surfing' – received the World Association of Non-Governmental Organizations (WANGO) Humanitarian Award in 2007 for their 'unique cutting edge solutions to alleviate human suffering in the Mentawai Islands' and the organization's ability to 'tap into the inherent values in the surfing community – individualism, courage, dynamism, and adaptability' (Taj Hamad, WANGO Secretary General, cited in SurfAid International, 2007, para. 5); and Skateistan won the 2009 Peace and Sport Non-Governmental Organization Award for its efforts in educating urban and internally displaced children in Kabul (see Thorpe and Rinehart 2010).

Acknowledging the complex relationships between alternative and lifestyle sports, identity, consumption, politics, and new forms of media, Wheaton (2007) describes lifestyle sport participants as 'individualistic *and* part of a collectivity: they are hedonistic *and* reflexive consumers, often politically disengaged yet environmentally aware and/or active' (p. 298, emphasis in original). Building upon Wheaton's thesis and drawing upon my previously published work with Robert Rinehart, I argue that, while many contemporary young physical cultural participants are politically engaged, their politics often take different shapes, and occur in different spaces and places, than in previous generations. Relying on traditional conceptions and 'conventional indicators' of what constitutes politics, however, we risk being 'blind' to some of the highly nuanced and variegated forms of political agency being expressed by youth in the early twenty-first century (Norris, 2002, p. 222). Thus, to reveal some of the diversity in the embodied political practices employed by snowboarders, I draw upon two recent theoretical perspectives – nonrepresentational theory and 'politics of affect' (Thrift, 2008), and third-wave feminism. In each theoretical discussion I offer brief examples from the snowboarding culture to further illustrate the unique embodied and affective strategies being employed by participants. In my discussion of the 'politics of affect', I offer the example of 'Protect Our Winters', a nonprofit organization that draws upon an array of new affective media to raise awareness about environmental issues, and particularly the threat posed by global warming to the snow-sport industry and culture. Following this, I offer some brief examples of the alternative bodily politics being employed by young women for both individual and collective change (e.g., Sweet Cheeks, Boarding for Breast Cancer).

'Politics of affect' and contemporary physical cultures

In his recent work on nonrepresentational theory, Thrift (2008) observes new forms of politics emerging in the 'affective swirl that characterizes modern societies' (p. 25). That is to say, he sees as one facet of the contemporary a self-reflexivity that focuses on emotive responses and relationships between individuals and the world. Introducing the concepts of 'politics of affect' and 'politics of hope', he argues

> a series of affective technologies that were previously used mainly in the corporate sphere to work on consumer anxiety, obsession and compulsion

are now being moved over into the political sphere with mainly deleterious consequences. However, this process of transmission also suggests some interesting counter-politics based on the cultivation of contrary affect motion. (Ibid., p. 26)

Here I briefly outline what a 'politics of affect' might look like as well as the countervailing 'politics of hope', and consider how these concepts might facilitate different ways of thinking about new forms of politics within youth-dominated physical cultures such as snowboarding.[1]

Politics of affect

Various politics have always deployed affect; powerful political technologies and actors have long intentionally married cognitions with emotion, and blurred result with process. Large corporations have also been 'influencing disposition through various methods of entrancement' since the early days of marketing (Thrift, 2008, p. 243). For Thrift, however, the manipulation of affect for political and commercial ends has reached new heights of impact in the present moment. He identifies (i) the 'sheer weight' of 'formal knowledges' (from both highly formal theoretical backgrounds such as psychoanalysis, and practical theoretical backgrounds like performance) regarding the ways of responding to affective pleas, (ii) the 'vast number of practical knowledges of affective response that have become available in a semiformal guise (e.g., design, lighting, event management, logistics, music, performance)', and (iii) the incredible amounts of salient cultural synergies that proliferate through the culture, as three key differences from previous time periods (Thrift, 2004, p. 67).

Another significant difference between political communications and marketing then and now, in Thrift's view, is the massive increase in the mediation of society, which allows for significant increase in acceptance and presentation of affective transmissions. New spaces and technological devices, such as the Internet and electronic tools like iPhone, are prime conductors of affect. Moreover, Thrift (2008) believes that, in such a highly mediated world, affect is 'much easier to trigger and diffuse' and thus 'much more likely to have grip at a distance' (p. 254). As discussed in Chapter 4, Thrift (2004) views the camera as a particularly important tool in enlarging and expanding moments of 'bare life': in its ability to capture the 'sense of small bodily movements' the camera 'can impose its own politics of time and space', thus allowing us to 'think of time as minutely segmented frames, able to be speeded up, slowed down, even frozen for a while' (p. 67).

New understandings of 'bare life' are not just being deployed knowingly but also politically: 'Now all kinds of corporate and state institutions are trying to formulate bodies of knowledge of ... complex affective states of becoming, "regimes of feeling" which are bound to be constitutive of new political practices' (Thrift, 2004, p. 68). In other words, those in power are turning deliberately to these 'registers of thought', 'regimes of feeling', and moments of 'bare life' for very politically charged attempts at heightened 'persuasion and manipulation': 'today the "dense series of counter-loops among cinema, TV, philosophy, neuro-physiology and everyday life" mean that we do recognize the realm between thinking and affects and are beginning to outline a "neuropolitics" (Connolly, 2002) that might work with them' (Thrift, 2008, p. 192). One of the results of new technologies and knowledge is that affective response is being 'designed into spaces, often out of what seems like very little at all' (Thrift, 2004, p. 68). Of course, these technologies of affect are not value-free. They represent overt attempts for control through 'power-knowledge'. Thrift (2004) is not, however, proffering a top-down understanding of power, knowledge, and politics; he does not assume all consumers are duped to technologies of affect – 'affective response can never be guaranteed' (p. 48). According to Thrift, the politics of affect may even offer us hope for modifying our engagement with political discourses by simply acknowledging that they exist in affective ways. In other words, as we discover these new manipulative techniques and discourses of affect, we also begin to understand more progressive ways of dealing with them.

Politics of hope

In proposing his notion of a 'politics of hope', Thrift (2008) claims that, in response to the 'increasingly toxic post-liberal' forms of politics 'proliferating around the world', various forms of counterpolitics are emerging:

> There seems to be a movement to new forms of sympathy – new affective recognitions, new psychic opportunity structures, untoward reanimations, call them what you like – forms of sympathy which are more than just a selective cultural performance and which allow different, more expansive political forms to be built. (p. 254)

According to Thrift (2004), while many critical citizens in postindustrial societies are 'less loyalist and deferential in orientation toward mass branch parties', they are becoming more actively engaged in different forms of political expression (p. 65). Thrift (2004) argues that this turn to alternative ways of thinking about and being political is particularly true among younger generations, and he describes politically engaged youth drawing upon new technologies, and particularly web tools, to produce 'highly disaggregated political performances' in ways that were not possible before (Thrift, 2008, p. 254; see also Chesters & Welsh, 2007; Norris, 2002). Some are also efficient at taking affect into their workings such that they are able to produce campaigns with 'real political bite' (Thrift, 2008, p. 254). Many alternative sport-related social movements are drawing heavily upon new knowledges and technologies, such as websites, YouTube, Facebook, MySpace, blogs, and DVDs, to produce new forms of passionate politics within local, regional, national, global, virtual, and imagined communities. Some also appear to be embracing the concepts of 'kinetic empathy' and 'regimes of feeling' that drive the linked politics of affect and politics of hope (see Thorpe & Rinehart, 2010). To illustrate some of the various technologies of affect employed by such organizations I offer the example of 'Protect Our Winters', a snowboarding-related climate change advocacy group.

'Protect Our Winters': powder politics and affective action

Established in 2007 by culturally renowned big mountain snowboarder Jeremy Jones, Protect Our Winters (POW) is a nonprofit organization dedicated to educating and activating snow-sport participants on issues relating to global warming. Jones describes his initial motivation as stemming from his personal observations of the effects of global warming on mountains, and in mountain communities, around the world, combined with the recognition that he had access to potentially useful resources (social, cultural, and financial) that could be fruitfully utilized to raise the awareness of snow-sport enthusiasts:

> Through snowboarding I started to see more and more the mountains were changing. Something needed to be done; I had built some great rela-tionships in the snowboard and ski industry; and, I felt like our culture needed to come together and slow down climate change. I went back and forth on the idea for a while, because I had a lot of thoughts of, 'Who am I to start this foundation? I'm not an environmental saint'. But it was something that just wouldn't go away. So I went full on into it, because I felt our industry really needed it (cited in McDermott, 2009, para. 2)

Drawing upon his extensive social and symbolic capital within the snow-sport industry, Jones garnered the support of various corporations, media agents, resorts, and professional snow-sport athletes. With the aim to 'unite and mobilize the winter sports community to have a direct and positive impact on climate change' (About POW, para. 6), POW focuses on four key areas of action: 'inspiring our members to become involved locally', 'educat-ing the next generation of environmental leaders', 'supporting innovative, alternative energy projects', and 'establishing corporate and resort partners as leaders in the fight against global climate change' (About POW, para. 8). Understanding the individualistic, and often short-range, perspectives of many young skiers and snowboarders, POW's marketing and educational documents and products (e.g., films, websites) tend to emphasize the direct consequences of global warming for snow-sport enthusiasts (e.g., shorter winters, resorts closing) and offer immediate and simple strategies that can be employed to help 'save the winters' for current, as well as future, genera-tions (e.g., carpool to the mountain; campaign local resorts to be more envi-ronmentally conscious in day-to-day management practices ranging from recycling to the use of snowmobiles).

As with many other alternative sport-related social movements, POW readily employs an array of new social media to educate and activate snowsport enthusiasts around the world (e.g., YouTube videos, Jones' personal blog, Twitter, Facebook). The Protect Our Winters Facebook page, for example, hosts more than 13,000 'fans', many of whom consume, produce, and respond to regular blogs, links to recent news items regarding POW and relevant environmental policies, as well as videos, photos, personal stories, comments and responses, and calls to action within local, national, global, and virtual communities. A discursive analysis of these various media, and other available interviews, press releases, websites, films, and articles, reveals POW staff and supporters (e.g., journalists, professional athletes) taking 'affect and entrancement' into their workings in an attempt to not only inform, but also evoke a political response from those in the snow industry and culture. Common affective discourses identified in the various documents include fear, remorse, guilt, cultural debt, hope, and individual and community responsibility. For example, a *Transworld Snowboarding* magazine journalist evokes guilt and fear in an attempt to move the predominantly young male readership to action:

> Let's be honest, pro snowboarders are fundamentally at odds with the environment. Their globetrotting ways are pretty damn detrimental to the globe and its increasingly fragile climate. ... It's in *your* best interests to get involved. This is no time for apathy. If *you* love snow and winter and predictable amounts of precipitation, become a part of the POW movement. *Your* lifestyle depends on it. (Variables, 2008, p. 62, emphasis added)

In contrast, POW-produced media emphasize discourses of inspiration, hope and optimism, based on an imagined sense of community agency and responsibility:

> As a community, *our* snowboarding and skiing culture has a lot of power to affect change and to get things going in a positive direction again. I've learned that making small changes in each of *our* daily habits can make a huge difference to fight the global warming battle – it's time to get this information out there and get *our* collective efforts reversing the damage. ('Jeremy Jones', 2007, para. 4, emphasis added)

> It's time for *us* to step up and take responsibility to save the lifestyle that *we* all value so much. POW was founded on the idea that if *we* harness *our* collective energy and put forth a focused effort, the winter sports community can have a direct influence on reversing the damage that's been done and ensure that winters are here for generations behind *us*. (www. protectourwinters.org, emphasis added)

Of course, readers' and consumers' affective responses to these discourses can 'never be guaranteed' (Thrift, 2004, p. 68). The technologies of affect being employed by staff and supporters of POW can have various effects ranging from apathy to the production of panic, fear, guilt, or worry, to personal reflection on lifestyle choices, and in some cases, behavioral changes. While some respond by supporting POW initiatives via donations, others are moved to action within their local, regional, national, and global communities. Many of the latter pitch their ideas on various POW-related social networking sites, such as Facebook, and gain feedback, advice and support from other environmentally conscious and politically engaged POW 'members' from around the world. This is what Thrift (2008) refers to as 'affective contagion', that is, how 'affect spreads and multiplies' (p. 223). Of course, this has not been a haphazard process. Rather, affect (in the form of guilt, remorse, anxiety, fear, accountability, cultural debt, or personal responsibility) is increasingly being choreographed and strategically engineered via an array of affective technologies which are then repeated and recycled throughout the existing global snow-sport industry, and cultural, social, and media networks.

Having appeared in more than 45 snowboarding films during his career, it is perhaps not surprising that Jones is particularly efficient at using this medium to communicate affective politics across the global snow-sport culture. The organization regularly posts short video clips on its website and YouTube. Directly targeting young snow-sport enthusiasts, many of these clips feature professional skiers and snowboarders proffering key information about the threat of global warming and other POW-related information (e.g., simple strategies for reducing personal energy consumption), carefully interspersed with evocative footage of the athletes skiing and snowboarding in deep powder, juxtaposed with images of snowless mountainscapes. In 2009, POW released *My Own Two Feet*, the first 'sustainable snowboarding film'. The film features Jones' and friends' predominantly human-powered backcountry expeditions (e.g., using a snow-plane and then hiking, climbing, and camping to access remote terrain) during the previous winter. As well as demonstrating Jones' exceptional big mountain snowboarding abilities in exotic locations, the film also provided space for him to discuss and illustrate some of the joys (and challenges) of pursuing personal and professional snowboard travel with a 'different mindset', that is, with the aim of minimizing his carbon footprint rather than 'run after run, after run' provided by heavily polluting helicopters and snowmobiles. Describing the sensual and affective pleasures offered by such an approach, Jones explains:

> It is a much more intimate experience with the mountains because I am not retreating back to the hotel room when nightfall comes or a storm blows in. I see every layer in the snowpack form as it falls. We watch our

projected lines day and night for weeks on end and get to learn their moods (Jones, 2009, para. 1)

As the recipient of eight 'Big mountain rider of the year' awards, Jones' cultural status lends much credibility to his initiatives. Jones is critically aware of the value of his cultural and physical capital for his campaign: 'leading with your actions will inspire others to do the same, and ultimately make a difference in global warming' (cited in 'The POW Perspective', 2008, para. 2).

More recently, POW partnered with outdoor sport conglomerate The North Face and snow sports film company, Teton-Gravity Research, to produce a 17-minute film titled *Generations: A Skiers' and Snowboarders' Perspective on Climate Change*. The North Face director of corporate sustainability and strategic marketing, Letitia Webster, emphasizes the desire to offer a more affecting and personal narrative of the global warming debate: 'We wanted to produce something that went beyond the traditional climate change speech. *Generations* takes the conversation a step further by relating global warming to real consequences and *personal affection*' (cited in 'Download TGR', 2009, para. 3, emphasis added). With the goal of designing a short film capable of evoking maximum affect, the three key agents worked together to strategically employ new technologies and an array of techniques, such as carefully edited music and lighting, highly evocative images of powdery snowscapes juxtaposed with snowless mountainous terrain, personal narratives from professional skiers and snowboarders, anecdotal evidence and narratives from long-time local residents, 'scientific' evidence of global warming, and a short sequence with young children playing in the snow and discussing their love of skiing and the snow. On its release, the film won a number of awards, including 'Best Environmental Message' at the Backcountry Film Festival. Perhaps more significantly, however, the film was screened as part of a January 2010 U.S. Congress conference on climate change. According to Congressman Jared Polis:

'Generations' provided a valuable and often overlooked component of the climate change debate in Washington. ... These athletes are on the front lines of this crisis, watching snow, ice and communities disappear all over the world. In sharing their story with Congress ... these individuals show us how we all stand to be personally affected by this global problem. (cited in 'Jeremy Jones', 2010, para. 5)

As these comments suggest, POW's use of various technologies of affect (including film and websites) has been effective in offering a form of counterpolitics – a 'politics of hope' – that continues to work towards mobilizing the snow-sport industry to initiate social change at the individual, local, national, and global level.

In sum, Protect Our Winters is a good example of the various kinds of 'new' practical affective politics currently being mobilized in the early twenty-first century. In particular, this case study illustrates how staff and supporters of Protect Our Winters strategically employ affective techniques to 'engineer intention and increase capability by constructing automatic reactions to situations which can carry a little more potential, a little more "lean-in", a little more commitment' (Thrift, 2008, p. 219). The affective practices and political strategies of alternative sport-related social movements and organizations, such as Protect Our Winters, deserve further critical exploration. Arguably, a Thriftian approach can facilitate such projects by encouraging us to pay closer attention to some of the 'diverse ways in which the use and abuse of various affective practices is gradually changing what we regard as the sphere of "the political"' in contemporary sport and physical cultures (Ibid., p. 173).

Third-wave feminism and female body politics

In light of women's professional ambitions, educational achievements, practices of cultural consumption, and participation in sport and leisure, some cultural commentators have begun to question the relevance of feminism: 'Is feminism dead?' asked *Time* magazine in 1998. Based on my observations in the snowboarding culture, I argue that feminism – the modern women's movement that seeks to change the existing gender order and its discriminatory practices against women – is not irrelevant to contemporary women. However, some young women are practicing a different type of politics to previous generations of feminists, which some refer to as third-wave feminism.[2] The body is intimately connected to third-wave feminist politics.

What is third-wave feminism?

Third-wave feminism refers to contemporary young women who, although often refusing or challenging the label 'feminist', are politically conscious and actively developing and practicing their own forms of praxis. Many women born in the last quarter of the twentieth century have different experiences from those of previous generations. Hence it should come as no surprise that their feminist questions and strategies differ from women of earlier historical junctures. Speaking on behalf of a younger generation of feminists, Baumgardner and Richards (2000) advocate a different form of feminism: 'being liberated doesn't mean copying what came before but finding one's own way – a way that is genuine to one's own generation' (p. 130). Whereas the first (1848 to mid-1920s) and second (1960s to early 1980s) waves of feminism emerged in historical periods more amenable to mass movement as the driving forces of social change, third-wave feminism (early 1990s to early 2000s) articulates itself in a different context. Today, young women's feminism is being shaped by both the sense of entitlement secured by second-wave feminism and the backlash against feminism provoked by those very successes (Cullen, 2001).

Feminism as a social movement confronted hard times during the 1990s. The mass media accused feminists of being man-haters and the term became synonymous with aggression rather than fairness. Some commentators accused feminists of seeking to turn the social order upside-down and of striving for ultimate female superiority (Faludi, 1991). Simultaneously, many beneficiaries of first- and second-wave feminism disavowed feminism as unnecessarily ideological and political, and superfluous. They pointed to women successfully holding positions working alongside men and to a relatively egalitarian gender order. During this period many young women felt ignored by the feminist organizations founded by earlier generations. Some of these younger women thought second-wave strategies 'didn't speak to their media-savvy, culture driven generation' (Baumgardner & Richards, 2000, p. 77). Third-wave feminism, which began speaking for itself in the early 1990s, came of age politically amid this backlash. Yet the emergence of this new branch of feminism has sparked tensions between second- and third-wave feminists, with many of the former accusing young women of being ignorant about their history and apathetic about their rights as women (Friedlin, 2002).

Responding to such accusations, third-wave feminists argue that their feminism articulates a generational difference and is a reaction against perceptions about feminists that have permeated society, not against the movement itself. Young feminists know that they are entitled agents and they attribute their opportunities to their predecessors. In the words of Baumgardner and Richards (2004), 'because of when we were born, younger women can take certain freedoms for granted...our entitlement is a mark of their success' (p. 63). Indeed, the first and second waves of feminism furnished this younger generation of women with greater choices about sexuality, more opportunities in education and employment, and new ways of asserting their autonomy and rights. Hence, Baumgardner and Richards (2004) conceptualize third-wave feminism as an evolutionary process 'building on previous generations' (p. 63). The struggles and strategies of third-wave feminists, however, differ in a number of key ways.

It has been argued that third-wave feminism is less ideological and more strategic than the second wave. Third-wave feminists 'embrace second-wave critique as a central definitional thread while emphasizing ways that desires and pleasures subject to critique can be used to rethink and enliven activist work' (Heywood & Drake, 1997, p. 3). Continuing, Heywood and Drake (1997) define feminism's third wave as 'a movement that contains elements of the second-wave critique of beauty culture, sexual abuse and power structures' while also acknowledging and making use of 'the pleasure, danger and defining power of those structures' (p. 3). One feminist describing this paradoxical perspective states, '[If violated] we're not afraid of lawsuits, boycotts, organized protests, or giving the deserving offender a good cuss-ing out...but we also recognize that there are times when winning requires a lighter touch. And sometimes a short skirt and a bat of the eye is not only easier but infinitely more effective' (Morgan, 1999, cited in Baumgardner & Richards, 2000, p. 163). Of course, the strategies employed by third-wave feminists are only possible in the context of legal and institutional support for women's rights.

In contrast to many second-wave feminists who argued that women as a biological group need to work collectively to change patriarchal practices, the ambitions and aspirations of third-wave feminists are often more indi-vidually focused, self-defined and self-oriented. Thus, the primary focus of third-wave feminism tends to be individual, not collective, action, and many express feminist ideas without labeling them as such (see Braithwaite, 2002; Jowett, 2004). Indeed, their simultaneous endorsement of feminist goals and purported defiance of feminism has led to labels such as the 'I'm not a feminist, but...' generation. Hence, a common perception is that young women today are not politically active. However, as 'everyday fem-inists', many advance their causes through 'stealth feminism' that draws attention to key feminist issues and goals 'without provoking the knee-jerk social stigmas attached to the word feminist' (Heywood & Dworkin, 2003, p. 51). Simply put, while many young women avoid adopting the feminist label, they are subtly drawing attention to feminist issues and goals in their everyday lives.

A major difference between second- and third-wave feminists is that the latter feel at ease with contradiction. Third-wave feminism is a product of the contradiction between ongoing sexism and greater opportunities for women. 'We are the daughters of privilege', claims Joan Morgan, a black feminist speaking on behalf of the younger generation; 'we walk through the world with a sense of entitlement that women of our mothers' generation could not begin to fathom' (Morgan, 1999, cited in Heywood & Dworkin, 2003, p. 41). Although 'sexism may be a very real part of my life...so is the unwavering belief that there is no dream I can't pursue and achieve sim-ply because "I'm a woman"' (Morgan, 1999, cited in Heywood & Dworkin, 2003, p. 41). This new social context fosters a third-wave feminism that explicitly embraces hybridity, contradiction, and multiple identities. Walker (1995) sets third-wave 'hybridity' in opposition to what she describes as a rigidly ideological second-wave feminism: 'For many of us it seems that to be a [second-wave] feminist...is to conform to an identity and way of living that doesn't allow for individuality, complexity, or less than perfect per-sonal histories' (p. xxxi).

Contemporary feminist politics have been described as highly 'aestheti-cized', entailing 'experimentation, boundary crossing and an ongoing determination to shock and unsettle' (Davis, 1997, p. 13). Not surprisingly, the body is a key site for this 'transgressive aesthetic' of 'performance and display' (Ibid). From the third-wave feminist perspective, binaries like masculine/feminine, active/passive, strong/weak, violent/peaceful, and competitive/cooperative belong to essentialist gender natures that have long ceased to have relevance (Heywood & Dworkin, 2003; Keenan, 2008). Challenging these binaries in playful and performative ways, third-wave feminism celebrates a 'politics of creative subversion without retreating to...the tactics of collective rebellion which belonged to body/politics in the 1970s' (Davis, 1997, p. 13). As discussed in Chapter 6, some female boarders disrupt conventional social dichotomies by embodying traditionally masculine traits and practices (e.g., risk-taking, aggression, competitiveness, and swearing), while simultaneously reveling in select elements of emphasized femininity, such as wearing brightly colored nail polish, jewelry, pink snowboarding clothing and equipment. Indeed, many female snowboarders represent a new generation of young women who are 'defining for themselves' how to use and celebrate their bodies 'not in ways that are assimilated to the male-dominated system, or that are in opposition to male-defined practices but *on their own terms*, "for themselves"' (Hargreaves, 2004, p. 194, emphasis added).

Scholars and commentators frequently argue that political action is not a priority for the current generation of young women. Dicker and Piepmeier (2003) call third-wave feminism a 'feminist free-for-all' that empties feminism of any core set of values and politics (p. 17). They proclaim that, while it is fine to challenge perceptions of what feminism is or to engage the world in a playful and individualistic way, feminist engagement has to take into account the power relations surrounding gender, race, class, and sexual orientation. Put simply, feminism must entail a politics that is transformative of both the individual and society. Baumgardner and Richards (2000) make the same point more playfully when they write: 'feminism for this younger generation is like fluoride. We scarcely notice that we have it...it's simply in the water' (p. 17). Continuing, they admit that 'while on a personal level feminism is everywhere', on a political level the movement is 'like nitrogen: ubiquitous and inert' (Baumgardner & Richards 2000, p. 18). Certainly, snowboarding culture presents many examples of young women embracing an apolitical and/or postfeminist attitude, as demonstrated in Dakides' response to an interviewer asking her opinion on the 'Girls Kick Ass' movement in snowboarding: 'Girls do kick ass but I'm not one to get all up in your face about it' (Yant, 2001b, para. 16). The following comment from American professional snowboarder Janna Meyen further illustrates the prevailing individualistic mentality among many young women: 'I'm not out there representing women's snowboarding. I'm out there doing it for myself. For me it's a totally individual thing' (Willoughby, 2004, para. 16). According to Susan Hopkins (2002), if 1970s feminism was built on ideals of authenticity and solidarity, feminism in the twenty-first century is built on the dreams of celebrity and self-advancement. In the view of many second-wave feminists, the idea of doing something for the greater good has become an anachronism for many young women in this context.

Based on my observations in snowboarding and various other youth-dominated physical cultures, such as surfing and skateboarding, I argue that, while some young women are apathetic about their rights, others are engaging in highly creative and variegated forms of political action. However, their alternative politics often go overlooked because they take a different shape from previous feminist generations. Young women, explains Harris (2001), have 'developed quite new ways of conducting political organization, protest, debate, and agitation' (p. 8; see also Harris, 2008). Indeed, many young female snowboarders cleverly exploit the resources of contemporary society, such as technology, popular culture, corporate sponsors, and the media. They use, and create, websites and chat-rooms (e.g., www. powderroom.net, www.bettygohard.com, www.snowgirls.co.nz), and voice their concerns in snowboarding magazines by sending emails to editors and writing columns. With the goal of producing more opportunities for professional female boarders and offering alternative discourses of femininity in the snowboarding culture, women have also developed their own companies (e.g., Fruition), snowboarding films (e.g., *As If*) and magazines (e.g., *Curl*); the latter provide important spaces for women to display their skills, gain cultural knowledge, and voice their opinions. Employing an array of new social media, and challenging observed inequalities and injustices in playful ways, many young women are subtly drawing attention to key feminist issues and goals without provoking the knee-jerk reactions so typical of many second-wave projects. Some socially conscious and politically engaged female snowboarders are also attempting to initiate broader social change. U.S. Olympic gold (2006) and silver (2010) snowboard half-pipe medalist, Hannah Teter, offers an excellent exemplar here.

After winning the gold medal at the 2006 Winter Olympics, Teter established 'Hannah's Gold', a company producing maple syrup with proceeds funding a clean water project for AIDS victims in Kirindon (Kenya) (see http://www.hannahsgold.com/). Teter attributes her social consciousness and philanthropist bent to the travel opportunities facilitated by her snowboarding career:

> For me, being raised in America, to go over there [Africa] and see what other people live through, it's just super heavy and grounding. It makes you so appreciative of what we have and what I have...I've been blessed to have enough to buy organic and have a house in Tahoe. I know I'm going to be able to eat. This way, *I can work it* [my snowboarding career] so that...I can give to charity. (cited in Pells, 2009, para. 11, emphasis added)

Teter dedicated all of her earnings from snowboarding competitions during the 2009 and 2010 winter season to the Kirindon project. As with many other third-wave initiatives, Teter also harnesses the assistance and support of various corporate sponsors. For example, Ben and Jerry's Ice-cream Company contributes a proportion of proceeds from their line of Hannah Teter 'Maple Blondie' products to the Kirindon project.

In early 2010, Teter also founded 'Sweet Cheeks', a company producing personally designed and politically inspired women's knickers to raise funds for various social causes. Every month the company offers a new design touting a political and/or social slogan relating to a current issue; US$5 from every pair is donated to the charity of the month. According to the company website:

> [Sweet Cheeks] is about giving with your heart, soul, and booty. When she's not on the slopes Hannah dedicates much of her time and interest to transformative gifting. Clean water, food, shelter, hope, grace, [and] mercy for those in need. It is Hannah's wish to share this experience of gifting with women everywhere in a fun and fashionable way. (www. sweetcheekspanties.com)

'Sweet Cheeks is Hannah's brainchild,' claimed her brother and manager, Amen Teter; 'she wanted to find a fun, sassy way of giving back and making a statement about it with your underwear' (cited in Helfrich, 2010, para. 1). Further embodying third-wave feminist politics, Teter used a photo-shoot in *Sports Illustrated* magazine to launch 'Sweet Cheeks'. In most of the images, Teter appears in various states of undress – wearing a bikini or lingerie and snowboard boots in an array of snowy settings (e.g., on a chairlift, in a gondola). One photograph, however, features Teter lying on a bed, her snowboard next to her, wearing just a pair of the Sweet Cheeks February knickers with the slogan 'Make love not war' emblazoned across the back. Her participation in the special feature titled 'The Hottest Women of the 2010 Winter Olympics', which also included hypersexual images of skiers Lindsey Vonn and Lacy Schnoor, and fellow snowboarder Claire Bidez, was not without controversy. In response to accusations that she was 'being exploited' and 'sexualizing the Olympics', Teter was adamant: 'I'm not suppressed...I don't believe in the criminalization of the body and I don't believe women should be ashamed of their bodies. That's just so wrong' (cited in Ginsburg, 2010, para. 3); she was also quick to remind critics that all earnings from the shoot were donated to the Kirindon water project. Teter's alternative body politics epitomize third-wave feminism. Not only is she vocal and proactive in her response to an array of political issues and social inequalities, she is also aware of her commodity value and has no qualms about marketing her femininity and sexuality to boost her public profile and image, and secure financial rewards for an array of charities and social justice organizations.

In contrast to Teter's largely *individualistic* philanthropic efforts, Boarding for Breast Cancer (B4BC) – a 'non-profit, youth-focused education, awareness, and fundraising foundation' with a mission to 'increase awareness about breast cancer, the importance of early detection and the value of an active lifestyle' (www.b4bc.org) – offers a good example of an extraordinarily prolific, creative, and variegated *collective* third-wave feminist organization. B4BC was founded in 1996 by a group of professional female snowboarders and members of the snowboarding industry after a mutual friend, Monica Stewart, was diagnosed with breast cancer. Before her death in 1996, Monica actively voiced her frustration about the lack of breast cancer awareness and education for young women. Inspired to initiate change, the cofounders of B4BC began collaborating with an extensive list of male and female artists (e.g., musicians, painters, and designers) and athletes, as well as marketing (including Billabong, Betty Rides, Burton, and Paul Frank) and media (e.g., ESPN X-Games, *Elle Girls*, Fuel TV, *Transworld Snowboarding*) sponsors and partners, to organize numerous educational and fundraising events, such as the Pink Ribbon Jibbin Rail Jam Contest, B4BC Board-A-Thon, and the Annual B4BC Snowboard and Music Festival. Since 1996, B4BC has raised more than US$500,000 for breast cancer research and education in the United States (see www.b4bc.com). Inspired by such efforts, top New Zealand female snowboarders established the inaugural Freestyling for Funds event held at Snowpark (Wanaka) and Turoa (Mt Ruapehu) in 2005. Freestyling For Funds is an all-inclusive, noncompetitive women's snowboarding event, in which female boarders share knowledge about breast cancer and participate in events such as the 'Bikini Downhill' and 'Boxes and Boobs Rail Jam'. Embodying a third-wave approach, some women choose to further celebrate this event, and the female body, by participating in bras or bikinis (see Figure 10.1). While this is a women-focused event, men's attendance and assistance is welcomed. All proceeds from the event are donated to the New Zealand Breast Cancer Foundation.

Clearly, not all young women are apathetic about their rights. The feminist philosophy 'the personal is the political' continues to hold true among some young women (and men). Yet contemporary young women express their politics differently to previous generations; their feminist questions and strategies are a reflection of the cultural context from which they emerged. In the early twenty-first century, many young women are redefining their bodies as points of celebration so that they are visible symbols of their agency and power; some are also engaging in an array of creative, variegated, and highly tenacious bodily politics to promote both individual and collective change in a new feminist context.

Snowboarding bodies in theory and practice: lessons from the field

Contemporary youth-dominated physical cultures are complex, multidimensional, and in a constant state of change and flux. While such features

Figure 10.1   Female snowboarders at the 'Snowgirls and Freestyling for Funds' event held at Snowpark in September 2005 wore bikinis, bras, and snowboarding stickers across their breasts, and pink ribbons on their beanies and bikinis, in celebration of the female body and breast cancer awareness (photo taken by Sally Norman) (image used with permission of event co-coordinator Fiona Duncan)

are often part of the appeal for participants and researchers alike, making meaning of such dynamic and multilayered social phenomena can prove challenging for both new and experienced scholars. Here I argue that future theoretical investigations seeking to construct nuanced social explanations of the body in contemporary physical cultures must embrace theoretical and conceptual reflexivity, and analytical dynamism and openness. I suggest that critical sociocultural scholarship that embraces a creative, adventurous, flexible, innovative, and political approach to theory and research, has the potential to be more personally and socially meaningful for researchers, readers, and physical cultural participants alike. In this final section I draw on my personal research journey to offer some suggestions for a physical cultural studies that is more accessible, politically engaged, reflexive, embodied, affective, theoretically playful and dynamic, and perhaps, even, pleasurable.

Making a difference: sociological contributions and physical cultural politics

Theory is the heart and soul of sociology and central to the discipline's contribution to 'the development of self-knowledge *and* the guidance of human society' (Waters, 2000, p. 1, emphasis added). While this discussion of snowboarding culture has privileged theory with the goal of developing new ways of knowing the physical cultural body, it is also important to consider the social responsibility and/or ethics of social theory: what constitutes socially responsible sociology? Here we might recall Marx's observation that 'philosophers have interpreted the world in various ways; the point, however, is to *change* it' (cited in Coakley & Dunning, 2000, p. xxxii). While sociologists seek to both understand society and change discriminatory practices within society, I believe social researchers need to make their work more accessible so that the general public can use it to reflexively interpret the social conditions of their existence and to change them accordingly. While the various social theories discussed in this book have much to offer in terms of providing frameworks for a range of descriptions and explanations of the contemporary social world, too often these theories remain highly abstract and thus inaccessible to the majority of those outside academe. I argue that the answer to the question 'what constitutes socially responsible sociology?' is not in how much change scholars can personally initiate, but rather our ability to explain and present theories and concepts in an accessible manner so that readers can use them to make sense of their own (and others') embodied and bodily experiences and inform their involvement in related practical and political issues.

Similar goals are at the heart of the emerging Physical Cultural Studies agenda. Andrews (2008) describes the field as committed to producing and disseminating 'potentially empowering forms of knowledge and understanding', particularly in relation to the role physical culture plays in reproducing, and sometimes challenging, power inequities and social injustices, which can then be used to 'illuminate, and intervene into, sites of physical cultural injustice and inequity' (Andrews, 2008, p. 54). A similar political impetus underpins this book. By engaging theoretical concepts in conversation with the snowboarding empirical, this book is a concerted effort to make social theory more accessible to wider audiences. I encourage readers to 'rummage' through this text to find those theoretical and methodological 'tools' that best help them identify and analyze some of the complex and highly nuanced forms of power operating on and through their own and others' physically active bodies (Foucault, 1974). Importantly, as well as facilitating intellectual projects and personal reflections, such knowledge may also be mobilized to imagine more 'politically expedient physical cultural possibilities', and perhaps develop more effective strategies for intervening in contexts of power (Andrews, 2008, p. 57).

Arguably, in our efforts to 'strategically disseminate' potentially empowering forms of knowledge to wider audiences (Andrews, 2008), we might also draw some salient lessons from physical cultural participants themselves in terms of their creative and savvy use of new social media (e.g., niche magazines, websites, and blogs), for sharing information, engaging in local, national, and transnational conversations, and inspiring individual and collective political action. Since 2005, for example, I have shared my research with the broader boarding culture as an occasional columnist for *Curl*, an Australasian female-specific glossy surf, skate, and snowboarding magazine. My columns help me to ascertain whether my research findings are consistent with the perspectives of cultural participants, and to promote reflexivity among the readership. According to the editor, Lynne Dickinson, an article entitled 'Women-only snowboard videos: Virtue or vice?' deriving from my Foucauldian-informed research on the snowboarding media 'really made people think' and prompted 'plenty of discussion and feedback' from male and female readers (personal communication, March 2007). My article, she said, also provoked considerable 'discussion around the office ... [among] lots of keen boarders and skiers' (personal communication, March 2007). In the subsequent issue, Dickinson (2007) commented that my article had impelled a reader to write an article for the magazine: 'Since the last issue we have had a huge response to Holly's article on the virtues and vices of all girls snowboarding DVDs. This got Cris thinking about whether girls preferred to snowboard with their girl or guy friends ...' (p. 54). As this example suggests, accessible, theoretically informed research can encourage people to reflexively interpret the social conditions of their existence and act on related practical and political issues. Arguably, alternative styles of representation can further enhance the accessibility of our theoretically informed research and help us raise critical social issues about various dimensions of the physical cultural body (e.g., reflexivity, power, ethics, identity, pleasure, pain, performance, and gender) among wider audiences (see Evers, 2010).

Social theory and the body: toward embodied theorizing

Too often theorizing about the body has been 'a cerebral, esoteric and, ultimately, disembodied activity' (Davis, 1997, p. 14). Much traditional theorizing on the body has distanced us from 'individuals' everyday embodied experiences' and, ultimately, from the 'dangers and pleasures of the body itself' (Ibid.). Arguably, developing more 'embodied theories' on physical cultural bodies requires 'interaction between theories about the body and analyses of the particularities of embodied experiences and practices' (Ibid., p. 15). Indeed, the dialogue between theoretical knowledge and cultural knowledge, gained from previous and current cultural participation combined with multiple modes of data generation, was central to this discussion of snowboarding bodies. Moreover, some of the methods employed in this project, such as participant-observation and sensual ethnography, further evoked the lived, embodied experiences of snowboarding. Of course, not all social researchers are able or willing to enter the field or participate in the sports or physical cultures they study; much quality scholarship is produced using less physical methods. Regardless of the methods employed, however, researcher reflexivity must be central to embodied theorizing in physical cultural studies. Recognizing that the theorist is always embodied, and paying theoretical attention to our own bodies, as well as those of our participants, can evoke tensions and contradictions (see Chapter 9). Yet becoming 'entangled', 'disturbed' or 'fascinated' by these bodily tensions can provide an important resource for further theoretical reflection (Davis, 1997, p. 15). Thus, rather than using social theory to 'distance' ourselves from the social world, and 'detach' ourselves from the body, 'embodied theorizing' asks that we use theory to draw the bodies of the social world a little closer and embrace the theoretical 'squirm' that this has the potential to induce.

The pains and pleasures of social theorizing: affective scholarship

Another important consideration when theorizing popular physical cultures, such as snowboarding, is whether critical social theorizing and leisure can be enjoyed at the same time. According to Barcan (2002), there is an 'intellectual bias towards pessimism' in critical theorizing, such that it is a practice marked by 'suspicion of hope or joy' (p. 345). Indeed, Leane and Buchanan (2002) report that, some (not all) students experience theoretical analysis as 'a form of robbery of unselfconscious pleasure' (p. 257) and a 'theft of enjoyment' (p. 254). Similarly, Grossberg (1992) explains that his students regularly oppose theoretical analyses on rock music because, in some sense, they know that 'too much intellectual legitimation will redefine the possibilities of its effectiveness; it will become increasingly a meaningful form to be interpreted rather than a popular form to be felt on one's body and to be lived passionately and emotionally' (p. 79). Admittedly, at various stages in this project, I struggled to keep in mind the pleasures inherent in the snowboarding experience. During my participant-observation phases, for example, I occasionally found it difficult to switch off my theoretically informed critical analyzing and simply enjoy the thrill and excitement of snowboarding down a mountainside.

Yet social theorizing does not have to be a gloomy experience. 'Despite the intellectual allure of pessimism, there is, in fact, nothing intrinsically or inevitably pessimistic about critical theory at all,' says Barcan (2002, p. 346). Describing cultural critic and landscape architect Dean MacCannell's use of theory, for example, Lippard (1999) writes: '[H]e deploys the speculative nature of theory in the service not of nitpicking cynicism but of freedom to dive in, to question everything about everything – especially those concrete phenomena that he has seen, experienced, and pondered firsthand' (cited in Barcan, 2002, p. 346). Certainly, while I regretted the loss of some of the 'unselfconscious' pleasures inherent in my snowboarding experiences prior to commencing this study, the adoption and application of various theoretical frameworks and conceptual schemas changed the way I see the world and understand the physical cultural body, such that I ultimately found much pleasure in this theoretical journey. Rather than adopting a position of 'cognitive estrangement,' in which we seek to separate ourselves from our thoughts and feelings, we should instead begin to explore the potential space in critical theorizing for affective processes, including 'hope and joy' (Leane & Buchanan, 2002, p. 257), and in so doing move toward a more self-reflexive engagement with social theory. Based on my own theoretical and research experiences, I believe theory, research, and leisure can, and should, be enjoyed at the same time, particularly when we introduce the element of 'play' into our embodied theorizing.

Sociological adventures: playing with social theory

Sociology hosts a wide variety of theories and theoretical perspectives, each drawing on different sets of assumptions about social reality and how it should be explained. The tendency in social theory has been to pick one primary theorist and regard the rest as secondary (Connell, 1987). There is often a sense that we should align ourselves with one theoretical school, or even one theorist. In the process of drawing from this work, the scholar defines him or herself as a particular type of researcher. Thus, using a theoretical work is not just a question of being interested in particular ideas but also how one represents oneself to others (Mills, 2003). However, scholars must be cautious about confining themselves to one theory or one theoretical tradition. As Andrews (2002) reminds us, there is a very real danger of being lulled into a 'false sense of conceptual security' (p. 116), in which individuals see only what fits into their preexisting schema and ignore conflicting evidence. Indeed, Barrett (1999) argues that theoretical disciplines offer a 'license to ignore', since disciplinary boundaries create 'an informal division of labour in which certain questions are assigned to one subject and can thus legitimately be ignored' by others (cited in McDonald & Birrell, 1999, p. 285).

Despite each theory claiming to best interpret the facts it identifies as significant, no single theory is adequate to deal with the wide range of phenomena studied by sociologists (Wilson, 1983). All theories have strengths and shortcomings and, because they are a matter of perspective, are always open to debate. If we approach our research with the knowledge that the search for the 'exact theoretical fit' is futile (Slack, 1996, cited in Andrews, 2002, p. 116), perhaps we can begin to use social theory differently, that is, with the aim to 'think differently than one thinks' and 'perceive differently than one sees' (Foucault, 1985, cited in Mills, 2003, p. 6). Rather than employing one theoretical perspective to frame our research, I suggest there is much to be gained by experimenting with a range of theoretical perspectives. Arguably, while there are obviously still gaps, the theoretical adventure embarked upon in this book paints a fuller, more complete, picture of the snowboarding body than would have been possible by focusing on a single critical social theory. In doing so, it is hoped that this project prompts fresh questions as to how we are using theory to understand and explain sport and physical cultures in historical and contemporary contexts.

Perhaps, social theorizing should be an 'adventure in the dialectics of cultural thought' (Alexander, 2003, p. 6), in which we set out to 'see things differently' (Baert, 2004, p. 367) and from multiple perspectives. According to Fredrick Jameson, we should 'learn theories like languages, and explore as every good translator does the expressive gaps between them – what can be said in one theory and not another' (cited in Leane & Buchanan, 2002, p. 254). Extending Jameson's metaphor, I suggest that once a researcher has gained a solid understanding of a particular theoretical vocabulary, and is able to speak a 'theoretical language' fluently and with confidence, there is much room for self-expression and creativity. I encourage physical cultural scholars to 'play' with theoretical concepts; pushing, pulling and stretching theories and concepts in relation to our empirical evidence can help us identify their strengths and limitations for explaining particular aspects of contemporary society and/or the physically active body. Indeed, sometimes those 'theoretical languages' that require the most 'struggling', or as Hall (1992) terms it, 'wrestling with the angels' (p. 280), can be the most fulfilling because they challenge us to think differently about the body and embodiment, and the social world around us.

Beyond boarding bodies: some final reflections

In sum, sociological theory can only be a legitimate and socially important enterprise if, according to Jeffrey Alexander (1991), it can 'make a claim to reason' (p. 147). To make a claim to reason is to suggest that sociological theory can 'achieve a perspective on society which is more extensive and more general than the theorist's particular life-world and the particular perspective of [his or her] social group' (Ibid.). Embracing a variety of theoretical perspectives and engaging these in extensive dialogue with empirical research, this project not only provided insights into the multidimensional snowboarding body, and the efficacy of numerous social theories and concepts for understanding various aspects of the physical cultural body, it also enabled me to make explicit what I previously unquestioningly accepted in my culture, to challenge deep-seated beliefs about the body, and to 'imagine socio-political scenarios other than the ones that are currently present' (Baert, 2004, p. 367). It is hoped that the suggestions offered here, for an embodied theoretical approach that embraces the creative, dynamic, adventurous, playful, pleasurable, and political aspects of social life, also prove valuable for those seeking to understand, explain, and perhaps intervene into, physical cultures in the twenty-first century and beyond.

Notes

1 Introducing a Sociology of Snowboarding Bodies

1. Citations from specific magazines, websites, videos and so on are listed in the Bibliography.
2. All interviewees received both an information sheet that outlined the project and their ethical rights, and a consent form. All interviewees had the choice to remain anonymous (full confidentiality), to be partially identified (e.g., occupation, and/or first name) or to be fully identified (full name and occupation), and signed the consent forms accordingly. While all but two agreed to be fully identified, in this book all interviewees have been given pseudonyms, except where the participant agreed to full disclosure and identifiers (e.g., age, occupation) help contextualize a particular comment or example included in the text. I have removed the full dates of interviews and personal communications.
3. Importantly, I was critically aware that entering virtual spaces for 'research' purposes raises many ethical issues, and thus I did not actively participate (e.g., post comments) on interactive websites or forums. Information published on publicly available travel, sport, and local websites, however, was used in conjunction with other cultural artifacts (e.g., magazines, films) with the primary intention of further developing and refining themes emerging in my fieldwork and interviews.
4. Of course, theoretical synthesis is not a new idea for feminists, some of whom have been combining the insights of two or more theoretical traditions for many years (e.g., Marxist feminism).

2 Remembering the Snowboarding Body

1. Early versions of some parts of this discussion originally appeared in *Sporting Traditions* (see Thorpe, 2010a).
2. In recent years, a myriad of snowboarding memorabilia collectors have also emerged, some of whom pay thousands of dollars for early snowboard equipment (especially snowboards).
3. Every historical artifact in the Salty Peaks Snowboard and Skateboard Shop and Museum is security tagged and inventoried; customers are under the surveillance of 28 video cameras.

3 Producing and Consuming the Snowboarding Body

1. Although his full name is Jake Burton Carpenter, Jake recently changed it to Jake Burton to avoid confusion. Hereafter I will refer to him as Burton, except where he has published under either Jake Burton or Jake Burton Carpenter.
2. There are different levels of sponsorship. Burton sponsors young riders at a 'factory level,' supplying them with snowboarding equipment. The next level is a 'rookie' sponsorship, where riders receive equipment and/or clothing, occasional

travel budgets and other incentives. The top level of sponsorship is Burton's Global Team, some of whom earn six-figure salaries.

3. According to a recent study conducted by the United States National Sporting Goods Association, only 11 percent of American snowboarders are members of racial/ethnic minority groups; 3.6 percent Asian, 2.3 percent Hispanic/Spanish/ Latino, 1.6 percent African American, 1.1 percent Native American, and 2.4 percent other (NGSA Newsletter, 2001).

4. *Transworld Snowboarding* stated that 44.3 percent of American snowboarders have a household income of US$75,000 a year or more (Hard Numbers, 2005, p. 58).

5. Clipping tickets is common practice among (typically younger) snowboarders and skiers on a tight budget; they approach patrons in the resort car park who appear to be heading home from a morning on the mountain, and offer them a cheap price for their used lift ticket (e.g., $20 for a lift ticket initially purchased for $80).

6. Since 1995 Chill has provided over 14,000 disadvantaged youths from 14 North American cities, as well as youth in Sydney (Australia) and Innsbruck (Austria), with the opportunity to learn to snowboard (for more information visit http:// www.burton.com/Home/chill,default,pg.html).

7. It is important to note that very few proponents of the notion of base and super-structure actually adopt such a determinist perspective. Moreover, Marx and Engels never held to such a doctrine. According to Engels, 'neither Marx nor I have asserted this. Hence if somebody twists this into saying that the economic factor is the *only* determining one, he transforms that into a meaningless, abstract, absurd phrase' (letter to J. Bloch, September 21–22, 1890, cited in Larrain, 1991, p. 47).

8. In these respects, post-Fordism 'overlaps to a good extent with some central aspects of post-modern theory' (Kumar, 1995, p. vii). A significant body of work links postmodernism and post-Fordism (e.g., Grossberg, 1992; Hall, 1989; Harvey, 1989; Jameson, 1991). For a critical discussion of such approaches, however, see Gartman (1998).

9. Theorization of the historical evolution and change from Fordism to post-Fordism has not passed unchallenged. In fact, post-Fordism is a hotly contested concept and, like the phenomena it seeks to understand, lacks a fixed and uniform interpretation. Hence, one must approach the literature on post-Fordism as a debate rather than a universally accepted theory of transition (see Nadesan, 2001).

10. This chapter has focused on the cultural positions of Western women as consumers and producers in the global boarding culture. Further research is necessary to examine how the positions of female snowboarders, as cultural consumers and producers, vary among different countries.

4   Representing the Boarding Body: Discourse, Power, and the Snowboarding Media

1. Earlier versions of some parts of this chapter originally appeared in *Journal of Sport and Social Issues* (see Thorpe, 2008).

2. The panopticon refers to Jeremy Bentham's design for a building that maximizes the working of power. Subjected to the 'omnipresent gaze of authority' in specially designed buildings, individuals scrutinize their own behaviors in a manner that 'renders them docile: they become their own supervisors' (Pringle & Markula,

2006, p. 43). Although Western states never implemented Bentham's design, Foucault (1991[1997]) identified panoptical power as a critical dimension of modern society.

3. As I have explained elsewhere (see Thorpe, 2008), the recent development of high-quality female-only snowboarding films (e.g., *As If* [2005], *Brighta* – Japanese all girl snowboard film [2007], *Stance* [2009]), also increasingly provide women with the opportunity to define their own criteria for inclusion, exhibit skills, create new meanings and values for women's snowboarding, and challenge dominant gender discourses.

4. Here 'discursive effect' refers to 'a momentary production of a phenomenon, such as the production of objects, subjects or conceptual understandings' (Markula & Pringle, 2006, p. 29).

5. A reverse discourse often uses 'the same vocabulary' as a dominating discourse but produces an opposing strategy or social effect (Foucault, 1978, p. 101).

5   Cultural Boarding Bodies: Status, Style, and Symbolic Capital

1. In this sense, there are some similarities between Bourdieu's conceptualization of social space and practice, and the concept of hegemony. Arguably, Bourdieu's conceptual schema is more useful because it is grounded in the 'real' and concerned primarily with the particular.

2. 'Going bigger' translates to more amplitude. 'Going fatter' means to perform the most technical maneuvers with style.

6   Female Boarding Bodies: Betties, Babes, and Bad-Asses

1. There are, of course, some notable exceptions. In the 1890s and early 1900s, for example, Sigmund Freud argued that gender and sexuality were socially constructed; the Frankfurt School then adopted his ideas in the mid-twentieth century. In the 1960s and 1970s, Michel Foucault also argued that all humans were social constructs – an argument that feminists adopted in the 1980s and 1990s with a Foucauldian stance.

2. An earlier version of this chapter originally appeared in *Sociology of Sport Journal* (see Thorpe, 2009).

3. Of course, feminine capital may also be used by men, and masculine capital may also be used by women.

4. However, perhaps due to his concern with the French working classes, Bourdieu tended to gloss over certain interclass differences (see Shilling, 2004), that would be pertinent to this discussion of intergroup gender relations within (and across) sports fields such as snowboarding, skateboarding and/or surfing.

5. Unfortunately, capturing the voices and understanding the lived experiences of 'pro-hos' proved difficult for this project, primarily because few women self-identify as 'pro-hos'. Rather, 'pro-ho' tends to be a label imposed upon 'other' women whose feminine dispositions and behaviors do not comply with the cultural valuation system within the snowboarding field. Some men are also identified as 'pro-hos' when they are perceived to be investing too heavily in social relationships with key figures in the sport or industry.

7 Male Boarding Bodies: Pleasure, Pain, and Performance

1. Scholars working in sport studies in the early 1990s enthusiastically embraced the concept of hegemonic masculinity because it offered both a way for feminists to explain women's complicity in their own subjectification in a post antidiscrimination law (e.g., Title IX) society, and an opportunity for men to 'deconstruct their own sexual politics' (Ingham & Donnelly, 1997, p. 390; Messner & Sabo, 1990; Pronger, 1990). Numerous scholars continue to use Connell's conceptual schema to facilitate understanding of the gendering processes related to sport, particularly the 'critiques of heavy contact, male-dominated sports such as American football and rugby union and the sexist and violent cultures that support such sports' (Pringle, 2005, p. 257).
2. Interestingly, the weight of logic and evidence offered by this new generation of gender scholars compelled Connell to 'reshape' her position (Connell & Messerschmidt, 2005, p. 845). Yet her suggested modifications failed to satisfy some of Connell's critics who proclaimed their arguments leveled against Connell's original conceptual schema continued to hold true. Rather than helping capture the complexities of gendered power relations in the twenty-first century, Connell's recommendations for reformulation appear to extend the shelf life of a problematic conceptual schema.
3. An earlier version of this chapter originally appeared in *Journal of Sport and Social Issues* (see Thorpe, 2010b).
4. See Chapter 9 for a discussion of the culturally exalted masculinities of big mountain snowboarders.
5. Young Australian male snowboarders, for example, are particularly notorious for their distinctive larrikin behavior. In Whistler, Canada, I overheard local residents joke that this is the one place in the world where there is 'racism against Australians' due to their drunken, obnoxious, violent, and often sexist behavior in bars and at parties, disrespect to local property (e.g., rental accommodation), and dangerous practices on the mountains (e.g., hiking out of bounds without safety equipment) (Field notes, November 2005; see Chapter 8).
6. The concept of hegemonic masculinity was 'originally formulated in tandem with the concept of hegemonic femininity – later renamed 'emphasized femininity' to acknowledge the asymmetrical position of masculinities and femininities in a patriarchal gender order. ... [Regrettably] in the development of research on men and masculinities, their relationship has dropped out of focus' (Connell & Messerschmidt, 2005, p. 848).

8 Transnational Boarding Bodies: Travel, Tourism, and Lifestyle Sport Migration

1. For some committed participants this discourse of transnationalism is such that a global snowboarding identity takes precedence over more traditional notions of identity (e.g., nationality). For example, when Haakonsen was asked to explain his highly controversial decision not to compete in the 1998 Winter Olympics, his response revealed stronger identification with the global snowboarding culture, and a transnational snowboarding company, than his nation state: 'Norway is a great country to live, but it's never supported me like my sponsors. My flag should be Burton not Norway' (cited in Reed, 2005, p. 135).

2. An earlier version of this discussion originally appeared in Maguire and Falcous (2010) *Sport and Migration* (see Thorpe, 2010c).
3. In light of government concerns about U.S. unemployment, the law was amended such that only 66,000 visas are available to 'alien' workers per year. Visas are spread out over 12 months and exclude from the cap workers who were employed in the United States during the previous three years. Prior to this law, the ski industry accounted for approximately one-third of all H-2B visas issued each year (H2B Visa Information, 2009). Recognizing the detrimental effects of this quota on the U.S. snow-sport industry, the National Ski Areas Association (NSAA) continues to actively lobby Congress to reconsider this law.

9 Sensual Snowboarding Bodies in Affective Spaces

1. The Alaskan heli-skiing phenomenon started in the mountains surrounding Valdez and Juneau during the early 1990s when local skiers and snowboarders convinced local pilots to give them a lift. 'There were probably only twenty people that were skiing or snowboarding in Valdez', recalls snowboarding cinematographer Mike Hatchett, 'there were no guides; it was total cowboy' (cited in Reed, 2005, p. 116). Hatchett's film *TB2: A New Way of Thinking* (1993) documented some of the first ever Alaskan heli-snowboarding footage. 'When people saw the videos of people making sick powder turns in Alaska, they wanted that. It became a fantasy', says early professional snowboarder Jeff Fulton. Heli-skiing and heli-boarding blossomed into a cottage industry where diehards make the long pilgrimage each spring, and a day snowboarding can cost anywhere upwards of US$1000; a price-tag covering both helicopter rides and the advice of highly trained guides. According to Brisick (2004), Alaska is 'the place to go if your dreams, board, wallet, and balls are big enough' (p. 119).
2. An extended version of this narrative appeared in *Sociology of Sport Journal* (see Thorpe *et al.*, 2011).
3. Not all core snowboarders participate in the hedonistic après-snow lifestyle to the same extent. For example, while professional Australian snowboarder Torah Bright enjoys socializing and dancing at snowboarding parties, as a devout Mormon she refuses to partake in the more salacious offerings at these events, and describes a 'constant battle' with her peers who regularly tempt and taunt her (cited in Karnikowski, 2010, para. 7). Some participants have also created alcohol- and drug-free snowboarding groups (see, e.g., www.ridersagainstdrugs.org).

10 Body Politics, Social Change, and the Future of Physical Cultural Studies

1. An earlier version of this discussion appeared in a special issue of *Sport in Society* (see Thorpe and Rinehart, 2010).
2. For historical convenience, many scholars and historians break feminism into waves. Thus far, the feminist movement consists of the first (1848 to mid-1920s), second (1960s to early 1980s), and third (early 1990s to 2000s) waves. The primary concern of first-wave feminism was women's suffrage. The 1960s marked a new, more adversarial, phase of feminism. Second-wave feminists focused on the radical reconstruction or elimination of traditional sex roles and the struggle for equal rights; their strategies were more radical than both their predecessors and

successors. Second-wave feminists built feminist organizations and fought for legislative changes regarding the family, sexual relations, reproduction, employment and education. Third-wave feminism emerged in the early 1990s in response to the perceived inadequacies of the second-wave. It was developed by feminists seeking to challenge and expand common definitions of gender and sexuality in contemporary society (e.g., Baumgardner & Richards, 2000, 2004; Heywood & Drake, 1997; Heywood & Dworkin, 2003; Walker, 1995). Put simply, the women's movement has followed periods of mass involvement, backlash, and 'quiet' periods, with different generations living through different stages of the cycle, which directly influence their experiences and attitudes toward feminism.

Bibliography

Aapola, S., Gonick, M., & Harris, A. (2005). *Young femininity: Girlhood, power and social change*. New York: Palgrave Macmillan.

Abbott, A. (1991). History and sociology: The lost synthesis. *Social Science History*, *15*(2), 201–238.

Abercrombie, N., Hill, S., & Turner, B. (2000). *The Penguin dictionary of sociology* (4th edition). London: Penguin Books.

'About POW'. (no date). Retrieved March 8, 2010, from http://protectourwinters.org/about/.

Abrams, P. (1982). *Historical sociology*. Ithaca, NY: Cornell University Press.

Adams, M. (2006). Hybridizing habitus and reflexivity: Towards an understanding of contemporary identity? *Sociology*, *40*(3), 511–528.

Adkins, L. (2002). *Revisions: Gender and sexuality in late modernity*. Buckingham: Open University Press.

Adkins, L. (2003). Reflexivity: Freedom or habit of gender? *Theory, Culture and Society*, *20*(6), 21–42.

Adkins, L. (2004). Introduction: Feminism, Bourdieu and after. In L. Adkins & B. Skeggs (Eds), *Feminism after Bourdieu* (pp. 3–18). Oxford: Blackwell.

Alexander, J. (1991). Sociological theory and the claim to reason: Why the end is not in sight? Reply to Seidman. *Sociological Theory*, *9*(2), 147–153.

Alexander, J. (1995). Modern, anti, post and neo*. *New Left Review*, *210*, 63–101.

Alexander, J. (2003). *The meaning of social life: A cultural sociology*. Oxford: University Press.

Allard, A. (2005). Capitalizing on Bourdieu: How useful are concepts of 'social capital' and 'social field' for researching 'marginalized' young women? *Theory and Research in Education*, *3*(1), 63–79.

Almendros, C. (2009, June 19). Interview with Russian snowboarder and photographer Dashika. *Cooler*. Retrieved January 18, 2010, from http://coolermag.com/features/-/interviews/interview-with-russian-snowboarder-and-photographer-dashika.html.

Althusser, L. (1977). *Lenin and philosophy and other essays*. London: New Left.

Amin, A. (1994). Post-Fordism: Models, fantasies and phantoms of transition. In A. Amin (Ed.), *Post-Fordism: A reader* (pp. 1–39). Oxford: Blackwell.

Amit, V. (2000) Introduction: Constructing the field. In V. Amit (Ed.), *Constructing the field: Ethnographic fieldwork in the contemporary world*. Florence: Routledge.

Anderson, E. (2009). *Inclusive masculinity: The changing nature of masculinities*. New York: Routledge.

Anderson, K. (1999). Snowboarding: The construction of gender in an emerging sport. *Journal of Sport and Social Issues*, *23*(1), 55–79.

Andrews, D. (1993). Desperately seeking Michel: Foucault's geneology, the body, and critical sport sociology. *Sociology of Sport Journal*, *10*(2), 148–167.

Andrews, D. (2000). Posting up: French post-structuralism and the critical analysis of contemporary sporting culture. In J. Coakley & E. Dunning (Eds), *Handbook of sports studies* (pp. 106–138). London: Sage.

Andrews, D. (2002). Coming to terms with cultural studies. *Journal of Sport and Social Issues*, *26*(1), 110–117.

Andrews, D. (2008). Kinesiology's *Inconvenient Truth* and the physical cultural studies imperative. *Quest, 60,* 45–62.

Ankersmit, F. (2005). *Sublime historical experience.* Stanford: University Press.

'Antifashion' (2002). *Transworld Snowboarding,* December, p. 30.

Appadurai, A. & Breckenridge, C. (1989). On moving targets. *Public Culture, 2,* i–iv.

Appleby, J., Hunt, L., & Jacob, M. (1994). *Telling the truth about history.* New York: W. W. Norton.

'Ask Dr Marco'. (2003, November 4). Retrieved March 12, 2009, from http://snowboarding.transworld.net/1000021203/uncategorized/ask-dr-marco/.

'Ask Dr Marco'. (2006). *Transworld Snowboarding,* February, p. 200.

Atencio, M., Beal, B. & Wilson, C. (2009). The distinction of risk: Urban skateboarding, street habitus and the construction of hierarchical gender relations. *Qualitative Research in Sport and Exercise, 1*(1), 3–20.

'Athlete Bio' (no date). Retrieved January 30, 2010, from http://www.lat34.com/snowboard/marc_frank.htm.

'Athlete Bios' (2002). Retrieved March 10, 2003, from http://expn.go.com/athletes/bios/DAKIDES_TARA.html.

Attwood, F. (2005). Tits and ass, porn and fighting: Male heterosexuality in magazines for men. *International Journal of Cultural Studies, 8*(1), 83–100.

Azzarito, L. (2010). Ways of seeing the body in kinesiology: A case for visual methodologies. *Quest, 62,* 155–170.

Baccigaluppi, J., Mayugba, S., & Carnel, C. (2001) *Declaration of independents: Snowboarding, skateboarding and music: An intersection of cultures.* San Francisco, CA: Chronicle Books.

Baer, A. (2001). Consuming history and memory through mass media products. *European Journal of Cultural Studies, 4*(4), 491–501.

Baerenholdt, J., Haldrup, M., Larsen, J., & Urry, J. (2004). *Performing tourist places.* Aldershot: Ashgate.

Baert, P. (2004). Pragmatism as philosophy of the social sciences. *European Journal of Social Theory, 7*(3), 355–369.

Bailey, R. (1998). Jake Burton: King of the hill. *Ski, 62*(6), 60–66.

Bakesale. (2009, December 9). Retrieved April 12, 2010, from http://www.snowboardingforum.com/snowboarding-general-chat/20572-resort-one-night-stand.html.

Baldwin, S. (2006). Riding high? Skiing, snowboarding and drugs. *Snowsphere.com.* Retrieved March 12, 2010, from http://www.snowsphere.com/special-features/riding-high-skiing-snowboarding-and-drugs.

Baldwin, S. (2006, January). Snowboarding vs skiing: The dying feud. *SnowSphere.com.* Retrieved March 12, 2009, from http://www.snowsphere.com/special-features/snowboarding-vs-skiing-the-dying-feud.

Bale, J. & Krogh-Christensen, M. (Eds) (2004). *Post-Olympism? Questioning sport in the twenty-first century.* Oxford: Berg Publishers.

Barcan, R. (2002). Problems without solutions: Teaching theory and the politics of hope. *Continuum: Journal of Media and Cultural Studies, 16*(3), 343–356.

Barnes, R. & Eicher, J. B. (Eds) (1992). *Dress and gender: Making and meaning.* New York: Berg.

Barr, M., Moran, C., & Wallace, E. (2006) *Snowboarding the world.* Bath: Footprint.

Basich, T. (with Gasperini, K.) (2003). *Pretty good for a girl: The autobiography of a snowboarding pioneer.* New York: Harper Collins.

Baumgardner, J. & Richards, A. (2000). *Manifesta: Young women, feminism and the future.* New York: Farrar, Straus and Giroux.

Baumgardner, J. & Richards, A. (2004). Feminism and femininity: Or how we learned to stop worrying and love the thong. In A. Harris (Ed.), *All about the girl: Culture, power and identity* (pp. 59–67). London: Routledge.

Beal, B. (1996). Alternative masculinity and its effects on gender relations in the subculture of skateboarding. *Journal of Sport Behavior, 19*, 204–221.

Beal, B. & Weidman, L. (2003). Authenticity in the skateboarding world. In R. E. Rinehart & S. Sydnor (Eds), *To the extreme: Alternative sports, inside and out* (pp. 337–352). New York: State University Press.

Beamish, R. (2002). Karl Marx's enduring legacy for the sociology of sport. In J. Maguire & K. Young (Eds), *Theory, sport and society* (pp. 25–39). London: Elsevier Science.

Benedek, D. (2009, August 8). David Benedek interviews Jake Burton Carpenter. *Snowboarder Magazine.* Retrieved January 12, 2010, from http://fresh.snowboardermard.com/feature.

Benedek, D. (2009, November 20). David Benedek interviews Terje Haakonsen. *Snowboarder Magazine.* Retrieved August 4, 2010, from http://fresh.snowboardermard.com/feature.

Berkley, A. (1999, August 13). Play misty for me: Three women redefine the chick flick. *Transworld Snowboarding,* Retrieved August 12, 2003, from http://www.transworldsnowboarding.com/snow/features/article/0,13009,245481,00.html.

Berra, L. (2006, January 16). Shread hot. Retrieved November 22, 2009, from http://sports.espn.go.com/espn/print?id=3693536&type=story.

'Beyond Hollywood'. (2006, February 16). Retrieved August 12, 2006, from http://www.beyondhollywood.com/gallery/category/gretchen-bleiler/.

Blackman, L. & Venn, C. (2010). Affect. *Body and Society, 16*(7), 7–28.

Blaikie, N. (2000). *Designing social research.* Cambridge: Polity.

Blehm, E. (2003). *Agents of change: The story of DC shoes and its athletes.* New York: Reagan Books.

Bleiler, G. (2005). Snowboarders are fashion victims. *Transworld Snowboarding,* January, p. 60.

Bleiler, G. (2005). To the gym or not to gym? *Transworld Snowboarding,* March, p. 58.

Blevins, J. (2007, April 17). Terrain-park safety becomes top priority after lawsuit. *The Denver Post.* Retrieved March 18, 2010, from http://www.denverpost.com/skiing/ci_5682314.

Blum, M. (1994). PC girl: take one (letter to the editor). *Snowboarder Magazine,* August, p. 9.

Blumberg, A. (2002). Launch. *Transworld Snowboarding,* January, p. 16.

Booth, D. (2002). From bikinis to boardshorts: Wahines and the paradoxes of the surfing culture. *Journal of Sport History, 28*(1), 3–22.

Booth, D. (2005). Paradoxes of material culture: The political economy of surfing. In J. Nauright & K. Schimmel (Eds), *The political economy of sport* (pp. 310–343), International Political Economy Series. New York: Palgrave Macmillan.

Booth, D. (2008). (Re)reading the surfers' bible: The affects of Tracks. *Continuum: Journal of Media and Cultural Studies, 22*(1), 17–35.

Booth, D. (2009). Politics and pleasure: The philosophy of physical education revisited. *Quest, 61*, 133–153.

Booth, D. & Loy, J. (1999). Sport, status, and style. *Sport History Review, 30*, 1–26.

Booth, D. & Thorpe, H. (Eds) (2007). The meaning of extreme. *Berkshire Encyclopedia of Extreme Sports* (pp. 181–197). Great Barrington, MA: Berkshire.

Borden, I. (2003). *Skateboarding, space and the city: Architecture and the body.* London: Berg.

Borden, M. (2009, January 14). Shaun White's business is red hot. *Fast Company.* Retrieved January 8, 2010, from http://www.fastcompany.com/node/1139303.

Bottomore, T. (Ed.) (1956). *Makers of modern social science: Karl Marx.* Englewood Cliffs, NJ: Prentice-Hall.

Bottomore, T. (Ed.) (1991). *A dictionary of Marxist thought* (2nd edition). Oxford: Blackwell.

Bourdieu, P. (1971). Intellectual field and creative project. In M. F. D. Young (Ed.), *Knowledge and control: New directions in the sociology of education* (pp. 161–188). London: Collier-Macmillan.

Bourdieu, P. (1977). *Outline of a theory of practice.* Cambridge: University Press.

Bourdieu, P. (1978). Sport and social class. *Social Science Information, 17*(6), 819–840.

Bourdieu, P. (1980). The production of belief: Contribution to an economy of symbolic goods. *Media, Culture and Society, 2,* 261–293.

Bourdieu, P. (1984) *Distinction: A social critique of the judgement of taste.* London: Routledge.

Bourdieu, P. (1985). The social space and the genesis of groups. *Theory and Society, 14,* 723–744.

Bourdieu, P. (1986). The forms of capital. In J. G. Richardson (Ed.), *Handbook of theory and research sociology of education* (pp. 241–258). New York: Greenwood Press.

Bourdieu, P. (1990a). *In other words.* Cambridge: Polity Press.

Bourdieu, P. (1990b). La domination masculine. *Actes de la Recherche en Sciences Sociales, 84* (September), 2–31.

Bourdieu, P. (1991). *Language and symbolic power.* Cambridge: Polity Press.

Bourdieu, P. (1992). *The logic of practice* (Trans. R. Nice). Cambridge: Polity Press.

Bourdieu, P. (1993). *The field of cultural production.* Cambridge: Polity Press.

Bourdieu, P. (2001). *Masculine domination.* Cambridge: Polity Press.

Bourdieu, P. & Wacquant, L. J. D. (Eds) (1992). The purpose of reflexive sociology. *An invitation to reflexive sociology* (pp. 61–215). Cambridge: Polity Press.

Bourdieu, P., Chamboredon, J., & Passeron, J. (1991). *The craft of sociology: Epistemological preliminaries.* Berlin & New York: Walter de Gruyter.

Bradley, S. (2010, January 28). Campaign targets boozy Brits on the piste. *Swissinfo.ch.* Retrieved March 12, 2010, from http://www.swissinfo.ch/eng/culture/Campaign_targets_boozy_Brits_on_the_piste.ht.

Braithwaite, A. (2002). The personal, the political, third-wave and post-feminisms. *Feminist Theory, 3*(3), 335–344.

Brayton, S. (2005). 'Back-lash': Revisiting the 'white negro' through skateboarding. *Sociology of Sport Journal, 22,* 356–372.

Bridges, P. (2004). Romain DeMarchi. *Snowboarder Magazine,* November, 94–105.

Bridges, P. (2005). The next Shaun White. *Snowboarder Magazine,* August, pp. 82–93.

Brisick, J. (2004) *Have board will travel: The definitive history of surf, skate, and snow,* New York: HarperCollins.

Brockmeier, J. (2002). Remembering and forgetting: Narrative as cultural memory. *Culture and Psychology, 8*(1), 15–43.

Brohm, J. M. (1978). *Prison of measured time.* London: Pluto Press.

Brooks, A. & Wee, L. (2008). Reflexivity and the transformation of gender identity: Reviewing the potential for change in a cosmopolitan city. *Sociology, 42*(3), 503–521.

Brooks, R. (2010). Success stories: Jake Burton charts a new course in snowboarding. *Success Magazine.* Retrieved January 7, 2010, from http://www.successmagazine.com.

Brown, D. (2006). Pierre Bourdieu's 'masculine domination' thesis and the gendered body in sport and physical culture. *Sociology of Sport Journal, 23*(2), 162–188.

Bull, J. (2009, April 1). Fluid snowboarding. Retrieved December 20, 2009, from personal blog, http://www.jamesbull.ca/blog/tag/snowboarding.

Bull, M., Gilroy, P., Howes, D., & Kahn, D. (2006). Introducing sensory studies. *Senses and Society, 1*(1), 5–7.

Burawoy, M. (2000). Introduction: Reaching for the global. In M. Burowoy, J. A. Blum, S. George, et al. (Eds), *Global ethnography: Forces, connection, and imaginations in a postmodern world*. Berkeley/Los Angeles, CA: University of California Press.

Burawoy, M., Blum, J. A., George, S., et al. (Eds) (2000). *Global ethnography: Forces, connection, and imaginations in a postmodern world*. Berkeley/Los Angeles, CA: University of California Press.

Burkitt, I. (1999). *Bodies of thought: Embodiment, identity and modernity*. London: Sage.

Burns, P. & Novelli, M. (Eds) (2008). Introduction. *Tourism and mobilities: Local-global connections* (pp. xvii–xxvi). Oxfordshire: CABI.

Burstyn, V. (1999). *The rites of men: Manhood, politics, and the culture of sport*. Toronto: University of Toronto Press.

Burton Carpenter, J. & Dumaine, B. (2002). My half-pipe dream come true. *Fortune Small Business, 12*(8), 64.

'Burton goes global'. (2005). Retrieved July 15, 2006, from http://www.burton.com/Company/Companyresearch.aspx

'Burton history'. (2005). Retrieved July 15, 2006, from http://www.burton.com/Company/Companyresearch.aspx

'Burton reports salary cuts' (2009, March 25). *Transworld Business*. Retrieved December 10, 2009, from http://business.transworld.net/14120/features/burton-announces-salary-cuts-5-staff-layoffs.

'Burton sponsors national Snowboard Team of China'. (2005, October 14). Retrieved from http://www.twsbiz.com/twbiz/print/0,21538,1119465,00.html.

Burton, J. (2003). Snowboarding: The essence is fun. In R. Rinehart & S. Sydnor (Eds), *To the extreme: Alternative sports, inside and out* (pp. 401–406). New York: State University Press.

Business Week (2009). The Burton corporation. Retrieved January 6, 2010, from http://investing.businessweek.com/research/stocks/private/snapshot.asp

Butt, D. (2005). Pro's and con's. *New Zealand Snowboarder*, July/August, pp. 88–92.

Butt, D. (2006a). Abby Lockhart interview. *New Zealand Snowboarder*, September/October, pp. 34–39.

Butt, D. (2006b). The 2006 NZ Snowboarder Magazine rider poll. *New Zealand Snowboarder*, July/August, pp. 52–60.

'Buyers guide' (2003). *New Zealand Snowboarder*, May/June, pp. 84–104.

'Buyers guide' (2004/2005). *Northwave, Drake, and Bakota Buyers Guide*, Winter, p. 16.

Buzinski, J. (2002). Snowboarder Ryan Miller: Out on the slopes. *OutSports*. Retrieved March 12, 2009 from http://www.outsports.com/local/2002/ryanmiller.htm

Canniford, R. (2005). Moving shadows: Suggestions for ethnography in globalized cultures. *Qualitative Market Research, 8*, 204–218.

Carlson, J. (1999). *Snowboarding: A ragged mountain press woman's guide*. Camden: Ragged Mountain Press.

Carrigan, T., Connell, R., & Lee, J. (1987). Hard and heavy: Toward a new sociology of masculinity. In M. Kaufman (Ed.), *Beyond patriarchy: Essays by men on pleasure, power and change* (pp. 139–192). Toronto: Oxford University.

Catsburg, M. (2005). Sibling rivalry? *Manual: New Zealand Skate and Snow Culture, 18*, pp. 110–116.

Cavanagh, K. (2005). Book review. The myth of empowerment: Women and the therapeutic culture in America, by Dana Becker. *British Journal of Social Work, 35*(8), 1423–1425.

Celsi, R. (1992). Transcendent benefits of high-risk sports. *Advances in Consumer Research, 19*, 636–641.

Chambers, C. (2005). Masculine domination, radical feminism and change. *Feminist Theory, 6*(3), 325–346.

Chapman, G. (1997). Making weight: Lightweight rowing, technologies of power, and technologies of the self. *Sociology of Sport Journal, 14*, 205–223.

Chesters, G. & Welsh, I. (2007). *Complexity and social movements: Multitudes at the edge of chaos.* Routledge: London.

Chronis, A. (2006). Heritage of the senses: Collective remembering as an embodied praxis. *Tourist Studies, 6*(3), 267–296.

Coakley, J. (1998). *Sport in society: Issues and controversies.* St Louis, MO: Times Mirror.

Coakely, J. & Dunning, E. (2000) (Eds). *Handbook of sports studies.* London: Sage.

Cohen, R. (1996). Diasporas and the nation-state: From victims to challengers. *International Affairs, 72*, 507–520.

Cole, C. & Hribar, A. (1995). Celebrity feminism: *Nike Style,* post-Fordism, transcendence, and consumer culture. *Sociology of Sport Journal, 12*, 347–369.

Cole, C. L., Giardina, M. D., & Andrews, D. (2004). Michel Foucault: Studies of power and sport. In R. Giulianotti (Ed.), *Sport and modern social theorists* (pp. 207–223). London: Palgrave Macmillan.

Coleman, A. G. (2004). *Ski style: Sport and culture in the Rockies.* Lawrence, KS: University Press of Kansas.

Coles, T. (2009). Negotiating the field of masculinity: The production and reproduction of multiple dominant masculinities. *Men and Masculinities, 12*(1), 30–44.

Confino, A. (1997). Collective memory and cultural history: Problems of method. *American Historical Review,* December, 1386–1403.

Connell, R. W. (1983). *Which way is up?* Sydney: George Allen and Unwin.

Connell, R. W. (1987). *Gender and power: Society, the person and sexual politics.* Cambridge: Polity Press.

Connell, R. W. (1995). *Masculinities.* St. Leonards: Allen and Unwin.

Connell, R. W. (2002). *Gender.* Cambridge: Polity Press.

Connell, R. W. & Messerschmidt, J. (2005). Hegemonic masculinity: Rethinking the concept. *Gender and Society, 19*(6), 829–859.

Connor, S. (2008). Introduction. In M. Serres, *The five senses: A philosophy of mingled bodies* (Trans. M. Sankey & P. Cowley) (pp. 1–16). London: Continuum.

Costios, D. (2005). Aussies behaving badly. *Australian, New Zealand Snowboarding,* p. 15.

Coyle, C. (2002). The siege at Summit. *Transworld Snowboarding,* September, pp. 128–135.

Coyle, C. (2004). 10 years of thinking outside the box. *Transworld Snowboarding,* March, p. 115.

Coyle, C. (2005). Japan: Land of the rising sons. *Transworld Snowboarding,* February, p. 154.

Craib, I. (1992). *Modern social theory* (2nd edition). Hemel Hempstead: Harvester Wheatsheaf.

Crane, L. (1996). Snowboard history timeline part 2 (1980s). Retrieved March 22, 2004, from http://www.transworldsnowboarding.com/snow/features/article/0,26719,246573,00.html.

Crane, L. (2008, February 29). Jake Burton and the snowboard conspiracy. Retrieved April 12, 2009, from http://www.leecrane.com/?p=398.

Crang, P., Dwyer, C., & Jackson, P. (2003). Transnationalism and the spaces of commodity culture. *Progress in Human Geography, 27*(4), 438–456.

Crossley, N. (2005). *Key concepts in critical social theory*. London: Sage.

Csikszentmihalyi, M. (1990). *Flow: The psychology of optimal experience*. New York: Harper and Row.

Csordas, T. (Ed.) (1994). *Embodiment and experience: The existential ground of culture and self*. Cambridge: University Press.

Cuff, E., Sharrock, W., & Francis, D. (1990). *Perspectives in sociology* (3rd edition). London: Unwin Hyman.

Cullen, D. (2001). The personal is political: Third-wave feminism and the study of gendered organizations. Retrieved June 14, 2004, from http://www.mngt.waikato. ac.nz/ejrot/cmsconference/2001/papers/gender/cullen.pdf

Curtes, J. Eberhardt, J., & Kotch, E. (2001). *Blower: Snowboarding inside out*. London: Booth-Clibborn Editions Ltd.

Dant, T. (1999). *Material culture in the social world: Values, activities, lifestyles*. Buckingham: Open University Press.

Davis, K. (1997). Embody-ing theory: Beyond modernist and postmodernist readings of the body. In K. Davis (Ed.), *Embodied practices: Feminist perspectives on the body* (pp. 1–23). Sage: London.

Davis-Delano, L. & T. Crosset. (2008). Using social movement theory to study outcomes in sport-related social movements. *International Review for the Sociology of Sport, 43*(2), 115–134.

Deemer, S. (2000, January 24). Snow business is booming in sunny Orange County. *Los Angeles Business Journal*. Retrieved from http://www.allbusiness.com/north-america/united-states-california-metro-areas/442072-1.html.

Denison, J. & Markula, P. (Eds) (2003). *Moving writing: Crafting movement in sport research*. New York: Peter Lang.

Denison, J. & Rinehart, R. (Eds) (2000). Introduction: Imagining sociological narratives: Special issue. *Sociology of Sport Journal, 17*(1), 1–4.

Dicker, R. & Piepmeier, A. (2003). *Catching a wave: Reclaiming feminism for the twenty-first century*. Boston, MA: Northeastern University Press.

Dickinson, L. (2007). Virtue or vice. *Curl*, January/February, p. 54.

Diehm, R. & Armatas, C. (2004). Surfing: An avenue for socially acceptable risk-taking, satisfying needs for sensation seeking and experience seeking. *Personality and Individual Differences, 36*, 663–677.

Dillman, L. (2010, February 21). Snowboarding's 'X Games vibe' an unlikely but profitable fit with Olympics tradition. *LA Times*. Retrieved March 1, 2010, from http://www.cleveland.com/olympics/index.ssf/2010/02/snowboardings_x_games_vibe_an.html.

Donaldson, M. (1993). What is hegemonic masculinity? *Theory and Society, 22*, 643–657.

Donnelly, M. (2003). Sweet spots and eye candy: Some problems with representing women's extreme sports culture. *Journal for the Arts, Sciences, and Technology, 1*(2), 147–150.

'Download TGR's new movie *Generations*'. (2009, December 4). *Free Skier*. Retrieved March 9, 2010, from http://www.freeskier.com/article/artide.php?article_id=4449.

Dresser, C. (2002, January 7). Mail 15.5. *Transworld Snowboarding*, retrieved August 12, 2003, from http://www.transworldsnowboarding.com/snow/magazine/article/0,14304,242495,00.html.

Dresser, C. (2003). The wildcats nine lives. Retrieved June 12, 2006, from http://www.transworldsnowboarding.com/snow/features/article/0,26719,424373,00.html

Dresser, C. (2004a). Mail. *Transworld Snowboarding*, March, p. 26.

Dresser, C. (2004b). Snowboarding Japan: A guide for the young professional. *Transworld Snowboarding*, November, pp. 125–127.

Dresser, C. (2005). Getting deep: The DCP interview. *Transworld Snowboarding*, January, pp. 132–149.

Dresser, C. (2006). Interpretations of style. *Transworld Snowboarding*, March, pp. 106–117.

Dreyfus, H. L. & Rabinow, P. (1982). *Michel Foucault: Beyond structuralism and hermeneutics*. Chicago, IL: University of Chicago Press.

Duncan, M. C. (1994). The politics of women's body images and practices: Foucault, the panopticon and *Shape* magazine. *Journal of Sport and Social Issues, 18*, 48–65.

Duncan, M. C. (2007). Bodies in motion: The sociology of physical activity. *Quest, 59*(1), 55–66.

Duncan, M. C. & Messner, M.A. (1998). The media image of sport and gender. In L. A. Wenner (Ed.), *Mediaport* (pp. 170–185). London: Routledge.

Duncan, T. (2008). The internationalisation of tourism labour markets: Working and playing in a ski resort. In C. M. Hall & T. Coles (Eds), *International Business and Tourism* (pp. 181–194). London: Routledge.

Dunk, T. (2000). Girl with attitude. *CLEO New Zealand*, February, pp. 20–22.

Dunning, E. (1994). Aspects of the relationship between history and sociology. Unpublished paper, University of Leicester.

Ebner, D. (2009, February 11). U.S snowboarder at top of fame mountain. *Globe and Mail*. Retrieved January 5, 2010, from http://licensc.icopyright.net/user/viewfreeuse.act?fuid=NjM5MTQ1MQ%3D%BD.

Edley, N. & Weatherell, M. (1995). *Men in perspective: Practice, power and identity*. London: Harvester Wheatsheaf.

Edwards, G. (2006). Attack of the flying tomato. *Rolling Stone, 995*(March), pp. 43–45.

Eliot, T. D. (1922). The use of history for research in theoretical sociology. *The American Journal of Sociology, 27*(5), 628–636.

Elliot, J. (2001, January 21). The 'It' girl. *SI Adventure*. Retrieved November 11, 2004 from http://sportsillustrated.cnn.com/features/siadventure/11/it_girl.

Elliott, A. (2008). *Contemporary social theory: An introduction*. London: Routledge.

Emler, N., & Reicher, S. (1995). *Adolescence and delinquency: The collective management of reputation*. New York: Blackwell.

Evers, C. (2004). Men-who-surf. *Cultural Studies Review, 10*, 27–41.

Evers, C (2006). How to surf. *Journal of Sport and Social Issues, 30*(3), 229–243.

Evers, C. (2009). 'The Point': Surfing, geography and a sensual life of men and masculinity on the Gold Coast, Australia. *Social and Cultural Geography, 10*(8), 893–908.

Evers, C. (2010). *Notes for a young surfer*. Melbourne: University Press.

'Fact sheet: Burton Snowboards' (2003). Retrieved from www.burton.com.

Faludi, S. (1991). *Backlash: The undeclared war against American women*. New York: Crown.

Fast, A. (2005, October 9). All girls all the time. *Transworld Snowboarding*. Retrieved on July 20, 2006, from http://www.transworldsnowboarding.com/snow/features/article/0,13009,1103511,00.html.

'Fastest growing sports' (no date). Retrieved March 14, 2005, from http://www.extrememediagroup.com/xchannel/xcha_main.html#4.

Featherstone, M. (1991). *Consumer culture and postmodernism*. London: Sage.

Featherstone, M., Hepworth, M., & Turner, B. (Eds), (1991). *The body: Social processes and cultural theory*. Newbury Park, CA: Sage.

Fincham, B., McGuinness, M., & Murray, L. (2010). *Mobile methodologies*. Palgrave Macmillan: Hampshire.

'Fishing a wider sea'. (2006, June 22). *Transworld Business*. Retrieved August 2, 2006, from http://www.transworldbusiness.com.

Floros, S. (2004, November 1). Snowboarding's rookie of the year: Leanne Pelosi. Retrieved from www.snowboardermag.com/columns/pelosi100704/index1.html.

Fong, T. (2000, April 28). Soapbox by Tracey Fong, owner of Deep. *Transworld Snowboarding*, retrieved June 7, 2004, from http://www.transworldsnowboarding.com/snow/snowbiz/article.

Ford, N. & Brown, D. (2006) *Surfing and social theory*. London: Routledge.

Foucault, M. (1974). Prisons et asiles dans le mécanisme du pouvoir. In D. Defert & F. Ewald (Eds), *Dits et Ecrits*, t. II. Paris: Gallimard.

Foucault, M. (1977). *Discipline and punish: The birth of the prison* (Trans. A. M. Sheridan). New York: Pantheon Books.

Foucault, M. (1978). *The history of sexuality volume 1: An introduction*. London: Penguin Books.

Foucault, M. (1981). The order of discourse. In R. Young (Ed), *Untying the text: A post-structuralist reader* (pp. 48–79). London: Routledge & Keagan and Paul.

Foucault, M. (1983). The subject and power. In H. L. Dreyfus & P. Rabinow (Eds), *Michel Foucault: Beyond structuralism and hermeneutics* (2nd edition) (pp. 208–226). Chicago, IL: University of Chicago Press.

Foucault, M. (1984). Polemics, politics and problematizations. In P. Rabinow (Ed.), *Foucault reader* (pp. 381–390). New York: Pantheon Books.

Foucault, M. (1985). *The use of pleasure: The history of sexuality, Volume 2*. London: Penguin Books.

Foucault, M. (1986). *The care of the self: The history of sexuality, Volume 3*. New York: Pantheon.

Foucault, M. (1987). The ethic of care for the self as a practice of freedom: An interview with Michel Foucault on January 20, 1984. In J. Bernauer & D. Rasmussen (Eds), *The final Foucault* (pp. 1–20). Cambridge, MA: The MIT Press.

Foucault, M. (1988a). Technologies of the self. In L. H. Martin, H. Gutman, & P. H. Hutton (Eds), *Technologies of the self: A seminar with Michel Foucault* (pp. 16–49). Amherst, MA: University of Massachusetts Press.

Foucault, M. (1988b). An aesthetics of existence. In L. D. Kritzman (Ed.), *Michel Foucault politics, philosophy, culture: Interviews and other writing 1977–1984*. London: Routledge.

Foucault, M. (1991[1977]). *Discipline and punish: The birth of the prison*. London: Penguin Books.

Foucault, M. (2000) (Edited by P. Rabinow). *Essential works of Foucault 1954–1984: Ethics*. London: Penguin.

Fowler, B. (2003). Reading Pierre Bourdieu's *Masculine Domination:* Notes towards an intersectional analysis of gender, culture and class. *Cultural Studies, 17*(3/4), 468–494.

Friedlin, J. (2002). Second and third-wave feminists clash over the future. Retrieved June 14, 2004, from http://www.womensenews.org/article.cfm/dyn/aid/920/context/cover

Frohlick, S. (2003). Negotiating the 'global' within the global playscapes of Mount Everest. *The Canadian Review of Sociology and Anthropology, 40*(5), 525–542.

Frohlick, S. (2005) 'That playfulness of white masculinity': Mediating masculinities and adventure at Mountain Film Festivals. *Tourist Studies, 5*, 175–193.

Frow, J. & Morris, M. (2003). Cultural studies. In N. Denzin & Y. S. Lincoln (Eds), *The landscape of qualitative research: Theories and issues* (pp. 489–530). London: Sage.

Funnell, N. (2010, January 5). Give young men a sporting chance. *Sydney Morning Herald*. Retrieved January 6, 2010, from http://www.smh.com.au/opinion/society-and-culture-give-young-men-a-sporting-chance-20100104-lq1k.html.

Gagnon, O. (2008, February). Snowblind. *Snowboarding Magazine*. Retrieved March 10, 2010, from http://www.snowboardermag.com/features/news/february-08-on-sale-now.

Galbraith, J. & A. Marcopoulos, A. (2004). Terje Haakonsen. *Frequency: The Snowboarder's Journal*, 3(3), 62–83.

Gartman, D. (1998). Postmodernism or the cultural logic of post-Fordism? *The Sociological Quarterly*, 39(1), 119–137.

du Gay, P., Hall, S., Janes, L., Mackay, H., & Negus, K. (1997). *Doing cultural studies: The story of the Sony walkman*. London: Sage.

Ghosh, S. & Wang, L. (2003). Transnationalism and identity: A tale of two faces and multiple lives. *The Canadian Geographer*, 47(3), 269–282.

Gill, R. (2008). Empowerment/sexism: Figuring female sexual agency in contemporary advertising. *Feminism and Psychology*, 18(1), 35–60.

Ginsburg, S. (2010, February 16). Hannah Teter defends her bikini shots. Retrieved March 1, 2010, from http://www.reuters.com/assets/print?aid=USTRE61F0UH20100216.

'Girls and snowboarding'. (2003, March 28). *Boardpass.com*. Retrieved January 19, 2004, from http://www.boardpass.com/search/snownews/replies.asp?IDCODE=829andMainCode=703.

Giulianotti, R. (2005). *Sport: A critical sociology*. Cambridge: Polity Press.

Goldstein, J. (Ed.) (1994). *Foucault and the writing of history*. Cambridge, MA: Blackwell.

Goldthorpe, J. H. (1991). The uses of history in sociology: reflections on some recent tendencies. *British Journal of Sociology*, 42(2), 211–230.

Goodman, D. (2003). Chairman of the board. *Yankee*, 67(1), 64.

Graves, T. (2010). *AR-2010. Project: Aries 2010*. Portland, OR: Endo Publishing LLC.

Griffin, L. J. (1995). How is sociology informed by history? *Social Forces*, 73(4), 1245–1254.

Grossberg, L. (1992). *We gotta get out of this place: Popular conservatism and postmodern culture*. London: Routledge.

Grossberg, L. (1997). Cultural studies, modern logics, and theories of globalization. In A. McRobbie (Ed.), *Back to reality? Social experience and cultural studies* (pp. 7–35). Manchester: Manchester University Press.

Grosz, E. (1994). *Volatile bodies: Toward a corporeal feminism*. Bloomington, IN: Indiana University Press.

Gruneau, R. (1991). Sport and 'esprit de corps': Notes on power, culture and the politics of the body. In F. Landry, M. Landry, & M. Yerles (Eds), *Sport... The third millennium* (Symposium Proceedings) (pp. 169–185). Les Saint-Foy: Presses de L'Univesite Laval.

Guarnizo, L. E. (1997). The emergence of a transnational social formation and the mirage of return migration among Dominican transmigrants. *Identities*, 4(2), 281–322.

Gurley, J. (1984, May). Marx's contributions and their relevance today. *The American Economic Review*, 74(2), 110–115.

'H2B visa information'. (2009, August 17). Available at: http://www.outbreak-adventure.co.uk/recruitment/visa.php.

Hagerman, E. (2002, November). The cool sellout. *Outside Magazine*. Retrieved March 27, 2008, from http://outside.away.com/outside/features/200211/200211/cool_sellout_2.html.

Hakes, R. (2000). Ladies room: insight into the female mind. *Transworld Snowboarding*. Retrieved from http://www.transworldsnowboarding.com/snow/snowboard_life/article/0,13009,243647,00html (accessed November 20, 2000).

Haldrup, M. & Larsen, J. (2006). Material cultures in tourism. *Leisure Studies, 25*(3), 275–289.

Hall, M. A. (1996). *Feminism and sporting bodies: Essays on theory and practice.* Champaign, IL: Human Kinetics.

Hall, S. (1980). Cultural studies: two paradigms. *Media, Culture and Society, 2*(1), 57–72.

Hall, S. (1981). Notes on deconstructing 'the popular'. In R. Samuel (Ed.), *People's history and socialist theory* (pp. 227–240). London: Routledge and Kegan Paul.

Hall, S. (1989). The meaning of New Times. In S. Hall & M. Jacques (Eds), *New Times: The Changing Face of Politics in the 1990s* (pp. 116–134). London: Verso.

Hall, S. (1992). Cultural studies and its theoretical legacies. In L. Grossberg, C. Nelson, & P. Treichler (Eds), *Cultural Studies* (pp. 277–294). London: Routledge.

Hall, S. & Jacques, M. (Eds) (1989). *New Times: The changing face of politics in the 1990s.* London: Verso.

'Hard numbers'. (2005). *Transworld Snowboarding*, September, p. 54.

Hardy, S. (1999). Where did you go, Jackie Robinson? Or, the end of history and the age of sport infrastructure. *Sporting Traditions, 16*(1), 85–100.

Hargreaves, J. (1987). The body, sport and power relations. In J. Horne, D. Jary, & A Tomlinson (Eds), *Sport, leisure and social relations* (pp. 139–159). London: Routledge & Kegan Paul.

Hargreaves, J. (2004). Querying sport feminism: Personal or political? In R. Giulianotti (Ed.), *Sport and modern social theorists* (pp. 187–205). Basingstoke: MacMillan.

Hargreaves, J. & Vertinsky, P. (Eds) (2007). Introduction. *Physical Culture, Power and the Body* (pp. 1–24). London: Routledge.

Harris, A. (2001, September). Not waving or drowning: Young women, feminism, and the limits of the next wave debate. *Outskirts: Feminisms along the edge*. Retrieved from http://www.chloe.uwa.edu.au/outskirts/index.html.

Harris, A. (Ed.) (2004a). *All about the girl: Culture, power and identity.* London: Routledge.

Harris, A. (2004b). *Future girl: Young women in the twenty-first century.* London: Routledge.

Harris, A. (2005). Discourses of desire as governmentality: Young women, sexuality and the significance of safe spaces. *Feminism and Psychology, 15*(1), 39–43.

Harris, A. (2008). *Next wave cultures: Feminism, subcultures, activism.* London: Routledge.

Harris, L. (1991). Forces and relations of production. In T. Bottomore (Ed.), *A dictionary of Marxist thought* (2nd edition) (pp. 204–206). Oxford: Blackwell.

Harris, C. & Wilson, E. (2007). Travelling beyond the boundaries of constraint: Women, travel and empowerment. In A. Pritchard, N. Morgan, I. Ateljevic & C. Harris (Eds), *Tourism and Gender: Embodiment, Sensuality and Experience* (pp. 235–253). Oxfordshire: CABI.

Harvey, D. (1989). *The condition of postmodernity.* Oxford: Basil Blackwell.

Harvey, D. (2001). The body as referent. *The Hedgehog Review, 3,* 2.

Harvey, J. & Houle, F. (1994). Sport, world economy, global culture, and the new social movements. *Sociology of Sport Journal, 11*(4), 337–355.

Harvey, J. & Sparkes, R. (1991). The politics of the body in the context of modernity. *Quest, 43,* 164–189.

Heino, R. (2000). What is so punk about snowboarding? *Journal of Sport and Social Issues, 24*(2), 176–191.

Helfrich, B. (2010, February 16). Bottoms up: Hannah Teter launches personal line of underwear. *Street and Smith's Sports Business Daily.* Retrieved March 20,

2010, from http://www.sportsbusinessdaily.com/index.cfm?fuseaction=archive.printArticle&artic...

Helmich, P. (2000, August 8). Chairman of the board. Retrieved from http://www.vermontguides.com/2000/8-aug/aug1.html.

Henderson, M. (2001). A shifting line up: Men, women, and *Tracks* surfing magazine. *Continuum: Journal of Media and Cultural Studies, 15*(3), 319–332.

Hervieu-Leger, D. (2000). *Religion as a chain of memory.* Oxford: Polity Press.

Heywood, L. & Drake, J. (Eds) (1997). Introduction. *Third-wave agenda.* Minneapolis, MN: University of Minnesota Press.

Heywood, L. & Dworkin, S. L. (2003). *Built to win: The female athlete as cultural icon.* Minneapolis, MN: University of Minnesota Press.

Heywood, L. & Montgomery, M. (2008). Ambassadors of the last wilderness: Surfers, environmental ethics, and activism in America. In K. Young & M. Atkinson (Eds), *Tribal play: Sub-cultural journeys through sport* (pp. 153–172). Bingley: Emerald Publishing Group, JAI Press.

Heywood, L. (2006). Producing girls: Empire, sport and the neoliberal body. In P. Vertinsky and J. Hargreaves (Eds), *Physical culture, power and the body* (pp. 101–120). London: Routledge

Higgins, M. (2010a, February 12). Swifter, higher... higher. *ESPN.com.* Retrieved March 1, 2010, from http://sports.espn.go.com/espn/print?id=4910112&type=story.

Higgins, M. (2010b, January 28). Freestyles are uptight about keeping clothes loose. *New York Times.* Retrieved January 29, 2010, from http://www.nytimes.com/2010/01/28/sports/olympics/28suits.html?emc=eta1&pagew.

Hills, L. (2006). Playing the field(s): An exploration of change, conformity and conflict in girls' understandings of gendered physicality in physical education. *Gender and Education, 18*(5), 539–556.

Hockey, J. & Collinson, J. A. (2007). Grasping the phenomenology of sporting bodies. *International Review for the Sociology of Sport, 42*(2), 115–131.

Hodgkin, K. & Radstone, S. (Eds) (2003). Introduction: Contested pasts. *Contested pasts: The politics of memory* (pp. 1–21). London: Routledge.

Holt, R. (2005). *Australian and New Zealand Snowboarding Magazine,* September/October p. 91.

Honneth, A. (1986). The fragmented world of symbolic forms. *Theory, Culture and Society, 3,* 55–66.

Hopkins, S. (2002). *Girl heroes: The new force in popular culture.* Sydney: Pluto Press.

Howe, S. (1998). *(SICK) A cultural history of snowboarding.* New York: St. Martins Griffin.

Howes, D. (2003). *Sensual relations: Engaging the senses in culture and social theory.* Ann Arbor, MI: Michigan University Press.

Howson, A. (2005). *Embodying gender.* London: Sage.

Howson, A. & Inglis, D. (2001). The body in sociology: Tensions inside and outside sociological thought. *Sociological Review, 49*(3), 297–317.

Hua, V. (2006, February 13). Diversity on the slopes an uphill climb. *SFGate.com.* Retrieved October 11, 2008, from http://www.sfgate.com/cgi-bin/article.cgi?f=/c/a/2006/02/13/MNG16H7I551.DTL&type=printable.

Huffman, J. (2006). 10 questions: Louie Fountain, *Transworld Snowboarding.* Retrieved October 18, 2007, from http://snowboarding.transworld.net/1000021814/uncategorized/10-questions-louie-fountain/

Hughes, K (1988, March). Surfboarding shifts to the ski slopes and cultures clash. *The Wall Street Journal.* Retrieved March 10, 2003, from http://global.factiva.com/en/arch/display.asp.

Humphreys, D. (1996). Snowboarders: Bodies out of control and in conflict. *Sporting Traditions, 13*(1), 3–23.

Humphreys, D. (1997). Shredheads go mainstream? Snowboarding an alternative youth. *International Review for the Sociology of Sport, 32*(2), 147–160.

Humphreys, D. (2003). Selling out snowboarding. In R. E. Rinehart & S. Sydnor (Eds), *To the extreme: Alternative sports, inside and out* (pp. 407–428). New York: State University Press.

Hunt, G., Moloney, M., & Evans, K. (2010). *Youth, drugs and nightlife*. London: Routledge.

Huppatz, K. (2009). Reworking Bourdieu's 'capital': Feminine and female capitals in the field of paid caring work. *Sociology, 43*(1), 45–66.

Hutton, F. (2004). Up for it, mad for it? Women, drug use and participation in club scenes. *Health, Risk and Society, 6*(3), 223–237.

Huyssen, A. (2003). *Present pasts: Urban palimpsests and the politics of memory*. Stanford, CA: Stanford University Press.

'In your head' (2005). *Transworld Snowboarding*, February, p. 54.

Ingham, A. G. (1997). Toward a department of physical cultural studies an an end to tribal warfare. In J. Fernandez-Balboa (Ed.), *Critical postmodernism in human movement, physical education, and sport* (pp. 157–182). Albany, NY: Statue University of New York Press.

Ingham, A. G. & Donnelly, P. (1997). A sociology of North American sociology of sport: Disunity in unity, 1965 to 1996. *Sociology of Sport, 14*(2), 362–418.

Irish, O. (2003, April 6). X-Files: Six superstars of board and bike. *The Observer*. Retrieved January 14, 2005, from http://observer.guardian.co.uk.print/0,3858,4639886,00.html.

Irwin-Zarecka, I. (1994,). *Frames of remembrance*. New Brunswick: Transactions Book.

'Is snowboarding a religion?' (2002, July). Retrieved June 7, 2004, from http://www.boardtheworld.com/magazine/editorial.php?month=2002–07–01.

Jackson, P., Crang, P. & Dwyer, C. (2004). Introduction. In P. Jackson, P. Crang, & C. Dwyer (Eds), *Transnational spaces* (pp. 1–23). London: Routledge.

'Jake Burton Carpenter Interview' (2008, February 10). *Transworld Snowboarding*, Retrieved November 16, 2009, from http://snowboarding.transworld.net/1000030391/photos/backcountry/jake-burton-carpenter-interview.

Jameson, F. (1991). *Postmodernism, or the cultural logic of late capitalism*. London: Verson.

Jenkins, D. (2002a). SurfAid International Annual Report 2002. *SurfAid International*. Retrieved October 12, 2009, from http://www.surfaidinternational.org.

Jenkins, R. (2002b). *Pierre Bourdieu* (Revised edition). London: Routledge.

'Jeremy Jones establishes Protect Our Winters (POW) in fight against global warming crisis'. (2007, March 28). Retrieved March 10, 2010, from http://www.snowboard-mag.com/node/19938.

'Jeremy Jones, POW and TGR meet with Congress'. (2010, January 29). *Powder Magazine*. Retrieved March 12, from http://blogs.powdermag.com/industry-news-and-events/jeremy-jones-pow-tgr-go-to-washington.

Jones, J. (2009, April 2). The dream has changed. Retrieved March 9, 2010, from http://blog.jonessnowboards.com/.

Jowett, M. (2004). 'I don't see feminists as you see feminists:' Young women negotiating feminism in contemporary Britain. In A. Harris (Ed.), *All about the girl: Culture, power and identity* (pp. 91–100). London: Routledge.

Kansteiner, W. (2002). Finding meaning in memory: A methodological critique of collective memory studies. *History and Theory, 41*, 179–197.

Karnikowski, N. (2010, February 19). Snow white golden girl. *The Age*. Retrieved May 25, 2010, from http://blogs.theage.com.au/executive-style/sportandstyle/2010/02/19/snowwhitegold.h...

Kay, J. & Laberge, S. (2002). The 'new' corporate habitus in adventure racing. *International Review of the Sociology of Sport, 37*(1), 17–36.

Kay, J. & Laberge, S. (2003) 'Oh say can you ski?' Imperialistic construction of freedom in Warren Miller's *Freeriders*. In R. Rinehart & S. Sydnor (Eds) *To the extreme: Alternative sports, inside and out*. New York: State University of New York.

Keck, N. (2008, November 24). Burton owners discuss controversy over snowboards. *Vermont Public Radio*. Retrieved December 12, 2009, from http://www.vpr.net/news.

Keenan, E. (2008). Who are you calling 'lady'? Femininity, sexuality, and third-wave feminism. *Journal of Popular Music Studies, 20*(4), 378–401.

Keh, A. (2009, December 4). Burton introduces 'Anti uniform' for U.S snowboarders. *New York Times*. Retrieved December 12, 2009, from http://vancouver2010.blogs.nytimes.com/2009/12/04/burton-introduces-anti-uniform-...

Kelly, D., Pomerantz, S., & Currie, D. (2005). Skater girlhood and emphasized femininity: 'You can't land an olly properly in heels'. *Gender and Education, 17*(3), 229–248.

Kelly, P. & Lusis, T. (2006). Migration and the transnational habitus: Evidence from Canada and the Philippines. *Environment and Planning, A38*(5), 831–847.

Kenway, J. & McLeod, J. (2004). Bourdieu's reflexive sociology and 'spaces of points of view': Whose reflexivity, which perspective? *British Journal of Sociology of Education, 25*(4), 525–544.

Kimmel, M. (1994). Masculinity as homophobia: Fear, shame, and silence in the construction of gender identity. In H. Brod & M. Kaufman (Eds), *Theorizing masculinities*. London: Sage.

Kirmayer, L. (1992). The body's insistence on meaning: Metaphor as presentation and representation of illness experience. *Medical Anthropological Quarterly, 6*(4), 323–346.

Klugman, M. (2009). *Passion play: Love, hope and heartbreak at the footy*. Melbourne: Hunter Publishers.

Knowles, C. (1999). Here and there: Doing transnational fieldwork. In V. Amit (Ed.), *Constructing the field: Ethnographic fieldwork in the contemporary world*. Florence, KY: Routledge.

Krais, B. (1993). Gender and symbolic violence: Female oppression in the light of Pierre Bourdieu's theory of social practice. In C. Calhohn, E. LiPuma, & M. Postone (Eds), *Bourdieu: Critical perspectives* (pp. 156–177). Cambridge: Polity Press.

Krais, B. (2006). Gender, sociological theory and Bourdieu's sociology of practice. *Theory, Culture and Society, 23*(6), 119–134.

Kumar, K. (1995). *From post-industrial to post-modern society: New theories of the contemporary world*. Oxford: Blackwell.

Kusz, K. (2007a). *Revolt of the white athlete: Race, media and the emergence of extreme athletes in America*. New York: Peter Lang Publishing.

Kusz, K. (2007b). Whiteness and extreme sports. In D. Booth & H. Thorpe (Eds), *Berkshire encyclopedia of extreme sport* (pp. 357–361). Great Barrington, MA: Berkshire Publishing.

Laberge, S. (1995). Toward an interpretation of gender into Bourdieu's concept of cultural capital. *Sociology of Sport Journal, 12*, 131–146.

Laberge, S. & Kay, J. (2002). Bourdieu, socio-cultural theory and sport practice. In J. Maguire & K. Young (Eds), *Theory, sport and society* (pp. 239–266). London: JAI.

Laberge, S. & Sankoff, D. (1988). Physical activities, body habitus and lifestyles. In I. J. Harvey & H. Cantelon (Eds), *Not Just a Game: Essays in Canadian Sport Sociology*. Ottawa: University Press.

Landan, J. (director and producer) (2008). *Against the grain: A documentary on the life of Tara Dakides*. Ventura, CA: The Background Collective.

Larrain, J. (1991). Base and superstructure. In T. Bottomore (Ed.), *A dictionary of Marxist thought* (2nd edition) (pp. 45–48). Oxford: Blackwell.

Lash, S. (1990). *The sociology of postmodernism*. London: Routledge.

Latham, R. (2002). *Consuming youth: Vampires, cyborgs, and the culture of consumption*. Chicago, IL: University Press.

Laurendeau, J. (2004). The 'crack choir' and the 'cock chorus': The intersection of gender and sexuality in skydiving texts. *Sociology of Sport Journal, 21*(4), 397–417.

Laurendeau, J. & Sharara, N. (2008). 'Women could be every bit as good as guys': Reproductive and resistant agency between two 'action' sports. *Journal of Sport and Social Issues, 32*(1), 24–47.

Laviolette, P. (2006). Green and extreme: Free-flowing through seascape and sewer. *Worldviews, 10*(2), 178–204.

Laviolette, P. (2010). Fearless trembling: A leap of faith into the devil's frying pan. *Senses and Society, 4*(3), 303–322.

Layder, D. (2004). *Emotion in social life: The lost heart society*. London: Sage.

Layder, D. (2006). *Understanding social theory* (2nd edition). London: Sage.

Leane, E. & Buchanan, I. (2002). What's left of theory? *Continuum: Journal of Media and Cultural Studies, 16*(3), 253–258.

LeFebvre, E. (2005, August 29). Shut the f – k up. *Transworld Snowboarding*. Retrieved April 1, 2006 from http://www.transworldsnowboarding.com/snow/features/article/0,13009,1099403,00.html.

'Letters 13.4'. (1999, November). Retrieved June 7, 2004, from http://www.transworld-snowboarding.com/snow/magazine/article/0,14304,245248,00.html.

Levitt, P. & Glick Schiller, N. (2004). Conceptualizing simultaneity: A transnational social field perspective on society. *International Migration Review, 38*(3), 1002–1039.

Lewis, M. (2005, February 5). Women's market: Not just a man's world. *Transworld Business*, retrieved from http://www.twsbiz.com/twbiz/women/article/0,21214,1060373,00.html.

Lewis, M. (2008a, April 1). New baggage charges sweep airline industry. *Transworld Business*. Retrieved August 12, 2009, from http://business.transworld.net/features/new-baggage-charges-sweeping-the-airline-industry.

Lewis, M. (2008b, December 5). Snow exposure meter: Andreas Wiig regains lead; captures 07–08 title. Retrieved April 12, 2010, from http://business.transworld.net/6233/exposure-meter/snow-exposure-meter-andreas-wiig-regains-lead-captures-07–08-title.

Lewis, M. (2008c, March 6). Transworld Business investigates: The Jake Burton children's book controversy. Retrieved April 12, 2009 from http://business.transworld.net.

Lewis, M. (2009a, April 20). March mountain lodgings dive 21.3 percent. *Transworld Business*. Retrieved August 12, 2009, from http://business.transworld.net/march-mountain-lodgings-dive-213-percent.

Lewis, M. (2009b, November 4). Annie Boulanger takes the Exposure-Meter reins. *Transworld Business*. Retrieved August 5, 2010, from http://business.transworld.net/22519/features/annie-boulanger-takes-the-exposure-mete...

Lidz, F. (1997). Lord of the board. *Sports Illustrated, 87*, pp. 114–119.

Lipton, N. (2009, October 7). Kumara Kelley's redemption hump day. *YoBeat.com*. Retrieved January 10, 2010, from http://www.yobeat.com/2009/10/07/kumara-kelleys-redemption-hump-day/.

Lipton N. (2010, February 26). High fives with Todd Richards: Olympic drag. *Yo Beat*. Retrieved March 2, 2010, from http://www.yobeat.com/2010/02/26/high-fives-with-todd-richards%E2%80%94olympic-drag/.

Lister, M. & Wells, L. (2005). Seeing beyond belief: Cultural studies as an approach to analysing the visual. In G. Stygall (Ed.), *Reading contexts* (pp. 431–459). New York: Thomson Wadsworth.

Lloyd, M. (1996). A feminist mapping of Foucauldian politics. In S. Hekman (Ed.), *Feminist interpretations of Michel Foucault* (pp. 241–264). University Park, PA: Pennsylvania State University Press.

Lorimer, H. (2005). Cultural geography: The busyness of being 'more-than-representational'. *Progress in Human Geography, 29*(1), 83–94.

Lorimer, H. (2008). Cultural geography: Non-representational conditions and concerns. *Progress in Human Geography, 32*(4), 551–559.

Lovell, T. (2000). Thinking feminism with and against Bourdieu. *Feminist Theory, 1*(1), 11–32.

Loy, J. W. (1991). Introduction – Missing in action: The case of the absent body. *Quest, 43*, 119–122.

Loy, J. W. (1995). The dark side of Agon: Fratriarchies, performative masculinities, sport involvement, and the phenomenon of gang rape. In K. H. Better & A. Rutten (Eds), *International sociology of sport contemporary issues: Festschrift in honour of Gunther Luschen* (pp. 263–282). Naglschmid: Stuttgart.

Loy, J. W., Andrews, D. L., & Rinehart, R. E. (1993). The body in culture and sport. *Sport Science Review, 2*(1), 69–91.

Macdonald, M. (2003). *Exploring media discourse*. London: Arnold.

Macdonald, N. (2001). *The graffiti subculture: Youth, masculinity and identity in London and New York*. London: Palgrave MacMillan.

Maguire, J. (1995). Common ground? Links between sports history, sports geography and the sociology of sport. *Sporting Traditions, 12*(1), 3–25.

Maguire, J. (1996). Blade runners: Canadian migrants, ice hockey, and the global sports process. *Journal of Sport and Social Issues, 23*, 335–360.

Maguire, J. (2002). Michel Foucault: Sport, power, technologies and governmentality. In J. Maguire & K. Young (Eds) *Theory, sport and society* (pp. 293–314). London: Elsevier Science.

Mahler, S. (1999). Engendering transnational migration: A case study of Salvaldorans. *American Behavioral Scientist, 42*, 690–719.

Mahler, S. & Pessar, P. (2001). Gendered geographies of power: Analyzing gender across transnational spaces. *Identities, 7*(4), 441–459.

'Mail'. (2005). *Transworld Snowboarding*, January, p. 48.

'Mail 15.5: Seeing red' (2002, January 7). *Transworld Snowboarding*. Retrieved on August 20, 2003, from http://www.transworldsnowboarding.com/snow/magazine/article/0,14304,242495,00.html.

Mandel, E. (1976). Introduction. In K. Marx, *Capital* (Trans. B. Fowkes) (pp. 11–86). New York: Penguin.

Marcus, G. (1995). Ethnography in/of the world system: The emergence of multi-site ethnography. *Annual Review of Anthropology, 24*, 95–117.

Markula, P. (1995). 'Firm but shapely, fit but sexy, strong but thin': The postmodern aerobicizing female body. *Sociology of Sport Journal, 12*, 424–453.

Markula, P. (2003). The technologies of the self: Sport, feminism, and Foucault. *Sociology of Sport Journal, 20,* 87–107.

Markula, P. & Pringle, R. (2006). *Foucault, sport and exercise: Power, knowledge and transforming the self.* London: Routledge.

Martin, A. (1994, January). Betty's. Retrieved on July 25, 2006, from http://www.heckler.com/articles/heckler_4/bettys.html.

Marx, K. (1964). *The economic and philosophical manuscripts of 1844.* New York: International Publishers.

Marx, K. (1970[1885]). *Capital: A critique of political economy.* London: Lawrence and Wishart.

Marx, K. (1982). *The economic and philosophic manuscripts.* Reprinted in A. Giddens & D. Held (Eds), *Classes, power, and conflict: Classical and contemporary debates* (pp. 12–19). Berkeley, CA: University of California Press.

Mason, J. (2002). *Qualitative researching* (2nd edition). London: Sage.

Massumi, B. (2002). *Parables for the virtual: Movement, affect, sensation.* Durham, NC: Duke University Press.

McCall, L. (1992). Does gender *fit?* Bourdieu, feminism, and conceptions of social order. *Theory and Society, 21,* 837–867.

McDermott, M. (2009, November 24). Interview with Jeremy Jones: Founder of Protect Our Winters. *Tree Hugger.* Retrieved April 5, 2010, from http://www.tree-hugger.com/files/2009/11/the-th-interview-jeremy-jones-protect-our-winters.php.

McDonald. M. G. & Birrell, S. (1999). Reading sport critically: A methodology for interrogating power. *Sociology of Sport Journal, 16,* 283–300.

McHoul, A. & Grace, W. (1998). *A Foucault primer: Discourse, power and the subject.* Dunedin: University of Otago Press.

McKay, D. (2005). Migration and the sensuous geographies of re-emplacement in the Philippines. *Journal of Intercultural Studies, 26,* 75–91.

McLeod, J. (2005). Feminists rereading Bourdieu: Old debates and new questions about gender habitus and gender change. *Theory and Research in Education, 3*(1), 11–30.

McNay, L. (1992). *Foucault and feminism: Power, gender and the self.* Cambridge: Polity.

McNay, L. (1994). *Foucault: A critical introduction.* Cambridge: Polity.

McNay, L. (1999). Gender, habitus and the field: Pierre Bourdieu and the limits of reflexivity. *Theory, Culture and Society, 16*(1), 95–117.

McNay, L. (2000). *Gender and agency: Reconfiguring the subject in feminist and social theory.* Cambridge: Polity.

McRobbie, A. (2004). Notes on 'what not to wear' and post-feminist symbolic violence. In L. Adkins & B. Skeggs (Eds), *Feminism after Bourdieu* (pp. 99–109). Oxford: Blackwell.

McRobbie, A. (2009). *The aftermath of feminism: Gender, culture and social change.* Los Angeles, CA: Sage.

'Media man Australian extreme directory' (no date). Retrieved November 19, 2009, from www.mediaman.com.au_profiles_snowboard.pdf.

Mellegren, D. (1998, January 7). AP reports Terje boycotting Nagano? *SOL Snowboarding Online,* www.solsnowboarding.com/compete/terje.html.

Merton, R. (1981). Forward: Remarks on theoretical pluralism. In P. Blau & R. Merton (Eds), *Continuities in structural inquiry* (pp. i–vii). Beverly Hills, CA: Sage.

Messner, M. (1987). The life of man's seasons: Male identity in the life of course of the jock. In M. Kimmel (Ed.), *Changing men: New directions in research on men and masculinity* (pp. 53–67). London: Sage.

Messner, M. (2002). *Taking the field.* Minneapolis, MN: University of Minnesota Press.

Messner, M. & Sabo, D. (Eds) (1990). *Sport, men, and the gender order.* Champaign, IL: Human Kinetics.

Midol, N. (1993). Cultural dissents and technical innovations in the 'whiz' sports. *International Review for Sociology of Sport, 28*(1), 3–32.

Mills, C. W. (1959). *The sociological imagination.* Oxford: Oxford University Press.

Mills, S. (2003). *Michel Foucault.* London and New York: Routledge.

Miller, T. (1998). Commodifying the male body, problematizing 'hegemonic masculinity'? *Journal of Sport and Social Issues, 22,* 431–447.

Misztal, B. (2003). *Theories of social remembering.* Philadelphia, PA: Open University Press.

'MLK day coverage: The top 10 Black snowboarders of all time'. (2009, January 19). *YoBeat,* retrieved August 10, 2009, from http://www.yobeat.com/2009/01/19/happy-birthday-mlk/.

Moi, T. (1991). Appropriating Bourdieu: Feminist theory and Pierre Bourdieu's sociology of culture. *New Literary History, 22,* 1017–1049.

Montoya, M. (2001, November 29). Marc Frank Montoya interview. *Transworld Snowboarding.* Retrieved April 2009, from http://snowboarding.transworld.net/2001/11/29/marc-frank-montoya-interview/.

Morford, R., & Clarke, C. (1976). The agon motif. In J. Keogh & R. Hutton (Eds), *Exercise and sports science reviews, Vol. 4* (pp. 167–168). Santa Barbara, CA: Journal of Publishing Affiliates.

Morley, D. (2000). *Home territories: Media, mobility and identity.* London: Routledge.

Morris, J. (2008, June). Research on the slopes: Being your own customer can be essential to success. *Change Agent: The Global Market Research Business Magazine.* Retrieved January 1, 2010, from http://synovate.com/changeagent.index.php.

Mottier, V. (2002). Masculine domination: Gender and power in Bourdieu's writings. *Feminist Theory, 3*(3), 345–359.

Mouzelis, N. (1995). *Sociological theory: What went wrong? Diagnosis and remedies.* London and New York: Routledge.

Mouzelis, N. (2007). Habitus and reflexivity: Restructuring Bourdieu's theory of practice. *Sociological Research Online, 12,* Retrieved May 5, 2008, from http://www.socresonline.org.uk.

Munslow, A. (1997). *Deconstructing history.* London: Routledge.

Murdock, G. (1997). Cultural studies at the crossroads. In A. McRobbie (Ed.), *Back to reality: Social experience and cultural studies* (pp. 58–73). Manchester: Manchester University Press.

Murphy, C. (2006, January 22). Sloping off to Mont Blanc. *The Post IE.* Retrieved December 2, 2009, from http://archives.tcm.ie/businesspost/2006/01/22/story11123.asp.

Murray, R. (1989). Fordism and post-Fordism. In S. Hall & M. Jacques (Eds), *New times: The changing face of politics in the 1990s* (pp. 38–54). London: Verso.

Muzzey, J. (2003, April). Interview: Romain De Marchi. *Transworld Snowboarding,* 126–139.

Nadesan, M. H. (2001). Post-Fordism, political economy, and critical organizational communication studies. *Management Communication Quarterly, 15*(2), 259–268.

Nauright, J. (2005). Conclusion: The political economy of sport in the twenty-first century. In Nauright & S. Schimmel (Eds), *The political economy of sport* (pp. 208–214). New York: Palgrave Macmillan.

Nayak, A. & Kehily, M. (2008). *Gender, youth and culture: Young masculinities and femininities*. Hampshire and New York: Palgrave Macmillan.

Nelson, J. (1989, January 26). Snowboarding: Riding the bank sideways. *New York Times*. Retrieved October 2006, from http://proquest.umi.com/pdfweb?did±157078 261&sid=2&Fmt=3&client.

'NGSA 2003 women's participation ranked by percent change' (2005a). Retrieved October 12, 2006, from http://www.nsga.org/public/pages/index.cfm?pageid=155.

'NGSA 2001–2004 participation by median age' (2005a). Retrieved October 12, 2006, from http:// www.nsga.org/public/pages/index.cfm?pageid=1358.

NGSA Newsletter (2001) Skiers/snowboarder profile continues to change, November 12, 3(21). Retrieved March 2005, from http://www.nsga.org

Nixon, H. (1993). Accepting the risks of pain and injury in sport. *Sociology of Sport Journal, 10*(2), 183–196.

Nonini, D. & Ong, A. (1997). Chinese transnationalism as an alternative modernity. In A. Ong & D. Nonini (Eds), *Ungrounded empires: The cultural politics of modern Chinese transnationalism* (pp. 3–33). London: Routledge.

Nora, P. (Ed.) (1996). *Realms of memory* (Vols 1–3, Trans. A. Goldhammer). New York: Colombia University Press.

Norris, P. (2002). *Democratic phoenix: Reinventing political activism*. Cambridge: Cambridge University Press.

Noy, C. (2004). 'This trip really changed me': Backpackers' narratives of self-change. *Annals of Tourism Research, 31*, 78–102.

O'Farrell, C. (2005). *Michel Foucault*. London: Sage.

O'Grady, H. (2005). *Woman's relationship with herself: Gender, Foucault and therapy*. New York: Routledge.

O'Hearn, M. (2008). *Jake Burton Carpenter and the snowboard*. Mankato, MN: Capstone Press.

'Onset: respect'. (1995). *New Zealand Snowboarder*, May/June, p. 9.

Osmond, G. & Phillips, M. (2004). 'The bloke with a stroke': Alick Wickham, the 'crawl' and social memory. *The Journal of Pacific History, 39*(3), 309–324.

Osmond, G., Phillips, M. & O'Neill, M. (2006). 'Putting up your Dukes': Statues, social memory and Duke Paoa Kahanamoku. *The International Journal of the History of Sport, 23*(1), 82–103.

Owen, A. Stein, S., & Vande Berg, L. (2007). *Bad girls: Cultural politics and media representations of transgressive women*. New York: Peter Lang Publishing.

Paasonen, S. (2007). Strange bedfellows: Pornography, affect and feminist reading. *Feminist Theory, 8*(1), 43–57.

Packard, S. (2006, March 15). French ski resort's lure leaves locals bruised. *The New York Times*, Retrieved January 17, 2010, from http://www.nytimes.com/2006/03/15/business/worldbusiness/15iht-chamonix.html.

Parkins, W. (2000). Protesting like a girl: Embodiment, dissent and feminist agency. *Feminist Theory, 1*(1), 59–78.

Pells, E. (2009, January 4). Board of education. *Los Angeles Times*. Retrieved March 12, 2010, from http://articles.latimes.com/2009/jan/04/sports/sp-dogsnowboard4.

Pennington, B. (2010, March 26). Playgrounds for skiers and snowboarders in New Hampshire. *The New York Times*, Retrieved June 3, 2010, from http://travel.nytimes.com/2010/03/26/travel/escapes/26loon.html.

Petrovic, G. (1991). Alienation. In T. Bottomore (Ed.), *A dictionary of Marxist thought* (2nd edition) (pp. 11–16). Oxford, Blackwell.

Phillips, M. (2004). Remembering sport history: Narrative, social memory and the origins of the rugby league in Australia. *The International Journal of the History of Sport, 21*(1), 50–66.

Picard, K. (2008, December 3). Antiviolence advocates ponder next move in Burton protest. *Seven Days: Vermont's Independent Voice*. Retrieved December 12, 2009, from http://www.7dvt.com/node/25372/print.

Pink, S. (2006). *Doing visual ethnography: Images, media and representation in research*. London: Sage.

Pink, S. (Ed.) (2007). *Visual interventions: Applied visual anthropology*. Oxford: Berghahn Books.

Pink, S. (2010). *Doing sensory ethnography*. Los Angeles, CA: Sage.

'Poll results: How many times have you snowboarded in a foreign country?' Online posting. Retrieved February 1, 2006, from: http://snowboard.colonies.com/Polls/PollResults.aspx?pollID=36&shouldShowPollResults=True.

'Porn conviction for snowboarder' (2005). Press release. Retrieved December 11, 2005, from http://www.boarderzone.com/forum/showthread.php?p=23394#post23394.

Poulantzas, N. (1978). *State, power, socialism*. London: New Left.

Powell, A. (2008). Amor fati? Gender habitus and young people's negotiation of (hetero)sexual consent. *Journal of Sociology, 44*(2), 167–184.

Pratt, G. & Yeoh, B. (2003). Transnational (counter) topographies. *Gender, Place and Culture, 10*(2), 159–166.

Press release. (2002, April). Gravis adds Torah Bright and JP Solberg. *EXPN.com*. Retrieved on March 20, 2003, from http://expn.go.com/snb/s/020425_gravis.html.

Press release. (2004, October 17). Burton teams with Mandalay Entertainment. Retrieved November 12, 2006, from http://www.transworldsnowboarding.com/snow/snowbiz/article/0,13009,710987,00.html.

Press release. (2007, November 8). Resorts of the Canadian Rockies focuses on terrain park safety with an industry leading initiative. *Snowboard Magazine*. Retrieved March 20, 2010, from http://www.snowboard-mag.com/node/28059.

Pries, L. (Ed.) (2001). *New transnational social spaces: International migration and transnational companies in the early twenty-first century*. London: Routledge.

Pringle, R. (2005). Masculinities, sport and power: A critical comparison of Gramscian and Foucauldian inspired theoretical tools. *Journal of Sport and Social Issues, 29*(3), 256–274.

Pringle, R. (2009). Defamiliarizing heavy-contact sports: A critical examination of rugby, discipline and pleasure. *Sociology of Sport Journal, 26*(2), 211–234.

Pringle, R. & Markula, P. (2005). No pain is sane after all: A Foucauldian analysis of masculinities and men's experiences in sport. *Sociology of Sport Journal, 22*(4), 472–497.

Probyn, E. (2004). *Blush: Faces of shame*. Minneapolis, MN: University Press.

Pronger, B. (1990). *The arena of masculinity*. New York: St Martin's Press.

'Question and answer' (2006, January 19). *Transworld Snowboarding*, retrieved March 22, 2008, from http://www.transworldsnowboarding.com/article_print.jsp?ID=1000027333.

'Questions for Torah Bright'. (2005, May 22). *The Sydney Morning Herald*. Retrieved August 8, 2006 from http://www.smh.com.au/news/Sport/Questions-for-Torah-Bright/ 2005/05/22/1116700581606.html.

Radley, A. (1990). Artifacts, memory and a sense of the past. In D. Middleton & D. Edwards (Eds), *Collective remembering* (pp. 46–59). London: Sage.

Rail, G. & Harvey, J. (1995). Body at work: Michel Foucault and the sociology of sport. *Sociology of Sport Journal, 12*, 164–179.

Randall, L. (1995). The culture that Jake built. *Forbes, 155*(7), March 27, pp. 45–46.

Reay, D. (1995). 'They employ cleaners to do that': Habitus in the primary classroom. *British Journal of Sociology of Education, 16*(3), 353–371.

Reay, D. (2004). 'It's all becoming habitus': Beyond the habitual use of habitus in educational research. *British Journal of Sociology of Education, 25*(4), 431–444.

Rebagliati, R. (2009). *Off the chain: An insider's history of snowboarding.* Vancouver: Greystone Books.

Reed, R. (2005). *The way of the snowboarder.* New York: Harry N. Abrams, Inc.

'Resort guide' (2005). *Transworld Snowboarding*, September, pp. 48–49.

Richards, T. (with Blehm, E.) (2003). *P3: Pipes, parks, and powder.* New York: Harper Collins.

Rigauer, B. (1981[1969]). *Sport and work.* New York: Columbia University Press.

Rinehart, R. (2000). Emerging/arriving sport: Alternatives to formal sports. In J. Coakley & E. Dunning (Eds), *Handbook of sports studies* (pp. 504–519). London: Sage.

Rinehart, R. (2005). 'Babes' and boards. *Journal of Sport and Social Issues, 29*(3), 232–255.

Rinehart, R. (2008). ESPN's X games, contests of opposition, resistance, co-option, and negotiation. In M. Atkinson & K. Young (Eds), *Tribal play: subcultural journeys through sport* (Vol. IV: *Research in the Sociology of Sport*) (pp. 175–196). Bingley: Jai.

'Risky maneuver lands snowboarder in a coma'. (2010, January 5). *ABC News*, Retrieved March 12, 2010, from http://abcnews.go.com/video/playerindex?id=9479741.

Roberts, S. (2002, February 7). Some winter stars prefer green to gold. *New York Times*, p. A.1.

Robertson, G., Mash, M., Tickner, L., Bird, J., Curtis, B, & Putnam, T. (1994). *Travellers' tales: Narratives of home and displacement.* London and New York: Routledge.

Robinson, L. (2002). *Black tights: Women, sport and sexuality.* Toronto: Harper Collins.

Robinson, O. (2006, December 7). Moving mountain: Bringing out the best in Beijing's boarders. Retrieved May 17, 2007, from http://www.thatsbj.com/blog/index.php/2006/12/07/sport_moving_mountains.

Robinson, V. (2008). *Everyday masculinities and extreme sport: Male identity and rock climbing.* New York: Berg.

Rodaway, P. (1994). *Sensuous geographies: Body, space and place.* London: Routledge.

Rodgers, A. (2001, December). Carving out a niche. Retrieved from http://www.fast-company.com/articles/2001/12/chorus.html.

Roenigk, A. (2004, February 23). Tara Dakides talks. *EXPN.com*, retrieved from http://expn.go.com/expn/story?pageName=040220_tara_talks_2.

Rojek, C. (2000). *Leisure and culture.* New York: St. Martin's Press.

Rojek, C. & Turner, B.S. (2000). Decorative sociology: A critique of the cultural turn. *Sociological Review, 48*(4), 629–648.

Rojek, C. & Urry, J. (Eds) (1997). Transformations of travel and theory. *Touring cultures: Transformations of travel and theory* (pp. 1–19). London: Routledge.

Rossi, P. (2002, December). Nothing snows him down: Marc Montoya: Professional snowboarder. *Latino Leaders: The National Magazine of the Successful American Latino.* Retrieved January 12, 2010, from http://findarticles.com/p/articles/mi_m0PCH/is_6_3/ai_113053352/

Rowe, D. (2004). *Sport, culture and the media* (2nd edition). Berkshire: Open University Press.

Rudofsky, B. (1986). *The unfashionable human body.* New York: Prentice-Hall.

Russo, J. (director) (2007). *Let it Ride: The Craig Kelly Story.* Montreal: Locomotion Films.

Samuel, R. (1994). *Theatres of memory, Vol. 1: Past and present in contemporary culture.* London: Verso.

Sands, R. (2008). Ethical ethnography: Epistemology and the ethics of good intentions. In. K. Young & M. Atkinson (Eds), *Tribal play: Subcultural journeys through sport.* Bingley: Emerald.

Sankey, M. & Cowley, P. (2008). Sense and sensibility. In M. Serres (Ed.), *The five senses: A Philosophy of mingled bodies* (Trans. M. Sankey & P. Cowley) (pp. vii–xiii). London: Continuum.

Saville, S. (2008). Playing with fear: Parkour and the mobility of emotion. *Social and Cultural Geography, 9*(8), 891–914.

Schultz, J. (2007). 'Stuff from which legends are made': Jack Trice Stadium and the politics of memory. *The International Journal of the History of Sport, 24*(6), 715–748.

'Scott goggle tan contest'. (2009). *Snowboarder Magazine* (Issue 16.3), Retrieved December 10, 2009, from http://snowboardermag.com/features/online-exclusives/scottgog/.

Seidler, V. (2006). *Transforming masculinities: Men, cultures, bodies, power, sex and love.* London: Routledge.

'Select snow brands to show at ASR'. (2004, December 2). *Transworld Business, Surf, Skate, Snow.* Retrieved from http://www.twsbiz.com.

Self, D., Henry, E., Findley, C., & Reilly, E. (2007). Thrill seeking: The type T personality and extreme sports. *International Journal of Sport Management and Marketing, 2,* 175–190.

Sensitive in SoCal. (2002). *Transworld Snowboarding,* September, p. 30.

Serres, M. (2008). *The five senses: A philosophy of mingled bodies* (Trans. M. Sankey & P. Cowley). London: Continuum.

Settimi, C. (2010, February 9). Top earning athletes of the 2010 Winter Olympics. *Forbes.com.* Retrieved March 1, 2010, from http://www.forbes.com/2010/02/09/top-earning-winter-olympic-athletes-business-sport... .

'Sex rot' (1994). *Flakezine.* Retrieved on August 12, 2003, from http://www.flakezine.com/fz11.html.

Shapiro, A. (1997). Whose (which) history is it anyway? *History and Theory, 36*(4), 1–3.

'Shaun White interview'. (2010). *Rolling Stone,* March, p. 43.

Sherker, S., Finch, C., Kehoe, E. J., & Doverty, M. (2006). Drunk, drowsy, doped: Skiers' and snowboarders' injury risk perceptions regarding alcohol, fatigue and recreational drug use. *International Journal of Injury Control and Safety Promotion, 13*(3), 151–157.

Sheller, M. & Urry, J. (Eds) (2004). Places to play, places in play. *Tourism mobilities: Places to play, places in play* (pp. 1–10). London: Routledge.

Sherowski, J. (2003a). Women on the verge: The future of female supershredding is now. *Transworld Snowboarding,* November, pp. 142–157.

Sherowski, J. (2003b). Q and A. *Transworld Snowboarding,* November, p. 48

Sherowski, J. (2003c). Your mom thinks freckles are cute. *Transworld Snowboarding,* November, p. 58.

Sherowski, J. (2004a). Notes from down-under. *Transworld Snowboarding,* April, pp. 104–117.

Sherowski, J. (2004b). Q and A: Should women get equal prize money, paychecks, and incentives in snowboarding? *Transworld Snowboarding*, February, p. 48.

Sherowski, J. (2005a). It's about damn time: Drake introduces the first-ever women's pro-model binding. *Transworld Snowboarding*, October, p. 54.

Sherowski, J. (2005b). What it means to be a snowboarder. *Transworld Snowboarding*, January, pp. 160–169.

Shilling, C. (1993). *The body and social theory*. London: Sage.

Shilling, C. (2003). *The body and social theory* (2nd edition). London: Sage.

Shilling, C. (2004). Physical capital and situated action: A new direction for corporeal sociology. *British Journal of Sociology of Education*, 25(4), 473–487.

Shilling, C. (2005). *The body in culture, technology and society*. London: Sage.

Shilling, C. (2007). Sociology and the body: Classical traditions and new agendas. *The Sociological Review*, 55(s1), 1–18.

Silk, M. (2005). Sporting ethnography: Philosophy, methodology and reflection. In D. Andrews, D. Mason, & M. Silk (Eds), *Qualitative methods in sports studies*. Oxford: Berg.

Silk, M. & Andrews, D. (2010). Call for papers: Physical Cultural Studies. Special issue of *Sociology of Sport Journal*. Retrieved December 9, 2009, from http://hk.humankinetics.com/ssj/SSJ_Call_for_Papers.pdf.

Simons, H. & Usher, R. (Eds) (2000). *Situated ethics in education research*. London and New York: Routledge.

Skeggs, B. (1997). *Formations of class and gender*. London: Sage.

Skeggs, B. (2004). Context and background: Pierre Bourdieu's analysis of class, gender and sexuality. In L. Adkins & B. Skeggs (Eds), *Feminism after Bourdieu* (pp. 19–34). Oxford: Blackwell.

Skelton, T. & Valentine, G. (Eds) (1998). *Cool places: Geographies of youth cultures*. London: Routledge.

'Ski tourism on the rise' (2007, August 14). Retrieved August 10, 2009, from http://news.holidayhypermarket.co.uk/Ski-Tourism-On-The-Rise-18244376.html.

Skocpol. T. (Ed.) (1984). *Vision and method in historical sociology*. Cambridge: University Press.

Slack, J. D. (1996). The theory and method of articulation in cultural studies. In D. Morley & K. H. Chen (Eds), *Stuart Hall: Critical dialogues in cultural studies* (pp. 112–127). London: Routledge.

Smith, M. P. (2001). *Transnational urbanism: Locating globalization*. Oxford: Blackwell.

Smith, M. P. (2002). Preface. In N. Al-Ali & K. Koser (Eds), *New approaches to migration?* London: Routledge.

'Snow sports industries America (SIA)' (2003–2004). Snowboard apparel. Retrieved June 7, 2004, from http://www.thesnowtrade.org/downloads/industry_research/03–04snowboard_apparel.pdf

'Snowboard shocker! Burton announces big layoffs'. (2002, April 12). Retrieved July 12, 2006, from http://www.skipressworld.com/us/en/daily_news/2002/04/snowboard_shocker_burton_announces_big_layoffs.html?cat=.

'Snowboarding and the Olympics'. Retrieved July 17, 2004, from http://www.burton.com/company/default.asp, pp. 22–23.

'Sold out in the cold contest' (2003). *Snowboarder*, February, pp. 42–44.

Sosienski, S. (1995, October 1). The herstory of snowboards. *Transworld Snowboarding*. Retrieved March 22, 2006, from http://www.transworldsnowboarding.com/snow/snowbiz/article/0,13009,246640,00.html.

Speer, S. (2001). Reconsidering the concept of hegemonic masculinity: Discursive psychology, conversation analysis and participant's orientations. *Feminism and Psychology, 11*, 107–135.

Spivak, G. (1989). Who claims alterity? In B. Kruger and P. Mariani (Eds.), *Remaking History: Dia Art Foundation Discussions in Contemporary Culture, Volume 4* (pp. 269–292). Seattle, WA: Bay Press.

Spowart, L., Hughson, J., & Shaw, S. (2008). Snowboarding moms carve out fresh tracks: Resisting traditional motherhood discourse? *Annals of Leisure Research, 11*(1&2), 187–204.

Stableford, D. (2005, January 31). Snow-mag renegades. *Folio Magazine: The magazine for magazine management.* Retrieved July 20, 2006 from http://www.foliomag.com/viewmedia.asp?prmMID=4469&prmID=249.

Star, L. (1999). New masculinities theory: Poststructuralism and beyond. In R. Law, H. Campbell, & J. Dolan (Eds), *Masculinities in Aotearoa/New Zealand* (pp. 36–45). Palmerston North: Dunmore.

Stassen, L. (2005a, June 10). Donna Burton Carpenter clears a path. *Transworld Business.* Retrieved July 2008, from http://www.twsbiz.com/twbiz/profiles/article/0,21214,1114933,00.html.

Stassen, L. (2005b, August 4). Women's market: Where the girls are(n't). *Transworld Business.* Retrieved from http://www.twsbiz.com/twbiz/women/article/0,21214,1090188,00.html.

'Stats confirm Australian invasion on NZ ski slopes' (2009, September 22). Retrieved November 14, 2009, from http://www.infonews.co.nz/news.

Stoddart, M. (2010). Constructing masculinized sportscapes: skiing, gender and nature in British Columbia, Canada. *International Review for the Sociology of Sport*, Online First, 1–17, doi: 10.1177/1012690210373541

Stoller, P. (1997). *Sensuous scholarship.* Philadelphia, PA: University of Pennsylvania Press.

Stone, J. & Horne, J. (2008). The print media coverage of skiing and snowboarding in Britain: Does it have to be downhill all the way? *Journal of Sport and Social Issues, 32*(1), 94–112.

Stravers, K. (2004). Ladies first. *SG Surf, Snow, Skate Girl*, December, 58–71.

'Stuff white people like: #31 snowboarding'. (2008). Retrieved October 12, 2008, from http://stuffwhitepeoplelike.com/2008/01/27/31-snowboarding/?cp=16.

Sugden, J. (2008). 'Anyone for football for peace?' The challenges of using sport in the service of co-existence in Israel. *Soccer and Society, 9*(3), 405–415.

Sweetman, P. (2003). Twenty-first century dis-ease? Habitual reflexivity or the reflexive habitus. *The Sociological Review, 51*(4), 528–548.

Swift, E. (2006). Eyes on the prize. *Sports Illustrated*, January 16, pp. 63–65.

'Tara-bly dangerous' (2000, December 19). *EXPN.com.* Retrieved March 10, 2004, from http://expn.go.com/xgames/wxg/2001.

'Teton releases new climate change film "Generations"' (2009, November). Retrieved March 18, 2010, from http://www.tetongravity.com/blogs/T-G-Rreleasesnewclimatechangefilm-Generations-1546892.htm.

'TGR releases new climate change film "Generations"' (2009). Retrieved March 9, 2010, from http://live.tetongravity.com/_TGR-releases-new-climate-change-film-Generations/BLOG/1546892/75233.html.

'The Aussie's take over Whistler' (2009, February). Retrieved December 8, 2009, from http://tysonclarke.spaces.live.com/blog/cns!9EDF684300D9B683!318.entry?sa=122810826.

'The mainstream media still don't get it'. (2010, January 5). *The Angry Snowboarder (blog)*. Retrieved January 10, 2010 from http://www.angrysnowboarder. com/?p=5497.

'The POW perspective: Jeremy Jones' Protect Our Winters campaign' (2008, January). *Future Snowboarding*. Retrieved March 10, 2010, from http://protectourwinters.org/ wp-content/uploads/2009/02/futurejanuary.pdf.

'The principles of snowboarding' (2002, August). Retrieved July 2008, from www. boardtheworld.com.

'The snowboard bible' (no date). Retrieved August 28, 2004, http://www.snowboard. com/articles/View.asp?U=461&I=4&Page=1.

'Theberge, N. (1991). Reflections on the body in the sociology of sport. *Quest, 42*(2), 123–134.

Thomas, H. & Ahmed, J. (Eds) (2004). *Cultural bodies: Ethnography and theory*. Malden, MA: Blackwell.

Thomas, P. (2009, February 20). For snowboarders, drug testing can be a real bummer. *LA Times*. Retrieved March 12, 2010, from http://articles.latimes.com/2009/ feb/20/sports/sp-snowboarding-drugs20.

Thompson, J. (2006, February 5). Boys (and girls) from the white stuff. *The Independent*. Retrieved March 3, 2010, from http://license.icopyright.net/user/viewFreeUse. act?fuid=NzMxMTc1Nw%3D%3D.

Thornton, S. (1996). *Club cultures: Music, media and subcultural capital*. London: Wesleyan University Press.

Thorpe, H. (2004). Embodied boarders: Snowboarding, status and style, *Waikato Journal of Education, 10*, 181–201.

Thorpe, H. (2005). Jibbing the gender order: Females in the snowboarding culture. *Sport in Society, 8*(1), 76–100.

Thorpe, H. (2006). Beyond 'decorative sociology': Contextualizing female surf, skate and snow boarding. *Sociology of Sport Journal, 23*(3), 205–228.

Thorpe, H. (2008). Foucault, technologies of self, and the media: Discourses of femininity in snowboarding culture. *Journal of Sport and Social Issues, 32*(2), 199–229.

Thorpe, H. (2009). Bourdieu, feminism and female physical culture: Gender reflexivity and the habitus-field complex. *Sociology of Sport Journal, 26*, 491–516.

Thorpe, H. (2010a). The politics of remembering: An interdisciplinary approach to physical cultural memory. *Sporting Traditions, 27*(2), 113–125.

Thorpe, H. (2010b). Bourdieu, gender reflexivity and physical culture: A case of masculinities in the snowboarding field. *Journal of Sport and Social Issues, 34*(2), 176–214.

Thorpe, H. (2010c). 'Have board, will travel': Global physical youth cultures and transnational mobility. In J. Maguire & M. Falcous (Eds.), *Sport and Migration: Borders, Boundaries and Crossings* (pp. 112–126). London: Routledge.

Thorpe, H. (In Press). Transnational mobilities in snowboarding culture: Travel, tourism and lifestyle sport migration. *Mobilities*.

Thorpe, H. & Rinehart, R. (2010). Alternative sport and affect: Non-representational theory examined. *Sport in Society* (Special issue: *Consumption and Representation of Lifestyle Sport*), *13*(7/8), 1268–1291.

Thorpe, H. & Wheaton, B. (In Press). The Olympic movement, action sports, and the search for generation Y. In J. Sugden & A. Tomlinson (Eds), *Watching the Olympics: Politics, power and representation*. London: Routledge.

Thorpe, H., Barbour, K., & Bruce, T. (2011). 'Wandering and wondering': Theory and representation in feminist physical cultural studies. *Sociology of Sport Journal, 28*(1).

Thrift, N. (2000). Still life in nearly present time: The object of nature. *Body and Society, 6*(3–4), 34–57.

Thrift, N. (2004). Intensities of feeling: Towards a spatial politics of affect. *Geografiska Annaler 86B*(1), 57–78.

Thrift, N. (2008). *Non-representational theory: Space, politics, affect.* London: Routledge.

Tomlinson, A. (2002). Pierre Bourdieu and the sociological study of sport: habitus, capital and field. In R. Giulianotti (Ed.), *Sport and modern social theorists* (pp. 161–172). Palgrave.

Tosh, J. (2000). *The pursuit of history* (3rd edition). Harlow: Pearson.

Turner, B. (1988). *Status.* Milton Keynes: Open University Press.

Turner, B. (2008). *The body and society: Explorations in social theory* (3rd edition). Los Angeles, CA: Sage.

Turner, J. (1991). *The structure of sociological thought* (5th edition). Belmont, CA: Wadsworth.

Turner, S. (Ed.) (1996). Introduction: social theory and sociology. *Social theory and sociology: The classics and beyond* (pp. 1–16). Cambridge: Blackwell.

Ulmer, K. & Straus, A. (2002). Action figures: the girls of extreme sports. Retrieved May 10, 2004, from http://www.maximonline.com/sports/girls_of_extreme_sports/dakides.html.

Urry, J. (1996). How societies remember the past. In S. Macdonald & G. Fyfe (Eds), *Theorizing museums* (pp. 45–65). Blackwell, Cambridge.

Urry, J. (2000). Mobile sociology. *British Journal of Sociology, 51*(1), 185–203.

Urry, J. (2007). *Mobilities.* Cambridge: Polity Press.

Urry, J. (2008). Foreword. In P. Burns & M. Novelli (Eds), *Tourism and mobilities: Local-global connections* (pp. xiv–xv). London: CABI.

Vamplew, W. (1998). Facts and artifacts: Sports historians and sports museums. *Journal of Sport History, 25*(2), 268–282.

'Variables: Protect our winters' (2008). *Transworld Snowboarding,* April, p. 62.

Veblen, T. (1970/1899). *The theory of leisure class.* London: Allen and Unwin Books.

Vertovec, S. (1999). Conceiving and researching transnationalism. *Ethnic and Racial Studies, 22*(2), 447–462.

Vertovec, S. (2009). *Transnationalism.* Oxon: Routledge.

Vivoni, F. (2009). Spots of spatial desire: Skateparks, skateplazas and urban politics. *Journal of Sport and Social Issues, 33*(2), 130–149.

Vogt, J. (1976). Wandering: Youth and travel behavior. *Annals of Tourism Research, 4,* 25–41.

'Volvo sports design forum' (2005). Retrieved from http://www.ispo-sportsdesign.com/english/forum/reports05/burton/index.html.

Wacquant, L. J. D. (1992). Toward a social praxeology: The structure and logic of Bourdieu's sociology. In P. Bourdieu & L. Wacquant, *An invitation to reflexive sociology* (pp. 1–59). Oxford: Blackwell.

Wacquant, L. J. D. (1993). On the tracks of symbolic power: Prefatory notes to Bourdieu's 'state nobility.' *Theory, Culture and Society, 10,* 1–17.

Wagner, A. & Houlihan, D. (1994). Sensation-seeking and trait anxiety in hang-gliding pilots and golfers. *Personality and Individual Differences, 16,* 975–977.

Waitt, G. (2008). 'Killing waves': Surfing, space and gender. *Social and Cultural Geography, 9*(1), 75–94.

Waitt, G. & Warren, A. (2008). 'Talking shit over a brew after a good session with your mates': Surfing, space and masculinity. *Australian Geographer, 39*(3), 353–365.

Walby, S. (2005). The sociology of gender relations. In C. Calhoun, C. Rojek, & B. Turner (Eds), *The Sage handbook of sociology* (pp. 367–380). London: Sage.

Walker, R. (1995). *To be real: Telling the truth and changing the face of femin*ism. New York: Anchor.

Wark, P. (2009, March 19). Skiing: Fun on the slopes or a risky business? *The Times*. Retrieved August 10, 2010, from http://women.timesonline.co.uk/tol/life_and_style/women/the_way_we_live/article5934246.ece.

Waters, M. (2000). *Modern sociological theory*. London: Sage.

Wearing, S., Stevenson, D., & Young, T. (2010). *Tourist cultures: Identity, place and the traveller*. London: Sage.

Weatherell, M. & Edley, N. (1999). Negotiating hegemonic masculinity: Imaginary positions and psycho-discursive practices. *Feminism and Psychology, 9*, 335–356.

Weber, M. (1978). *Economy and society*. Berkeley, CA: University of California Press.

Webster, S. (1996). Pamela Bell interview, *New Zealand Snowboarder*, August, p. 43.

Wellard, I. (2009). *Sport, masculinities and the body*. New York: Routledge.

Westcot, J. (2006). Onset. *New Zealand Snowboarding*, July/August, p. 18.

'What sucks in snowboarding right now?' (2004). *Transworld Snowboarding*, March, p. 48.

Wheaton, B. (2000a). Just do it: Consumption, commitment, and identity in the windsurfing subculture. *Sociology of Sport Journal, 17*(3), 254–274.

Wheaton, B. (2000b). 'New lads?' Masculinities and the 'new sport' participant. *Men and Masculinities, 2*, 434–456.

Wheaton, B. (2002). Babes on the beach, women in the surf: Researching gender, power and difference in the windsurfing culture. In J. Sugden and A. Tomlinson (Eds), *Power games: A critical sociology of sport* (pp. 240–266). London and New York: Routledge.

Wheaton, B. (2003a). Lifestyle sport magazines and the discourses of sporting masculinity. In B. Benwell (Ed.), *Masculinity and men's lifestyle magazines* (pp. 193–221). Oxford: Blackwell Publishing.

Wheaton, B. (2003b). Windsurfing: A subculture of commitment. In R. Rinehart & S. Sydnor (Eds), *To the extreme: Alternative sports, inside and out* (pp. 75–101). New York: State University of New York.

Wheaton, B. (2004). Selling out? The globalization and commercialization of lifestyle sports. In L. Allison (Ed.), *The global politics of sport: The role of global institutions in sport*. London: Routledge.

Wheaton, B. (2007). Identity, politics, and the beach: Environmental activism in 'Surfers Against Sewage'. *Leisure Studies, 26*(3), 279–302.

Wheaton, B. & Beal, B. (2003). 'Keeping it real': Sub-cultural media and discourses of authenticity in alternative sport. *International Review for the Sociology of Sport, 38*, 155–176.

Wheaton, B. & Tomlinson, A. (1998). The changing gender order in sport? The case of windsurfing subcultures. *Journal of Sport and Social Issues, 22*, 251–272.

Whiskey: The Movie (1994). Canada: Boozey the Clown Productions.

Whitehead, S. (1998). Hegemonic masculinity revisited. *Gender, Work and Organization, 6*(1), 58–62.

Whitehead, S. (2002). *Men and masculinities: Key themes and new directions*. Cambridge: Polity.

Whitson, D. (1990). Sport in the social construction of masculinity. In M. Messner & D. Sabo (Eds), *Sport, men and the gender order* (pp. 19–29). Champaign, IL: Human Kinetics.

Whyte, C. (2009, January 14). Pat Bridges interview. *ESPN.com*, retrieved January 10, 2010, from http://espn.go.com/action/snowboarding/blog?post=3832429.

Wiles, J. (2008). Sense of home in a transnational social space: New Zealanders in London. *Global Networks, 8*, 116–137.

Williams, P. W., Dossa, K. B., & Fulton, A. (1994). Tension on the slopes: Managing conflict between skiers and snowboarders. *Journal of Applied Recreation Research, 19*(3), 191–213.

Williams, S. & Bendelow, G. (1998). *The lived body: Sociological themes, embodied issues*. London: Routledge.

Willoughby, S. (2004, January 18). Snowboarding: Meyen seeks to raise the women's bar. *Denver Post*, p. C.03. Retrieved November 14, 2006, from http://proquest.umi.com/pdf web?did=526548421&sid=1&Fmt=3&clientld=8119&RQT=3097VName=PQD.

Wilson, B. (2007). New media, social movements, and global sport studies: A revolutionary moment and the sociology of sport. *Sociology of Sport Journal, 24*(4), 457–477.

Wilson, J. (1983). *Social theory*. Englewood Cliffs, NJ: Prentice-Hall.

Wilson, R. & Dissanayake, W. (1996). Introduction: Tracking the global/local. In R. Wilson & W. Dissanayake (Eds), *Global/local: Cultural production and the transnational imaginary* (pp. 1–18). Durham, NC: Duke University Press.

'Women we love'. (1994). *Flakezine*. Retrieved August 12, 2005, from http://www.flakezine.com/fz13.html.

'Women's market heats up' (2001). *Transworld Snowboarding*. Retrieved March 21, 2005, from http://www.transworldsnowboarding.com/snowbiz/article.

'Women's sports and fitness facts and figures' (2005, August). *Women's Sports Foundation*. Retrieved March 19, 2006, from http://www.womenssportsfoundation.org/binary.

'Women's tech: Questions and answers' (2006). *Burton Catalogue, 29*, pp. 8–9.

Woodward, K. (2009). *Embodied sporting practices: Regulating and regulatory bodies*. Hampshire: Palgrave MacMillan.

Wright, K. H. (2001). 'What's going on?' Larry Grossberg on the status quo of cultural studies: An interview. *Cultural Values, 5*(2), 133–162.

Wulf, S. (1996). Triumph of hated snowboarders. *Time*, January, *147*, 69.

Yant, N. (2001a). Marc Frank Montoya interview. *Transworld Snowboarding*. Retrieved May 10, 2004, from http://www.transworldsnowboarding.com/snow/magazine/article/0,14304,242627,00.html

Yant, N. (2001b). Tara Dakides interview. *Transworld Snowboarding*. Retrieved May 10, 2004, from http://www.transworldsnowboarding.com/snow/magazine/article/0,14304,243261,00.html

'Yellow snow'. (2002). *Transworld Snowboarding*, September, pp. 204–206.

Young, F. (1965). *Initiation ceremonies*. New York: Bobbs-Merrill Co. Inc.

Young, K., White, P., & McTeer, W. (1994). Body talk: Male athletes reflect on sport, injury, and pain. *Sociology of Sport Journal, 11*, 175–194.

Index

CPSIA information can be obtained at www.ICGtesting.com
Printed in the USA
LVOW07*2148230714

395655LV00002BA/9/P